The Ancient Egyptian State

This book focuses on the development of Egypt in its formative phase, from c. 5200 BC, when Egyptians first began farming wheat and barley, until 2055 BC, as Egypt's central government weakened and appears to have fallen into disorder. During these millennia, which coincide with the Predynastic, early Dynastic, and Old Kingdom Periods, Egyptian civilization became increasingly complex, and many of its greatest pyramids and other monuments were built. Robert J. Wenke examines this cycle of ancient Egypt's development by analyzing Egyptological, anthropological, and other forms of evidence, which are set into the larger context of early civilizations that developed in various areas of the world. Written in an accessible style, with many anecdotes, quotations, and personal reflections, this book is intended for use in undergraduate and graduate courses on early civilizations and states.

Robert J. Wenke, a scholar of ancient Egyptian civilization, taught at the University of Washington before he retired. A former director of the American Research Center in Egypt, he has conducted fieldwork throughout the world and is the author of *Patterns in Prehistory*, now in its fifth edition.

D1112069

Case Studies in Early Societies

Series Editor
Rita P. Wright, New York University

This series aims to introduce students to early societies that have been the subject of sustained archaeological research. Each study is also designed to demonstrate a contemporary method of archaeological analysis in action, and the authors are all specialists currently engaged in field research. The books have been planned to cover many of the same fundamental issues. Tracing long-term developments and describing and analyzing a discrete segment in the prehistory or history of a region, they represent an invaluable tool for comparative analysis. Clear, well organized, authoritative, and succinct, the case studies are an important resource for students, and for scholars in related fields, such as anthropology, ethnohistory, history, and political science. They also offer the general reader accessible introductions to important archaeological sites.

Other titles in the series include:

Ancient Mesopotamia
Susan Pollock

Ancient Oaxaca
Richard E. Blanton, Gary M. Feinman, Stephen A. Kowalewski, and Linda M. Nicholas

Ancient Maya
Arthur Demarest

Ancient Cahokia and the Mississippians
Timothy R. Pauketat

Ancient Puebloan Southwest
John Kantner

Ancient Middle Niger
Roderick J. McIntosh

Ancient Jomon of Japan
Junko Habu

Ancient Tiwanaku
John Janusek

The Ancient Egyptian State

The Origins of Egyptian Culture (c. 8000–2000 BC)

Robert J. Wenke

University of Washington

CAMBRIDGE
UNIVERSITY PRESS

CAMBRIDGE UNIVERSITY PRESS

Cambridge, New York, Melbourne, Madrid, Cape Town, Singapore, São Paulo, Delhi

Cambridge University Press
32 Avenue of the Americas, New York, NY 10013-2473, USA

www.cambridge.org
Information on this title: www.cambridge.org/9780521574877

First published 2009

Printed in the United States of America

A catalog record for this publication is available from the British Library.

Library of Congress Cataloging in Publication data
Wenke, Robert J.
    The Ancient Egyptian State : the origins of Egyptian culture
    (c. 8000–2000 B.C.) /
    Robert J. Wenke.
        p.   cm. – (Case studies in early societies ; 8)
    Includes bibliographical references and index.
    ISBN 978-0-521-57377-1 (hardback) – ISBN 978-0-521-57487-7 (pbk.)
    1. Egypt – Civilization – To 332 B.C.   I. Title.   II. Series.
    DT61.W547 2009
    932'.011 – dc22   2008025449

ISBN 978-0-521-57377-1 hardback
ISBN 978-0-521-57487-7 paperback

For Chris and Anna Wenke, *Requiescat in Pace*

Contents

List of Illustrations

List of Tables

Preface

Novelist F. Scott Fitzgerald said that the "test of a first-rate intelligence is the ability to hold two opposed ideas in the mind at the same time, and still retain the ability to function."

This book requires something similar. On the one hand, the reader is asked to use the book to *analyze* the origins of the Egyptian state and civilization. To do this one must use the analytical methods of anthropology, history, ecology, Egyptology, and other disciplines to try to understand the dynamics of a remarkable process of cultural evolution that occurred in Egypt between about 6000 and 2000 BC. During this period the small groups of hunter-foragers whose ancestors had lived in North Africa for many hundreds of millennia were succeeded by farmers who lived in small villages and towns; and then, within just a few centuries, these unprepossessing peasant farming communities were transformed into elements of a glorious civilization. In this book the reader is invited to join generations of scholars who have attempted to analyze Egypt's development, to explain how and why this state and civilization evolved, and to account for both its similarities to, and its differences from, other early civilizations.

At the same time, the reader is invited to use the book simply to experience and enjoy early Egyptian civilization as a unique and fascinating culture. Ancient Egypt's brilliance in art, architecture, literature, philosophy, and other fields can instruct us and enrich our lives; the study of Egypt in this sense needs no justification in terms of an analytical science of history.

These two views of the Egyptian past are not, of course, contradictory: One can marvel at the Egyptian pyramids, for example, and at the same time try to analyze the fact that several other ancient states, such as Mexico, Mesopotamia, and North America, also built massive pyramids, and to consider what role such structures played in these evolutionary histories.

The reader is forewarned that this book is neither a comprehensive anthropological analysis nor a detailed Egyptological description of the early Egyptian state. Space limitations necessitated a highly selective treatment of the subject, and I have concentrated on anthropological analyses to the exclusion of many important Egyptological topics. Also, I have had to focus on only the first part of pharaonic history, from about 5000 to 2055 BC. Nonetheless, I have used examples from Egyptian culture after 2000 BC to illustrate certain points.

This book is intended for use in college courses; it is in no sense a sourcebook for professionals, as space limitations precluded an in-depth review of the many topics considered. I've included many quotations from lyric poets and archaeologists and other scholars, and I've tried to set the book in the context of world literature, philosophy, politics, and other disciplines – all in the hope of making it more readable and contributing to the reader's liberal education. This book contains many of the cliches concerning Egypt, from Herodotus's observations of Egyptian life to debates about how the pyramids may have been built. Although these are overly familiar to professional Egyptologists and archaeologists, long experience has taught me that they are not to many students – the target audience of this book. For similar reasons, the book contains many references to popular accounts of Egyptian archaeology and commonly available reference books. The book is also partly a personal account of my experiences. It may strike the professional reader as overly self-referential, but here too my goal is readability.

I greatly appreciate the saintly patience of my editors (Rita Wright, Beatrice Rehl) in waiting for the finished manuscript. I am particularly grateful to Janis Bolster, the production editor; Phyllis Berk, the copy editor; and Lin Maria Riotto, who indexed the book. Their combined contributions verge on coauthorship. I especially thank Emily Teeter, Douglas Brewer, John Nolan, Wilma Wetterstrom, Bruce Smith, Paul Johnson, Donald Redford, Matthew P. Adams, Mike Brass, Richard Redding, and Mark Lehner for answering many questions. John and Deborah Darnell graciously provided a photograph of their discovery at Gebel Tjauti. The anonymous reviewer for Cambridge made many useful suggestions. Elizabeth Saluk organized the illustrations and permissions with great efficiency; I thank her for her invaluable work, and Deborah Rosenzweig as well. Danette Newcomb did an able job on the bibliography.

I also thank Nanette M. Pyne for her invaluable editing of the early drafts of this book, and for her many contributions to our field work projects over nearly thirty years.

I am grateful to the National Science Foundation, the National Geographic Society, the National Endowment for the Humanities, the Bioanthropology Foundation (via Roxie Walker), and the University of

Washington Graduate School Research Fund for the financial support that allowed me to spend many years doing archaeology in Egypt. I am also particularly grateful in this regard to Maurice and Lois Schwartz, who funded part of my first archaeological project in Egypt when I was an archaeological refugee from revolutionary Iran. David H. Koch funded our radiocarbon analyses of the pyramids, and I'm very grateful to him.

I also thank the American Research Center in Egypt for facilitating my research in Egypt, particularly Amira and Amir Khattab, Mai Trad, Albert, and also Ibrahim, Hassan, and Salah – all loyal comrades-in-arms at the old American Research Center in Egypt. I am also sincerely and deeply grateful to Zahi Hawass and other members of the Egyptian antiquities services for facilitating my field research.

Most of all, I thank Ilene VanZandt, David Wenke, Lorence Wenke, Dennis Wenke, Judy Joling, and Joy McCorriston for their support and encouragement. Geoffrey Wenke was a continuing inspiration.

1 The Significance and Character of Ancient Egyptian Civilization

> Concerning Egypt I shall extend my remarks to a great length, because
> there is no country that possesses so many wonders, nor any that has
> such a number of works that defy description.
>
> Herodotus (c. 440 BC)

Introduction

King Pepy II, or *Neferkare*, to use one of the several names by which his
subjects knew him, died in what was probably the year we designate as
2181 BC. As his embalmers laid his cold corpse out on the mortuary
slab, they were likely looking at the wizened remains of the only king
they – or, for that matter, most of their parents – had ever known.
Ancient texts suggest that Pepy ruled for ninety-four years. His reign was
probably shorter (the texts are ambiguous), but lying there in front of the
embalmers would have been the mortal remains of the man who for
decades had embodied everything that it meant to be "Egyptian."

Yet Pepy's embalmers no doubt methodically proceeded with their
work. The precise details of the mummification process as it was practiced at the time of Pepy's death remain obscure, but we know something about them from tombs and remains from Pepy's Old Kingdom
ancestors (Taylor 2001) and his successors. If later texts describing
Egyptian mortuary arts accurately reflect Old Kingdom practices (and
they may not), the mummification process and its associated rituals
lasted about seventy days. The embalmers would have begun by
scooping his brain out through his nose with a metal spoon and evis-
cerating him through an incision in his abdomen. After his organs were
removed, dried, and placed in separate containers, they desiccated his
body by packing it in salts for forty (or perhaps seventy) days. Then they
coated the corpse with various unguents and wrapped it in linen strips,
individually wrapping each finger and toe and his penis. Once Pepy had
been mummified, various rites were performed. His mouth was ritually
opened, for example, so that he could eat and chat with other dead

people and perhaps communicate with his gods (the "opening of the mouth" ceremony remains a matter of much dispute). Following these rituals, his body was placed in a wooden coffin. The priests then carried the corpse in its coffin, along with the rich store of the things Pepy hoped to enjoy in eternal life, into his tomb, which had been carved into the limestone bedrock of the Saqqara plateau, a few kilometers south of modern Cairo, on the west side of the Nile (Figure 1.1). Once they placed his coffin in his granite sarcophagus, they sealed the tomb and no doubt returned to their quarters at nearby Memphis, Pepy's erstwhile earthly home, serene in their conviction that he already had ecstatically rejoined his fellow gods, high in the starry nights.

Unlike modern morticians, Pepy's embalmers were not engaged in some pathetic effort to make his corpse presentable for public display. Instead, they worked diligently to transport him safely into eternity and furnish him with all the provisions he would need there, including a reasonably intact physical body. His embalmers were trying to make Pepy's corpse resemble Pepy as he was in life, so that one form of his "soul" could recognize the corpse when this soul returned to take up residence in his tomb.

But these embalmers and priests were also trying to do something with an importance that went far beyond Pepy's personal fate: They were attempting, with the earnestly entreated aid of all the great and ancient gods of Egypt, to perpetuate in good order not only Pepy but also the entire universe. They strove mightily in mummifying and entombing him, and performing the last rites and rituals, in hopes of counteracting the forces of death, decay, and disorder, and of reasserting good order in the cosmos.

They were not entirely successful. The universe continues, it is widely hypothesized, but Pepy's body has long since disappeared, his empty sarcophagus a sad witness to his fate. His tomb was probably looted within a few decades or centuries of his death, thereby abruptly wrenching him out of the vehicle he had hoped would – and, we can hope, nonetheless did – carry him into an eternal pleasant afterlife.

We know little about the specifics of Pepy's life. He may have been homosexual (Parkinson 1995), a fault in the Egyptian view, for how could such a king maintain the universe in good order while he himself was so at odds with good order? Yet he *was* the king and thus deserved all the rituals and rights of newly dead kings. Pepy's pyramid, tomb, and temple, nonetheless, were small and cheap compared to those of his illustrious ancestors, and he is remarkable among kings chiefly for the supposed length of his reign. But his life and death are a good place to begin a study of the origins of ancient Egyptian civilization, because Pepy II was among the last rulers of the illustrious Old Kingdom Period

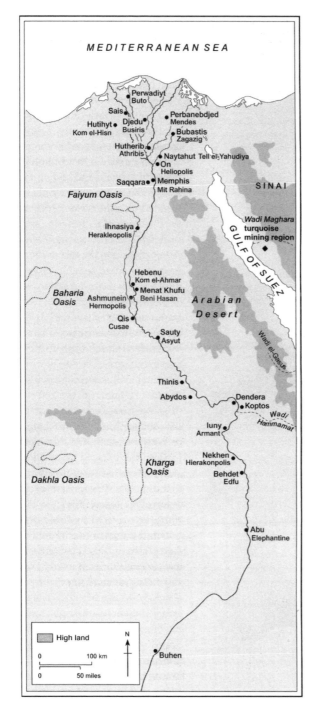

Figure 1.1. General topography of Egypt and the locations of some important ancient settlements. *Source:* Reproduced by permission of Oxford University Press from Shaw 2000, p. 22. © Oxford University Press 2000.

Table 1.1. Major Periods in Ancient Egypt's
Chronology

Paleolithic	c. 700,000–8800 BP*
Saharan Neolithic	c. 8800–4700 BC
Lower Egyptian Neolithic	c. 5300–4500 BC
Predynastic	c. 4500–3000 BC
Early Dynastic	c. 3000–2686 BC
Old Kingdom	2686–2160 BC
First Intermediate	2160–2055 BC
Middle Kingdom	2055–1650 BC
Second Intermediate	1650–1550 BC
New Kingdom	1550–1069 BC
Ramessid	1295–1069 BC
Third Intermediate	1069–664 BC
Late	664–352 BC
Ptolemaic	332–30 BC
Roman	30 BC–AD 395

*BP = Before the Present.
After Shaw 2000: 479–483.

(c. 2686–2160 BC), the "Pyramids Age," and his death is thought to have ushered in a century of chaos and economic and political retraction in Egypt. In later periods, the Egyptian state reconstituted itself and produced works and ideas that make the Old Kingdom seem primitive, but Pepy II's death is significant. Table 1.1 shows his place in the chronology of ancient Egypt.

Pepy's reign completed a great developmental cycle that began about 4000 BC. At that time most Egyptians lived in small villages and subsisted on simple farming of wheat, barley, and a few other crops, supplemented by domesticated sheep, goats, pigs, and cattle, as well as the proceeds of hunting, fishing, and foraging. There were no glorious temples, tombs, or pyramids. Each tiny village was largely a world unto itself, with few economic, social, or political connections to the outside world. Every community, in fact, performed nearly all the economic and social activities of every other community: They were "functionally redundant," in the terms of modern economic theory. Most people's lives were largely encompassed within the extent of their farm fields and livestock pastures and the circumference of their village's walls.

Yet by the time of Pepy II's death, Egypt was a great nation-state, with a written language, a diversified and productive economy, a complex bureaucratic hierarchy, a powerful army, lavish temples and tombs, and substantial towns. Indeed, by the time of Pepy's demise, Egypt had already been a great *civilization* and a powerful *state* for nearly a millennium. In his dotage Pepy could – and probably did – count among his royal ancestors more than thirty-five kings who had ruled before him. And he probably died with the consoling thought that many kings would come after him, as indeed they did.

The primary focus of this book is this *first Dynastic cycle*, from about 4000 to 2055 BC, when Egypt first became a great state and civilization and then, after many centuries of stability and prosperity, apparently devolved abruptly into a century of anarchy and poverty. As we shall see, this developmental cycle, like similar cycles in other ancient civilizations, has engaged the attention of scholars for millennia. Attempts to "explain," or in some larger sense understand, these cycles range from appeals to such "authorities" as God's will to the elaborate interpretations of twentieth-century French social anthropology. None, as noted in Chapter 7, has been entirely successful.

It must be admitted from the outset that defining the terms "state" and "civilization" remains a matter of inconclusive and largely unedifying debate. Indeed, legions of scholars have dismissed these terms as sterile typologies based on untenable assumptions about historical and cultural transformations (Shanks and Tilley 1987a, 1987b; McGuire 1983; Yoffee 2005). Some of the scholars whose focus is ancient Egypt also reject these terms and the analytical perspective from which they derive, for similar reasons (e.g., Wengrow 2006). These critical appraisals are considered in detail in subsequent chapters, but the concept of the state and civilization used here are intended as simple descriptive summaries of complex patterns of cultural change, and they are used in the same sense that many scholars have applied them, not just to Egypt but to other early polities as well (e.g., Trigger 2003; R. McC. Adams 1966; Butzer 1976; Bard 2000; Maisels 2001; R. Wright in press).

In the sense in which the concepts of state and civilization are used in this book, they can be thought of in terms of several salient features. The ancient Egyptian state was, for example, *functionally differentiated* and *integrated*. After about 2700 BC, Egypt's economy was based on the integrated labors of scores of occupational specialists – farmers, fishermen, herdsmen, potters, porters, bakers, brewers, masons, metalsmiths, tax agents, generals, priests, painters, sculptors, provincial governors, judges, and many others. And like all other early states, the ancient Egyptian state was a complex system in which everyone depended on these specialists for at least some goods and services. If the military forces weakened, for example, the "barbarians" could soon be at the national gates, and several times, in fact, foreign armies did overrun

Egypt. If administrators did not tax, store, and redistribute part of the harvests, the many artisans, politicians, soldiers, and other professionals who did not produce their own food could not be supported, and too many years of poor harvests could, and occasionally did, result in misery and starvation. Thus, from the poorest farmer to the king himself, these people were linked in mutually dependent, hierarchically arranged, and complex socioeconomic and political relationships.

All Egyptian kings, including Pepy, no doubt led a life of wealth and privilege, but like everyone in the society, they too had a job to do. "Uneasy lies the head that wears the crown," as Shakespeare said of Henry IV. Pepy was considered by his people to be both a man and a god – but a god who could intercede on behalf of Egyptians with other gods, and who had the responsibility to do so effectively. A king whose reign was cursed by lost wars or poor harvests could be blamed for such obvious signs of the gods' displeasure. In some sculptures, the king is portrayed with a falcon (Figure 1.2), a representation of the great god, sitting on his shoulders, ready to offer advice. The implication was that although the king was considered a deity of sorts, he was a god who needed the help and protection of other gods on occasion.

Figure 1.2. King Khafre (c. 2558–2532 BC) rules under the tutelage of the god Horus, represented by the falcon. Sculpted in black basalt. Though considered a god, the king was believed to be guided by other gods. *Source:* Delimont, Herbig & Assoc.

The ancient Egyptian state, like all early states, operated through a *bureaucratic hierarchy*. Dynastic Egypt saw the emergence of *Homo hierarchicus*, in the place of *Homo aequalis*, to use Louis Dumont's terms (1980). Like all kings before and after him, Pepy II had numerous aides and advisers, and much of the daily operation of the Egyptian state was administered by officials many levels below him in the bureaucratic hierarchy. Yet one of the vital lies of Egyptian political theory was that the king personally directed these thousands of officials who collected taxes, adjudicated legal disputes, interceded with the gods through rituals, and in a thousand other ways managed the state's business. In fact, such complexly differentiated and highly integrated states could operate only by means of an administrative hierarchy that was itself highly differentiated and complexly integrated. Thus, even the poorest Egyptian farmer bore the weight in his daily life of many levels of bureaucrats above him, from the village headman, through provincial tax collectors and governors, to state administrators, and ultimately to the king himself. Ancient Egyptians probably found bureaucracies of all kinds as oppressive in their profusion and inefficiencies as we do, but they, too, seem to have had a sense that such hierarchies were fundamental to a well-ordered state and universe, and they believed that they were established by the gods to further that goal.

Any attempt to analyze the pharaonic past in general terms must consider the evolution of these administrative institutions.

Like all other early states, Egyptian society was also based on *institutionalized inequalities*, in the sense that some people had disproportionate access to wealth, power, and prestige – and, moreover, this unequal access either was inherited or was dictated by elites. Marxists and some others (e.g., Crone 1989: 101–102) restrict the use of the term "class" to industrial societies with specific kinds of economic and social relations that did not appear in developed form in ancient Egypt. But Egyptian society was sharply defined in terms of various inequalities, ranging from simple distinctions based on age and gender to precise calculations of one's familial proximity, if any, to the ruling elites. Thus, Pepy and other kings and nobles were at the apex of Egypt's social pyramid, and below them were many other groups, ranging from leisured elites to enslaved war captives. Social "mobility" – moving up the socioeconomic ladder – was possible, with luck and pluck. Becoming a scribe (Figure 1.3), for example, allowed a person to join a privileged meritocracy. Most people, however, inherited their class status and bore it for life. Probably 90 percent or more of ancient Egyptians existed at the bottom of social, wealth, and power hierarchies, where they labored as farmers, fishermen, potters, bakers, or other tiny cogs in the state apparatus. Yet they, like the

Figure 1.3. Seated scribe statue. Numerous figurines of scribes have been found, such as this individual from the Fifth Dynasty (painted limestone). Many early Egyptian representations of people have a static formalized quality, but they could represent ordinary individuals in what we consider a "naturalistic" fashion, with such things as rolls of belly fat faithfully illustrated. *Source:* The Louvre Museum, Réunion des Musées Nationaux/Art Resource, NY.

lowest classes in most ancient societies, apparently accepted these inequalities as their fate and the will of the gods: There is no clear evidence that proletarian revolutions ever occurred in ancient Egypt, nor did the ancient Egyptians unite in powerful groups that tried to advance their groups' interests through strikes and revolts. Egyptian menials knew they were at the bottom of society; they just did not see anything they could do about it that would not violate their religious and political beliefs, or would have any chance of improving their lot.

At this point it is worth considering how restrictive such social hierarchies can be. The United States of America, for example, was founded by some elites, but the vast majority of immigrants were small-time European farmers and tradesmen. Out of that genetic mix has come one of the most powerful and creative societies in history, approaching even fifth-century BC Greece and eighteenth- and nineteenth-century Great Britain.

Perhaps the most important aspect of Egypt's ancient specialized occupational system, as well as its hierarchically arranged bureaucratic administrative structures and its institutionalized forms of economic and social inequalities, is that very similar cultural forms appeared in many areas of the ancient world, from China to Peru. Moreover, most of these early states and civilizations developed largely independently, and at about the same time – 4000 BC–AD 1000.

A fundamental issue considered here is how we are to understand and explain these parallel culture histories. But that is not the only issue. This book is also concerned with questions about how we are to understand and appreciate Egyptian civilization, and what – in the largest possible sense – we can learn from it.

The Nature and Significance of Ancient States (Part 1): Aesthetic and Philosophical Appreciations of Egypt as a Unique Civilization

Earth has not anything to show more fair;
Dull would he be of soul who could pass by
A sight so touching in its majesty. . . .

> (William Wordsworth [1770–1850], "Lines Composed
> upon Westminster Bridge")

It is difficult to resist the temptation to become morbidly sentimental about ancient Egypt. Many people find Egypt's past and its remains profoundly affecting. This book includes enough "purple prose" to fit the definition of sentimentality about ancient Egypt. Wordsworth's paean was to London, but his musings are equally applicable to the relics of ancient Egypt. Dull, indeed, too would be the soul who could view these pyramids, temples, and tombs without a profound sense of awe, pleasure, and curiosity.

We need not consider grand questions about the meaning of the past and the "science" of history in order to benefit from the contemplation of Egypt's wonders. Nor do we have to choose between *analyses* of the Egyptian past and an aesthetic *appreciation* of that past; these are complementary perspectives. The book allots more space to analyses of the socioeconomic dynamics of the Egyptian past than to appreciation of it, but both are necessary for a comprehensive understanding of this culture.

Ancient Egypt's potent cultural themes, like those of ancient Greece and Rome, have reverberated throughout history, in such diverse forms as the Bible, Plato's *Dialogues*, William Shakespeare's plays, and Giuseppe Verdi's masterful opera *Aida*. And Egyptian architectural and aesthetic forms have inspired artists for millennia, from ancient Rome to the oddities of contemporary Las Vegas in the United States. A trivial but more tangible example of ancient Egypt's lingering cultural influence can be found on the reverse side of the U.S. dollar bill. On the left side is a pyramid, with an eye below the capstone, and the inscription "ANNUIT COEPTIS" (Latin shorthand for "God has favored our undertaking") above it. Below the pyramid is written "NOVUS ORDO SECLORUM," Latin for "a new order of the secular ages [is created]." There are thirteen levels to the pyramid, representing the original states, and it is left unfinished in anticipation of great things to come. Many believe that these symbols and ideas were incorporated in American currency because mystical ideas about ancient Egypt influenced some secret societies, such as Freemasonry, to which many politically important Americans of the nineteenth century belonged (including most of the signers of the Constitution). At least thirteen presidents have been members, from George Washington to George W. Bush.

Think about it. The people who built the pyramids and other wonders of Egypt's first civilization have been *pulvis et umbra*, dust and shadows, for 4500 years and more. Why do their works and eschatology captivate people of so many diverse epochs and cultures? The answer in part is that the remains of Egyptian civilization constitute a multifaceted work of art that, like all great art, enriches and resonates through many people's lives. One can argue that there are no aesthetic absolutes, but only the most cloddish are unmoved, for example, when they first see the Sphinx and the Great Pyramids at Giza (Figure 1.4). Viewed early in the morning they are a spectacular sight, as the warm red sun rolls up over the horizon, sparkles the Nile, accents the vivid greens of the floodplain farms, and then slowly reveals the pyramids and Sphinx in honey-colored tones.

Or consider ancient Egyptian texts, arguably the most beautiful written language in human history. Formal Old Kingdom hieroglyphic inscriptions (Figure 1.5) have knife-edge clarity and engaging symmetry unequaled by any other script. There is a "certain slant of light," as Emily Dickinson observed in another context, that imbues objects with profound meanings, and Egypt's raking evening and morning sunlight gives monumental hieroglyphic inscriptions remarkable depth and presence. Even the ordinary Egyptian texts – the bills, contracts, deeds, graffiti, and so forth – were written in the appealing "hieratic" script, for Egyptian scribes did not "write" as we do; they literally painted their texts with brushes and colored inks, and they did so in many media and with considerable grace (Figure 1.6).

Even in the small and common Egyptian relics, such as the stone statues of husband and wife (Figure 1.7), we find poignant expressions of individual lives and loves. In none of the world's other earliest civilizations do we find so many celebrations in art of the simple domestic felicity of husband and wife and their pairing even into the afterlife.

Such contemplations of ancient Egypt need no ultimate justification. We need not denature them by analyzing them into their components and relating them to ponderous theories of history.

Figure 1.4. The Great Sphinx at Giza, with Khafre's pyramid in the background. *Source:* Werner Forman / Art Resource, NY.

Figure 1.5. Example of Old Kingdom hieroglyphs. The inscriptions and depictions of items inscribed in relief on this limestone panel well represent the clarity and aesthetic appeal of Old Kingdom hieroglyphs. It is from the offering chapel of Rahotep, at Meidum. *Source:* © The Trustees of the British Museum.

Figure 1.6. Hieratic papyrus from the pyramid complex at Lahun. These and similar documents provide much information about the exchange of goods and services during this age (c. 1950 BC), just following the end of the Old Kingdom. *Source:* The Trustees of the British Museum.

Figure 1.7. Old Kingdom "seated-pair" statues. These were commonly included in the tombs of the upper classes in early Egyptian antiquity. Here Katep and Hetepheres share what we can only hope is a pleasant afterlife together. The ancient Egyptians thought that the efficacy of such representations depended on its realism, and so this statue is carefully painted. Limestone, c. 2500 BC. *Source:* The Trustees of the British Museum.

Ancient Egypt offers us not only beautiful things but also fascinating ideas. J. W. von Goethe said, "*Wer fremde Sprachen nicht kennt, weiß nichts von seiner eigenen*" – roughly, "he who does not know foreign languages, knows nothing of his own." The same is true of cultures. One must fully experience another culture to become truly aware of one's own. Egypt offers a view of life, death, and the universe that differs intriguingly and instructively from ours. To our own, essentially Greek, minds, for example, the Egyptians' conception of the *meaning* of things in relation to *representations* of things is difficult to comprehend (Hornung 1999). In provisioning a dead king's tomb for his eternal life (Ikram and Dodson 1998), for example, the Egyptians apparently saw no *essential* difference in placing in the tomb real loaves of bread, or wooden models of bread, or paintings of loaves on the walls, or even paintings of people making bread. All could sustain the deceased in the afterlife. The Egyptians obviously knew that a living person could not eat the wooden models of loaves of bread or the paintings of bread with which they furnished tombs, or eat the other foods and tools illustrated on a tomb wall, but they had a sense that such representations could indeed sustain the deceased in some way. Similarly, some richer tombs included formulaic texts that promised offerings of food and goods to the deceased. Simply by reading these texts and saying the individual's name, the Egyptians believed that they could feed the deceased and keep him or her "alive" after death. Writing or saying the person's name would allow him or her to participate in the society of the living, at least to the extent that the deceased's appearance, words, and identity were remembered.

Cremation of human remains has a long history and is emerging as a preferred method of disposing of the dead in Western society, but it would have been anathema to the ancient Egyptians, for they would have viewed it as the loss of their most precious asset in negotiating a pleasant afterlife. For example, millions of tourists file past King Tutankhamun's coffin every year, and just by saying his name, according to ancient Egyptian belief, they "cause him to live, as he so fervently wished, every minute of every day, around the vastness of a modern world he could never have imagined" (N. Reeves 1990: 209).

We have not rid ourselves completely of superstitious confounding of word and deed, as anyone who has repeatedly postponed making a will – or, conversely, refrained from speaking of a desired future event for fear of "jinxing" it – can understand. But in the Egyptian view, the word and the object were in a sense the same, and therefore the powers inherent in the word could be used for good or to mitigate evil. Consider, for example, "mutilated" hieroglyphs (Allen 2000: 317). Their precise significance remains obscure, but some scholars suggest that if it were linguistically necessary in composing, let's say, a tomb inscription with the hieroglyphic sign in the shape of a bird, the Egyptian scribe could prevent the bird thereby called into existence from eating the baskets of grain included in the tomb offerings – or even the grain in baskets pictured in tomb inscriptions – by mutilating the hieroglyph of that bird, such as by representing it without a head. Thus, the inscription could still be read, but a peckish bird would not threaten the deceased's rations (Davies 1987). Similarly, in some inscriptions the character in the form of a snake, necessary to convey a specific sound in the spoken language, could be depicted as cut with knives and thereby rendered impotent to harm the deceased (Figure 1.8)

The ancient Egyptians identified many powerful supernatural forces in their cosmos, many of them malignant, and all of them – especially the king – had to come to terms with these forces and their own place in relation to them. For us, life's many reverses – including illnesses, financial privations, marital woes, and so forth – are just the expected and inescapable consequences of being human in this particular inexplicable universe; for us, even death is often viewed as sad but not tragic, if the deceased is aged – and if it happens to someone other than ourselves or our relatives. As we shall see, the ancient Egyptians had a very different view of misfortunes, and they had religious weapons that they could wield to mitigate or even overcome all ills, even death.

These aspects of ancient Egyptian cosmology may seem primitive to us, but the Egyptians would no doubt see our own cosmologies as equally bizarre. "Western science" was only possible once scholars stopped using analytical units composed of visible entities, such as earth, water, and fire, and the many other *things*, the enumeration and categorization of which were the true sources of knowledge to the Egyptians. For the Egyptian, the image *was* the thing, and to picture the thing and to know its name was to understand it, and in a sense control it. For us, in great contrast, science requires that we abandon these familiar things and think instead in terms of quarks, genomes, black holes, string theory, and the rest of the cosmic stew of phenomena that in most cases cannot be seen, only deduced (Dunnell 1982). And in place of the actions of the gods to create and shape the world, we must believe in such absurdities as an ever-expanding universe that originated as a single super massive object about the size of an atom, which exploded in the "Big Bang" and created the expanding universe in which we live. At this point, the skeptical reader is invited to enter the term "Boltzmann brain problem" in his or her Internet search engine, and to consider the chance that the reincarnation of Pepy II, for example, according to at least a few reputable cosmologists, is not only possible but possibly inevitable.

Figure 1.8. The sharp definition of characters in monumental inscriptions gives them particular distinctiveness as the sunlight changes angle. Note that knives are shown as cutting the snake character – a protection against a bite from the snake called into existence by this representation of it. From the tomb of Kheruef in Western Thebes, Theban Tomb 192, dating to the reigns of Amenhotep III–Amenhotep IV, c. 1355 BC. The text is part of a sun hymn. The word with the knives through the determinative is *kednw*, "to encircle." *Source:* Photograph courtesy of Emily Teeter.

The ancient Egyptians conceptualized their world in terms that we can think of metaphorically as a cosmic turbine. They believed that the moving parts of their universe, including the stars in their courses, the sun's daily transit, the ebb and flow of the Nile, the succession of seasons, human transitions through birth, life, death, and afterlife – all the elements of this eternal armature – could be kept in proper operation only through the efforts of both the gods and the living. It was through their own performance of rituals in temples, and the activities of the priests and rulers, they believed, that they assisted the gods in keeping the universe in continuous good operation.

In these and many other diverse ways, the Egyptians saw themselves and their world differently than we do. Yet we know from their literature that they were also much like us in essential ways. In one poem of the New Kingdom (c. 1540–1070 BC), for example, a young man is prostrate, stricken with the adolescent passions that poetry celebrates in all cultures:

Why, that girl's better than any prescription...
...
At the sound of her voice my heart leaps to her tune,
And then when I kiss her, feel her length breast to thigh,
Love's evil spirits fly clean from my system –
God, what a girl, what a woman!
And that bitch has been gone for a week!   (Foster and Davies 1992: 58–61)

Poetry, Robert Frost said, is what is lost in translation, and this is probably particularly true of Egyptian poetry, so different from English in sound and semiotics. In love, however, the ancient Egyptians seem much like us. They even resemble us in the small human virtues. As we do, they lavished love on cats, dogs, and other pets, even mummifying and naming them in ways necessary to ensure their eternal life. Such rituals probably did much to remove some of the sting of the death of even a pet cat, for one could assume that in the afterworld one would be reunited with it – a hope with which we can sympathize, even if few of us believe in it.

Egypt's record of dynastic life is so rich that we are tempted to believe that we can get "into their skins" and know how they experienced life. French sociologist Marcel Mauss expressed (1979) a similar idea in his concept of *habitus*, meaning the habitual experiences, particularly those "anchored in the body." These daily practices of individuals and groups, including all of our learned habits, tastes, preferences, styles, bodily skills, and other knowledge, form such a basic foundation of ordinary life that the word means something like "it goes without saying." The rich texture of the Egyptian material from the past gives us the illusion that

Box 1. Cats in Ancient Egypt

For I will consider my Cat Jeoffry
For he is the servant of the Living God, duly and daily serving him.
. . .
For he keeps the Lord's watch in the night against the adversary,
For he counteracts the powers of darkness by his electrical skin and glaring
   Eyes.
For he counteracts the Devil, who is death, by brisking about the life.
. . .
For he purrs in thankfulness when God tells him he is a good Cat.
For he is an instrument for the children to learn benevolence upon.
For every house is incomplete without him, and a blessing is lacking in the
   spirit. . . .

(Christopher Smart [1722–1771], "Jubilate Agno")

The authority of the Bible must be questioned on the grounds that it inexplicably fails to celebrate cats, surely one of God's better creative efforts. The ancient Egyptians, in contrast, wisely made the cat a potent religious symbol (Malek 1997). The goddess Bastet, for example, was depicted as having the body of a woman and the head of a cat or a lion. Already by the Second Dynasty (c. 2890–2686 BC), she was considered a primary goddess of northern Egypt, especially the Delta. She was associated with war and was also considered to be a ferocious protector of the pharaoh; in later periods her image was softened and she also became associated with aspects of love, fertility, and house cats.

Cats were an integral part of ancient Egyptian life, both as cherished household pets and valued bounty hunters of birds and rodents. Herodotus reported that when a pet cat died, members of the bereaved household shaved their eyebrows to express their grief. A tomb of the Twelfth Dynasty (c. 1985–1773 BC) at Abydos contained seventeen cat skeletons, and the excavator, Sir Flinders Petrie, inferred that a row of tiny rough pottery bowls found in this tomb once contained milk to "feed" the dead cats. In one tomb at Tell Amarna (c. 1353 BC), the sarcophagus of a pet cat was inscribed with her name, "Osiris, the Lady Cat." This obviously adored pet was depicted on the sarcophagus as sitting next to an offering table with a feline-headed *shabti*, a figurine of an individual placed in a tomb to help the deceased in the afterlife, "as if the cat were a deceased member of the family" (Brewer, Redford, and Redford 1994: 109). In a vault carved out of the stone bedrock of the area near Saqqara, more that three hundred thousand cat mummies were discovered. Some were buried with mummified mice to feed them after death. Killing a cat, except as an offering to the goddess Bastet, was punishable by death.

The Egyptian word for cat can be transliterated as *"myw,"* and it does not take a trained cryptographer to see the connection.

Cat skeletons have been found in Southwest Asian villages that date to about 7000 BC, but the skeletal differences between wild and early domestic cats are minor; indeed, the common house cat's proportions are nearly the same as a lion's, when allometrically scaled to a lion's size. Thus, it is not clear when and where they were first "domesticated" – a vague term that does not really capture the willful solipsists that all cats, paradoxically, are. When people in Southwest Asia became cereal farmers, ten thousand years ago, they inevitably attracted mice and rats to their homes, and mice and rats attract cats. It is out of this conjunction that cats probably entered their ambivalent relationship with people. Douglas Brewer, Donald Redford, and Susan Redford note (1994: 105) that the control of breeding has been the key to the domestication of most animals. But people have been laughably inept at controlling cats' reproductive strategies and tactics; thus, cats have not lost the primary adaptive traits of their wild relatives: retractile claws, keen hearing and smell, remarkable night vision, a muscular and supple body, excellent memory, and an impressive aptitude for learning from observation and experience.

I expatriated to the United States a stray Egyptian cat, Shireen, who, previous to her abrupt transition to Seattle, had been eking out a living by importuning fish offal from fishermen near the houseboat on which I lived in Cairo. She was a most grateful immigrant and proved to be a marvelous animal in every way. She had some of the coat colors and characteristics of her wild relatives, and she also had that special stare of all cats, in which they look at their putative owner as if considering purchasing him or her (as Mark Twain observed). She regularly assassinated rodents and birds and proudly laid their bleeding corpses on my best oriental rug. But she was the very embodiment of gentleness and affection in her dealings with me, and on occasion she would even coolly acknowledge the presence of other people.

we can see the world and life in much the same terms as the Egyptians did themselves, even in such matters as their ideas about their cats.

We must remind ourselves, however, that Egypt's many artifacts, from pyramids to amulets, were not just aesthetic expressions intended simply for display but were *used*, in a complex system of symbols and meanings that we can only partially access. And they did not make the same sharp distinctions that we sometimes draw between decorative forms, the media in which they are produced, and their entire range of functions.

Egyptian views about death and the afterlife seem particularly compelling to the modern mind. Ancient Egypt confronts us vividly with the idea of inescapable personal death, and with our own selves in relation to the infinity of time and the abyss of history. Some people (including me) have had their first memorable encounter with a dead person in the form of an Egyptian mummy in a museum (Figure 1.9). On such occasions the ancient maxim "as you are now, I once was; as I am now, you soon will be" comes irresistibly to mind. The Egyptians remind us that we too shall soon be dead and remain so for what to all evidence will be a rather long time. And they too had their existential fears and anxieties. The Roman sentiment *Timor mortis conturbat me*, "the fear of death disturbs me," is common to all but the insane and/or religious zealot. And although many

Figure 1.9. Mummy of Pharaoh Ramses II. He looks rather well for a man who died about 3,020 years ago. In his prime he sent large Egyptian armies into Syro-Palestine, where he directed massive battles at Qadesh and other locations. The military result seems to have been a draw, but Ramses presented it as a great victory and celebrated it in tomb and temple inscriptions and other documents. Old Kingdom mummification was probably not as good as that used on Ramses II. From the early Dynastic Period onward, a well-mummified and well-supplied corpse was considered important for negotiating a happy afterlife. *Source:* Scala / Art Resource, NY.

devout ancient Egyptians may have "solved the Great Riddle" (i.e., died) in their faith with more equanimity than many moderns, some apparently did not. One text records a person's idea of a debate between two forms of his soul and concluded pessimistically: "Make holiday! Do not weary of it! See, no one can take goods with him. See, no one who [has] departed returns again."

We know relatively little about Egyptian beliefs about destiny and the nature of the human soul(s). Meskhenet, a goddess associated with childbirth, seems to have had some role in predicting the social roles of people, and various other gods were associated with the notion of human destiny, but little is known about such ideas as the people in the periods that are the main focus of this book might have conceived them. In general, however, unlike theologian John Calvin, who made the powerful observation that an omniscient God, by definition, must know who is predestined for eternal salvation and who is doomed to hell, the ancient Egyptians seem have had a much looser sense of destiny (Assman 2002, 2005). They had no conception of heaven or hell like that of Christianity or Islam, at least for the vast majority of people. Moreover, the Egyptians had the comforting belief that eternal life could be gained through good works, not just faith.

Despite the ancient Egyptians' extravagant mortuary cults and ideologies, even a cursory study of their past reveals that they were neither obsessed with death nor intoxicated with eternity. Their love of life simply was such that they tried mightily to perpetuate it beyond death. Indeed, life in ancient Egypt, seen from our vantage point, appears to have been enviably pleasant. They were a comely people who lived in a salubrious climate and a beautiful country; they enjoyed relaxed notions of sexual propriety; they do not generally appear to have been weighed down by neuroses or fear of death and damnation; they drank excellent wines and beers; and their insularity, both cultural and geographical, meant that most avoided the paths to military glory that abruptly led many an ancient Syro-Palestinian, Hittite, Persian, Greek, and Roman to an early grave.

Egypt, in fact, was so renowned in the ancient world for its many charms that at about 620 BC, God himself felt compelled to command the Israelites not to leave the unprepossessing area that was Syro-Palestine in order to relocate in the lush environs of Egypt. And God confided his plans to his prophet Jeremiah in minatory terms:

But if ye say, We will not dwell in this land; so that ye obey not the voice of Jehovah your God, saying, No; but we will go into the land of Egypt, where we shall see no war, nor hear the sound of the trumpet, nor have hunger of bread; and there will we dwell:

now therefore hear ye the word of Jehovah, O remnant of Judah: Thus saith
Jehovah of hosts, the God of Israel, If ye indeed set your faces to enter into
Egypt, and go to sojourn there;

then it shall come to pass, that the sword, which ye fear, shall overtake you
there in the land of Egypt; and the famine, whereof ye are afraid, shall follow
hard after you there in Egypt; and there ye shall die.

So shall it be with all the men that set their faces to go into Egypt to sojourn
there: they shall die by the sword, by the famine, and by the pestilence; and none
of them shall remain or escape from the evil that I will bring upon them.

(Jeremiah, Chapter 42, American Revised Version)

Nonetheless, despite its many virtues and allures, we should not
romanticize ancient Egypt. To begin with, it was in no sense a Jeffersonian
democracy. The elites disparagingly referred to commoners with the word
for "larks," meaning the tiny crested birds that one still encounters by the
millions everywhere in Egypt; and they believed that it was their God-
given right to expropriate the labor and wealth of these masses. The
average farmer or herdsman probably performed many difficult and
dangerous tasks. And although Egyptian women of the dynastic age seem
to have had remarkable status and civil rights compared to women in
other early states, ancient Egyptian society was, too, thoroughly dominated by men.

The Egyptians were also somewhat xenophobic; they considered most
foreigners to be inherently at odds with the true gods, the gods of Egypt,
particularly the rebarbative "sand dwellers," or Asiatics, on their
northeastern border. The Egyptians associated them with "chaos," the
opposite of the concept of "good order," represented by the deity Maat.
The Egyptians had military conflicts with these people throughout their
history, from before 3000 BC and often during the period covered by
this book (Redford 1992: 229–233). It is probably unfair to characterize
them as "racists," however. They were ethnocentric to a fault, but
throughout their history they seem to have believed that anyone, no
matter what his or her ethnic origins or skin color, who spoke Egyptian
and followed Egyptian customs was for all practical purposes an Egyptian. Thus, in later periods at least, the Egyptians permitted their
ostensible inferiors from Nubia and Syro-Palestine to become, on
occasion, powerful and wealthy members of the elites.

Although Egypt was no Hobbesian world of unrelenting competition
for sustenance, there were bad years in which the Nile flood was particularly low and unrewarding, and these hard times must have been
fresh in the memory of older people. The bones of many ancient
Egyptians, who were small in stature, show signs of nutritional stress

during childhood, probably from inadequate diet and parasitic worms; few lived into their fifties. Occasionally the widening gyre of provincial and national wars engulfed them. Indeed, for all we know, most of Egypt's poorest farmers were just a beer or two away from pouring out their simmering resentments about death, taxes, and outrageous fortune's many other slings and arrows. Government officials, for example, who surpassed even the confiscatory agents of the U.S. Internal Revenue Service in rapaciousness, taxed them unmercifully. And although there are many competing ideas about how the pyramids and other monumental structures were built, one thing is certain: They could only have been constructed through the hard labor of hundreds of thousands of commoners toiling over many years.

In person they were probably insufferably provincial and monolingual – resembling in this regard many Americans. Few of them traveled outside the homeland, except for trade or warfare, and for centuries they resisted even such useful foreign innovations as domesticated horses and war chariots until forced to do so by military necessity.

Yet for all these societal ills and oddities – at least as we perceive them from our own vantage points in time and history – there remains much about the Egyptian past that can instruct us and enrich our lives – and much that seems attractive. The *Westcar Papyrus*, an ancient Egyptian text, for example, records that Sneferu (c. 2613–2589 BC), the first king of the Old Kingdom's Fourth Dynasty, was wandering through his palace one day in search of diversion. Here was a man who had unlimited entrée to Egypt's most desirable nubilia; he had wine stewards ready to ply him with Egypt's grandest vintages; he had teams of magicians, jesters, acrobats, and entertainers of every sort. And yet he was thoroughly and existentially bored out of his skull. The text records that one day

[Sneferu said] "Go, bring [to] me the chief lector-priest, the scribe of the books, Djadja-em-ankh!" He was brought to him straightaway. His majesty said to him: ["I have gone through all the rooms] of the palace in search of relaxation and found none." Djadja-em-ankh said to him: "May your majesty proceed to the lake of the palace. Fill a boat with all the beautiful girls of your palace. Your majesty's heart will be refreshed by seeing them row . . . rowing up and down. As you observe the fine nesting places of your lake, as you observe the beautiful fields and shores, your heart will be refreshed by it."   (After Lichtheim 1973: 216)

Well, "it's good to be the king," as we all know, and Sneferu's imperious recreational prerogatives may rankle modern sensibilities, but such texts reveal that the ancient Egyptians were not the untutored primitives who, as we sometimes erroneously imagine, preceded us in history.

The Nature and Significance of Ancient States (Part 2): Egypt and Comparative Analyses of Early Civilizations

The most important issue confronting the social sciences is the extent to which human behaviour is shaped by factors that operate cross-culturally, as opposed to factors that are unique to particular cultures.   (Bruce Trigger 2003: 3)

It is regrettable that we must approach the marvels of ancient Egyptian civilization by traversing the arid plains of cross-cultural analyses, but in this quotation the late, brilliant anthropologist and Egyptologist Bruce Trigger confronts us with a difficult and complex question – a question that sums up the central issue in centuries of academic debates about comparative history and anthropology.

To begin with, what can we hope to know about Pepy II and the Egyptian history of which he was a part? And what can we know about the human past and history in general? What are the dynamics that have caused people and their cultures to change as they have? What forces propelled Egypt from simple farming to "high civilization"? Why, for example, was Egypt fundamentally similar in its developmental trajectory and characteristics to other ancient civilizations? Why and how was it different? And why were these early civilizations different from "less complex" societies in aboriginal Australia, Hawaii, Scotland, California, and many other places?

These are difficult questions, without easy answers. From our perspective, the independent evolution of these ancient states may seem to be natural, almost inevitable outcomes of history. In our experience, civilizations not only change; they *advance*, at least in the sense of the evolution of technology, socioeconomy, and political integration. Yet there is nothing *necessary* about this evolutionary pattern. While dynastic Egypt and similar societies around the world were emerging as complex states and civilizations, the vast majority of the world's populations were not. In most areas of the world, the people who lived at the same time that Egypt's civilization was flowering were still following the ancient hunting-foraging way of life of their ancestors from thousands of years earlier (Figure 1.10). Indeed, in much of the world, hunting and foraging remained the basis of human life until just a few millennia ago, and in some areas until just a few centuries ago. "Aborigines," for example, have lived for about forty thousand years in Australia, and when the first Europeans encountered them they found a people whose technology and social organization had changed very little over all that time (though even seasoned ethnographers find their ideology nearly impenetrably complex). Moreover, in

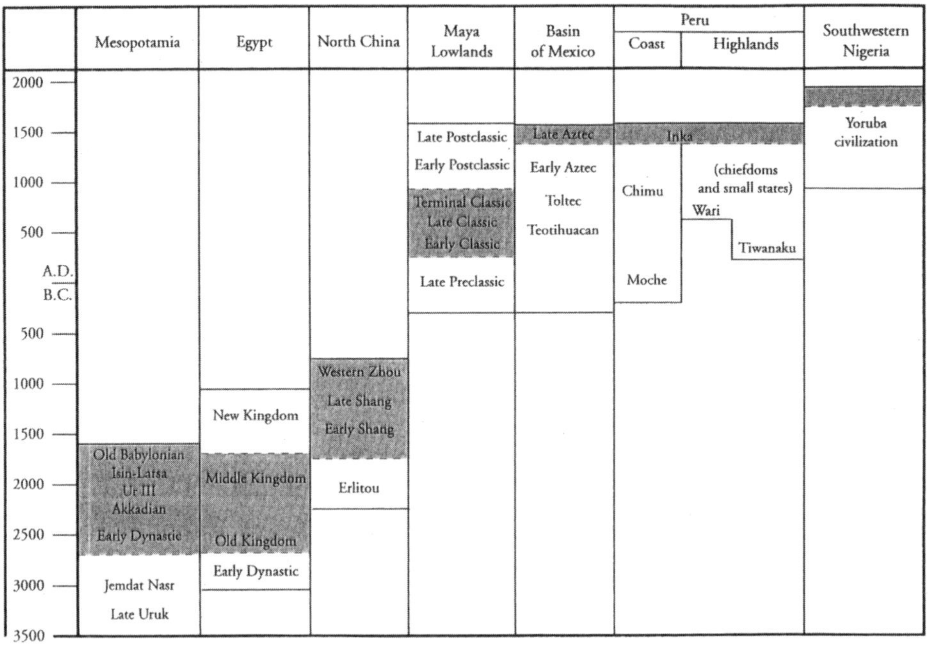

	Mesopotamia	Egypt	North China	Maya Lowlands	Basin of Mexico	Peru Coast	Peru Highlands	Southwestern Nigeria
2000 —								
1500 —				Late Postclassic	Late Aztec	Inka		Yoruba civilization
1000 —				Early Postclassic	Early Aztec	Chimu	(chiefdoms and small states)	
500 —				Terminal Classic Late Classic Early Classic	Toltec Teotihuacan		Wari	
A.D. B.C.				Late Preclassic		Moche	Tiwanaku	
500 —								
1000 —			Western Zhou					
1500 —		New Kingdom	Late Shang Early Shang					
2000 —	Old Babylonian Isin-Larsa Ur III Akkadian	Middle Kingdom	Erlitou					
2500 —	Early Dynastic	Old Kingdom						
3000 —	Jemdat Nasr	Early Dynastic						
3500 —	Late Uruk							

Figure 1.10. Comparative chart of early civilizations by the late Bruce Trigger. Trigger briefly summarized the developmental quality of the polities – they all appeared after centuries of accumulated cultural changes. He tried to examine a wide range of complex cultures, and so he included the Yoruba while leaving out of this chart much earlier and more complex cultures, such as the Harrapan civilization of the Indus Valley. The earlier appearance of Old World states (except the Yoruba), compared to New World civilizations, has been attributed to the absence in the New World of large domesticted stock animals, steel tools (particularly guns), war horses, long-distance sailing craft, and so forth. *Source:* Reprinted with the permission of Cambridge University Press and the American University in Cairo Press from Trigger 2003: © Cambridge University Press 2003.

other parts of the world, some people, such as the yam farmers of Polynesia and the maize-beans-squash horticulturists of New Mexico, made the transition to agriculture but never developed a state apparatus (Figure 1.11).

It is important to remember that a century of archaeological research has shown that the world's early civilizations were not formed by people walking, metaphorically speaking, in a single file, in lockstep and at a continuous rate, from Neolithic farming to royal splendor. We cannot simply identify a sequence leading inexorably from a barbarous Neolithic Age to a great civilization, and then productively apply that paradigm to all early states. Instead, the evidence shows that developmental changes occurred at varying rates and through different mechanisms to form ancient states.

Yet the developmental parallels in ancient states raise interesting questions. Why, for example, does warfare seem to have been so common in history, when there would seem to be such advantages to cooperation and peace among people who had just mastered the agricultural skills that allowed them to live in villages? Do economic forces really "drive" history, as Karl Marx argued, so that we can understand the Egyptian state in terms of technological and socioeconomic dynamics? Or do great ideas and powerful individuals determine the course of history? Does "the past" really exist in some analyzable form and sense, or is what we call the past – even as seemingly vivid a past as that of Egypt – just our evanescent imaginings about something that we cannot truly reconstruct or understand? Does the past tell us anything of interest about ourselves, or are we just "leaves on a stream," irresistibly borne along by time and circumstance? Is the most important feature of ancient states and civilizations their general similarities, or is it the great variability they displayed in culturally constructing their individual worlds?

These issues are reviewed in Chapter 7 of this book, but we can begin our inquiry into Egypt's place in this context with a few observations. Trigger, for example, analyzed early civilizations in great detail (1993, 2003), and he found that in every single early state, elites were somehow able to confiscate economic surpluses and use them to their advantage, at the expense of the poorer classes. From such observations, he concluded: "I have documented significant variation from one early civilization to another only in terms of art styles and cultural values" (1993: 110).

If Trigger's observations are accurate, how can we go about explaining this lack of variability and the strong similarity he ascribes to these early states? To begin with, numerous archaeologists (e.g., Yoffee 2005; Richards and Van Buren 2000) have challenged the idea that early states were as fundamentally similar as traditional models of state origins have suggested; they also dispute the notion that ancient states are the products of general, universal forces. They highlight the many significant differences among early states – a term itself that they see as imprecise. The Harrapan civilization of the ancient Indus Valley, for example, appears to have been much less finely divided by inherited and differential

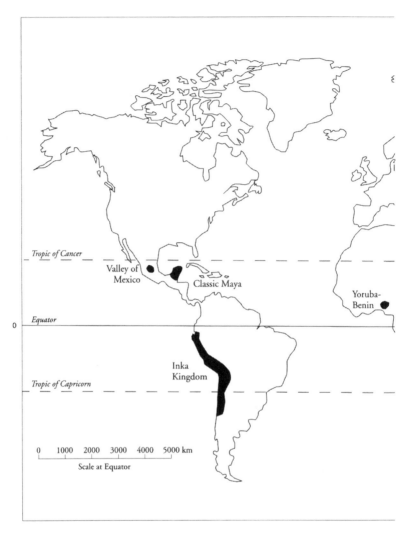

Figure 1.11. Locations of some early complex societies. Note that all occur in a narrow range of latitude. The northwest African examples all appeared several millennia after such civilizations as Egypt and Mesopotamia, but seem to have arisen mainly in response to regional factors, not simply contact with older polities. *Source:* Reprinted with the permission of Cambridge University Press from Trigger 2003. © Cambridge University Press 2003.

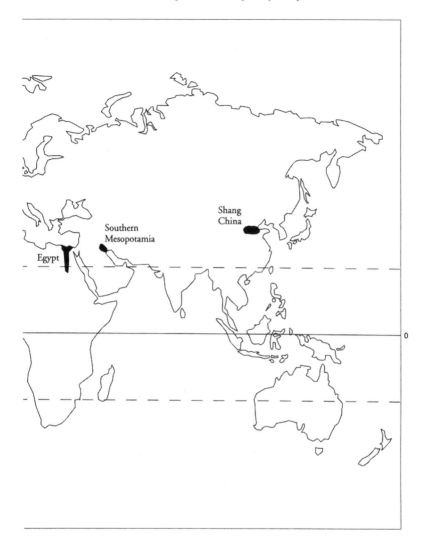

access to wealth, power, and prestige than were the other early states (R. Wright in press). These critics of traditional explanations of early state origins also emphasize the importance of ideologies in shaping cultures and their histories, not just the environmental, demographic, and technological forces in these cultures and histories. David Wengrow, for example, has argued that Egyptian cultures, from the Neolithic to the pharaonic era, express various continuities that "are not adequately accounted for either by evolutionary models which stress the progressive growth of technological and organizational complexity, or by evoking the internal structural and symbolic coherence of 'high cultures' and 'great traditions'" (2006: 9). The alternative analyses Wengrow and others suggest are in complex terms that are largely beyond the scope of this book, but some of these analyses and terms are discussed in subsequent chapters.

In any case, we must assume that there were diverse paths to the social organisms we loosely call "ancient states." Trigger himself, in his last major summary of this topic (2003), identified more variability in the evolutionary processes that produced early states, and in their characteristics, than he did in earlier works. Nonetheless, there *are* general similarities among early states, and any comprehensive analysis of early civilizations must explain *both* their differences and their similarities.

Many factors have been postulated as causes of the cultural changes that resulted in ancient civilizations and their inherent similarities: population growth, climate change, warfare, irrigation agriculture, and technological evolution have all been closely examined as primary factors, but none seems to explain much about early states' parallels and differences. None of the explanations based on such factors constitutes a satisfactory and powerful explanation of the Egyptian past, or of other ancient states, and few contemporary scholars are pursuing general unified analyses of ancient cultural change in terms of these factors.

Some contemporary scholars have attacked the very assumption that the human past can be usefully analyzed *scientifically* in almost any sense. Archaeologists Michael Shanks and Christopher Tilley, for example, have argued (1987a, 1987b, 1989) that the human past cannot be usefully analyzed in terms of an empirical science that "explains" history, in any traditional sense of that term. Other scholars (e.g., Dunnell 1982; Lyman and O'Brien 2000), in sharp contrast, argue that the past can be analyzed scientifically, and that archaeology can be as much a science as geology, paleontology, and biology.

Most scholars occupy the middle ground between these extremes, and apply concepts and analyses from a broad range of perspectives.

The Theoretical Perspective of This Book

History is philosophy teaching by examples.

                                        (Dionysius of Halicarnassus, c. 40 BC)

My premise is that Egypt's antiquity has greater significance than simply as an imagined "Disneyland" of an exotic extinct civilization. The assumption here is that we can enjoy Egypt as a beautiful and unique civilization, but that we can also attempt to place Egypt in the context of other early civilizations and consider the dynamics that produced them all, their similarities as well as their dissimilarities.

This is not a new or controversial perspective; many scholars have adopted this approach (reviewed in Trigger 2003). Nonetheless, the great majority of the scholarly literature concerning ancient Egypt is devoted to the specifics of this history, not its role in the context of general analyses of early states. Here, too, Pepy II provides a good example. Elaborate tombs like his have been found in China, Peru, Mexico, Iraq, and many other places; ancient Egypt, like these other cultures, was a social system based on the expropriation of wealth by elites and validated by a national religion. And so Pepy, when placed in a comparative analytical context, brings us back to the most basic and important questions of historical analysis: Why, for example, did these societies, Old and New World alike, all evolve social systems based on inherited privilege and wealth, in which the great mass of humanity labored mainly for the benefit of a small elite class? And how are we to explain the differences among these polities, such as the Harrapan example presented previously?

The reader is forewarned that this book does not conclude triumphantly with comprehensive answers to such questions, or with powerful explanations of the Egyptian past. It is narrowly focused on a particular interval of dynastic history, and space limitations do not permit a systematic comparison of Egypt to other early states. Instead, a few general ideas are presented and evaluated with evidence from the Egyptian past. Most of these ideas may appear to the reader as elaborations of the obvious, or too complex to be evaluated with our fragmentary and adventitious evidence from Egypt. But the history of science teaches us that advancements in understanding and explanation demand the accumulation not just of "facts" but also of concepts that dictate what kinds of "facts" are relevant, and how they should be collected and interpreted.

The development of powerful general analyses of ancient civilizations may seem premature and ultimately unlikely, but as the nineteenth-century sociologist Herbert Spencer observed in a different context, the greatest sin in evaluating methods of analyses is "contempt prior to investigation."

2 Introduction to the Ancient Egyptians and Their Country

Egypt...is an acquired country, the gift of the [Nile].

Herodotus (c. 450 BC)

Introduction

Images from space (Figure 2.1) reveal Egypt to be an elongated oasis, sinuously traversing the stark emptiness of the eastern Sahara. The ancient Egyptians may not have appreciated the obvious metaphor of their country's shape as a lotus flower – a national symbol – writ large, because in the few pharaonic maps we know of, they sometimes put the south at the top.

This idea would have appealed to them, nonetheless, for they saw their world as a beautiful whole, built of such dualities as cultivated land/desert land, delta/valley, east/west, life/death, sacred/profane, and order/chaos. The reconciling and balancing of such binaries were central elements in Egyptian ideology.

The ancient Egyptians understood and valued their country as the gift of the Nile many millennia before Herodotus made his often-repeated observation. No civilization is entirely the product of its physical environment, of course. Modern Cairo, for example, bears little resemblance, except in location, to its ancestral communities of the pyramids age. Yet all civilizations have deep roots in their physical environment, and this is particularly true of Egypt. John Wilson (1951) characterized Egypt as a "sealed test tube" in which pharaonic civilization could flourish in its own unique environment, relatively sheltered from outside influences. Egypt was much more open to the outside world than Wilson supposed, but there is some truth to his characterization. Because of the productivity of the Nile Valley and its sharply defined borders, the pharaonic state controlled an area that was roughly the same size (see Figure 1.1) for more than three thousand years, a territorial stability no other early civilization experienced; and within that area they created a culture of unique brilliance.

The objective of this chapter is to present a summary – a stereotype – of ancient Egypt's people, environment, and culture. All stereotypes are

31

Figure 2.1. Satellite image of Egypt. This image emphasizes Egypt's isolation by the Sahara and Sinai, but cultural connections between Egypt and Southwest Asia began as early as 7000 BC. The large dark area west of the Nile and south of the Delta is the Faiyum Oasis, which contains evidence about Egypt's first cereal farmers (c. 5000 BC). *Source:* Courtesy of Paul Buck.

false to some extent, and we cannot suppose that Egypt as it existed during the period of primary interest in this book, circa 4500–2000 BC, can be accurately and completely inferred from the evidence of later periods. Yet Egypt was highly conservative in many of its cultural elements, and some of these persisted throughout the dynastic ages.

A note on the terminology used in this book is required here. "Pharaoh," as a term referring to the king, was used only relatively late in Egypt's dynastic history. In most of this book, the term "Dynastic" is used to refer to the entire sequence of kings and the periods in which they lived. Also, there are many variant spellings of names, archaeological sites, monuments, and so forth. Some of these variants are given here, but in general the most common appellations appear in this book.

The Origins of Dynastic Egyptians

Victory has a thousand fathers, but defeat is an orphan.

(Attributed to John F. Kennedy and others)

Debates about the physical anthropology and origins of ancient Egyptians concern biologically trivial issues, such as variations in hair texture and skin color, but these discussions reveal much about ideas concerning "race," ethnicity, and the relative merits of cultures.

Some nineteenth-century scholars, for example, doubted that a "high civilization" such as Egypt could be the product of Africans, and thus they concluded that invaders from Syro-Palestine had created pharaonic culture. In bitter contrast, some "Afrocentrists" have long argued that ancient Egypt was part of the "Negro world," and that all African cultures were influenced by Egypt (Diop 1974: 23). Others have argued that "Black" Africa was the ultimate source of European civilizations as well (e.g., Asante 1990). W. E. B. Du Bois, the American Civil Rights advocate, wrote, " [T]he shadow of a mighty Negro past flits through the tale of Ethiopia [and] of Egypt [and] the Sphinx. Throughout history, the powers of single blacks flash here and there like falling stars"([1903] 1995). And in his beautiful poem "The Negro Speaks of Rivers" (2002 [orig. 1926]), Langston Hughes wrote, "I looked upon the Nile and raised the pyramids above it." The evidence that few "Nubians" apparently participated in building the pyramids is of interest only to academics.

More recently, historian Martin Bernal has charged that for centuries racist Western scholars have maliciously minimized the historical roles of Semitic and African peoples. The title of his book *Black Athena* (1987; also see 2006) reflects his contention that the goddess Athena was Egyptian in origins, and – more important – that Greek and Roman cultures were influenced more directly by African and Semitic cultures than previous scholars have supposed. He claims, for example, that 40 percent of the classical Greek vocabulary was derived from Egyptian and Semitic languages, and thus he concludes that the evidence refutes what he calls the "Aryan Model" of the origins of classical Greek culture.

In this politically sensitive era, such arguments have achieved a level of debate far beyond their merits. Most scholars have concluded that the origins of Western civilization were mainly in the Mediterranean world, and that the origins of central elements of "Western" cultures are fundamentally in classical Greece and Rome, with significant influences from Southwest Asia (Burkert 1992), but few from "Black Africa" or elsewhere (Lefkowitz 1996).

In any case, these quarrels about ancestry are largely irrelevant to debates about the origins of states and civilizations; no one can rationally deny that people of genius have graced every culture, or that the world's centers of cultural florescence have shifted throughout history. England, for example, was a cultural backwater of illiterate hunter-foragers (despite their construction of Stonehenge at about 3000 BC) when the civilizations of Egypt, Mesopotamia, India, and China were already centuries old. Yet nineteenth-century England was able to dominate or exploit each and every one of these ancient civilizations. On this evidence alone, one might logically conclude that "cultural achievement," however defined, is not causally related to "race."

In any case, patterns of human physical variability seem best understood not in terms of races but as "clines" and "clusters" of human physical variability (Brace et al. 1993). Consider, for example, the variations in skin pigmentation along the gradient between northern Europe and southern Africa. Such variations can only be crudely described as "white" or "black." Moreover, human physical characteristics vary to some extent *independently*. Natives of southern India, for example, have skins as dark as many sub-Saharan Africans, but they typically have the straight hair texture and facial proportions of Caucasians and East Asians. Both southern Africans and southern Indians have dark skins because this genetically based trait evolved to protect people against skin cancers and other tropical maladies. Relatively lighter skin colors are typically found in northern climates where lighter skins facilitate vitamin D synthesis during long, dark winters, and where dark skin is largely unnecessary to protect from skin cancers.

The skin tones of dynastic Egyptians were likely the result of several factors. Hunter-foragers lived in what are now Egypt's Eastern and Western Deserts – but were once vast grasslands dotted with lakes – for long intervals before about six thousand years ago, and some of these people must have contributed their genes to what eventually became dynastic Egyptians. But after the world's glaciers began to retreat about twelve thousand years ago, northeast Africa became progressively drier, and the expanding deserts of the Sahara restricted the movement of people (and their genes) from elsewhere in Africa, except through the narrow southern Nile Valley, where turbulent rapids impeded navigation and, to a limited extent, human migration. Migration into Egypt was easier through the many land and sea routes that connected it to Syro-Palestine and the rest of the Mediterranean world. It is instructive, for example, that in much of their art the Egyptians depicted Nubians with the dark skins and hair styles of sub-Saharan Africans (Figure 2.2).

C. Loring Brace and his colleagues (1993) measured many different features on a sample of ancient Egyptian crania and used these data to estimate the genetic affinities of the ancient Egyptians to other groups. They concluded that ancient Egyptians were most closely related to Europeans (probably those closest to the Mediterranean) and to the people of North Africa, Somalia, Nubia, and India. They were most

Figure 2.2. Ethnic distinctions in Egyptian art. The Egyptians usually depicted the peoples to their south in skin tones, hairstyle, and dress different from their own. This scene, from Theban Tomb 40 of Huy, shows the reception of Nubians at the court of Tutankhamun, c. 1325 BC. Painted limestone. They also used distinctive hairstyles and dress to distinguish themselves from Asiatic "sand-dwellers." *Source:* Courtesy of the Oriental Institute, University of Chicago.

distant from native Australians, Melanesian peoples, and East Asian people, including "Native Americans."

The genes contributed to the Egyptian gene pool after about 1000 BC by Persians, Greeks, Romans, Arabs, Europeans, and other conquerors of Egypt have had some impact, but Brace et al. suggest that Egyptian physical traits have remained approximately the same for the past ten thousand years (although they did find one skull from the Old Kingdom pyramid complex at Giza that was very unlike ancient Egyptians and most closely resembled a Neolithic German).

It is a standard observation in elementary statistics that the average adult human has one breast and one testicle, and a similar statistical confusion applies to attempts to capture the average ancient Egyptian. For example, some apparently looked much like Mediterranean peoples, others like modern Sudanese. Still, there are certain characteristics we can surmise with some confidence. They were, on average, shorter than many Europeans and Americans of today; men averaged less than 5 feet, 5 inches tall (165 cm), and women about 5 feet, 1 inch (155 cm). In this they were not much different from medieval Europeans, and perhaps for the same reason: Parasites, diseases, and meager diets stunted many people's growth. Many of them probably had darker complexions than do natives of northern latitudes today, and their hair varied from curly to straight. Figure 2.3 is a depiction of an Old Kingdom nobleman – probably made to the specifications of the nobleman himself, that is, somewhat idealized.

Egyptians of different socioeconomic classes may have had slightly different physical appearances, however. Andrew Johnson and Nancy Lovell (1994; Lovell 1999) found that in three cemeteries at Predynastic (c. 4000–3000 BC) Naqada, in southern Egypt, human skeletal remains show variations in their physical characteristics that correlated with the relative size and wealth of their tombs and graves. They interpreted these differences to be too minor to have been the result of invasions of foreigners; it is more likely, they suggested, that these differences resulted from a long-term mating pattern in which people tended to marry within the socioeconomic classes into which they were born.

Figure 2.3. Statue of Old Kingdom nobleman. This painted limestone statue is of a nobleman named Nenkheftka, who lived at about 2400 BC. Such nobles were usually presented in this classic form and coloring, with left foot striding purposefully, and the whole composition in a rigid pose. *Source:* © The Trustees of the British Museum.

Another of the many factors that played a role in shaping the physical characteristics of the ancient Egyptians concerns political changes. Until the first Egyptian states brought both the Delta and Valley peoples under unified administration (at about 3000 BC), it is likely that the peoples of these two regions varied somewhat physically. And even after political unification, these differences probably persisted – as they still do today. A walk through the southern city of Aswan and then through the northern city of Alexandria demonstrates some of these differences.

In a sense, these issues concerning genetics are less important to an understanding of ancient Egypt than the Egyptians' idea of *ethnic identity*. The concept of ethnicity has been corroded with racism and bloodshed throughout human history, yet it still has great impact on contemporary human affairs. In contemporary Iraq, for example, brutal battles are being fought between people who are essentially identical in physical characteristics and genomes but different ethnically. Ancient Egyptians, too, had a strong sense of ethnic identity, one that transcended racial categorizations to some extent. Still, so long as immigrants to Egypt, whether from Syro-Palestine, Sudan, or elsewhere, spoke Egyptian and adopted Egyptian cultural values, they achieved a degree of acceptance in Egyptian society.

But, like most ancients, pharaonic Egyptians considered themselves different from, and superior to, all other peoples. They proudly called themselves *Remet-en-Kemet*, meaning the "people of Egypt."

Egypt's Physical Environment

The higher Nilus swells,
The more it promises; as it ebbs, the seedsman
Upon the slime and ooze scatters his grain,
And shortly comes the harvest.

   (William Shakespeare [1564–1616], *Antony and Cleopatra*, II. vii)

In these lines, Shakespeare captures the essential agricultural mechanics of ancient Egypt. Geologist Karl Butzer, more prosaically but no less succinctly, stated, "Major segments of ancient Egyptian history may be unintelligible without recourse to an ecological perspective" (1976: 15).

One cannot simply infer causal relationships between Egyptian ecological facts and all forms of Egyptian culture, of course; much depends, in a sense, on how the Egyptians uniquely and *culturally constructed* their culture and society within the limitations and possibilities offered by their physical environments.

Climate

American novelist Herman Melville rhapsodized that the "climate of Egypt in winter is the reign of spring upon earth . . . and summer [is] tranquility in the heat." Today's visitors to Egypt may marvel at the fact that many nineteenth- and early-twentieth-century Europeans and Americans – especially the tubercular among them – went to Egypt for the purity of its air and water.

For most of the past ten thousand years, Egypt's climate was much like that of today, with mild, frost-free winters, pleasant springs and autumns, and torrid summers. Summer temperatures in southern Egypt regularly reach 42°–49° C (c. 108°–120° F), and so intense is the sun that even with adequate water many crops will not survive. On even the hottest summer days, however, humidity is usually low, and shady palm groves along the Nile are pleasantly cool. Summer winds from the Mediterranean sometimes penetrate as far south as Cairo and bring blessed relief. From October to March, Egypt's climate is simply sublime.

At times in the period circa 2900–1900 BC, rainfall patterns were slightly more variable than those of the present day, with brief intervals of cooler annual temperatures and greater rainfall, but these intervals always ended with the return of hyperarid conditions. Egypt's Mediterranean coastline receives about four inches of midwinter rainfall annually, but there is no appreciable rain in the Nile Valley south of the modern Faiyum.

Still, Egypt's climate is nearly optimal for preindustrial agriculture. Its warm winters, springs, and autumns permit year-round agriculture; and even in summer, fodder crops, orchards, and a few other garden plants (Figure 2.4) grow well in the intense heat. Its latitude is such that it gets relatively intense solar radiation, but it is semiarid and thus not enveloped in jungle-like vegetation that would compete with crops. Nor were there dense forests that had to be cleared or thick grasslands that required plowing to be farmed. It is no accident that dynastic culture, and some of the world's other earliest civilizations, including Mesopotamia, the Indus Valley, China, and Andean South America, appeared in semiarid environments crossed by large rivers that flooded annually and reliably, and were located a roughly predictable distance away from the equator.

Fundamentals of Nile Geography, Hydrology, and Ecology

Herodotus was famously right that Egypt is the gift of the Nile, but he was curious about its annual fluctuations in height. He hypothesized that

Figure 2.4. Cultivating perennial gardens. Wheat and barley were the foundations of the Egyptian diet, but many garden vegetables, spices, and flowers were produced by a form of "raised-bed" gardening. Rectangular plots were laid out, planted (see man kneeling on right using a stick to create a hole), and hand-watered by men carrying water pots. This scene also illustrates the two-dimensional perspective in most Egyptian paintings and reliefs. The garden squares imply a three-dimensional perspective simply by their representation as three tiers of squares. From the tomb of Mereruka, Saqqara, c. 2300 BC. *Source:* After Kemp 1989, fig. 3. Reproduced by permission of Barry J. Kemp.

some of this variability was caused by seasonal variations in temperature, and thus evaporation rates. He was wrong, but his inference illustrates the penchant for scientific inquiry into seemingly simple questions that were so much a part of Greek culture. It is a measure of how "Greek" we are that we think it is just "common sense" to wonder why rivers rise, and to try to explain such phenomena in terms of natural causes. The Egyptians, too, had a lively interest in their natural world, and they carefully recorded the annual height of the Nile floods, but there is little evidence that they ascribed the Nile fluctuations to anything other than the will of Hapy, god of the inundation, and to other deities.

They may have been right, ultimately, but the proximate cause of the Nile's annual flood cycle is fluctuations in seasonal rains in the mountains of central and eastern Africa (Adamson et al. 1980). Rivers connected to Lake Victoria and other lakes in central Africa flow northward to form the "White Nile," which contributes about 17 percent of the volume of the Egyptian Nile. In Sudan, near Khartoum, the White Nile is joined by the "Blue Nile," which is fed by summer monsoon rains in the Ethiopian highlands. About two hundred miles north of Khartoum, the Nile is joined by the 'Atbarah and Sobat Rivers, which also drain the

Ethiopian highlands. In all, rainfall in the Ethiopian highlands from May to September contributes the remaining 83 percent of the Nile's volume. The White Nile's volume does not vary much from year to year, but that of the Blue Nile and the 'Atbarah do, and thus so do annual Nile flood levels. At times during the late Pleistocene (c. 12,000–10,000 BC), streams and rivers from what is now eastern Chad also connected to the main Nile (Keding 1998).

The few hunter-foragers who lived in Egypt from about 12,500 to 12,000 years ago must have witnessed awesome annual floods because the Nile then was a much more vigorous river – the "Wild Nile" as it has been called. Its rushing floods carried massive loads of suspended gravel, sand, and clay. These sediments were deposited in the Valley in the form of levees and riverbanks, and in the Delta as mounds of sand and gravel, or "turtle backs" (*gezira* ["sing"] in Arabic). Some of these geziras are only a few hundred square meters in area and less than a meter high, while others are several meters or more in height and many hectares in area. In the Delta, ancient Egyptians concentrated their settlements on higher and larger geziras. Since about ten thousand years ago, enough of the annual Nile flood's sediment load has reached the Delta to raise its height at a rate of about twenty centimeters a century, and to extend its coastal margin by about fifty kilometers during the past five thousand years (Coutellier and Stanley 1987).

During the millennia after the end of the last glacial age, about ten thousand years ago, the Nile's regime became gentler, but it varied significantly from year to year in its maximum flood levels. In pharaonic times the Nile's main channel annually averaged between eight hundred and a thousand meters in width, and about ten to twelve meters in depth – smaller than the Mississippi and the Amazon, but still one of the world's largest rivers. Before dams were built in the twentieth century, and in times of dramatically lower floods, the Nile at its lowest stage was probably not a single stream; the floodwaters would have been divided among several branches that flowed weakly northward, if they flowed at all.

In years of normal or higher Nile floods, the river overflowed its banks. These floods did not usually submerge their entire banks completely, even at maximum flood levels; instead, floodwaters flowed through low points in the banks, temporarily submerging inland areas and leaving the highest levees near the main channel as islands. During periods of maximum flooding, areas farther away from the main channel were more deeply inundated than the levees closer to the river, forming large basins of floodwaters (Figure 2.5).

Thus, the Nile and its adjacent landforms were different from those of some other ancient civilizations. In the Tigris-Euphrates Valley, for

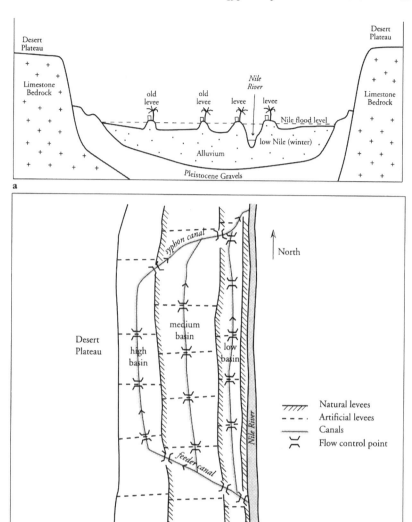

Figure 2.5. Mechanics of dynastic flood-basin agriculture, according to Bruce Trigger's reconstruction. Drawing (a) shows a cross section of the ancient Nile. Drawing (b) indicates the basics of agriculture in the main Nile channel in Upper Egypt. The river formed natural levees, but the Egyptians diverted some of the floodwaters through canals with control points so that water could be distributed to different areas of land. *Source:* Reprinted with the permission of Cambridge University Press from Trigger 2003, p. 296. © Cambridge University Press 2003.

example, the main river channels shifted dramatically and repeatedly, eventually creating a relatively level plain of redeposited levee and channel sediments that we call "Mesopotamia" (Figure 2.6). In contrast, the Nile's main floodplain shifted back and forth only a few kilometers during pharaonic history, and the cultivable area remained for many millennia just a thin strip of land on both banks of the main channel. The main Nile Delta distributaries, however, did change considerably in size and location during the pharaonic era.

In farming, Egypt had some advantages over Mesopotamia, where intensive canalization disastrously reduced water flow and eventually converted huge areas into salt flats worthless for farming (Pollock 1999: 37–38). In Egypt the annual floods washed away excess salts, and also brought fertilizing minerals from the mountains of East Africa. Egyptian farmers may have complemented this natural fertilization by herding cattle and sheep on fields after the harvest, so that their manure enriched the soil. They also planted nitrogen-fixing crops such as clover, but the great fertility of their land was largely a product of the river.

Nile Valley Ecology

In dynastic times, the main Nile Valley's environs were a complex mosaic of landforms and plant distributions (El-Hadidi and Springuel 1989; Wetterstrom 1997; Butzer 1976: fig. 1). The river's main channel was permanently submerged, but shallower areas along the banks would have supported reeds and other water-loving plants. Adjacent but slightly higher areas would have been submerged part of the year, but these would also have supported reeds and other marsh plants. Areas that were seasonally inundated for shorter periods would have been seasonal meadows of perennial grasses, with patches of reeds, some annual plants, and perhaps a few palm trees. Tamarisk trees and shrubs dominated higher areas that were only occasionally inundated. On higher ground, the levees' flora were primarily acacia and tamarisk trees, and shrubs. Once farming began, after about 5000 BC, farmers grazed animals on the levees, and cut trees and shrubs there for lumber, fuel, and fodder. Low vegetation and palm trees flourished in more open areas that had high water tables.

In the early pharaonic era, most of the farming was probably concentrated in the seasonally inundated areas that in their unfarmed state would have been meadows. With clearing and intensive weeding, these areas would have been very fertile and easily cultivated. Herodotus reports that these fields were not even plowed prior to planting; farmers simply waited until the floods receded and then sowed grain on the muck and sent in

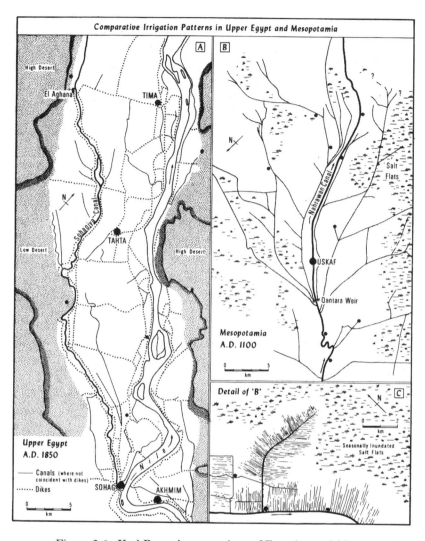

Figure 2.6. Karl Butzer's comparison of Egyptian and Mesopotamian farming. Many differences between ancient Mesopotamian and Egyptian cultures must be directly attributed to their differing river regimes. On the left is an example of the linear, flood-basin type of irrigation as it existed in an area of Upper Egypt at about AD 1850. On the right is an example of the Mesopotamian system, just south of Baghdad at about AD 1100. Clearly the Mesopotamian pattern required many more canals, both large and small, but it also permitted high population densities. *Source:* Butzer 1976, fig. 6 (see his references). © 1976 by the University of Chicago. Courtesy of the University of Chicago Press.

herds of pigs and other animals to trample in the seeds. Herodotus may have been misinformed in this regard, as there are scenes in ancient Egyptian art of wooden plows in use from about 2500 BC onward.

The Nile's gradient, periodicity, and other attributes are such that complex irrigation systems using dams and feeder canals upriver became important only fairly late in Egypt's history, perhaps not until about 1500 BC. However, during earlier periods, Egyptians probably made small dikes to trap part of the Nile floods in flood basins along the main channel, to be released later to increase the area of cultivable land and to irrigate summer vegetable crops and orchards. We do not know the extent to which the king and his administrators were involved in the management of water (Figure 2.7), but it was probably managed locally. People had to work together to build dams and clear canals.

Delta Ecology

Although the origins of Egyptian civilization were primarily in the south, the Delta was the agricultural heartland of the country for much of later dynastic history, famed for its wines, wheat, fruit, and cattle. The Delta also linked the Nile Valley to the cultures of the Mediterranean world and Southwest Asia; throughout the pharaonic period the Delta became increasingly important as a staging ground for armies, and as a nexus of overland and maritime trade routes (Figures 2.8, 2.9).

Figure 2.7. Royal control of irrigation works? The "Scorpion King," perhaps, inaugurating an irrigation project, at about 3100 BC. There is little evidence that there was much state control of local irrigation works, and this scene may be symbolic in the sense that the Egyptians thought of the king as the author and inspiration of all good works and things. *Source:* Butzer 1976, fig. 2 (see his references). © 1976 by the University of Chicago. Courtesy of the University of Chicago Press.

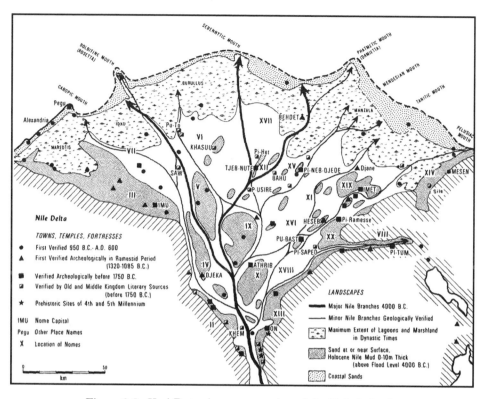

Figure 2.8. Karl Butzer's reconstruction of the Delta's landscape evolution in dynastic times. Note that the courses of the Nile distributaries changed repeatedly in location and volume. This explains why major ancient Delta cities are presently located relatively distant from modern branches of the Nile. Note, too, that the ancient "nomes" (provincial administrative units) were established on the basis of their connection to distributaries. The coastline would have been retracted southward through much of the dynastic era. Also, the geziras (see text) would be favored places to live. *Source:* Butzer 1976, fig. 4 (see his references). © 1976 by the University of Chicago. Courtesy of the University of Chicago Press.

The ancient Egyptian name for the Delta may derive from the word for "flooded land" (Goedicke 1988), but geological studies (de Wit and van Stralen 1988: 138) suggest that marshy conditions did not greatly restrict agriculture or settlement in this region. Indeed, archaeologists have found many archaeological sites in the Delta that date to 3200–2000 BC, the period when the first Egyptian states formed and expanded. Northern

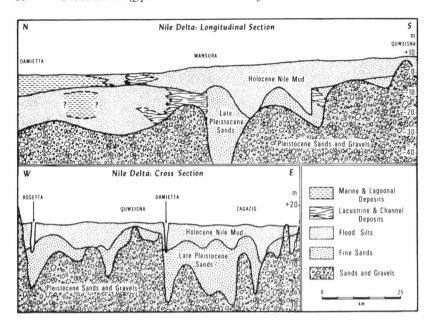

Figure 2.9. The Delta subsurface in longitudinal and transverse sections. *Source:* Butzer 1976, fig. 3 (see his references). © 1976 by the University of Chicago. Courtesy of the University of Chicago Press.

coastal areas of the Delta were marshes and lagoons, with frequent incursions of salt water from the Mediterranean Sea, which rose substantially between 9000 and 7500 BC, as the glaciers retreated. The Mediterranean's expansion covered areas that were once prime hunting-fishing-foraging lands with salt water, erasing or burying any archaeological remains that might have existed there (Butzer 2002, 1976: fig. 36).

Over the millennia, Nile distributaries incised several large channels through the Delta, all running roughly from south to north. Throughout the dynastic era at least some Delta tributaries were navigable and provided cultural connections to the Nile Valley and the Mediterranean world. Land routes to southwestern Asia followed the southeastern border of the Delta.

Deserts and Oases

Even just a few kilometers from the Nile, the desert is eerily silent and, to all appearances, lifeless. So silent is this region that if one sits quietly for a few minutes, the beating of one's own heart slowly becomes audible – a communion with one's mortality that can be a bit unnerving.

As one crests the last desert hills bordering the valley, however, one sees the beautiful stark contrast of green palm trees and fields against the deep blue of the Nile, the whole bracketed by the desert's reds, browns, and yellows, and the air comes alive with the thrumming of insects and frogs, and the voices of birds, livestock, and people.

Millions of years ago, a huge sea covered what is now Egypt, and for millions of millennia sediments precipitated from this sea formed a thick limestone formation on the seabed. This limestone formation is strewn with the fossilized teeth of the huge sharks and other animals that roamed these ancient seas. Today, just a few kilometers inland from the Nile's borders are vast seas of sand, ripped open by massive crests of basalt and granite that millions of years ago erupted through the limestone formation that underlies much of Egypt. Most of the building blocks used in Egyptian public architecture came from this formation. In southern Egypt, Dynastic Egyptians quarried basalt, granite, and other hard stones, and used them to spectacular decorative effect in making sarcophagi, obelisks, statuary, columns, and other architectural elements.

One of the humblest mineral resources of the desert was also one of its most important: The ancient Egyptians had no access to cheap metals for their basic tools, but the deserts provided them with an unlimited supply of fine-grained *chert* (or "flint"), from which they made sickle blades, awls, arrow and spear points, knives, and other implements (Figure 2.10).

A saline lake in the Wadi Natrun, in the desert west of the Delta, provided "natron" (mainly hydrated sodium carbonate), which was used to preserve mummies.

Throughout the pharaonic era, Egypt's desert margins were the favored locations for temples, tombs, and towns. Running east and west from the Nile, and far out into the deserts that border the Nile Valley, are many ancient erosional channels (*wadi* [sing.] in Arabic). They mark the course of rivers and streams that during wetter periods tens of thousands of years ago carried rainwater runoff to the Nile. In the south of Egypt, the wadis that ran through the Eastern Desert to the Red Sea probably linked Egypt to ships sailing from Mesopotamia and Arabia.

From at least 6000 BC, Egypt's deserts have been insignificant agriculturally, but in the period just before, during, and after the most recent retreat of the world's great glaciers (c. 12,000–10,000 BC), they supported gazelles, hares, ibexes, addaxes, rodents, and many other animals, as well as the predators – lions, wolves, foxes, hyenas, jackals, hawks, and people – who were attracted by this movable feast. This explosion of life in what for millennia had been nearly lifeless deserts was the result of a fortunate coincidence of climatic change. Periodically,

0 ——————————— 5cm

KOM EL- HISN

Figure 2.10. Egypt's deserts provided many tools for dynastic Egyptians. The most basic were chert sickle blades, knives, awls, and scrapers. Stone toolmaking began by striking a nodule of chert with a hammer-stone to detach a flake such as the one illustrated here. By chipping and grinding, a variety of tools could then be made. *Source:* Photograph by Robert J. Wenke.

summer rainfall patterns moved northward, and Mediterranean winter rains moved southward, and together they produced a verdant landscape dotted with lakes and streams, amidst vast grasslands. At the same time, the Nile was a much more vigorous river than it is today, and it created huge flood basins and a unique and productive ecosystem. The people who lived in the grasslands on the Nile's margins and along the Nile may, in fact, have been the distant ancestors of the peoples of the Neolithic and pharaonic ages (see Chapter 4).

The most important oasis in Egyptian history is the Faiyum (or "Fayum," or "Fayyum") (see Figure 2.1). It covers about 1,800 square kilometers (700 square miles), and parts of it are 45 meters (about 148 feet) below sea level. In pharaonic times, a secondary Nile channel, the Bahr Yusef, carried Nile floods into the Faiyum depression. As a result, the Faiyum encloses what was once the only freshwater lake in Egypt, known as the *Birket Qarun* in modern Arabic; to the ancient Egyptians it was *She-resy* ("southern lake"), and later *Mer-wer* ("The Great Lake").

To the ancient Egyptians, the Faiyum Lake was a holy place, sacred to Sobek, the crocodile god, whose material manifestations swarmed the lake's beaches. Beginning at least nine thousand years ago, when the connection to the main Nile formed, the Faiyum Lake rose and fell annually with the river, and when the Nile crested in late spring, floodwaters inundated much of the Faiyum. As the floods receded in summer and autumn, some of the lake's fertile bottom was exposed, providing exceptionally productive agricultural land. Wheat and barley were farmed in these areas as early as 5000 BC. Later, the higher areas along the ancient shorelines of the lake were favored sites for temples, towns, tombs, and cemeteries.

After about 1500 BC, the Egyptians built dams and weirs to restrict the river's connection to the Faiyum Lake, and to reclaim parts of the lakebed for farming. Land reclamation over the centuries has reduced the lake to less than 20 percent of its original extent, and today irrigation runoff of salts has made it so saline as to be nearly sterile.

Other Egyptian oases, formed around natural springs, dot the Western Desert between Egypt and Libya. Already by about 3000 BC, these oases served as military outposts, cult centers, and staging points for overland trade and exploitation of the desert's minerals, metals, and other resources. Dakhla Oasis (see Figure 1.1), for example, supported a large town by at least 2700 BC.

Egypt and Its Neighbors

From at least 7000 BC onward, products and people from the outside world found their way into Northeast Africa, beginning with animal and plant species that had been domesticated in Southwest Asia. Over succeeding centuries the variety and volume of this exchange increased, so that by the time the first elements of dynastic Egyptian culture appeared, Egypt was already a central node in the circulation of commodities such as gold, silver, copper, and a variety of other metals and minerals from the Sinai. Lapis lazuli and other semiprecious stones from Afghanistan, cedar wood and aromatic resins from Lebanon, copper from Palestine, tropical woods, ivory, spices, live baboons, and ostrich feathers from Nubia and tropical Africa, and hundreds of other commodities were imported (Figure 2.11). To pay for them, Egypt probably exported linen, preserved fish, cereals, wine, gold from the Sinai, papyrus, and other goods – although few archaeological traces of the exchange of the biodegradable goods have been found outside Egypt.

The use in Egypt of imports as prestige markers and in religious rituals is discussed in subsequent chapters.

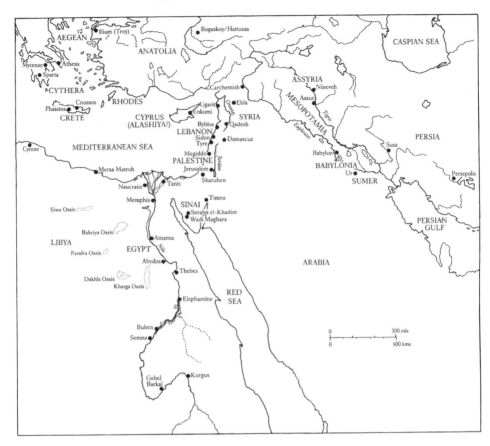

Figure 2.11. Egypt and its neighbors. The mountains and deserts that bordered the Nile Valley and Delta sheltered it from outside influences to some extent, but archaeological evidence indicates that some of Dynastic Egypt's most important domesticated plants and animals came from Southwest Asia before 5000 BC. We also know that Egypt traded with Syro-Palestinians from the very beginnings of its state. The Egyptian and Mesopotamian states were the two most powerful polities in this region for much of the period between 4000 and 2000 BC, but there were many other smaller but competitive polities between the two. *Source:* © The Trustees of the British Museum.

Cultural Geography

The Nile's dynamics and the Valley and Delta described earlier are merely the stage, as it were, on which the baroque history of pharaonic Egypt played out. To understand Egyptian civilization we must relate the blunt forces of floods, fields, and climate to the ancient Egyptians' conceptualization of their world.

Ancient Egyptians thought of their country as composed of two different geographical units: from the Nubian border to just south of where modern Cairo is situated lay *ta-shema*, the "land of the shema-reed"; north of that, including the Delta, was *ta-mehu*, the "land of the papyrus plant." Today archaeologists refer to this division as "Upper Egypt" (the south) and "Lower Egypt" (the north) – terms that reflect the gradient of the Nile. "Middle Egypt" extends from about the entrance to the Faiyum Oasis south to about the modern city of Asiut.

Ancient Egyptians called Egypt *Kemet*, literally "black land," after the dark alluvial sediments that sustained their crops, and thus themselves; the deserts they called *Deshret* – "red land." Along the Nile Valley's margins, so sharp is the demarcation between these landforms that, as the cliché has it (and as is literally true), one can stand with one foot on the red desert sands and the other foot on the black irrigated croplands.

From the earliest kings to the last, it was a royal obligation to protect the unity of the whole country. Kings took as one of their names a title that meant "He of the Two Ladies," a reference to the protection of the king both by the cobra-goddess Wadjet of Lower Egypt, associated with the community at Buto in the Delta, and by the vulture-goddess Nekhbet of Hierakonpolis in Upper Egypt (Figure 2.12).

The Nile was the lifeblood and central nervous system of the ancient Egyptian state. Egypt's efficiency in day-to-day operations, and in dealing with crucial problems, whether it was a low Nile flood or an invading army of Asiatics, depended on gathering accurate information and acting on it expeditiously. A king and his agents could make good and timely economic or military decisions only if they had current and relevant information, and also the means to communicate their decisions promptly to their administrators. The ancient Egyptians used the Nile to link the country and its administrators to the central government. In fact, they built few major roads and no large bridges, and they probably used land transportation – by simply walking or loading and riding domestic donkeys – mainly for short-distance travel to reach areas that the Nile did not, or for trade with Syro-Palestine.

From the capital at Memphis (near modern Cairo), an official sailing south could reach (with the help of oarsmen) one of the government's outposts at Elephantine, near Aswan, in about ten to fourteen days. The trip back took a week or less. Thus, a royal military advisor sent by the pharaoh to assess, for example, the military situation in Nubia could report back to the king in about three weeks. By our standards this is slow, but in no other ancient civilization was so much of the country so quickly and easily accessible to administrators and others.

1

2

Figure 2.12. "He of the Two Ladies." This was one of the names each king took from the First Dynasty onward. The two ladies referred to are the cobra-goddess Wadjet and the vulture-goddess Nekhbet. The top illustration is from an ivory tag found in King Aha's tomb at Naqada. The bottom, an ivory label depicting the pairing of the two goddesses, is from the tomb of Qa'a at Abydos. *Source:* From *Early Dynastic Egypt*, Toby A. H. Wilkinson, Copyright © 1999 Routledge. Reproduced by permission of Taylor & Francis Books UK.

The Agricultural Cycle

Tell me what you eat, and I will tell you what you are.
(Jean A. Brilla-Savarin, eighteenth-century French gastronome)

Before the Nile was damned in modern times, rising muddy waters in southern Egypt in late spring heralded the onset of the annual flood. The Egyptians anxiously observed the river's rise and hoped it would peak at about eight meters above the annual average low point. If the floods were low, the area refreshed with water and fertilizing sediments was reduced; but if it was too high, water covered farm fields well into the summer, and crops planted late would wither in the heat. Even so small a difference in the Nile's flood as fifteen to twenty centimeters, too high or too low, could

Box 2. Egyptian Agriculture and Chronologies

To think of time – of all that retrospection,
To think of to-day, and the ages continued henceforward.
Have you guess'd you yourself would not continue?
Have you dreaded these earth-beetles?
Is to-day nothing? is the beginningless past nothing?
If the future is nothing, they are just as surely nothing.

(Walt Whitman [1819–1892], "To Think of Time")

The Egyptians drew their measures of time directly from their natural world, particularly the Nile's flood cycle and the transits of the sun, moon, and stars. They used both a solar calendar and a lunar calendar, as well as several other methods of tracking time.

Most lunar calendars are based on sighting the new, full, and waning moon. This "synodic month," as it is termed by modern astronomers, is about 29.53 days long, giving the twelve lunar months either 29 or 30 days, with an annual total of about 354.36 days – about 11 days shorter than the solar year. Today, for example, Muslim Egyptians use a lunar calendar to celebrate the month of *Ramadan*, during which they may not eat, drink, or smoke during daylight hours. Because Ramadan is based on a lunar calendar, it "moves" progressively each year around the solar calendar (years in which Ramadan occurs in the hot, long days of summer require particular piety of those who have to work outside). In the Christian calendar, Easter is celebrated on the first Sunday after the full moon that occurs after the vernal equinox – but the ecclesiastical vernal equinox is fixed at March 21, and special tables are needed to determine the date of the full moon, which is not exactly and always the astronomical full moon.

A lunar calendar is not very useful for scheduling and tracking agricultural work because it does not remain correlated with the changes of the seasons or with the sun's annual variations in apparent visibility. Thus, the Egyptians complemented their lunar calendar with calendars based on the Nile floods, and on the solar year (Figure 2.13). The Nile-based calendar consisted of three seasons of four months each. The New Year began on June 21 and was marked by five days of feasting and celebrations. The period of flooding, from about June 21 to October 21, was called *akhet*, which probably meant "inundation." Most crops were planted between October 21 and February 21, a season called *peret*, or "time of emergence," in the sense that the farmland emerged as the floods receded. The harvest season, or *shemu*, was from February 21 to June 21, the driest period of

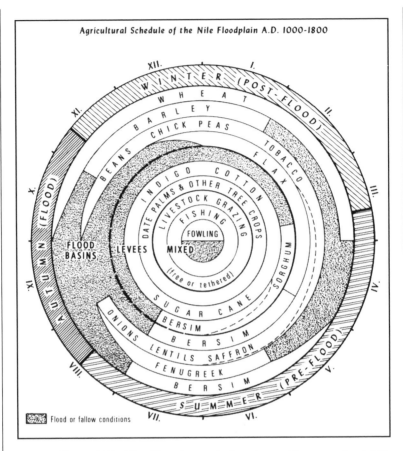

Figure 2.13. The Egyptian agricultural year. Between about AD 1000 and 1800, the Egyptian cropping cycle and agricultural calendar looked much like this reconstruction by Butzer. Except for tobacco and other exotics, the dynastic cycle was probably similar. Note that the twelve months of the agricultural year are indicated by Roman numerals on the periphery. *Source:* Butzer 1976, fig. 10. © 1976 by the University of Chicago. Courtesy of the University of Chicago Press.

the year (this section of this book, incidentally, is being written on March 8, AD 2007, which is III Shemu 21 in the Egyptian agricultural calendar). The actual dates of the Nile floods, their retreats, and the period of harvest varied by about two weeks over the length of Egypt.

The agricultural calendar based on the Nile was a useful device for locating oneself in relation to the seasons, but the ancient Egyptians were also much concerned with accurately measuring the lengths of reigns of kings, the dates of particular battles to be commemorated, the scheduling of royal rituals performed by the king on a periodic schedule, and many other activities that required precisely measuring the passing of the years. To meet this need, they developed a solar calendar, based on astronomical observation, which was somewhat complicated but rather clever. It was based on a year of 365 days – and thus was what astronomers call a "wandering year," because it was a quarter of a day shorter than the actual solar year. The Egyptian solar year would thus wander backwards in relation to the seasons of the year unless some correction was introduced, such as our "leap year." They had measured the solar year to an accuracy such that they obviously knew that a 365-day calendar was about a quarter of a day shorter than the solar year, but they probably saw no pressing need to adjust their calendars.

This solar calendar had an added element, which we call the "Sothic cycle" (Mackey 1995; Kitchen 1991). It was based on observations of the star that the Greeks knew as Sothis, we know as Sirius, and the Egyptians knew as *Spdt*. Because of the earth's rotation, Sirius appears to us to rise in the east and set in the west, and the sun appears to make a complete circle among the stars once a year. Sirius is invisible for a period of about seventy days each year during the period just before, during, and after the time that the earth, the sun, and Sirius are aligned. After this annual period of invisibility, Sirius is first visible above the eastern horizon for a few moments before the sun's brilliance renders it invisible until the next dawn. This first fleeting appearance of Sirius after seventy days of invisibility is called the "heliacal rising" of this star. A Sothic cycle is a period of 1,461 years of 365 days each in the Egyptian calendar. Over the course of a Sothic cycle, the 365-day year "loses" enough time that the start of the year once again coincides with the heliacal rising of Sothis. This rising occurred within about a month of the onset of the annual Nile flood; thus, the rising of Sothis marked the beginning of the New Year.

Heliacal risings of Sothis were recorded in the reigns of Pharaohs Senwosret III (1870–1831 BC), Amunhotep I 1525–1504 BC), Thutmose III (1479–1425 BC), and Ramesses II (1279–1213 BC), and these are used as fixed points in the absolute chronology of ancient Egypt – although debates about precisely when and where these sightings were made, and thus the precise royal chronology, continue. There is fragmentary and disputed evidence of sightings of heliacal risings of Sothis in earlier periods, and – given the Egyptians' profound interest in all things astronomical – it is possible that these sightings were made centuries before Egyptian writing was available to record them. But these dates are somewhat uncertain, and there are many other unanswered questions about ancient Egyptian chronologies (Hornung, Krauss, and Warburton 2006).

Many calendars use a reference point, similar to our "AD/BC" system, in order to chart events over the long term. The ancient Egyptians used reference points, such as lists of kings and the lengths of their reigns, so that events could be dated to a specific day in a specific year in the reign of a particular king. They also used a periodic national census of cattle as a reference point in time, to count the years of a king's reign, but we do not know if these censuses were made every year, or every other year, or on some other schedule. They also recorded the dates of festivals the king celebrated, and of his military and other signal events, but we simply do not know the accuracy with which they made these observations or the literalness with which they understood them (Assman 2002).

have a devastating impact on agricultural production. The Nile's annual volume appears to have declined by an average of about 30 percent between about 2600 and 2000 BC, for example, and this may have been a contributory cause of the socioeconomic and political decline that ensued after the death of Pepy II (c. 2184 BC) (Butzer 1976: 17).

Primary Elements in Ancient Egyptian Farming

The archaeological record of the *origins* of domestication and agriculture is analyzed in Chapter 4, but it is useful here to provide a general sense of the farming system that sustained Egyptians throughout the five thousand years of the pharaonic age. Figure 2.13 illustrates the cropping cycle of Egypt in the recent past. Except for fodder, cereal, and garden plants, however, and the times when they were planted, this modern cycle does not closely resemble the ancient one.

Farming in ancient Egypt was very productive, relative to other places in the world, but it still required a lot of sweat and effort. Before oxen were first used to pull plows, probably between circa 3000 and 2700 BC, the ancient Egyptians may have used wooden plows pulled by groups of men. Nile alluvia are exceptionally fertile but also somewhat difficult to till. Today on traditional Egyptian farms one can still see men with heavy mattocks working the thick soil from humid dawn to torrid dusk, in much the same way that their ancestors have for seven millennia. The handles of their heavy hoes are short, and the work is backbreaking.

Some scenes in Egyptian art show the sowing of prepared fields, which was done apparently by a man with a sack of seeds draped on his chest so that he could broadcast the seeds using both hands. The main crops were wheat and barley, but many other plant varieties were farmed as well (see Chapter 4).

Farm labor was considered so menial in ancient Egypt that some prisoners of war were forced to do it, and farmers shared with herdsmen and fishermen the lowest stratum of society. So onerous did ancient Egyptians find farming that already by Old Kingdom times, some elites were entombed with figurines (called *shabtis*), representing people who were expected to spring to life after the deceased elites were entombed and do the chopping, hewing, hoeing, and weeding for them. The people represented by these figurines probably were not expected to work for the individual tomb occupant but rather in place of the deceased, if the tomb owner was drafted for corvée labor for the gods in the afterlife. Crude clay figurines of people have been found in Predynastic graves, and by about 2600 BC limestone shabtis were in use; these continued as a standard part of funerary cults throughout pharaonic history. Until about 1900 BC, most of these shabtis appear to have been involved in food preparation, but later they were associated with many other activities.

Evidence suggests that among the lowest-ranking ancient Egyptian farmers were contracted workers who labored on other people's land – "sharecroppers," in effect. They could profit from their own labor, but the landlord took a large share of the harvest. The landlord in turn had to save about 10 percent of cereal crops for next season's seed and pay about 10 percent to the government in taxes.

In subsistence farming, as ancient Egyptians practiced it, even small children and aged grandparents could contribute to the extended family's food and resources. Small children tended animals (Figure 2.14) and collected firewood; older people labored in the fields; and the most aged could sew, cook, and care for children. One of the barriers encountered by modern administrators trying to promote population control in subsistence agricultural economies is the simple fact that the only source of "social security" for the aged is to have a large family with many children and grandchildren, all of whom could support them in their old age. The same was true for most ancient Egyptian farmers.

The ancient Egyptian harvests required many specialized tools and techniques, as well as hard work. Farmers harvested their cereals by cutting the stems of ripe wheat with wooden sickles fitted with sharp flint

Figure 2.14. Even small children could contribute to family income in rural Egypt. These two children are taking water buffalo out for a stroll. They will tend them while they feed along the Nile marshes and bring them back home. These animals provide wonderfully fat milk and yogurt, and then at a certain age will be slaughtered – usually for sale to others, as this (el-Hibeh) is one of the poorer villages in Egypt. *Source:* Photograph by Robert J. Wenke.

blades. They probably sawed the heads off the grain, rather than scything the plants, as one would do with a modern sickle. Scenes in their art show men carrying heavy baskets of grain suspended on long poles. Baskets of harvested grain heads were thrown on a threshing floor, and animals were driven over it repeatedly until the grain was separated from the "chaff," the husks that enclosed each seed. They then winnowed the grain by tossing it into the air so that the wind could blow the chaff away. They used the straw for brickmaking, animal bedding, and other purposes.

Cereals were usually stored in mud-brick silos that were carefully plastered inside and out to protect against damp and insects and rodents. Men had to carry heavy baskets of grain up ladders and then pour it into the silos, from which it was rationed out through small doors at the silo's base.

Most of the wheat and barley was made into bread and beer; grain was also cooked whole and served as a complement to meat and vegetables, added as a thickener to soups, crushed and boiled into a

Box 3: Egyptian Beer

Lo! The poor toper whose untutor'd sense,
Sees bliss in ale, and can with wine dispense;
Whose head proud fancy never taught to steer,
Beyond the muddy ecstasies of beer.

(George Crabbe [1754–1832], "The Village")

Like the English peasants Crabbe satirized, ancient Egyptians found in beer the subtleties of flavors we usually associate with wine. Once they discovered that cereals could be conveniently stored in a nutritious and entertaining form by fermentation, they produced vast quantities of beer of several different kinds. Modern attempts to make beer using ancient Egyptian recipes and methods have had mixed results: The Egyptians had no hops, and so their beer would not taste like our own (one modern re-creation substituted coriander for hops). We probably will never know the exact recipes for Egyptian beer or recover the yeast strains they used. But the simplest kinds of Egyptian beer were probably thick, dark, and "hearty." Indeed, if an ancient Egyptian farmer were ever revived through the terrible alchemy of modern sciences, he would probably describe modern mass-produced beers with urological references to cows.

Painted murals in tombs tell us much about how Egyptians made beer (Figure 2.15). The process began with women who ground barley on stone mortars and then sieved it to remove the husks. This flour was then mixed with water in pottery vats and kneaded by men. Yeast was probably added at this step, perhaps simply by adding uncooked dough from previous bread making – although at least by about 1500 BC (and probably two millennia earlier) Egyptians were using selected strains of yeast for some baking and brewing (H. Wilson 1988: 14). The evidence is unclear but it suggests that the dough was then made into cakes. Perhaps these cakes were baked at a very low temperature so that the yeast would not be killed. The loaves were then crumbled into the water, or perhaps the Egyptians poured water on the cakes and sieved the resulting solution through cloth into large vats (Kemp 1989: 123). They probably added flavorings to this liquid, such as dates, other fruit, herbs, or malted grain (i.e., grain steeped in water until it begins to germinate, which produces enzymes that facilitate the conversion of starches to fermentable sugars), and then left it to ferment. Beverages produced by fermentation in pottery vessels easily become vinegar if exposed to air and stray bacteria, and some of the flavorings used in beer and wine may have been intended to disguise a vinegary taste.

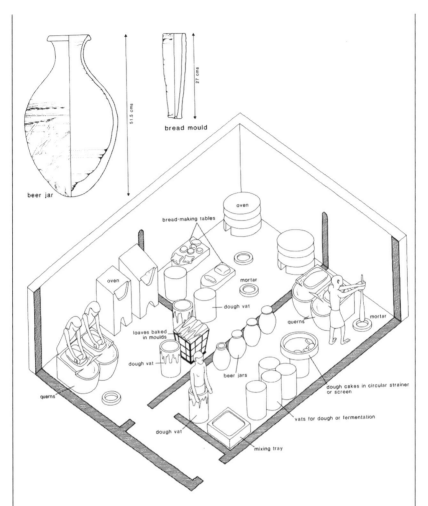

Figure 2.15. Baking and brewing. This model from an
Eleventh Dynasty tomb at Thebes illustrates the process of
baking bread and brewing beer. The two types of ceramics in
the upper left comprise a large percentage of the Egyptian
archaeological record. They varied somewhat over time and
place, but their basic functions were perfectly met by these kinds
of vessels. *Source:* Figure 42, *Models of Daily Life in Ancient
Egypt from the Tomb of Meket-Re' at Thebes*, by H. E. Winlock,
from the series: *Publications of the Metropolitan Museum of Art
Egyptian Expedition*, v. 18; published for Metropolitan Museum
of Art by Harvard University Press, 1955; reproduced with
permission.

In time, yeast would convert the solution into a beer that was probably clouded by particles of bread, stone, and husks. By filtering, flavoring, and varying fermentation times, the Egyptians produced a variety of tastes, aromas, and bodies. Their beer, filtered or not, would have contained significant amounts of carbohydrates, B vitamins, and minerals, and it was undoubtedly safer to drink than river and canal water. The Egyptians considered beer necessary to good health and a happy life, but they saw in it additional significance: We do not know precisely when beer first became a standard element in richer tombs, and thus was "socially necessary for the proper commemoration of the dead" (Wengrow 2006: 98), but evidence suggests that already by the late fourth millennium BC, beer had acquired that status.

The Egyptians occasionally drank to excess. In a text from about 1200 BC, for example, a student scribe was warned about drunkenness: "I am told . . . you go from street to street where everything stinks to high heaven of beer. Beer will turn men away from you and send your soul to perdition. You are like a broken rudder on a ship . . . like a shrine without its god, like a house without bread" (quoted in H. Wilson 1988: 19). But most ancient Egyptians would have agreed with Benjamin Franklin, the eighteenth-century American polymath, who suggested, "Beer is proof that God loves us and wants us to be happy." And as a restorative after a hard day of dragging stone blocks up a pyramid or hoeing endless fields of grain in the searing sun, beer would have been a nutritious rehydrant – as well as a mild antidepressant.

---

porridge, or ground and mixed with oil or water and then fried or baked into pancakes.

Peas, beans, and other legumes were also important foods in ancient Egypt. Meat from cows, sheep, and other animals was probably expensive, to the extent that the poorest 80 percent or so of the population probably ate meat only rarely. Nonetheless, cattle bones are found in nearly every site, no matter how small the community. Pigs were a common source of meat in nearly every community. And subsistence agriculture can provide nutritious food out of even poor ingredients. Legumes cooked with scraps of meat and bones, for example, provide much protein and other nutrients. And for the truly poor, protein in the form of fish and fowl was readily available.

Clover (*bersiim* as it is called in Arabic today) was the principal fodder crop in pharaonic times. It requires a lot of water, but clover fixes nitrogen in soils and thus, along with animal wastes, fallowing, and crop

Box 4. Egyptian Wines

And much as Wine has play'd the Infidel
And robb'd me of my Robe of Honour – well,
I often wonder what the Vintners buy
One half so precious as the Goods they sell.

(Edward Fitzgerald [1809–1883], *The Rubaiyat of Omar Khayyám*)

The ancient Egyptians loved their wines. Among the most common tomb furnishings of royalty and other elites were pottery jars of different kinds of wine, all intended to entertain and nourish the deceased in the afterlife as much as wine had enlivened them in this world. The Egyptians made wine out of many fruits, including dates and perhaps pomegranates, but they, like many other people, eventually and accurately concluded that the gods created grapes for the specific purpose of making wine.

The grapes (*Vitis vinifera*) grown by the ancient Egyptians were probably a strain they had domesticated (or imported as a domesticate) far back in their history. Grape seeds have been found in a grave at El-Omari dating to about 4500 BC, and from about 3200 BC onward, grapes and jars of wine were included in richer tombs. Some of these may have been imported from Syro-Palestine, but tomb paintings of grape cultivation and wine making are common themes. They indicate that grapes were made into juice; they were either treaded upon in vats or were put into bags to be constricted by groups of men turning poles in opposite directions. "Wild" yeast, which occurs naturally on grape skins, would begin to ferment the juice as soon as it was produced. Egypt's warm climate is such that the wine probably contained significant quantities of alcohol in less than a week – although one hopes that they did not drink the vile liquid it would have been at that stage (Brewer, Redford, and Redford 1994: 56). Egyptian wines were probably sweeter than the wines that dominate the modern market; the relatively hot summers and autumns probably reduced their wines' complexities and acidity – which no doubt meant that they sometimes produced vintages inferior even to today's many regrettable "House Chardonnays."

Egyptian texts mention white, red, and black wines, but we cannot accurately reconstruct how they produced these variations. Grape juice is generally clear when freshly squeezed; a wine's color is largely determined by whether or not the grape skins are fermented along with the juice. The wines we prize today are all the products of aging, which brings out subtle flavors. Jesus himself observed that "no man . . . having drunk old wine straightway desireth new: for he saith, the old is better"(Luke 5:39) – and he made this infallible observation in reference to wine that must have been made in much the same way as the dynastic Egyptians made it. The Egyptians laid down their better wines to age them, but they lacked the oak casks and corks that add to wine's subtleties. Many of the jars of wine recovered from tombs were sealed with a cap of mud and straw and stamped with the year of the king's rule, the district where the wine was grown, and sometimes the name of the grower. So perhaps royalty, at least, included some connoisseurs. Some of these jars had holes drilled into the stopper or neck of the wine jar to allow carbon dioxide from residual fermentation to escape. Wines were apparently blended when they were served, rather than in the jars in which they were stored.

Drinking to excess was common in ancient Egypt – some scenes show overindulgers vomiting – but it was considered a vice. The Fourth Dynasty King Menkaura, who was buried in the Third Pyramid at Giza, was the first ruler, so far as we know, who was accused of excessive drunkenness – although he might be excused on the grounds that his medical advisors had told him he had only a short time to live (Brewer, Redford, and Redford 1994: 60). Despite wine's potential for abuse, a liter of palm wine a day would provide an Egyptian with 100 percent of his or her recommended daily amount of vitamin C, as well as much potassium, riboflavin, and lysine (Brewer et al. 1994: 48).

rotation, improves soil structure and fertility – although it is unlikely that ancient Egyptians practiced this kind of fallowing on their primary agricultural fields, because Nile silts provided the nutrients necessary for productive farming.

Orchard crops are celebrated in Egyptian art, and excavations reveal that dates, for example, were very important parts of the diet, both as fruit and for producing wine. All agricultural crops in ancient Egypt had complex socioeconomic contexts. Orchard crops require great faith in the future, for example, because it takes many years for a date tree or a fig tree to become an economic asset; and in their immaturity they require much labor and water and give back nothing in return. But orchard crops constituted one of the few long-term investment opportunities in Egypt's moneyless economy. There were no government bonds to buy and hold, but an orchard could be expected to provide part of a lifelong income, subject, of course, to the government's bloodsucking taxes on every tree and load of fruit.

As for other vegetables and fruits, the ancient Egyptians had many to choose from, including lettuce, onions, garlic, leeks, fava beans, radishes, melons, and perhaps pomegranates. They also used numerous condiments to improve the taste of their simple cuisine. Salt, of course, was the mainstay; black pepper was probably imported in quantity, from India, only after about 300 BC. Black cumin and fenugreek were probably used in the early pharaonic era, and there is some evidence as well of coriander, parsley, rosemary, dill, chervil, fennel, and poppy seeds.

Animal Use

I was a vegetarian, until I started to lean toward the sunlight.

(Comedian Rita Rudner)

Cattle, sheep, goats, pigs, pigeons, quail, ducks, geese, and fish were the primary sources of animal products throughout dynastic times. Diet no doubt varied by class, but the remains of most common animals have been found in the deposits of even the smallest hamlets. Pork, in particular, seems to have been consumed by most socioeconomic groups throughout the dynastic era (Hecker 1982).

A major incentive to animal husbandry in preindustrial economies is that animals can convert into edible meat and milk the kinds of foods that people cannot or will not eat. Subsistence villages produce large amounts of garbage, ranging from spoiled food to reeds and weeds. There is great economy is recycling these foods, and barnyard fowl and animals, especially geese, pigs, sheep, and goats, convert these wastes into portable, storable, and high-quality food. Egyptians may also have recycled "night soil" (human feces) in the form of fertilizer or as food for pigs – as many farmers in Asia still do (an archaeologist of the author's acquaintance became a vegetarian after watching pigs and chickens sort through his own recent feces).

Goats, too, are justly famed for their ability to convert low-quality vegetation into fleece, meat, and milk. On one occasion, goats entered our dig-house in the Delta while we were out, and when we returned we discovered them eating with evident gusto our surplus onions and soiled newspapers and clothes.

Today, even in the poorest Egyptian villages where beef and meat from water buffalo are prohibitively expensive for most, one finds ducks, geese, chickens, and pigeons in profusion, as well as milk, eggs, cheeses, and yogurt. Herodotus reports that the Egyptians ate ducks and other small birds raw. A breakfast consisting of a raw, recently murdered duck does not bear thinking about, but food preferences are largely cultural, not genetic, and meat from raw ducks is probably more nutritious than the cooked variety. Today, as in pharaonic times, farmers build aviaries ("dovecotes") from mud brick and pottery to serve as roosts for pigeons. They collect the eggs and also squab-nap the chicks and grill them. The dovecotes also retain bird droppings, which can be collected and used as fertilizer.

In pharaonic Egypt, from at least 3000 BC onward, cattle provided power for plowing, and already by 3500 BC donkeys provided transport for people and provisions. The ancient Egyptians may have known of camels in early pharaonic times, but they did not become an important part of the Egyptian transport system (or diet) until the first millennium BC, when Persian and Assyrian invaders introduced them.

The Egyptians also kept various pets, particularly dogs and cats. The elites even enjoyed keeping monkeys and baboons as pets.

The Natural History of Ancient Egypt

The ancient Nile Valley and Delta comprised a lush semitropical setting in the middle of one of the world's harshest deserts. The Valley and Delta can be viewed as an extension of the central African ecozone, and lions, giraffes, and some other central African flora and fauna inhabited Nubia and even parts of Upper Egypt into the late prehistoric period.

If one were to generalize from tomb paintings and contents, Egyptians thoroughly exploited the resources of their rich world. They highly prized flowers, for example, particularly poppies, cornflowers, blue and white lotus, and larkspur. Flowers placed in tombs were often made into garlands with acacia branches or other leaves – and some of these have survived. The ancient Egyptians apparently developed "aromatherapy" far in advance of contemporary Californians: Paintings show them deeply savoring the scents of oils, perfumes, and flowers at banquets.

Papyrus is a graceful flowering reed (now rarely found in Egypt) that grew throughout Egypt's marshes in dynastic times. People fashioned its tough outer fibers into ropes, mats, sandals, and other items, and they used the softer core of the plant as the raw material for paper. Fibers from flax were used to make linen, which was the primary textile for clothes. Linen and other forms of flax were probably a main export used by Egypt to pay for precious and semiprecious stones and metals imported from abroad. Egyptians seem to have preferred plain linen clothes for almost all occasions, although wool was used for clothing in Roman Egypt. Herodotus claimed that wool clothes were forbidden by pharaonic religion. In any case, linen offered a cheap alternative to wool.

Lumber for roof beams and many other items was made from acacia, sycamore, and palm trees. None of these, however, offers the close-grained and straight lengths of timber prized for boatbuilding and other fine carpentry, and so larger Egyptian vessels were built of cedar imported from Syro-Palestine. Cedar was also used for coffins and other expensive craft items.

The Nile was not only the source of Egyptian agricultural wealth; its flora and fauna also sustained the hunter-foragers of the prepharaonic era, as well as the farmers who followed them. The Nile perch, for example, lived in the ancient river in huge numbers and could easily be netted or harpooned. Today's perch in Lake Nasser are overfished, but one recently caught was more than two meters long and weighed 175 kilograms (Brewer and Friedman 1989: 74). In ancient times these fish offered a rich and reliable source of protein. The Nile also teemed with tilapia, an almost tasteless but firm-textured fish, as well as catfish and other bottom feeders. Annual floods carried fish into even small flood basins distant from the river, and as the flood ebbed these basins would shrink and concentrate huge numbers of fish in small ponds where they could be easily caught. Fish were abundant, available at all times of the year, and easily preserved by drying or pickling. Fine screening of archaeological deposits in domestic remains almost always yields nearly uncountable numbers of fish bones. Rural dynastic Egyptians probably cooked fish in much the same way as our household staff did during our work in the Faiyum Oasis: They made a small fire of wood and straw, let it burn down to embers, and then placed the fish on them, turning the fish over just once. The skins were covered with ash, but these were easily peeled away to reveal perfectly cooked flesh with a faint smoky flavor, which when dressed with a dash of salt and fresh lemon juice made an excellent repast.

Ancient Egyptian tomb paintings include scenes of the process of netting waterfowl. And even after some species of these birds were domesticated, Egyptians exploited the seasonal migrations of wild ducks and geese (huge flocks of which pass through Egypt as they flee European winters) by netting, snaring, or hunting birds with bows and arrows. Egyptians also lived amidst vast numbers of pelicans, cormorants, ibises, falcons, vultures, herons, owls, and many smaller species of swallows and martins. Even in today's crowded Nile Valley and Delta, a rich array of bird life persists.

Although crocodiles are reestablishing themselves in Lake Nasser, south of the Aswan Dam, they have long since disappeared from the Egyptian Nile and Delta. In pharaonic times they were numerous, and some were huge. Mummies have been found of people who appear to have suffered the kinds of grievous injuries a crocodile can inflict (Figure 2.16). The hippopotamus, too, was both a predator and prey in ancient times. Royalty killed them for sport with bows and arrows and spears, but hippos are vicious when disturbed, and over the centuries they no doubt killed many an Egyptian.

Lions, too, no doubt "selected out" unwary travelers and workers. Quarrymen sent to extract limestone blocks on the desert margins were sufficiently threatened by lions that many wore amulets invoking the protection of the gods against them.

Rodents would have overrun Egyptian farms were it not for predatory birds, foxes, and snakes. Lice, flies, fleas, mosquitoes, scorpions, and other pests plagued ancient Egyptians as they do people today, but in ancient times there were far fewer people, and thus less fly-breeding

Figure 2.16. Caring for cattle. Old Kingdom herdsmen had some difficult moments, such as illustrated in this relief in the tomb of Princess Seshseshet (c. 2345–2181 BC) at Saqqara. They are trying to move cattle across a river, while such threats as the crocodile pictured beneath them wait for an opportunity. *Source:* Werner Forman / Art Resource, NY.

Box 5. Egyptian Snakes

A NARROW fellow in the grass
Occasionally rides;
You may have met him – did you not?
His notice sudden is.

The grass divides as with a comb,
A spotted shaft is seen;
And then it closes at your feet,
And opens further on.
. . .
Several of nature's people
I know, and they know me;
I feel for them a transport
Of cordiality;

But never met this fellow,
Attended or alone,
Without a tighter breathing,
And zero at the bone.

(Emily Dickinson [1830–1886], from *The
Complete Poems*, Part II, Nature)

Emily Dickinson knew a thing or two about snakes – or at least human reactions to them. Snakes, especially cobras, are frequent and unwelcome visitors to Egyptian archaeological excavations, particularly in the Delta where they favor the sparse vegetation that grows on the gravel mounds that underlie most sites there.

The Egyptian cobra (*Naja haje*) is particularly venomous and gives force to the quip that in some instances a "snake-bite emergency kit is a body bag" (Mitch Hedberg). Howard Carter, discoverer of King Tutankhamun's tomb, for example, had a favorite donkey that died within a few hours of being bitten on its lip by a cobra – or so the story goes. Cobras are largely nocturnal, but they take a perverse pleasure in basking in early morning sunlight on the mounds of newly excavated sand and gravel that archaeological work produces. Thus, the morning walk to an archaeological site is often interrupted by the sight or sound of snakes slithering into the brush. For most people, a day that begins with a snake encounter is a day badly begun. We once found the shed skin of a cobra about 1.4 meters in length in one of our shallow excavation pits – which moved one staff member to inquire about the possibilities of archaeological research in snake-free Ireland. Perhaps the most attractive aspect of cobras is that among their prey animals are other snakes. But they are also attracted to the fowl and rodents common in farming villages and stealthily invade homes there. Cobra anti-venom is stocked in many rural Egyptian medical clinics.

The Egyptian cobra has a relatively painless bite and a fast-acting poison. The fabled "asp" Cleopatra used to commit suicide – if this hoary story is true – was probably a cobra. The cobra was a symbol of the goddess Wadjet, the primary deity associated with Lower Egypt, and the irony would not have been lost on her. The ancient Egyptians were ambivalent about cobras: They had incantations intended to rid their villages of them, but the cobra image remained an essential part of the pharaonic regalia.

The small sand vipers (*Cerastes cerastes*) found along the desert margins of the Nile Valley today are not aggressive, nor are they as deadly as cobras, but they can kill. Workers on our archaeological research projects in the deserts around the Faiyum Oasis called them the "one cigarette snake," because they believe that a person once bitten has little recourse, in the absence of rapid medical help, but to enjoy a last cigarette and meditate on life's reversals of fortunes.

---

garbage, and there was much less standing water in which mosquitoes could breed. Still, to live in rural Egypt in any period was to live in intimacy with insects and other pests.

Fundamentals of Egyptian Demography

Demography is that rather austere science that expresses in mathematical summaries the variability in the causes and rates of changes in birth, disease, and death over time and space, as well as the causes and effects of the distribution of human populations through time and across space.

Ancient Egyptian records of life events are sparse and highly selective: For every royal elite's life story recorded on tomb walls, thousands of peasants presumably lived and died without attracting the attention of history. Yet from the surviving documents, and with some rather brave inferences, we can estimate aspects of ancient Egyptian demography.

So grand are the physical remains of the Egyptian past that it is difficult to believe that Egypt's total population during the time the pyramids at Giza were built probably never exceeded about 1,600,000 people. Estimates (Butzer 1976; Figure 2.17) of Egypt's demographic history probably contain significant errors, but Karl Butzer's analysis is

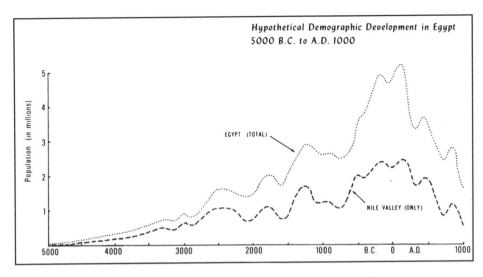

Figure 2.17. Dynastic Egyptian demographics. Karl Butzer's
hypothetical estimates of population sizes at various points in
dynastic history. The discoveries of major towns at Giza and
settlements of different kinds and periods in the Delta may require
adjustment of these estimates, but the general pattern is probably
accurate. *Source:* Butzer 1976, fig. 13. © 1976 by the University
of Chicago. Courtesy of the University of Chicago Press.

probably roughly accurate. Population growth in Egypt was apparently
slow, and densities were low in most areas until late in the pharaonic era.
This supports Butzer's assessment that land shortages and other kinds of
population stress were rarely if ever major factors in the formation of the
first Egyptian states.

Southern (Upper) Egypt was the most densely populated area of the
country in the early phases (c. 3100–2800 BC) – although we must
always qualify such statements with the fact that we know little about
Nile Delta demography. After about 2800 BC, population densities
appear to have grown more rapidly in Lower Egypt, especially the Delta.
Butzer estimated that in the middle of the Old Kingdom Period
(2500 BC), about 1,040,000 people lived in the Valley (including Giza
and Memphis) and about 540,000 in the Delta. Recent research in the
Delta (e.g., van den Brink 1992) suggests that Butzer may have
underestimated the Delta's population in the early periods of occupation. If Egypt's developmental focus after about 3100 BC moved from

Upper Egypt to Lower Egypt and the Delta, as the evidence suggests (see Chapter 5), then the Delta's rapid population growth after that time may be an indication of this shift (Butzer 2002).

Recent research suggests that the populations of large towns such as Abydos and Hierakonpolis may have been underestimated. The town associated with the building of Menkaure's pyramid at Giza, for example, likely had a population well in excess of 20,000.

Life and Death in Ancient Egypt

If the heats of hate and lust
In the house of flesh are strong,
Let me mind the house of dust
Where my sojourn shall be long.

(A. E. Housman [1859–1936], *A Shropshire Lad*)

Daily life in pharaonic Egypt was radically different for individuals, depending on one's gender, age, social class, and the period in which one lived. Still, there seem to be generalities that apply to most of pharaonic Egypt. Many, for example, died young – men averaged about thirty-five years and women about thirty. Thus, a fifty-year-old was considered aged, and by sixty, one would probably have few contemporaries with whom to bemoan the decadence of the times and the black ingratitude of one's children.

The lower classes probably lived shorter lives than the elites, but death was everywhere. Infant mortality rates were probably depressingly high, given the many direct disease vectors a preindustrial village offers in the form of rudimentary sewage systems and high population densities. The ancient Egyptians would have known that an abdominal pain or some other minor symptom might well be the first sign of The End. An ancient Egyptian would likely have known people who died soon after contracting what seemed a minor cold, and other people who recovered from seemingly terminal illnesses. Nonetheless, they would have been spared the awful certainty of impending death that comes with modern diagnoses of metastatic cancers and other ills.

Tuberculosis was common and leprosy may have afflicted many in later periods. The lungs of some mummies show the blackening of anthracosis, or "black-lung disease" – probably the result of living in rooms heated and lighted by burning oils and clouded with smoke from cooking fires. Some mummies show degenerative disease in the form of arteriosclerosis, or "hardening of the arteries." One factor in this disease is obesity. The mummy of Pharaoh Ramesses III (c. 1184–1153 BC)

Box 6. The Egyptian Village Milieu

[A goose] spends the summer ravaging dates, the winter destroying the seed grain, and its free time of the year pursuing farmers. One cannot snare it or offer it in the temple – sharp-eyed bird that does not work!
(An ancient Egyptian's lament, after Brewer, Redford, and Redford
1994: 122, citing Houlihan 1986)

Archaeologists who have spent time in rural Egyptian villages experience much of what the ancient Egyptian farmers' lives must have been like, including the many small felonies of geese that gave rise to this lament.

The archaeological remains of ancient Egyptian farming communities reflect similarities to contemporary Egyptian village houses: Both are composed of complexes of adjoining rectangular rooms formed by sturdy mud-brick walls, and individual homes usually share common walls with other residences. Rooms typically are used for several different activities; it is common, for example, for people to drink tea and socialize during the day in rooms that at night are used for sleeping.

Mud-brick structures are quite cool in summer and warm in winter, but flies, fleas, and mosquitoes abound. One's sleep is often interrupted by the cries of donkeys, cattle, and other animals penned in areas attached to the houses, and by crowing roosters and ubiquitous barking dogs. Archaeologist Sir Flinders Petrie recounted more than a century ago how he would rise in the middle of the night to fling stones at barking village dogs; he learned, as we did, that this only adds to their rich discourse.

Life in an Egyptian village gives one a clear sense of just how thoroughly modern industrialized societies shelter most of us from the simple, stark facts of life. The ancient Egyptians, for example, had a practical and unsentimental approach to farm animals. Numerous tomb paintings show them slaughtering cattle, force-feeding geese, spearing fish and hippos, depriving calves of their mothers' milk, and so forth – all without evident qualms. Most foreigners do not adapt well to such direct encounters with animals as one still sees in rural Egypt, where animals of all types urinate, defecate, and procreate without regard for human sensibilities. When we lived in a small village during our excavations (Wenke 1980a) at el-Hibeh, in Middle Egypt, our neighbors occasionally invited us to slit the throat of a condemned calf, goat, or water buffalo. There were no volunteers. The villagers were much amused by our reticence and did it themselves, using all elements of these animals with impressive efficiency – except for the spilled blood, which feral dogs lapped up. It is all a very long way, indeed, from the sterility of the meat aisle in one's local food market.

Washing clothes and cooking utensils are intensely social and communal events in Egyptian villages; still today, groups of girls and women gather daily at wells and canal banks to do these chores, while talking and laughing. One can easily imagine that the same was true for ancient Egyptians. Thus, it is not surprising that modern developers have found that villagers do not view the prospect of municipal water systems as an unmixed blessing.

Numerous contemporary Egyptians have emigrated from small rural villages to the larger cities, and they often remember their village childhoods with great fondness; many return to their villages for holidays and to enjoy the relative tranquility of the family farm. Archaeologists, too, can appreciate the charms of village life after a foray into the maddening din of modern Cairo. Although many Egyptian villagers today are relatively poor, they tend to be friendly, gregarious, and generous, and there is much peace in the reassuring rhythms of their lives. The simple pleasures of a rural village were probably much the same for ancient Egyptians.

But the industrialized world is quickly intruding on even small and remote Egyptian villages. It is a rare village today, for example, whose nocturnal "call to prayer" is not rebroadcasted on village loudspeakers from audiotapes or big-city radio stations. And during our excavations in the Nile Delta, men from a tiny nearby village invited us join them to watch football's World Cup, though on a black and white television powered by a car battery. These broadcasts always ended with Giacomo Puccini's great aria "Nessun Dorma" ("None shall sleep") – which seemed oddly appropriate in the lively Egyptian evenings.

---

indicates that he had heart disease and was obese – something one would not know from his depictions in official statuary.

Worms plagued ancient Egyptians, and long-term anemia caused by parasites and inadequate diets no doubt stunted the growth and shortened the lives of many. The eggs of "roundworms" (*Ascaris*), for example, are easily transmitted by fecal contamination of food, which probably occurred everywhere in ancient Egypt. Toilets for the more prosperous consisted of wood seats set over pottery bowls containing sand, and located in small mud-brick privies. In the *Tale of Sinhue*, a probably fictional account of the wanderings of an Egyptian nobleman of about 1950 BC, Sinhue boasts that the king gave him a residence so princely that it even had a bathroom (Parkinson 1997: 42). For the working classes, however, the great outdoors probably served this function. Thus, no doubt they frequently contaminated their food, as roundworm eggs are easily spread from human feces to salad vegetables, fruit, and other uncooked foods. In 1971 I suffered a roundworm infestation in Iran (although I probably acquired the infection during several previous months in Turkey). I lost 20 percent of my then inconsiderable weight in just five months. The cure for worm infestations at that time involved medicines that poison the patient, yet poison the worms more severely so that they lose their grip on the intestines and are excreted. The process is revolting but not painful; still, those who have endured this indignity never feel quite the same about their bodies ever again – intentional infection with roundworms is unlikely ever to gain popularity as a weight-loss alternative to bariatric surgery.

Tapeworms (*Cestoda*) were probably also common in ancient Egypt, as one can easily contract them by eating undercooked meat or fish. The largest species of this worm can grow to eight meters or more in length; they feed on digested foods in the gastrointestinal tract of people and animals and thus rob them of nutrients. Initial infection does not usually produce symptoms, and even today many people only discover their plight when they see soul-searingly hideous worm segments in their toilet bowl.

On intensely hot summer days, agricultural canals fed by the Nile look invitingly cool, and like their ancient forebears, modern Egyptians enjoy swimming in them; but their quiet backwaters harbor a particularly gruesome parasite, bilharzia (*Schistosoma*). These parasites invade the unlucky swimmer's urethra and multiply to the point that they can fatally damage the kidney, bladder, and intestines (Armelagos and Mills 1999). Male breast enlargement and morbidly enlarged penises and scrota are also dismaying effects of this disease.

Life's other burdens for ancient Egyptians, as inferred from mummies and texts, included smallpox, gout, hernias, arthritis, ulcers, skin cancer, osteoporosis, cataracts, and many other maladies. Dwarfism, cleft palates, deformed spines, and other commonly inherited afflictions affected the ancient Egyptians, too. Some crania show signs of dental abscesses, which can be fatal if untreated, and which in any event remind us that some pharaonic Egyptians spent much time in pain.

In addition to these illnesses and disabilities, we must also assume that many people died of traumas suffered while building pyramids or in hand-to-hand combat, or by presuming upon too slight evidence that no cobras, crocodiles, hippos, lions, or wolves were about. On the brighter side, comparatively few ancient Egyptians appear to have died from cancer, perhaps because they died relatively young, but also because they were spared the effects of some modern horrors, such as asbestos and tobacco.

Life had its full share of miseries specific to women. Ethnographic studies indicate that in the absence of professional medical care, a few women of every hundred who give birth will die in childbirth or soon thereafter, either from mismatched cervical/fetal head sizes, or of blood poisoning, heart attacks, or infections. The skeleton of an Egyptian woman of the fifth century AD indicates that she died in childbirth and must have endured indescribable pain, for she was born without a sacroiliac joint, without which the pelvis cannot expand during child-birth (C. Reeves 1992).

Various texts suggest that a woman would deliver her baby while squatting on two large bricks, each decorated with scenes to invoke the magic of the gods for the health and happiness of mother and child. An example of these bricks has been found at Abydos, in deposits dating to some time in the Middle Kingdom (c. 2055–1650 BC). A scene on the brick shows a mother with her newborn child. They are attended by women and by Hathor, a goddess associated with birth and motherhood. The Egyptians drew a parallel between the birth of a child and the rising of the sun. They believed that a newborn baby needed protection against the chaotic and evil forces present at the daybreak of his or her life. Joseph Wegner (1998) suggested that a princess named "Raseneb" was one of the women who used the brick at Abydos. Such bricks are sometimes well worn, and one can only imagine the pain, but also the joy, of those who used them so many centuries ago.

Today's physicians can at least offer some cures and hope – and palliatives in their absence. Ancient Egyptians could deal with broken arms and a few other traumas and illnesses, but by and large their medicine did not work (C. Reeves 1992). They did not seem to know much about the principles of mammal physiology, which is odd because butchered animals were an ordinary part of their lives, and because the priests who performed the evisceration that was part of the mummification process must have been struck by the similarities between human and animal organs. Not that they could have done much to treat even simple appendicitis, for example, even had they known its etiology. We must remember, too, that it was not until the seventeenth century AD that Vesalius detailed the nature of human physiology and anatomy.

Ancient Egyptian physicians apparently developed treatments through experience, made their own medicines, and had their own trade secrets, which they passed from generation to generation. They had rudimentary dentistry, including at least one courageous try at a bridge. According to

Herodotus, both men and women could be healers; they believed that the human body consisted of thirty-six parts, and that the care of each was the responsibility of a particular god or goddess.

Some respite from life's pains and rigors was provided by wine and beer; more profound out-of-body experiences may have been induced by the atropine and scopolamine found in some plants. In later periods, opium mixed with honey, which has natural antibiotic powers, was probably an effective anodyne.

Ancient Egyptians could pay priests to recite incantations over one during illnesses. Like many people today, they saw no conflict in treating illnesses with both prayer and medicine.

Fundamental Egyptian Cultural and Ecological Correlates

We can correlate many elements of the ancient Egyptians' physical world with their culture, but it is far more difficult to understand the meaning and significance with which they invested these correlations. Examples of these issues are considered in later chapters of this book, but a few examples are presented here to illustrate the point.

Butzer, for example, asserted, "[T]here is growing evidence that the economic history of ancient Egypt was primarily one of continuous ecological readjustment to a variable water supply, combined with repeated efforts to intensify or expand land use in order to increase productivity. It is in this sense that hydraulic civilization in Egypt remains inconceivable without its ecological determinants" (1976: 15–16). Nilotic environments directly offered both possibilities for and limitations on cultural forms and histories.

One aspect of the river's determining effects is evident in the basic political units. The Egyptian state was constructed by the socio-economic and political integration of discrete geographical provinces, known by their Greek name as "nomes." Most of these nomes' borders were defined by natural features, such as bends in the Nile or areas enclosed by adjacent Nile Delta tributaries. Marks found on pottery in these nomes suggest that the southern nomes were recognized as discrete cultural areas as early as about 3700 BC, centuries before the whole of Egypt was brought under state rule. Each nome had its own cult symbol and religious significance. The nome structure was probably first established in the south, and then developed into a national administrative structure later in pharaonic history as the central governmental bureaucracy matured. This nome structure divided ancient Egypt into effective administrative units, but it also provided the basis for the eternal struggle for power and wealth between the central government and provincial elites. When Egypt's central government weakened, there was a reversion to greater autonomy for the nomes for brief periods.

Various texts describe social disruptions that may be associated with flood-level (and thus agricultural productivity) fluctuations, but the Egyptian state evolved some mechanisms to cope with these problems. Throughout the pharaonic era, the primary responsibility of the pharaoh was the "containment of disorder" – which in its active sense meant the perpetuation of order, stability, and good governance. Pharaohs did this in part by defining clear boundaries to "Egypt," and by fortifying these borders, defending them, and establishing order within them.

Egypt's relative cultural homogeneity and conservative character resulted in part from its geographical and ecological situation. Nile tributaries led the river into the Mediterranean and Aegean worlds, but these northern harbors were poor, and great swamps and lagoons along the coastline channeled most of the traffic in and out of Egypt into the small shallow branches of the Nile. To the south, the steep rapids on the Nubian border barred boat traffic. Also, nomad interactions with the early states were not major influences on the culture of Egypt, as they were in Mesopotamia and China, for example. Rainfall in North Africa was too little for most of the Dynastic era to support large groups of nomads along the Nile Valley heartland.

The impact of the configuration of the Nile on Egyptian life and culture is obvious. Thus, where Mesopotamia, for example, was open and often in the process of cultural transformations stimulated by interactions with its many neighbors, Egypt was an idiosyncratic universe. The Southwest Asian system of writing in cuneiform on clay tablets, for example, which originated somewhere between southwestern Iran and the western part of Mesopotamia, spread west into Asia Minor and throughout Persia and beyond; but Egyptian hieroglyphic writing was never used outside the Nile Valley and Delta, except in a few trading communities.

Egyptians apparently had a real fear and loathing of the outside world, where rivers ran backwards (from north to south), water fell from the sky, and clouds and forests blocked their view of the daily procession of the gods across the skies (Hoffman 1980a). It was particularly important to an Egyptian that he or she be buried in Egypt. This is poignantly illustrated by the (probably fictional) story of *Sinuhe* (Lichtheim 1973: 228), who fled from Egypt to Palestine in about 1962 BC, in fear for his life because he was suspected in a plot to assassinate the pharaoh: "Whichever god decreed this flight, have mercy, bring me home! Surely you will let me see the place in which my heart dwells! What is more important than that my corpse be buried in the land in which I was born?"

Egypt seems to have been spared some of the conflict of ideologies so evident in Mesopotamia, where state religions and entire cosmologies and cosmogonies collided and replaced one another, or were amalgamated in radically new forms. Egypt had its internal religious revolutions and reformations, but the continuity of its religious and philosophical traditions, compared to Mesopotamia, is impressive. Egypt's physical environment helped shape a culture that was relatively self-absorbed, conservative, and homogenous – at least compared to other civilizations. Yet, as we shall see, this culture was affected from its very inception by foreign cultures, and in many of its periods Egypt was enmeshed in ever-widening spirals of trade, warfare, and international power politics.

In summary of this chapter, we have reviewed the "nuts and bolts," the fundamentals of the ecological adaptation of the ancient Egyptians and some aspects of their daily lives and times. But the description of the ordinary elements of ancient Egyptian life presented here lacks an essential element: We must consider the whole range of *ideas* that was part of the Egyptians' conception of their lives and what it all "meant." Butzer was accurate in arguing that civilization in Egypt remains inconceivable without its ecological determinants, but it is also true that the Egyptian past is largely incomprehensible without reference to its social and religious ideologies. The evolution of this unique world and life view is considered in detail in subsequent chapters.

3   Introduction to the Evidence and Interpretation of Egyptian Antiquity

The past is a foreign country: they do things differently there.

L. P. Hartley (1895–1972), *The Go-Between*

Introduction

Before commencing a review of early Egyptian state origins, it is useful to contemplate the nature of the evidence we must consider in analyzing this ancient society. To begin with, the "past" is a cultural construct. Every culture, every individual, reads the past uniquely. Consider, as a minor example, the varying interpretations of the damage to the face of the Great Sphinx at Giza (see Figure 1.4). Some have blamed Napoleon's soldiers for blasting the Sphinx with artillery. But one "Afrocentric" interpreter (Diop 1974) has claimed that Europeans disfigured the Sphinx to mask its supposed Negroid features. Some historians of Islam (e.g., Haarman 1996), in contrast, argue that medieval Egyptian documents record that a Muslim ruler tried to obliterate the Sphinx's face because he considered it an expression of pre-Islamic paganism.

These debates about the Sphinx concern a historically trivial matter, but they raise fundamental issues. It may seem obvious that everyone has historical and cultural biases that color his or her views of the past. But before considering the evidence about Egyptian antiquity, one should meditate on this salient fact: Scholars regularly discuss ancient Egyptian temple rituals, social classes, population growth, craft production, and other cultural phenomena that we cannot directly *observe*; all must be *inferred* from fragmentary texts, ruined buildings, broken pottery, and the other detritus of Egyptian antiquity.

Reconstructions of the Egyptian past typically are based on the principle known to the Romans as *ex ungue leonem*, literally, "from the claw to the lion," or the notion that from a part we can know the whole through the processes of analogy and inference. Not only is analogy a weak form of argument (especially when applied to Egyptian civilization instead of lions), but many of the scholars who made these analogies and

79

inferences have also viewed these remains of ancient Egypt through the prism of Western culture – not necessarily a bad thing, but still a unique and culturally bounded view of that world.

Studies of ancient Egypt have become almost geologically encrusted with interpretations that draw on other interpretations that drew on earlier interpretations, and so on, reaching from the dynastic Egyptians themselves to cassical Greek historians, and then century after century to the present day – and to this book as well.

Even if we could somehow take a neutral, objective perspective on ancient Egypt, we face other obstacles. Only a tiny proportion of Egyptian texts has been preserved, for example. So we must consider both what is and what is not there. Because the ancient Egyptians made little mention of agricultural irrigation in the surviving texts we have, we might conclude that there was little state-directed irrigation agriculture. But it is also possible by the accidents of preservation that few documents involving this topic have been found, or that the allocation of water was an important but mundane activity unlikely to be immortalized in the tomb and temple inscriptions that constitute most of the preserved texts.

In sum, we must infer the Egyptian past through our unique cultural lenses, and on the basis of texts and artifacts that cannot be expected to reflect every aspect of ancient Egyptian life. Even if we had a nearly complete textual record from ancient Egypt, most of the nontextual remains to which they refer – the towns, temples, and other material remnants of ancient Egypt – have long since been looted, damaged, or destroyed. In no sense, then, can we hope to "whip off the cloth" concealing ancient Egypt, to reveal it as it truly was. As novelist David Lodge expressed this sentiment, "every decoding is another encoding."

Yet it is the major premise of this book that we *can* know much about the Egyptian past, through the application of traditional scientific methods and historical analyses. It may seem odd that one must defend the application of these methods and analyses, but a strong current in social sciences is an extreme form of "relativism." Absolute relativists would argue, for example, that the varying interpretations of the damage to the Sphinx have an equal claim to the "truth," and, much more significantly, that all interpretations of the past have equal "validity," in a sense (Leone, Potter, and Schackel 1987).

This book, in contrast, is based on the traditional assumptions and methods of historical analysis. Our efforts to know the Egyptian past may be corrupted by our biases and shaped by our personal sociopolitical agendas, but the assumption here is that through analyses of empirical data, our knowledge of the past can transcend the limitations of personal and cultural biases and idiosyncrasies. The reader should note, however, that many scholars utterly reject this perspective (see Chapter 7).

The Rediscovery of Egyptian Antiquity

Egyptian antiquity was never entirely "lost," of course, in the sense that knowledge of it entirely disappeared from human consciousness. Even after about 700 BC, when, successively, Persians, Greeks, and Romans conquered Egypt, many Egyptian cultural elements remained much the same as they had been for millennia. Most of the millions of Egyptians in these eras spoke Egyptian, worshipped Egyptian gods, and lived very much as their ancestors had for thousands of years.

The Greeks were among the first foreigners, at least as far as we know, to record their observations of ancient Egyptian culture. Elements of the "Western" (e.g., European and North American) view of ancient Egypt can be traced to the fifth-century BC Greek historian Herodotus, the "father of history," who is among the earliest scholars (of whom we know, at least) who studied foreign cultures and tried to write narrative histories, and even to try to understand these histories mainly in terms of natural and cultural causes and effects – that is, to write *historiography*.

As much as Herodotus admired the Egyptians (though some scholars wonder if he ever went there), he considered their customs peculiar. First of all, they did not live in a *polis*, a quasi-democratic city-state, as the Greeks did; and though wise in many things, they were more mystically inclined than the Greeks. And his interpretations of Egyptian culture therefore were profoundly shaped by his culturally ingrained prejudices and experiences. The Egyptians no doubt returned the favor, for they considered anyone not Egyptian to be their inferiors.

When the Roman Empire succeeded Greece's, many Egyptian ideas, as well as artifacts, were brought back to Rome and other cities of the empire and influenced Roman culture. Despite the invasions of Egypt at the time of the tangled sexual and political relationships between the Egyptian Queen Cleopatra and the Roman Consul Mark Antony (35 BC), Egyptian culture was still much as it had been for thousands of years. But when Augustus Caesar defeated Antony and Cleopatra at the battle of Actium (31 BC), he decapitated Egypt's Ptolemaic Dynasty, and the end of ancient Egyptian civilization itself was just a few centuries away. In AD 380 the Byzantine Emperor Theodosius declared Christianity the state religion of Egypt and prohibited all others. In AD 391 Christians massacred the community of Egyptian priests at Memphis and later converted many ancient temples to churches, stables, and storerooms.

Box 7. Herodotus on Egypt

Very few things happen at the right time, and the rest do not happen at all. The conscientious historian will correct these defects.

(Attributed to Herodotus and others)

Herodotus's account of Egypt perhaps borrowed from other Greek travelers and historians, and he seems prone to accept as true some rather fantastic accounts from the Egyptians he met. Still, he was the first foreigner we know of who tried to describe Egyptian life in detail – as problematic as some of these descriptions may seem. The biblical Old Testament contains some information about Egypt, but Herodotus and a few other Greek scholars are the only sources we have for what is assumed to be eyewitness accounts of pharaonic society as it existed toward the end of the long Egyptian dynastic tradition. The following are excerpts from Herodotus's account (trans. Grene 1987):

From the coast inland as far as Heliopolis [near modern Cairo] the country is flat, without springs, and full of swamps. . . . From Heliopolis to Thebes [near modern Luxor] is about nine days' sail up the river. Not only is the [Egyptian] climate different from that of the rest of the world, and rivers unlike any other rivers, but the [Egyptians] exactly reverse the practice of mankind. The women attend the market and trade, while the men sit at home at the loom. . . . The women urinate standing, the men crouching. They eat their foods out of doors in the streets, but retire for the purposes of defecating to their houses. . . . They are the only people in the world – they at least and those who have learned the practice from them – who use circumcision. When they write, [unlike] the Greeks from left to right, they move their hand from right to left. . . . The priests shave their whole body every other day. . . . Their dress is entirely of linen and their shoes of the papyrus plant. . . . [E]very day bread is baked for them . . . and a plentiful supply of beef and of goose flesh . . . and also a portion of wine. . . . Fish they are not allowed to eat; and beans, which none of the Egyptians either sow or eat . . . the priests will not even endure to look at, since they consider [them] unclean. . . . Some male [cattle] . . . if clean are used for sacrifices by the Egyptians universally, but the females are not . . . since they are sacred to [the goddess] Isis. Almost all the names of the gods came into Greece from Egypt. The Egyptians first made it a point of religion to have no intercourse with women in the sacred places and not to enter them without washing, after such an act. . . . The crocodile is esteemed sacred by some of the Egyptians, by others he is treated as an enemy. In [some] places they keep one crocodile . . . who is taught to be tame. . . . [They] embalm him when he dies and bury him in a sacred repository. With respect to the Egyptians themselves . . .

for three successive days in each month they purge the body by means of emetics and douches . . . since they have the persuasion that every disease . . . is occasioned by the substances on which they feed. . . . Many kinds of fish are eaten raw, either salted or dried in the sun. Quails also, and ducks and small birds they eat uncooked, merely salting them first. All other birds and fishes . . . are either roasted or boiled. In social meetings among the rich, when the banquet is ended, a servant carries round . . . a coffin, in which is a wooden image of a corpse. . . . [A]s he shows it to each guest in turn, the servant says "Gaze here, and drink and be merry, for when you die, such will you be. . . ." Medicine is practiced among them on a plan of separation; each physician treats a single disorder, and no more. . . . Cheops [i.e., Khufu, 2589–2566 BC] succeeded to the throne . . . and plunged into all manner of wickedness. He closed the temples, and forbade the Egyptians to offer sacrifices, compelling them to labor, one and all, in his service. Some were required to drag blocks of stone down the Nile from the quarries in the Arabian range. . . . [O]thers received the blocks after they had been conveyed in boats across the river, and drew them to the range of hills called the Libyan. A hundred thousand men labored constantly, and were relieved every three months by a fresh lot. It took ten years' oppression of the people to make the causeway for the conveyance of the stone, a work not much inferior, in my judgment, to the pyramid itself.

We shall probably never know the identity of the last native speaker and writer of ancient Egyptian, but versions of it were probably spoken until at least the fourteenth century AD. Some elements of the ancient Egyptian language (though written in Greek) are preserved today in the Coptic Christian Church's liturgy. But as Arabic-speaking Muslims invaded Egypt in AD 640s, they eradicated almost all traces of ancient Egyptian ideas. Islamic Egyptian culture, like Byzantine Christianity, was itself a unique and brilliant civilization, but Islam and Christianity submerged not only the intellectual traditions of ancient Egypt but also much of its archaeological record. Historical records suggest, for example, that medieval Islamic rulers stripped the pyramids of the fine white limestone blocks that sheathed them and used the blocks to build palaces in Cairo.

Christianity and Islam did not completely transform Egyptian socioeconomic life, of course. An ancient Egyptian transported to today's Nile Delta farming villages would even now find much that was familiar in its agricultural and cultural rhythms. Civilizations do not so much become extinct as *change*; they are transmuted by time and circumstance to the extent that they appear almost unrelated, if viewed at widely spaced points along the continuum of the unknown past to the ever-changing present.

Some ideas of ancient Egyptian culture remained alive in European thought in the late first millennium AD, mainly in biblical and Greek and Roman references to Egypt. Europeans visited Egypt during the Crusades (c. 1096–1204) and marveled at the pyramids and other wonders. In the sixteenth and seventeenth centuries, Europeans traveled to Egypt specifically to bring back mummies, sculptures, and other treasures. The German scholar Athanasius Kircher (1602–1680) was among the first to try his hand (largely unsuccessfully) at deciphering ancient Egyptian writing. And the English astronomer John Greaves (1602–1652) was one of the first foreigners to study the precise geometry of the pyramids. The destruction of Egyptian's ancient remains continued, however (Fagan 1975). Many Egyptian mummies were ground into powder and used as medicine in Europe, or were brought back as curiosities. Today in Europe and North America, even many small museums have a mummy or two in their collections – typically some unfortunate of the Greco-Roman Period (c. 332 BC–AD 395), who no doubt had hoped to spend eternity in the land of his or her gods.

Among the most egregious of the nineteenth-century despoilers of Egypt was the Italian adventurer Giovanni Belzoni. He crept and crawled through many ancient Egyptian tunnels and tombs, and described his depredations as follows:

[Al]though, fortunately I am destitute of the sense of smelling, I could taste that the mummies were rather unpleasant to swallow. After . . . a passage of perhaps six hundred yards, nearly overcome, I sought a "resting place" . . . but when my weight bore on the body of an Egyptian, it crushed like a band-box. . . . I sank altogether among the broken mummies, with a crash of bones, rags, and wooden cases. . . . [E]very step I took I crushed a mummy. . . . I could not pass without putting my face in contact with that of some decayed Egyptian; but as the passage inclined downwards, my own weight helped me on: however, I could not avoid being covered with bones, legs, arms, and heads rolling from above. . . . The purpose of my researches was to rob the Egyptians of their papyri.

(Quoted in Daniel 1967: 49).

The French Emperor Napoleon provided an admirable contrast to such blatant looting and destruction. He directed that about 160 scholars be sent to Egypt with his armies to document every aspect of Egyptian life, both ancient and contemporary. The resulting compilation, *Description de l'Égypte* (1802), stands as one of the great academic accomplishments of recent centuries.

Then European looters in search of antiquities invaded Egypt in the nineteenth and early twentieth centuries. When the French and the British, heirs to the defeated Ottoman Empire, ruled Egypt, shiploads of antiquities were exported to the British Museum, the Louvre Museum in Paris, and elsewhere. The obelisks that adorn Paris, Rome, and New York were exported from Egypt in the early nineteenth century with the connivance of Egyptian officials. In the late nineteenth century the French adventurer E. Amélineau even was rumored to have smashed stone and pottery vessels from the tombs of Egypt's first kings at Abydos in order to increase the price of surviving objects for the art collectors who had financed him. The French scholar August Mariette (1821–1881) tried to stem the looting of Egypt by creating an Egyptian national museum and a governmental service to protect antiquities. But it is a measure of European colonialism that European museums were well stocked with Egyptian antiquities before the first museum appeared in Egypt, in the late 1850s.

The Decipherment of Ancient Egyptian Language

The Moving Finger writes: and, having writ,
Moves on: nor all thy Piety nor Wit
Shall lure it back to cancel half a Line,
Nor all thy Tears wash out a Word of it.

(Edward Fitzgerald [1809–1883], *The Rubaiyat of Omar Khayyám*)

The "rediscovery" of many elements of Egyptian antiquity was possible only when its written language was deciphered (see Davies 1987 for a good introduction to the history and methods of Egyptian writing). By the early nineteenth century, scholars had correctly identified the meanings of a few characters, but no one could really understand any text. They did not recognize that the key to reading these documents was that some characters and combinations of characters in certain contexts represented sounds in the spoken language, rather than simply what they pictured.

All ancient written languages probably began with pictures – or "ideograms" – that represented things, such as the sun or a river, and some languages eventually linked these pictures arbitrarily to sounds in the language, to form "phonograms." In ancient Egyptian, for example, the representation of a human mouth could mean "mouth," but it also had the sound value of "r" and could be used in combination with other symbols to write words of the spoken language that had nothing to do with "mouth" (Quirke and Spencer 1992: 129–130). Thus, ancient

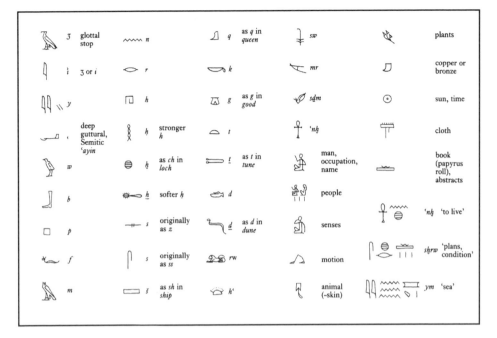

Figure 3.1. Simplified Egyptian hieroglyphic writing. This
simplified chart is of the sound and/or meaning of ancient Egyptian
hieroglyphs, but the grammar and syntax are complicated.
Arguments continue about the origins of the script, but note that
many of the characters are animals or tools common in Egypt,
and very unlike any other writing system. *Source:* © The Trustees
of the British Museum.

Egyptian, like some other early written languages, evolved as combinations of characters that could mean either what they depicted or sounds
in the spoken language (Figure 3.1). The reader decided the characters'
meaning on the basis of context and whether or not a *determinative stroke*
was present. If the stroke was present, the picture in the text usually,
but not always, meant what was pictured. Other kinds of determina-
tives indicated the category of meaning of words, spelled out in
consonants.

In contrast, the Mesopotamian cuneiform written language in use at
the same time as early written Egyptian was based on signs that gave a
syllabic value comprising one consonant and one vowel.

The individual sounds that comprise most spoken languages can
be precisely rendered in writing with a combination of about thirty

"letters" – that is, distinct vowels and consonants. In such *alphabetic* systems, writing and reading, as well as learning to read and write, are comparatively easy. Ancient Egyptian included signs that can be understood as semivowels, but it never evolved into an alphabetic system, nor did any other ancient written language except one: The first truly alphabetic written language appears to have developed shortly before about 1000 BC, among Semitic-speaking peoples in north-western Syro-Palestine (who may have been influenced by Egyptian writing). In the tenth or ninth centuries BC, the Greeks appear to have adapted the Syrian or Phoenician variant of these early alphabets to their own language, and reduced the number of signs to fewer than thirty. This Greek alphabet became the basis for all modern European written languages, including Cyrillic.

The Egyptians did not develop distinct signs for most vowels, and other Middle Eastern languages have a similar basis. Although formalized texts in Arabic, for example, were often written with diacritical marks that indicated the vowels intended, the reader of Arabic and some other ancient Southwest Asian languages, including Hebrew, often had to supply the vowels based on knowledge of what groups of consonants representing syllables meant in terms of the spoken language. Ths snds dffclt bt s nt. Still, ancient Egyptian scribes had to master hundreds of unique combinations of consonants and other signs and grammatical markers, which meant that they had to undergo long and intensive training.

It is erroneous, nonetheless, to think of the Egyptians as stalled in some kind of natural evolution toward an alphabet. The Egyptians seem to have had little interest in sacrificing beauty for efficiency in their writing system. But Egyptian scribes did seek some form of efficiency in writing by developing *hieratic*, a script that was much easier to write – especially as it was painted with a brush and ink on papyrus paper – than the highly stylized hieroglyphs typically carved in stone (although they were sometimes used in paper documents as well). Hieratic was probably developed soon after hieroglyphs were first used, about 3100 BC (see Figure 1.6).

An aid to the decipherment of ancient Egyptian languages was the discovery in 1799 of the "Rosetta Stone" (Figure 3.2) in the northern Delta by Napoleon's soldiers. This text is an unremarkable tribute to Pharaoh Ptolemy V, dated to what in our calendar was March 27, 196 BC. It bears the same text in Greek and both Egyptian hieroglyphic and *demotic* scripts. Demotic was a vernacular version of written Egyptian, used in everyday transactions and correspondence from about 700 BC to AD 500. It is a cursive script, and therefore relatively

Figure 3.2. The "Rosetta Stone." It was found at Rashid in the Delta in building debris. The same document is written in hieroglyphs (top register), demotic, a cursive form of late Egyptian (middle register), and Greek (lowest register). Although the Rosetta Stone was an important document in the rediscovery of the art of reading written Egyptian, Champollion depended mainly on his encyclopedic knowledge of other Greek and Coptic documents and other hieroglyphic texts to decipher the language. *Source:* The Trustees of the British Museum.

easy to write, but its resemblance to other Egyptian scripts is so remote that originally modern scholars found it difficult to read and translate.

The Greek version of this text on the Rosetta Stone could be easily read, however, and scholars tried to correlate the Greek and Egyptian versions. But since the hieroglyphic version was the most damaged and was considered by some to be an impenetrable language of mystic symbols, progress was slow at first. Various scholars made small advances in deciphering written Egyptian, but it was Jean-François Champollion (1890–1832) to whom we are most indebted for our understanding of written Egyptian. Champollion, born in France, was fluent in Latin, Greek, and Coptic when he was just sixteen. A key to his success in deciphering Egyptian script was his extensive knowledge of ancient Egyptian texts.

Champollion's decipherment of the name of the pharaoh we know as "Ramses" clearly demonstrates his insight that written Egyptian was a mixture of characters, some of which represented syllables in the spoken language, others that represented things and concepts. He knew that the Egyptians wrote the names of their kings in a *cartouche*, that is, within an oval (to the French it resembled a rifle cartridge, hence its name). He also knew that *Ra* means "sun" in Coptic, and he recognized that the sun-disk character in the name represented the idea "sun," with the sound-value "ra" in Egyptian. The sign at the end of the cartouche was used to write the letter "s" in the name (which he inferred from the Greek form of the name of the pharaoh "Ptolemaios" on the Rosetta Stone). Champollion could read "ra-? -s-s," and from this he guessed correctly that the middle sign should read "m." He thus read the name as *Ramses*, which he could infer from his knowledge of Coptic as *Ra-mise* or "Ra is the one who gives birth to him." In this way he came to the critical realization that some signs in Ramses' name represented concepts associated with the picture represented in the inscription, while others represented sounds. (For an accessible and interesting account of the decipherment and nature of Egyptian languages, see Quirke and Spencer 1992: 118–147).

Champollion made mistakes and later scholars have extended his work, but soon after his research, the basic meaning of many Egyptian texts could be understood. There remained, however, many ambiguities in the syntax and other grammatical structure of the various ancient Egyptian written languages. We shall never be able to comprehend entirely the subtle meanings of these texts, especially their earliest forms, and as they changed over the millennia of Egyptian civilization.

Contemporary Studies of Egyptian Antiquity:
The Integration of Egyptology and Other Disciplines

Though nothing can bring back the hour
Of splendour in the grass, of glory in the flower;
We will grieve not, rather find
Strength in what remains behind. . . .
             (William Wordsworth [1770–1850], "Intimations of Immortality")

Since Champollion's time, methods of Egyptological and archaeological
research have evolved. Egyptologists, for example, are now incorporating ideas from social sciences (e.g., Weeks 1979; Lustig 1994;
Wengrow 2006; Trigger 2003). Modern Egyptology has also incorporated recent technological advances. Computerized imaging of ancient
monuments can help scholars understand and preserve them, and even
"reconstruct" them. Numerous Egyptologists are currently engaged in
preserving this past by recording texts, by photographing and making
architectural drawings of temples, tombs, and so forth, and by physically
reconstructing monuments. The "Epigraphic Survey" of the University
of Chicago, a world leader in this field, has been responsible for
recording hundreds of inscriptions that appear doomed to destruction in
a few short years, because of rising water tables and other forces.

Computer-assisted studies of word frequency, word choice, grammatical structure, and other elements in ancient Egyptian texts show
some promise in refining our understanding of the language. Yet texts
and monuments can tell us only so much about the world of the ancient
Egyptians; a comprehensive understanding of ancient Egyptian civilization can only be gained through the integration of Egyptology and
other disciplines.

Who Studies Egyptian Antiquity?

Most scholars who study Egyptian antiquity have a Ph.D., a "Doctor of
Philosophy" degree, or the equivalent. This degree is usually awarded
after five to ten years of postgraduate study. Egyptologists are all trained
in the Egyptian language, but some make the language itself the primary
focus of their research, while others concentrate on Egyptian art, religion, architecture, and archaeology. Non-Egyptologists who specialize
in ancient Egypt are primarily anthropological archaeologists, few of
whom are trained in Egyptian languages. They specialize instead in
anthropological studies, excavation and survey methods, geological,
floral, or faunal analyses, and other research.

The study of Egypt's past is a thoroughly international endeavor. English is emerging as the primary language of publication, but no scholar can read the relevant literature without some fluency in French, German, and Italian. Publications in those languages go back more than two centuries and continue today.

As Egyptologists have broadened their discipline by integrating their research with social sciences and other approaches, non-Egyptologists who study the Egyptian past have come to recognize that their analyses can only be fully understood by considering them in the context of Egyptological data and methods. Large and long-term research projects involving excavations typically have on their staffs Egyptologists, anthropologists, and other specialists. Many projects also include graduate students who need field experience to become professionals in their own right.

Financial support for these scholars' research usually comes in part from their governments. In Cairo there are large research centers sponsored by the German, French, American, Swiss, and other governments. American scholars have increasingly relied on individual and corporate donations, but also on such agencies as the U.S. National Science Foundation, the U.S. National Endowment for the Humanities, and the National Geographic Society. The Egyptian government allocates funds mainly to Egyptians, who annually conduct many surveys, excavations, and restoration projects.

Most people have the potential to be competent field archaeologists, in the sense of doing the digging, drawing, surveying, and other ordinary tasks of fieldwork. The better excavators, however, have a natural talent for spatial reasoning and a sharp eye for slight variations in the color and consistency of archaeological depositional strata. *Sitzfleisch* – the ability to sit and work for long hours in any conditions while drawing pottery or other artifacts – is also an indispensable requirement for an archaeologist (Figure 3.3). Fortunately, the six to ten years that archaeologists and Egyptologists must spend in college and graduate school classes and in libraries winnow out most people ill-disposed to the rigor and focus of academic life and field archaeology.

Doing Archaeological Field Research in Egypt

To do archaeology in Egypt, one must first submit a proposal to a committee of Egyptian scholars and officials, specifying where one hopes to conduct the research, the research goals, and a list of project personnel and their qualifications. Project directors must provide evidence that they are qualified, which usually means that they have doctoral degrees and considerable experience in Egyptian archaeology. Once a

Figure 3.3. Analyses of excavated materials at Kom el-Hisn. Dr. Karla Kroeper, of Berlin University, drawing pottery from our excavations at Kom el-Hisn. Many archaeological analyses require repetitive tasks done precisely. *Source:* Photograph by Robert J. Wenke.

director has been given the "concession" for a site or area, he or she typically has exclusive permission to work there indefinitely – so long as competent fieldwork continues on a regular basis.

Foreign scholars who do research in Egypt do so in collaboration with Egyptian officials and scholars. Researchers submit a preliminary report of the season's research before leaving Egypt and a final report, in both English and Arabic, within a short time after fieldwork ends. An Egyptian "inspector" is assigned to each field project, usually a young man or woman with an undergraduate degree in archaeology who participates in the fieldwork and ensures that government rules are followed. He or she also provides valuable help by assisting in directing workmen employed by the project and facilitating interactions with the antiquities service.

Archaeological field projects in Egypt vary widely in number of personnel, but staffs typically include five to fifteen foreign scholars and ten to forty Egyptian employees. The director is usually a senior scholar whose "day job" is as a university professor or museum curator. Specialists typically assist him or her in the identification of plant and animal remains, geology, and ceramics. Graduate students supply necessary expert labor. The project director has the heavy responsibility of trying to ensure that the project objectives are achieved – which usually means trying to do twenty weeks of work in ten weeks, on an inadequate budget. This results in some stresses. Most project directors lie awake nights scheming as to how they can accelerate the work schedule and cover project costs.

Living conditions in the field vary from the palatial to those that would violate the Geneva Convention's rules on the treatment of prisoners of war. "Chicago House," the headquarters of the University of Chicago's Epigraphic Survey, in Luxor, for example, is a lovely villa, boasting a garden, library, laboratories, and an excellent cook; it is an ideal venue for the essential work the project members do, which is the recording and preservation of ancient inscriptions threatened with destruction by rising groundwater levels. In contrast, Sir Flinders Petrie, one of the greatest archaeologists ever to work in Egypt, was notorious for quartering himself and his staff in mud-brick hovels and eating little other than canned food (Figure 3.4). Some of his students composed a satirical hymn to tuna, as canned varieties of the fish had been their primary food.

Directors of long-term and well-financed projects typically build a "dig-house" to serve as living quarters and archaeological laboratories.

Figure 3.4. Sir Flinders Petrie and Amy Urlin, his sister-in-law, at their quarters at Abydos, in the early twentieth century. Petrie is bearded and wearing a kaffiya, a bandana type of head covering. He is seated across from Amy Urlin. *Source:* Courtesy of the Egypt Exploration Society.

Some expeditions rent houses in villages near the site they are excavating. If the site is far from available housing, one must resort to tents. These can be quite comfortable at night, but in summer they produce near-thermonuclear interior daytime temperatures and attract scorpions and reptiles to the shaded sand below them.

Experienced project directors know that adequate food is a key to a happy and productive crew, yet it is difficult to satisfy the diverse food preferences of a large international staff. Project directors can accurately estimate where they are in the field season schedule simply on the basis of the level of food fantasies expressed. This desperation, especially in remote situations where project staff members must prepare meals, has given the culinary world such regrettable innovations as "Mature Water Buffalo Stroganoff," "Old Goat Curry," and "Rabbit Enchiladas" (without the refried beans, jalapenos, *queso*, or tortillas). However, necessity really is the mother of invention: One of the graduate students on our staff managed to make a batch of world-class margaritas. He borrowed limes from a nearby orchard that "needed thinning" (to quote Mark Twain), and then used our Japanese generator to run our Egyptian refrigerator to produce ice cubes. He combined the lime juice, ice cubes, and the last bottle of duty-free tequila in a container that he tied to the violently vibrating generator. Needless to say, he has since gone on to a successful career in academia and archaeology.

Archaeological projects tend to form rather intense communities, as one might expect when people of different ages, nationalities, and personalities live for months in close quarters, deprived of many of their usual comforts, with few diversions, and engaged daily in hard, healthy physical labor. Novels have been written about the unique psychodrama of life on a dig (e.g., the wildly improbable *Murder in Mesopotamia*, by Agatha Christie). The field experience is well known to stimulate romantic relationships, but there is little privacy. Many archaeological staff members have done extensive research on the hypothesis that it is possible to have enthusiastic sexual encounters in excavation quarters on a quiet night without the whole expedition staff knowing about it; more research, no doubt, will be needed.

Life on a project can also exacerbate personality conflicts – sometimes to felonious levels. Staff members must share limited bathrooms, food, drink, recreational reading, and so forth. All in all, it is not surprising that vicious arguments break out over seemingly trivial matters. In the author's experience, for example, angry exchanges have occurred about where to get the best pizza in Seattle, the relative merits of Wagner and Puccini, the length of time some individuals spend in the shower, a person's position in a romantic triangle, and many, many other of the world's most pressing issues. But the experience of doing fieldwork together also forms many lifelong friendships. The crew (Figure 3.5.) on the 1986 excavation season at Kom el-Hisn was remarkable in this regard.

Local Egyptian workers do most of the heavy lifting on Egyptian archaeological projects. Some of them become quite skilled at carefully revealing slight changes in, for example, occupational deposits – once they get a clear sense of what the excavator is trying to do. Larger projects also hire laundresses, guards, drivers, housecleaners, and cooks, some of whom are excellent. Some are not. While doing research in the Faiyum Oasis, for example, we hired a man who confidently claimed to be a cook. This putative chef did not believe in the germ theory of disease, insisting instead that our frequent digestive illnesses resulted from our unwise consumption of foods whose mystical "hotness" and "coldness" had nothing to do with ostensible temperature. His specialties

Figure 3.5. The 1986 crew at Kom el-Hisn. First Row, left to right: Dr. Richard Redding (University of Michigan), Janet Long, Dr. Robert J. Wenke (University of Washington), Dr. Karla Kroeper (Berlin Museum), the late Dr. Lech Krzyzaniak (Poznan Museum); Background, left to right: Dr. Paul Buck (University of Nevada), our Egyptian Antiquities assistant, then Kim Honor, and Dr. Michal Kobusiewicz (Poznan Museum). Seated behind Prof. Krzyzaniak is Dr. Wilma Wetterstrom (Harvard Botanical Museum). *Source:* Photograph by Kom el-Hisn Archaeological Project staff.

were what the crew came to know as "salt soup" and "fire-cracked ox." Worse, much worse, one day he convinced the project's driver to let him drive one of our trucks, and he promptly hit a motorcycle and killed three men. Like the useful fiction of the king's personal direction of the Egyptian state, archaeological project directors are in theory responsible for everything that happens on a project. I quickly learned all verb forms derived from the infinitive "to kill." Fortunately, the killer's extended family was able to collect enough money to pay off the deceased men's families – not, however, before I had spent some long hours considering a career change, such as becoming a florist or a pathologist. If Shakespeare were to write a drama about archaeological project directors, he could simply adapt *King Lear.*

Merchants near archaeological projects soon learn to stock extra supplies of toilet paper, beer, insect spray, antibiotics, chocolate, benzodiazepines, and so forth. In the field, archaeologists whose mechanical expertise previously extended to, but did not include, changing a washer in a water faucet find themselves rebuilding carburetors, wiring laboratories, and disassembling clogged toilets.

Minor illnesses are common, and colorful descriptions of one's digestive processes and products are an accepted, even anticipated, feature of mealtime conversations.

Many people imagine the life of an archaeologist to be one of romantic adventure. It is, and it isn't. A lot of Egyptian archaeology occurs at uncongenial hours (dawn) and seasons (summers). Many long, hot afternoons are spent drawing pottery, mapping rather unspectacular sequences of cultural debris, and drawing one another's attention to the heat. On first acquaintance, one might hold a five-thousand-year-old pottery sherd and meditate profoundly on time and history, but sorting and drawing a few thousand more much like it tends to diminish the romance of it all. The vast majority of the ceramics at Old Kingdom residential sites are crudely made bread and beer containers, and thousands have been drawn and published, but most projects require that all pottery sherds with a rim or base or decoration be drawn.

Also, many difficult decisions have to be made each day. In excavating the remains of a large ancient community, for example, one is continually deciding where to excavate and how fast. Go too fast, and one loses too much evidence; go too slowly, and one can spend months in a corner of the garbage dump of a single provincial town. And accurate execution and interpretation of the most important forms of archaeological data – "profile drawings" of layers of sediments and objects visible in the cleanly scraped walls of excavation pits – require much time and expertise (Figure 3.6).

Figure 3.6. Complex stratigraphy at Mendes, central Delta. More than a century of excavations (which continue) at this town has produced a complex sequence of depositions. The letters in white mark some of these. "A" indicates the foundation slabs of a stone tomb. "B" indicates thick layers of Old Kingdom deposits that were leveled and used to make a foundation for the tomb and others nearby. The redeposited layers once covered the entire area exposed here. "C" indicates the lowest level of excavations by Donald Hansen (1967). "D" indicates the top courses of the remnant of an early Dynastic wall. "E" indicates the well-preserved floor of a well-preserved early Dynastic building, one of whose walls was "D." Inscribed clay sealing of the First Dynasty was found on this floor. "D" was built over early deposits of the early Dynastic Period, indicated by "F." "G" is a remnant left by Hansen's excavations in the 1960s. "H" indicates deposits that immediately predated "D." "I" indicates the lowest point of our excavations, dating to the transition from Predynastic to early Dynastic occupations. Auger samples from below the water table in area "I" retrieved artifacts that appear to be of Predynastic date. *Source:* Photograph by Mendes Archaeological Project staff. Stratigraphic labeling by Robert J. Wenke.

Everyone on the staff works hard. Still, except in midsummer and spring sandstorms, Egypt's climate is lovely, and there are simple pleasures to be had in hard, disciplined work on temperate days, as well as a sustained sense of curiosity about what one might find in excavations. And for all the toils and troubles of fieldwork, most academics relish their temporary deliverance from being "bitten to death by ducks" in the form of faculty meetings and other duties of the academic grind. Nonetheless, many project directors often find compelling academic reasons, once the season's fieldwork in Egypt is concluded, to visit Italy, Bavaria, France, or similar environs known for their food, wine, and bucolic peace.

Archaeology, Artifacts, and the Egyptian Archaeological Record

Archaeology is about Facts; if you want the Truth, go next-door to the Philosophy Department!

(Professor "Indiana" Jones, dialogue from the film *Indiana Jones*)

One can only see what one observes, and one observes only things that are in the mind.

(Alphonse Bertillon, French criminologist [1853–1943])

"Archaeology" can be defined as a body of theories and methods used to study the past (Dunnell 1971). The fundamental unit of analysis is the "artifact," which can be defined as anything that owes any of its physical characteristics or its place in time or space to human activity. Thus, Khufu's great pyramid at Giza is an artifact, but so is the smear of charcoal that is all that remains of burned grain in the Delta's moist soil. Even the footprints left in the lunar dust qualify as artifacts.

"Site" is an imprecise term widely used to refer to relatively dense concentrations of artifacts. Thus, an Egyptian tomb constitutes a site, but so does a small scatter of stone flakes and bones in the desert where some hungry prehistoric Egyptian hunter disassembled a gazelle. A "feature" is an even more imprecise category; it is used to refer to clusters of artifacts that reflect repeated activities, such as hearths and toilets, as well as other patterns of artifacts that are unique and often complex. The term "occupation" is equally imprecise. In its simplest sense, it means a specific location where people or their distant ancestors once lived. But in the case of ancient Egypt, it typically refers to complex layers of artifacts. These are often found in deeply stratified layers of deposits. Some of these occupations continued over millennia. Others show radical breaks where a site was abruptly abandoned, often to be reoccupied at a later time. An occupation can consist of a single hearth in the desert where hunter-foragers once spent a day or two camped out, but it can also refer to sites that we continually occupied for centuries, even millennia.

The term "archaeological record" refers collectively to all the physical remains of the past. The major premise of all archaeology is that much of what we shall ever know about our origins, our history, and perhaps even our destiny must be read in the patterns as they are reflected in the archaeological record. The archaeological record gives us the *sequence* and time depth and diversity of information that must be the basis for analyzing history. Historical documents can tell us much about ancient societies, but they also contain the usual propaganda and misconceptions of their authors. The material remains, however, as disturbed and fragmented as they may be, are a physical record of what *did* happen, not what someone *said* happened. As noted previously, interpreting what "actually did happen," as reflected by the archaeological record, must be done through the filter of the cultural constraints of the interpreter. Yet if the archaeological record is carefully dissected and recorded, it can provide a body of data useful even in widely varying interpretations.

In a sense, the data provided by, for example, a text, and that provided by excavating the bones, bricks, stones, and so forth of the community from which the text came, are incommensurable. An argument can be made that the excavated materials can be treated scientifically, but the textual information is of a completely different kind. But for the simple purpose of trying to understand the Egyptian past, *all* forms of evidence are useful.

Much of the Egyptian archaeological record consists of the remains of small villages and towns that were continuously occupied for decades or centuries or even millennia. These sites contain many superimposed layers of collapsed mud-brick structures and other debris. Thousands of these mounds (sing: *Tell* in Arabic) can be found throughout Egypt and elsewhere in the Middle East and, in fact, throughout the world. In Egypt their locations are usually obvious because they rise above cultivated fields, and their surfaces are often densely covered with broken pieces ("sherds") of ancient pottery, fragments of stone tools, and other debris – and sometimes by standing stone temples or other monuments. The locations of most of the larger sites of Egypt have been known for many years, but previously unknown and smaller sites are constantly being discovered, often as a result of new construction projects.

Mud-brick buildings were the primary architectural elements of most Egyptian towns and villages. Mud-brick buildings are ideally suited to the Middle Eastern environment; they are easily made from materials that are abundantly available nearly everywhere farming is possible (Figure 3.7). They offer excellent insulation against winter cold and summer heat. After some decades or even centuries, however, they deteriorate to the point that it becomes cheaper and easier to rebuild rather than repair them. Wooden beams used to support the ceilings and to form the door and windows can be salvaged, and thus rebuilding is

Figure 3.7. Making mud bricks. From at least 3500 BC to the present day, mud bricks have been an important element in Egyptian architecture. Constructions of mud brick are cheap, maintain moderate temperature throughout the year, and can easily be repaired or rebuilt. This photograph shows newly formed bricks, with the heaps of straw that is mixed with alluvial deposits to temper them. In contemporary Egypt, unfired bricks are still widely used, but firing them has become increasingly important. In some areas the government has tried to restrict mud-brick manufacturing, as it uses up alluvial deposits that are no longer annually replenished because of dams in Upper Egypt. *Source:* Photograph by Robert J. Wenke.

mainly a matter of leveling the old structure down to the first few courses (layers of bricks or stones), filling it with trash and construction debris, and then rebuilding on the same area. People probably rebuilt on the ruins of earlier communities, rather than start anew in another location, in part because this meant that no additional land was taken out of cultivation. Also, many Egyptian communities were built on the desert margins, just beyond the extent of the annual floods. And once there they would have had several inducements to remain at this same location: Community graveyards were typically established in the arid sands nearby, and animal pens, gardens, and the other fixed features of village life were built near the main residences. It is the systematic excavation of these mound sites that provides us with much of our knowledge about the Egyptian past.

Archaeologists working in Egypt are materially aided by the extraordinary natural *preservation* of artifacts. Organic decay is a chemical reaction, and preservation is best when there is not enough water, heat, or oxygen for decay to occur. Stone tools are almost indestructible, if buried, and ceramics will survive well for centuries even in water, if the pH is near neutral. Egypt's aridity is such that even ancient mud-brick walls many courses high (some more than five thousand years old) still stand in some areas. And the preservation of organic remains can be startling. In our excavations at El-Hibeh (Wenke 1980a), in Middle Egypt, for example, we found a two-thousand-year-old reed sandal with much of a human foot preserved inside it – the spoils of tomb robbers. Preservation of communities on the desert margins is often so good that one finds fragments of straw baskets, tiny fish bones, date pits, and other organic remains. Preservation is even fairly good in the humid and wet margins of the Nile and in the Egyptian Delta, except in uppermost levels where artifacts are exposed to the salt crust that formed as salt-laden Nile waters evaporated.

But Egypt's archaeological record is in great peril. Even the great Sphinx at Giza has suffered much damage to its lowest levels, where evaporation of groundwater has formed salt crystals on its surface. These crystals expand as they dry and exfoliate the stone. These same conditions are destroying temple and tomb inscriptions throughout Egypt.

How Do We Date the Objects and Events of the Egyptian Past?
Chronological Seriations of the Egyptian Archaeological Record

Chronology is essential to archaeological analyses because it is key to analyzing cultural changes and causes and effects in culture histories. If one were to hypothesize, for example, that pressure from human population growth caused the first Egyptian state to appear, we would test that hypothesis by dating the various sites and occupations in hopes of showing that population rose significantly in the period before the first state appeared. A chronology is also essential for analyzing change over time in such diverse remains as the written language, building methods and architectural styles, pottery styles, economic organization, and many other aspects of dynastic culture.

Our chronologies of ancient Egypt are based on: 1) ancient texts that appear to record lists of kings and their reigns and other chronological data (see Chapter 2); 2) various physiochemical methods, particularly radiocarbon dating; 3) the sequence of depositional events; and 4) *seriations* of artifact styles. All of these sources of evidence contain potential and real errors, but when combined they form a fairly precise chronology.

A major *textual* resource for establishing Egyptian chronologies derives from Manetho, an Egyptian priest who lived and wrote in the third century BC. He wrote an orderly account, in Greek, of the history of the Egyptian kings, which is still the basis of our conventional numbering of the dynasties. But Manetho lived three thousand years after Egypt's first kings, and some errors must be assumed. Thus, reconstructions of the ancient Egyptian chronology are based on the correlation of Manetho's account and other records and forms of evidence. There are inscriptions in hieroglyphics that apparently record the reigns and some of the events of the Egyptian past, and these are discussed in detail in subsequent chapters.

Physiochemical Dating Methods

Scholars have tried to develop a *radiocarbon* chronology for Egypt's history (Hassan and Robinson 1987; Haas et al. 1987; Bonani et al. 2001), often as an adjunct to chronologies based on texts, but also to date materials used before texts existed.

The details of radiocarbon dating (Higham, Ramsey, and Owen 2004) are beyond the scope of this book, but the method is based on carbon found in all biological organisms. When the organism dies, the isotope Carbon-14 trapped in its cells begins to revert to nitrogen. Because we know that approximately half of any given quantity of Carbon-14 will disintegrate in about 5,730 years, we can estimate the time an organism has been dead by measuring the amount of Carbon-14 remaining in its cells in ratios to other isotopes. The concentrations of carbon isotopes in the atmosphere have varied considerably over time; thus, correction factors are needed to infer a date for a particular sample (Figure 3.8). A major advance in radiocarbon dating was the development of the AMS method – accelerator mass spectrometry – to date samples. This method allows reliable dates to be obtained from samples the size of a match head, whereas older methods require about a small handful of carbon for a reliable date.

AMS methods were used, for example, to date the "Shroud of Turin," a cloth that appears to bear the image of a man. For centuries, many people have believed that the shroud was used to wrap the body of Jesus Christ. Scientists took three samples of cloth (each about the size of a postage stamp) and sent them to three different laboratories, in England, Switzerland, and the United States. Using AMS methods, scientists at the three laboratories all concluded

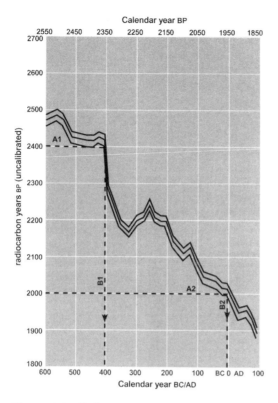

Figure 3.8. Carbon-14 correction curves. The concentration of the isotope Carbon-14 has not been constant in the atmosphere. Thus, radiocarbon dates must be calibrated. Calibration is based on samples taken from individual growth rings of long-lived trees (e.g., the bristlecone pine) and logs sunken in bogs and thus preserved for millennia. By matching the growth-ring patterns, archaeologists have produced correction curves. The central line of the graphed function is the median estimate; the two outside lines are within one standard deviation of it. Dates that fall between 2400 and 2300 BC cannot be precisely converted to calendar dates. The science of radiocarbon dating is progressing quickly, however, and much more sophisticated mathematical models than the one illustrated here have been developed. *Source:* Reproduced by permission of Oxford University Press from Shaw 2000, p. 3, after Pearson 1979. © Oxford University Press 2000.

independently that the linen used for the shroud was made about AD 1260–1390.

Still, radiocarbon dating has some limitations in seriating the archaeological record. For example, this method dates the time of death of the tree, person, or other biological entity from which the carbon sample comes, not the use of the materials to produce artifacts.

Our (Haas et al. 1987; Bonani et al. 2001) radiocarbon analyses of the Egyptian pyramid complexes illustrate this and other problems associated with the radiocarbon method. Not a single ancient text from the age when the pyramids were built has ever been found that precisely describes their construction or dates them, or records how long it took to build them and in what sequence. Thus, the pyramids have been dated primarily on the basis of names on inscriptions in temples and tombs in areas near the pyramids. Ancient king lists purport to give the length of reigns of specific kings, and so Egyptologists have been able to estimate the sequence of kings and how long each ruled.

We designed a research program to test the accuracy of the reconstructed sequence of kings in the Old Kingdom. In 1982 (and again in 1995) we attempted to date the pyramids using *radiocarbon analyses*. Our application of radiocarbon dating of the pyramids was based on the observation by Egyptologist Mark Lehner that the mortar used to level and bind in place the stone blocks of most pyramids contained visible pieces of carbon (Figure 3.9). The Egyptians produced this mortar by burning gypsum to create a powder that was combined with water and other materials. We reasoned that if these charcoal fragments could be dated, then we could estimate when the brush, trees, and so forth had been cut to get the fuel to burn the gypsum, and from this we could

Figure 3.9. A carbon sample from the pyramids. This speck of carbon was found by breaking a piece of mortar used to set the blocks on Khufu's Pyramid, at Giza. Though small, this sample is sufficient for radiocarbon dating. *Source:* Photograph by Robert J. Wenke.

estimate the age of the pyramids. We recognized that no single date could be assumed to be an accurate age indicator because of various errors inherent in the method. Radiocarbon dates for samples from the age of the pyramids typically have estimated error margins of about a hundred years – and traditional chronologies suggested that the major pyramids were probably built in less than a century. Thus, we collected hundreds of samples from many pyramids and other monuments and hoped to find a general convergence of dates around the times that the traditional chronologies dated these monuments. We hoped that if we took a lot of samples in sequence, from the base to the top of each pyramid, we even might arrive at some estimate of how long it took to construct them and the sequence in which they were constructed.

After having obtained the necessary permissions, we started at the first course, or row, of the Great Pyramid of Khufu and began extracting bits of carbon out of the mortar. Starting at the base of a Pyramid 146 meters tall is somewhat intimidating (Figures 3.10, 3.11). We also took straw from mud-brick walls and other materials from constructions associated with the pyramids (Figures 3.12, 3.13).

We used both AMS and earlier methods to estimate the ages of our samples. Many of the age estimates produced were one hundred to three hundred years older than most Egyptologists would estimate for these various pyramids. We presented a paper on our results at a scientific conference and were promptly informed by most Egyptologists that our radiocarbon dates (Figure 3.14) had little to do with the ages of the pyramids. Various scholars suggested that our dates came out too old because: 1) the ancient Egyptians used old wood in the fires to produce the mortar, or 2) the carbon came from plants that naturally absorb relatively large amounts of radioactive carbon, or 3) the mortar itself had contaminated the carbon, or 4) the correction curves we used were wrong. Because of "wiggles" (see Figure 3.8) in the correction curve, for example, for any particular sample, one might be able to read three or more different dates from the graph, none of which is more likely than the other dates.

All these factors may, in fact, have played a role in producing our dates, and even though we tried to control for as many of them as we could, we still are in no position to conclude that the traditional Old Kingdom chronology is wrong. We hope to extend our analysis by collecting additional samples, and by identifying the plants whose carbonized remnants we analyzed. If we find, for example, that most of our samples come from straw, reeds, or other short-lived plants, we can conclude that the Egyptians were not burning massive trees to make the mortar. In any case, as the explanation indicates, radiocarbon

Figure 3.10. Collecting carbon samples from Khufu. We began prospecting for carbon samples at the first tier of Khufu's Pyramid (the largest). There are twenty-two major Old Kingdom pyramids, many of them large; thus, some optimism was required. Photograph shows Robert Wenke and Melinda Hartwig beginning the process of obtaining the samples from Khufu's Pyramid at Giza. *Source:* Photograph by Pyramids Dating Project staff.

dating can be very useful, but interpretations of radiocarbon dates are usually difficult and necessarily include errors and ambiguities. One might consider that because most of our carbon-based age estimates had an error range of one hundred to two hundred years, and because most of the largest Old Kingdom stone pyramids were built in less than two hundred years (according to king lists), our radiocarbon estimates are irrelevant.

What is significant is the central tendency of the dates in Figure 3.14. Each of our many radiocarbon dates from Khufu's Great Pyramid may have an error margin of one hundred to two hundred years, but all of the dates taken together can give us some confidence about the age of this monument (although for statistical reasons, these dates cannot simply be averaged).

Other scholars (e.g., Spence 2000) have attempted to correlate the dates of the pyramids by associating their orientation and placement

Figure 3.11. Sampling Khufu. Egyptologists Mark Lehner and
Melinda Hartwig about a third of the way up Khufu's Pyramid, as
we looked for carbon samples. Acrophobiacs need not apply for
such work. The sensation is one of clinging to a slightly tilted
forty-eight-story building. Khufu's Pyramid is 146 meters in height
(c. 480 feet), and the angle is about 52 degrees. Legend has it that
many people have died climbing it. The steps are sometimes narrow
and covered by sand and stone rubble. The view from the top,
however, is unique. *Source:* Photograph by Robert J. Wenke.

with astronomical data. Other methods of physical dating have also
been developed and applied to archaeological problems, particularly
concerning Egypt in the period before ancient texts and radiocarbon
dating can be used. All of these techniques have inherent expected
margins of error, and all are still somewhat experimental. In a recent
analysis of Egypt in the period between about 170,000 and 70,000
years ago, scientists on a project directed by Fred Wendorf, Romuald
Schild, and Angela Close (see bibliography) applied an impressive
array of different dating techniques, including *uranium series dating* of
carbonates and tooth enamel; *thermoluminescence dating* of deposits,
both with traditional techniques and the newer optical methods; *elec-
tron spin resonance* dating of tooth enamel and other materials; and
amino-acid analyses of eggshells. The details of these methods are
beyond the scope of this book, but they have proved useful, especially

Figure 3.12. Sampling uncharred remains. Some of the samples taken to try to date the pyramids were bits of straw and wood from mud-brick walls of tombs and temple enclosures that were contemporary with the pyramid. We assumed that straw, reeds, and other short-lived organisms would provide the closest approximation to the construction date of the monuments. *Source:* Photograph by Robert J. Wenke.

when used in combination. The chronology they have established seems to be very accurate and to accord well with evidence about climate change and other factors.

Stratigraphy: Relative Dating by Depositional Sequence

In general, simply mapping the relative depths of a sequence of archaeological deposits allows one to estimate the relative ages of particular archaeological records. But this can be quite complex (see Figure 3.6). If ancient Egyptians dug deeply into earlier deposits to make a well or a "foundation trench" for a large building, for example, the stratigraphy may be "reversed." Also, many depositional events, such as flooding or leveling the ground for new constriction may produce irregular patterns of deposition that vary in size and shape both horizontally and vertically. Often it is difficult to correlate depositional histories if excavations are widely separated over a large area.

Relative Seriations of Artifact Styles

Chronological seriations of artifacts are based on the principle that the "styles" of artifacts change over time. In Egyptian archaeology the

Figure 3.13. Sampling logs in the core body of the Step-Pyramid. The very first application of radiocarbon dating to Egyptian remains involved the logs visible in this photograph. It was the disparity between the radiocarbon dates from these logs and the text-based chronology that caused Egyptologists to question Carbon-14 dating. But Willard Libby and the other developers of the Carbon-14 method did not know that a correction curve was needed. These logs are cedar and seem to extend far back into the core body of Djoser's Step-Pyramid. We took samples from the outer rings of these logs in hopes that they would provide an estimate of when these trees were cut. The results remain ambiguous. *Source:* Photograph by Pyramids Dating Project staff.

styles of stone tools and pottery are the primary evidentiary basis for such chronologies. Archeologists with long experience working with Egyptian pottery can, for example, walk onto a site they have never visited before and just by examining a few pieces of broken pottery can give a very reliable estimate of the age of the occupation of that site. Age estimates based on stylistic changes are *relative* dates, in the sense that they simply order samples in a sequence but do not estimate the precise years during which the samples were made. *Absolute* dates are those that associate a sherd or other artifact with a specific calendrical date (e.g., radiocarbon dating).

Archaeological Research Design and Analytical Methods

Most archaeologists have been asked at one time or another the question, "How do you know where to dig?" Archaeologists very rarely set out

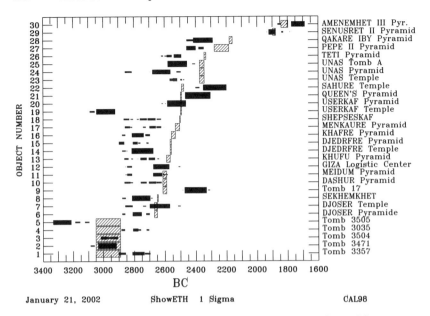

Figure 3.14. Problems of interpreting radiocarbon dates. Many problems inherent in the Carbon-14 dating method are illustrated in this figure. The left vertical axis ("Object Number") refers to the various pyramids and other monuments of the Early Dynastic and Old Kingdom Periods (listed by name on the right vertical axis. The figure illustrates the relationship of the dates for these monuments as dated from texts and other inferences (indicated by cross-hatched blocks (Clayton 1994), with those obtained by calibrated Carbon-14 dates (indicated by black boxes). The width of the black boxes is proportional to the probability of finding the true age within one standard deviation of the date indicated. The general pattern seems to be one in which the Carbon-14 dates are earlier, but there are points of agreement and reversals of the general pattern. *Source:* Courtesy of Georges Bonani.

blindly in hopes that something interesting will turn up. Most choose to excavate known sites that are likely to produce evidence about some specific problem or issue.

Many scholars focus on important cultural changes. Thus, Fred Wendorf and Romuald Schild (1976, 1998) and with their associates (1980, 1989, etc.), for example, have spent many years surveying and excavating archaeological sites in the Egyptian deserts, studying tens of millennia of cultural change in this area. They have sought to measure changes in climate and human occupation during the hundreds of thousands of years that *Homo sapiens*, ancestors of us all, migrated through this area to Southwest Asia, Europe, and beyond. Wendorf et al. have been searching for changes in kinds of stone tools and other evidence of how, when, and why this displacement might have occurred – and if it did. They have also excavated sites that date to the period when the peoples of the areas that are now deserts were adjusting to growing aridity and were, it seems, forced into the Nile Valley by these climate changes some ten thousand years ago. This migration may have been a factor in the change from hunting-foraging to farming.

The archaeological record of ancient Egypt provides a rich resource for studying many different kinds of cultural change, including such important problems as the transition from hunting-foraging economies to food-producing agricultural economies, the impact of Southwest Asian cultures on the rise of the first Egyptian states, the reasons for variations over time in Old Kingdom pyramid construction, and the eventual transformation of dynastic Egyptian settlement patterns.

Archaeological analyses are not always attempts to measure cultural change over time: Excavations of large towns and cemeteries, for example, are often focused on studying a narrow slice of time in the Egyptian past in great detail. Predynastic Hierakonpolis and Abydos (see Figure 1.1), for example, have been excavated for more than a century. Research at these sites is often focused on the period of about 3200–3000 BC, when the Egyptian state was in its early formative stages.

The Kom el-Hisn Project

The Kom el-Hisn archaeological project, directed by the author and Richard Redding (Wenke, Buck, et al. 1988; Buck 1989; Cagle 2001; Moens and Wetterstrom 1989), is offered here as an example of anthropological archaeological research – not because it was a model of its kind. In fact and in retrospect, we would have changed many aspects of our research, but that is always the way it is with archaeological projects. Nonetheless, this project, which involved three main seasons of excavations, in 1984, 1986, and 1988, illustrates some aspects of archaeological analyses as they are applied to Egyptian residential sites.

Beginning at least by 2500 BC, Kom el-Hisn (Figure 3.15) was the *nome* capital of an Old Kingdom Delta region. Our primary goal in designing the Kom el-Hisn project was to try to understand what the Old Kingdom Egyptian state was like in terms of its relations with its

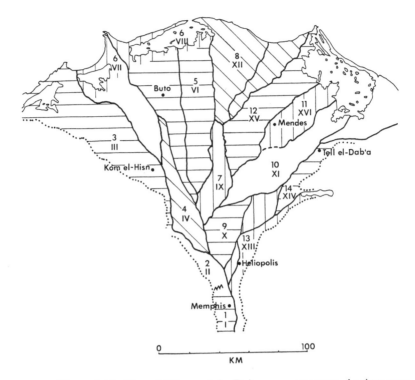

Figure 3.15. Kom el-Hisn and the Delta nome structure. Ancient texts suggest that Kom el-Hisn was the capital of the IIIrd nome ("province"). In this figure, the Ptolemaic nome numbers are indicated with Roman numerals; earlier nome designations are indicated by Arabic numbers (after Bietak 1979). *Source:* Wenke, Buck, et al. 1988. Courtesy of the *Journal of the American Research Center in Egypt.*

provincial components, and also the role that the Delta in general played in the first Egyptian states. First, we hypothesized on the basis of research by various scholars in the early 1980s in particular that – contrary to earlier opinions – the Delta was densely populated at the time the first Egyptian states formed and matured (i.e., 3500 – 2000 BC). Second, we knew that only a few Old Kingdom sites in the Delta had ever been extensively excavated, and that most were obscured by later occupations. Large areas of Kom el-Hisn's Old Kingdom occupations, however, had been exposed by farmers who had removed later occupations. Old Kingdom styles of pottery were scattered over most of the site. This meant that the remains of occupations of primary interest to us were relatively accessible. Third, we knew from mapping the area in which pottery sherds on the surface of the site were examined that Kom el-Hisn was a large settlement. The site's topography (Figure 3.16) indicated that it was a diverse settlement, and our test excavations indicated that most of the Old Kingdom remains were above the water table – making it possible to excavate it at reasonable cost and scale.

To get money for the fieldwork we wrote a proposal to the U.S. National Science Foundation. To be successful in obtaining a grant from this agency, one must specify in detail how the expected results of the excavations would contribute to an understanding of general problems of anthropology and historical analysis. In our research at Kom el-Hisn, we did this by developing somewhat contrasting "models" about the economic, political, and social composition of ancient Kom el-Hisn. We were particularly interested, for example, in its relationship with provincial Old Kingdom communities and the royal capital at Memphis, as well as with regional towns and villages. We were trying to understand the dynamics of the socioeconomic and political functioning of the early Egyptian state in order to evaluate various ideas about early states in general. Our two "models" of ancient Kom el-Hisn can be briefly characterized in the following as expressions of "the New Archaeology," which was popular about 1960–1990, as archaeology struggled to become a more rigorous and "scientific" discipline. Few Egyptian archaeological projects have been set in this theoretical context.

Model I. Kom el-Hisn was established as a *pious donation* (i.e., land set aside and made tax-free by the government to supply commodities to the royal courts), to provide cattle and orchard products to the central government. As a regional center it imported some products from central government workshops, but it was largely self-sufficient, and most of its external supplies came from regional markets. Its populace consisted mainly of agriculturists, who were administered by a resident agent of the provincial government and, thereby, the pharaoh. Except for this agent and, perhaps, a few elite families, most people lived in simple mud-brick houses that differed little in construction or contents. Because of the heavy centralization of economic and political power at Memphis, Mendes, and perhaps a few other centers, Kom el-Hisn was a tiny community compared to these centers, and supplied them and nearby communities with only a few goods and services.

Model II. Kom el-Hisn's initial settlement was in response to both local and national socioeconomic factors, and the community

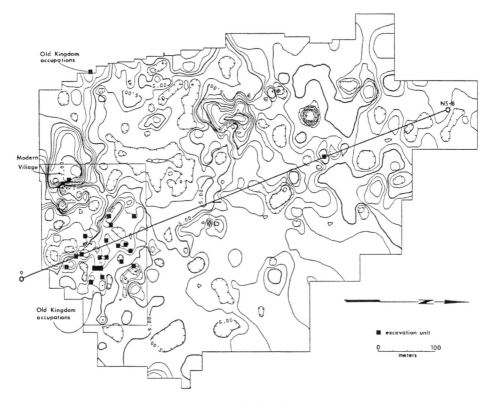

Figure 3.16. Map of Kom el-Hisn. This map indicates the general topography of Kom el-Hisn, including our excavations. Our augerings and test excavations indicate that much of the surface visible here is underlaid with Old Kingdom and earlier occupations. New Kingdom remains once covered the northern half of the site. A remnant of the Middle Kingdom is in the most southern quarter of the site, but most of the Middle Kingdom deposits were taken to build up agricultural fields that now border the southern edge of the site. First Intermediate Period remains extended over much of the southeastern portion of the site, but these were excavated before 1950. The line indicates the sequence of auger samples we took. The black squares are excavation units. Note that the modern village covers an area in the middle of our excavations of Old Kingdom occupations. Thus, it is possible that this village covers what was the center of the Old Kingdom community. *Source:* Wenke, Buck, et al. 1988. Courtesy of the *Journal of the American Research Center in Egypt.*

served a large hinterland with goods and services. Although participating in the national economy, it was itself functionally quite complex, producing a wide range of agricultural and craft products for internal consumption and export. Its inhabitants were mainly farmers but included specialists and administrators, so that there was significant social stratification and preferential access to the community's wealth, power, and prestige. Interactions between the people of Kom el-Hisn and the rest of Egypt were sufficiently frequent that its artifact styles reflect regional and national influences.

We recognized that many plausible alternative models could be constructed, that few of these hypothesized characteristics are mutually exclusive, and that these characteristics are not likely to have unique reflections in the archaeological record. The accuracy of any such models could never be conclusively "proven," and we used them mainly as a basis for specifying the variable interactions of potential importance to our analyses. We designed our research strategy so that we could also gain information about change over time in the community at Kom el-Hisn.

We also tried to test several specific ideas. Some scholars have suggested, for example, that Kom el-Hisn would show signs of contacts with the "Libyan" cultures to the west. In fact, our analyses of pottery styles and other artifacts showed them to be indistinguishable from Old Kingdom sites throughout the Delta and Nile Valley, and wholly different from Libyan or other North African cultures. Nor did we find any animal bones, plant remains, or other artifacts that were significantly different from other Old Kingdom sites in the Delta and Nile Valley. We also wanted to establish the chronology of the site. Vague textual references seem to identify occupations there from about 2900 BC onward, and the site was well documented as a large community into the New Kingdom and even the later periods.

Excavation Strategy

In our research we tried to find evidence with which to evaluate the relative "fit" of these models to various ideas about the nature of the Old Kingdom state. We hoped that our analyses would lead to a greater understanding about Kom el-Hisn but also to anthropological ideas about the nature and functioning of early states – ideas that link our research to that of others in different parts of the world.

Also, explicitly specifying these ideas required a particular field methodology, involving sampling, screening of deposits (Figure 3.17),

Figure 3.17. Screening deposits. Screening of deposits is essential
for recovering small but important artifacts. At Kom el-Hisn we used
the tripod method. One simply makes a tripod of three pieces of
lumber, each about three meters long, and then suspends ropes to
which are tied a fifty by fifty by ten centimeter box. The bottom of
the box is covered with a fine screen. Excavated materials are
dumped on the screen and shaken violently until most of the material
has passed through. In this manner even small bones, beads, and
thumbnail-size seal impressions can be recovered. *Source:* Photograph
by Robert J. Wenke.

and other techniques. In most archaeological instances when a large site
is located and preliminary excavation plans are made, one must develop
a *sampling design*. The essentials of statistical sampling are familiar to
most people. Polling organizations regularly ask a few thousand people
how they are going to vote in an election and use this information to
make very reliable predictions about the voting behavior of the larger
population (all the people who actually vote). Defining the target
population – that is, what it is that one is trying to estimate – is the key to
valid statistical analyses.

In our work at Kom el-Hisn we were particularly interested in
defining the size of this settlement, both in terms of its horizontal
extent and its depth. We also wanted to gather samples such that we

could estimate the community's use of plant and animal foods, the kinds and styles of the pottery and stone tools used by this community and so forth. Thus, as a first step, we designed a random sampling program in which we excavated a sample of two by two meter units (see Figure. 3.16). Random sampling works best when the data of interest are randomly distributed over a given space, and this is manifestly not true of ancient towns. In such communities many activities from garbage dumping to stone-tool manufacture may be consistently concentrated in the same place. Still, random sampling is the best way to get some general sense of the community and the span of time during which the site was inhabited. Such sampling designs are usually *stratified*, in the sense that one divides the entire site into discrete areas. In our case we divided the site into the main occupational mound, the perimeter of the modern village that overlies ancient deposits, and other different areas.

One limitation of such sampling is that widely dispersed two by two meter excavations reveal only small areas that were occupied at about the same time, and it is often difficult to correlate depositional histories of widely dispersed areas (Figure 3.18). Thus, we also made large *horizontal excavations* (Figures 3.19, 3.20). We found, for example, that we could identify the remains of many mud-brick buildings that seemed

Figure 3.18. Complex stratigraphy at Kom el-Hisn. Here, project member Maureen King is sorting out the depositional sequence consisting of several discrete levels of mud-brick architecture. Plant roots and rodent burrows complicate the discrimination of depositional events in the Delta's wet, thick sediments. *Source:* Photograph by Robert J. Wenke.

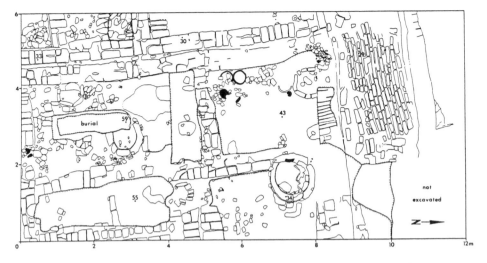

Figure 3.19. Old Kingdom architecture at Kom el-Hisn. Numbers indicate depths from surface. Areas in black are relatively complete ceramic vessels or features in situ on the floor underlying the walls. Plant and animal remains and artifacts within the walls and on the floor suggest food preparation and domestic activities. *Source:* Wenke, Buck, et al. 1988. Courtesy of the *Journal of the American Reserch Center in Egypt.*

to be occupied at about the same time and were adjacent to each other. And we used our initial small sample to identify large areas of the settlement that appeared to be contemporary. Then we concentrated on excavating a large horizontal area of the site that offered a view of what the community was like during a short span of time in the Old Kingdom.

Even our relatively intensive sampling of Kom el-Hisn, however, does not guarantee accurate inferences. We found, for example, almost no *debitage*, that is, the flakes of stone that are produced when people shape flint nodules into hoes, arrowheads, sickle blades, knives, and so forth. Perhaps Kom el-Hisn imported these tools in finished form – but it is more likely that our sampling design simply did not happen to locate the area where these tools were made. Such ambiguities are always the case, however, and all the archaeologist can do is design the best sampling program that can be afforded and then make shaky inferences from the statistical results.

Many different research designs have been applied to the Egyptian archaeological record. For example, archaeological surveys that have the

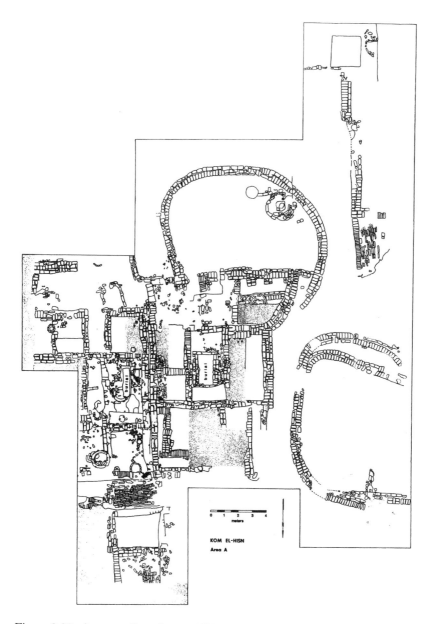

Figure 3.20. An area of contiguous Old Kingdom architecture at Kom el-Hisn. The drawing is a glimpse of the community as it existed for about a decade in the Sixth Dynasty. The rectangular structures were all walls preserved to a depth of 0.5–1.0 meter, but the ovoid structures were just .20 meter high. Perhaps some of their upper courses were removed to build agricultural fields, but is also possible that they were constructed to mark out animal enclosures, or for some other purpose. *Source:* Wenke, Buck, et al. 1988. Courtesy of the *Journal of the American Research Center in Egypt.*

objective of simply documenting the locations and occupational periods of sites are still are an important part of Egyptian archaeology, especially in the deserts, where huge areas remain largely unsurveyed. The majority of archaeological investigations in Egypt, however, are less concerned with the testing of sociological hypotheses than with the bones, stones, bricks, and other remains of the Egyptian past.

Artifact Recovery. Again, to use Kom el-Hisn as an example, we employed a variety of techniques to recover, conserve, and record artifacts. The site's surface is a salt crust about ten centimeters deep, and in those ten centimeters the pottery is so corroded by salt that it is virtually useless for analysis. As in many other sites in Egypt, several species of plants ("camel-thorn") can survive the salt and send down long roots to the water table. After many millennia, the entire site is like a gigantic Swiss cheese, with thousands of traces of plant roots that disturb the site's contents – not to mention burrowing animals. Also, there is clear evidence that much of the surface of Kom el-Hisn has been removed by local farmers, who prize these deposits as fertilizer and soil to build up their fields.

Once the salt-encrusted layer was removed, we found large and well-preserved layers of the remains of the Old Kingdom community at Kom el-Hisn. Excavating it required the coordinated labors of the professional staff and local workmen, and we employed on average fifteen to twenty-five local workmen to help us. Some skill is required when using a trowel, which is employed primarily to shave the walls and floors of the excavated units. Only if "sections," or walls, of the excavation are precisely straight can one interpret the cultural and geological process that created the site. One must look for the changes in color and texture that may signal a badly decomposed mud-brick wall, hearth, burial pit, and so forth (Figure 3.21). The sediments at a Delta site like Kom el-Hisn are often damp and difficult to force through screens, but we sieved most of the house floors and other intact domestic debris through screens, finding many beads, small bones, and – of particular importance – fragments of inscribed clay sealings.

Reconstructing Ancient Environments and Cultural Ecologies. Archaeologists working in Egypt often begin their analyses by trying to understand the physical environments in which a particular segment of the archaeological record was formed. In the Delta, for example, one can reconstruct changes in the location of distributaries of the Nile and relate them to particular ancient settlements. Many ancient settlements were on major Nile distributaries that today are quite a few

Figure 3.21. Domestic features at Kom el-Hisn. The term "feature" is imprecise, but it is commonly used to describe the deposits that seem to indicate long-term and repeated use. The circular object in this photograph could have been used as a kiln (although there was no pottery-firing debris near it) or a domestic oven. Its floor was lined with broken pottery and the interior exhibited much burning. It appears to be set in the corner of a simple domestic Old Kingdom room. *Source:* Photograph by Robert J. Wenke.

kilometers from the settlement. In the Delta, too, if one is interested in locating early sites, one tries to identify them by such means as walking surveys and analyses of aerial photographs and satellite images (Brewer et al. 1996). These often reveal the locations of the hundreds of raised mounds of sand and gravel (*gezira* [sing.] in Arabic) deposited by Pleistocene floods and enlarged, perhaps, by subsequent sandstorms.

Geoarchaeology, the combination of archaeological and geological analyses, is a particularly important part of contemporary research in Egypt. To reconstruct tens of thousands of years of local environment, for example, deep borings have been made with the use of augers. Pollen, sediment types, faunal remains, and other materials from these augerings can yield a surprisingly complex and detailed climate and environmental history.

Ancient dynastic ecology can also be partially reconstructed from faunal and floral remains. The study of animal remains, or *faunal analysis,* is a complex discipline in which, in most cases, the archaeologist is trying to reconstruct human diet and local environments. Animal bones preserve fairly well even in Kom el-Hisn's wet sediments (Figure 3.22). Faunal analysts usually tally the numbers and kinds of

Figure 3.22. Faunal preservation at Kom el-Hisn. Some bones, such as this jaw of a sheep/goat, preserve reasonably well, despite the site's thick, wet sediments. *Source:* Photograph by Robert J. Wenke.

animals represented by the remains they find, and then use statistical methods to estimate food values, the ages and sexes of the animals involved, changes in diets over long periods of time, and the physical characteristics of the animals being exploited. The presence of certain kinds of shrews and other rodents, for example, can indicate that the ancient environment was heavily irrigated by canals or natural watercourses, while other rodents indicate desert conditions.

Floral analysis, or *paleoethnobotany*, is no less complex. Specialists in this field must be skilled in recovering seeds, pollen, and other minute remains (including phytoliths, which are microscopic mineralized elements in the stalks of most plants). Carbon is chemically quite stable, and so charred plants and seeds preserve well. Carbonized plant remains can be retrieved by *flotation:* Excavated sediments are mixed with water or some other fluid and the charred plant fragments rise to the surface, where they can be skimmed off and identified. But in dry sites these plant remains must be sorted out with tweezers because some of them literally explode from expansion when placed in water.

The genera and frequencies of the many floral remains found in our samples of the 1984 and 1986 seasons are listed in Table 3.1.

Faunal remains from Kom el-Hisn reflect the typical ancient Egyptian combination of mammals, birds, and fish, as shown in Table 3.2. Domesticated sheep, goats, and pigs were the principal mammals represented in our samples. The ratio of pigs to sheep/goats is about 1:1.3 (pigs yield on average 1.5 times as much meat as the average sheep/goat). We have only small samples of bones useful in constructing age and sex distributions, but these samples do suggest that most of the pigs were eaten before maturity, and that the sheep/goats have a sharply bimodal age distribution, with most of the mortality within the first year or in late maturity. The taxa and their proportions in our samples are very much what one would expect from a dynastic settlement, except in the frequency of cattle bones. Not only are there relatively few cattle bones but they are all from animals of less than two years of age. Their significance in terms of the possible role of Kom el-Hisn as a cattle-breeding center is a complex issue and must be interpreted in the context of the floral remains.

Most of the fish were of varieties common in the immediate environs – though there seems to have been little use of the large varieties of *Lates* usually found in the main Nile. One species, *Sparus auratus*, is a marine fish that can survive brackish water. Its presence in the Kom el-Hisn assemblage may indicate import from the coast or from estuaries close to Kom el-Hisn. At the Neolithic-Predynastic site of Merimde, in the western Delta, 23 percent of the *Synodontis* remains were neurocranial fragments, but at Kom el-Hisn these amounted to less than 5 percent of the remains of this genus; this may indicate that these fish were brought to Kom el-Hisn primarily as dried, decapitated fish (a form illustrated in some tomb paintings).

Our statistical analyses of the patterns of spatial association of animal taxa continue, but bird bones and fish bones seem to be found in many of the same deposits. This may reflect the traditional ancient Egyptian practice of combining fishing and duck hunting during a certain period of the year. However, none of the identifiable bird bones comes from the domestic geese and ducks so common in Egyptian villages of all periods. In addition, animal and plant remains from Kom el-Hisn reflect the common ancient Egyptian combination of mammals, birds, and fish, along with cereal grains and other plant foods.

Most of the floral remains are carbonized straw, field weeds, reeds and sedges, and fodder plants. Marie-Francine Moens and Wilma Wetterstrom (1989) concluded that these floral remains were mainly the products of burning dung-cakes for domestic cooking. Floral remains

Table 3.1. Floral Remains from Kom el-Hisn

Plant Taxa (Common & Latin names	Number	Percentage of Total	Class Total	Class Percentage of Total
Cereal grains			251	02.18
Barley (*Hordeum vulgare*)	175	01.52		
Emmer (*Triticum dicoccum*)	76	00.66		
Cereal rachises			2600	22.59
Barley (*Hordeum vulgare*)	93	00.80		
Emmer (*Triticum dicoccum*)	2507	21.78		
Field weeds			2728	23.70
Canary grass (*Phalaris paradoxa*)	1325	11.51		
Darnel (*Lolium temulentum*)	1168	10.15		
Mayweed (*Anthemis* sp.)	161	01.40		
(None) (*Scorpirus muricata*)	71	00.62		
Vetchling (*Lathyrus* sp.)	3	00.03		
Reeds and sedges			2450	21.29
Reed (*Phragmites australis*)	1316	11.43		
Sedge (*Carex* sp.)	835	07.25		
Bulrush (*Scirpus* spp.)	133	01.16		
Fimbristylis (*Fimbristylis* spp.)	47	00.41		
Nutgrass (*Cyperus* Spp.)	47	00.41		
Spikerush (*Eleocharis*)	6	00.05		
Fodder plants			3171	27.55
Clover (*Trifolium* sp.)	2393	20.79		
Mustard (*Brassica* sp.)	383	03.33		
Dock (*Rumex* sp.)	213	01.85		
Vetch (*Vicia* spp.)	168	01.46		
Medick (*Medicago* sp.)	14	00.12		
Other plants			310	02.69
(None) (*Lapulla* sp.)	144	1.25		
Grass (*Bromus* sp. Et al.)	83	00.72		
Goosefoot (*Chenopodium* sp.)	50	00.72		
Grape (*vitis vinifera*)	3	00.03		
Pink family (*Caryophyllaceae*)	11	00.10		

Carpet weed (*Aizoaceae*)	1	00.01
Carpet weed (*Glinus* sp.)	1	00.01
Little mallow (*Malva parviflora*)	11	00.10
Purslane (*Portulaca oleracea*)	6	00.05
TOTAL	11,510	100

Summary of identified floral remains from Kom el-Hisn. Fewer than 5% of our samples have been analyzed, so these data may not be good estimators of the total assemblage at Kom el-Hisn. Most of these plant remains may be from cattle dung that was burned in the Old Kingdom community. Darnel, one of the most common weeds in our samples, grows almost exclusively in cultivated fields, and *Scorpirus* and canary grass are common invaders of grain fields. Mayweed and vetchling also commonly grow in grain fields. Seeds of all these plants were found in grain offerings in tombs at Saqqara – probably as contaminants. Reeds and sedges are common in wet marshy areas and may have been eaten by cattle or used as temper for dung–cakes.
Source: Wenke, Buck, et al. 1998, p. 22. Courtesy of the *Journal of the American Research Center in Egypt.*

from Kom el-Hisn are predominantly from plants commonly used as fodder, such as clover, and from weeds commonly found in fodder crops, including medick, vetch, dock, and mallow. The emmer seeds and rachises could have come from dung-cakes rather than directly from the plants, as wheat straw is commonly used to temper dung-cakes. Moens and Wetterstrom suggest that the Kom el-Hisn cattle were fed, perhaps in pens, rather than allowed free browsing in pastures. This is consistent with the kinds and proportions of plant remains in their dung.

Only a few pieces of sheep/goat dung were found in the Kom el-Hisn samples; and since such pellets are commonly preserved in domestic hearth fires elsewhere in Egypt and Southwest Asia, their absence supports the inference that cattle dung was the primary fuel (see Table 3.1).

Given this botanical evidence, as well as the low frequency of cattle bones in our samples, we might conclude that Kom el-Hisn was a specialized cattle-rearing center. Cattle may have been raised at Kom el-Hisn by people who subsisted primarily on other animals and foodstuffs and were charged with supplying cult centers near Memphis with herds of cattle. The use of Delta sites for this purpose is well documented in early dynastic documents and tomb scenes.

Finally, the only grape seeds recovered from Kom el-Hisn come from Middle Kingdom deposits. Artistic representations and inscriptions suggest that the Delta was an important area of viticulture from Early Dynastic times onward, but we have no evidence of this in Old Kingdom times at Kom el-Hisn.

Table 3.2. Faunal Remains at Kom el-Hisn

Taxa	(Nisp) Number of Identified Specimens	
		%
Sus	397	(30.01)
Fish	330	(24.90)
Ovis/Capra	311	(23.35)
Birds	178	(13.45)
Equus	41	(3.10)
Alcelaphus	16	(1.21)
Bos	14	(1.06)
Canis	12	(0.91)
Ostrich egg shell	9	(0.68)
Suncu	2	(0.15)
Felis	1	(0.07)
Lepus	1	(0.07)
Addax	1	(0.07)
Snake	1	(0.07)
Gazella	1	(0.07)
Trionyx	1	(0.07)

Summary of identified animal remains found in excavations at Kom el-Hisn. The distribution of fish by genus was *Tilapia* = 109 (33.30%), *Sparus auratus* = 96 (29.09%), *Synodontis* = 83 (25.15%), *Bagrus* = 23 (6.9%), *Clarias* = 6 (1.82%), *Tetradon* = 4 (1.20%), other = 4 (1.20%). Unidentified fish remains totalled 259.3 g; unidentified mammal remains totalled 14,626.1 g. The birds are all migratory water-fowl, many of them the teal, *Anas crecca*.
Source: Wenke, Buck, et al. 1998, p. 19. Courtesy of the *Journal of the American Research Center in Egypt*.

Human bodies are treasure troves of information for archaeologists, particularly if they are mummified. Unfortunately, the only bodies we found at Kom el-Hisn were badly decomposed and probably later than the Old Kingdom.

Analyses of Ceramic and Lithic Artifacts. Aside from ancient buildings, in sheer bulk the largest part of the Egyptian archaeological record is made up of pottery fragments (called "sherds") (Figures 3.23, 3.24, 3.25, 3.26).

Most Egyptian pots were made from either Nile alluvial sediments or marl (a mineral found primarily in the desert). The processes of manufacturing pottery out of these materials were rather complex and

Figure 3.23.
Meidum bowl sherds
from Kom el-Hisn.
This tray contains
many rim fragments
of "Meidum bowls,"
red-slipped and
carinated bowls
made in different
sizes and shapes but
found at every Old
Kingdom site, from
desert oases to the far
northern Delta. The
large field numbers
written on each sherd
reference the sherd
to a particular point
on the site. These
numbers are
removed after
analysis and
rewritten with
additional data in
permanent ink
Source: Photograph
by Robert J. Wenke.

produced a wide range of vessels (Dorthea Arnold 1981; Bourriau 1981). Some clays seem to have been soaked in water ("levigated") to make them workable and to mix in tempering materials, such as straw, sand, crushed limestone, and crushed pottery. Inelastic tempering materials help prevent pottery from fracturing during firing or subsequent heating.

The sherds of thousands of handmade vessels, for example, mark almost every site of the Old Kingdom Period – and other periods as well. These seemed to have been produced simply by taking a lump of processed clay and forming it into a vessel, then firing it. By the Old Kingdom, Egyptian potters were using stands of some sort to rotate the vessel in its manufacture. There are basically two kinds of potter's wheels. One kind can be rotated with sufficient speed that centrifugal force allows the potter to "throw" the pot by precisely shaping its

Figure 3.24. Reconstructed red-slipped bowl from Kom el-Hisn.
Very few whole pottery vessels were found at Kom el-Hisn. These
bowls – probably used to serve and eat food – are one of the
more common types in the Kom el-Hisn collection. Although they are
common at Old Kingdom sites, minute variations in shape may be
useful indicators of place of manufacture and the specific dynasty in
which they were made. *Source:* Photograph by Robert J. Wenke.

contours as the pot spins rapidly around a central point. A "turntable,"
in contrast, revolves much more slowly. These appear to have been used
for making smaller vessels and for applying decoration and in other
finishing touches. Both the fast wheel and the turntable appear to be
represented in tomb paintings, but there are still ambiguities about
wheel-made Egyptian pottery. Tomb inscriptions and paintings show
different kinds of pottery in use, giving us a basis for inferring the
functions of various forms of pottery.

Once finished, a pottery vessel was usually set to dry in open air
(probably in shade) until it had a leather-like consistency. Then the
potter could smooth the surface by scraping it, or rubbing it with a cloth,
and it could be colored with a coating of pigment and water (a "wash")
or clay and water (a "slip").

The final stage – firing – we know primarily from tomb inscriptions
that appear to depict the process. The ceramics were stacked in a kiln,
and fuel in the form of wood, brush, straw, and so forth was fed into the
bottom. Careful control of internal kiln temperature and length of firing
was required to produce the finished artifact.

One of the most common classifications of pottery in archaeology has
been in terms of *functional* types. Archaeologists working in Egypt, for
example, typically refer to "beer jars," "bread molds," "jugs," "jars,"
"plates," and so forth. Obviously, imagination plays a role in creating

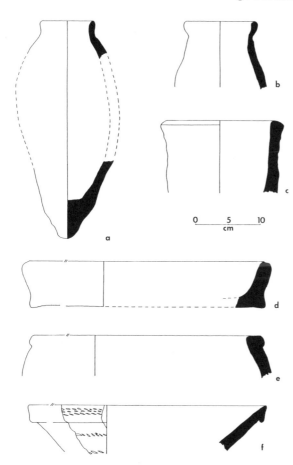

Figure 3.25. Some examples of "crude" Old Kingdom ceramics from Kom el-Hisn. The vast majority of pottery found was in the form of crude beer jars and bread molds. *Source:* Wenke, Buck, et al. 1988. Courtesy of the *Journal of the American Research Center in Egypt.*

functional types, particularly when archaeologists are dealing with extremely old remains left by people who lived in cultures very different from our own. But tomb paintings depict many of these vessels as they were apparently used. Also, high-powered microscopes reveal wear patterns on stone tools, and other technical advances have given archaeologists more confidence in their ability to infer the functions of artifacts. In some pottery jars from Egyptian sites dating to about 3200 BC, traces of the organic compounds found in wine are still preserved. Still, there will always be an element of speculation, inference, and error in these typologies.

Another widely used archaeological classificatory approach employs *chronological* types. Chronological types are artifacts whose combination

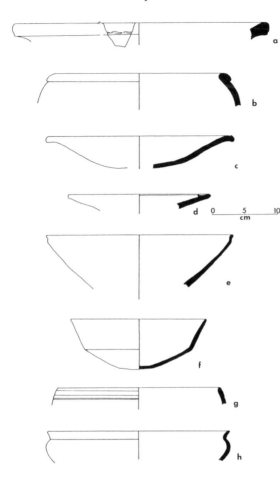

Figure 3.26. Some examples of relatively fine Old Kingdom ceramics from Kom el-Hisn. These bowls and plates were probably used for food preparation and service. *Source:* Wenke, Buck, et al. 1988. Courtesy of the *Journal of the American Research Center in Egypt.*

of attributes is known to be limited to particular time periods. Stylistic elements such as pottery decorations and house architecture have limited distribution in time, and by sorting artifacts into groups based on their similarity of stylistic elements, we can often devise relative chronologies of archaeological remains (Figure 3.27). Archaeologists assume that communities with approximately the same stylistic elements in their pottery are approximately contemporary in time. Also, pottery that is distinctively Southwest Asian or Nubian, or of distinctive styles of particular areas of Egypt, can be taken to indicate cultural interactions. Thus, thousands of pottery sherds must be drawn precisely and compared to published illustrations.

Figure 3.27. Constructing a typology of Old Kingdom ceramics. Emily Zartman, a former graduate student at the University of Washington, was Sherd-Master of the 1988 Kom el-Hisn project. After washing, the sherds (each identified by number) are placed into boxes of similar sherds. Systematic arrangements of pottery sherds have many inherent ambiguities. Traditional Egyptian typological systems, for example, are based on changes over time both in style and in function, which does not necessarily change over time. Various methods of analyzing a sherd by measuring different attributes of it have been employed, instead of just adding the individual sherd to a pile of similar items. *Source:* Photograph by Robert J. Wenke.

Production of stone tools is relatively simple but does involve some skill. When a chunk of fine-grain stone is struck with sufficient force at the proper angle with another rock or with a wood or bone baton, a shock wave will pass through the stone and detach a flake of the desired size and shape (3.28, 3.29). Through experimentation, some archaeologists are able to produce copies of almost any stone tool type used in antiquity.

Flint sickle blades that have been used to cut cereals – which have strong abrasive stalks – typically develop "sickle sheen," a glossy pattern of wear. Many of the stone tools found at Kom el-Hisn were sickle blades with this pattern.

Kom el-Hisn produced a wide range of beads, small animal figurines, and other "small finds," including cylinder and stamp seals and sealing (Figure 3.30) and one bronze mirror (Figure 3.31), all of them commonly found at Old Kingdom sites.

In sum, analyzing ancient Egypt's complex archaeological record requires many skills and much labor, often in difficult living conditions (Figure 3.32).

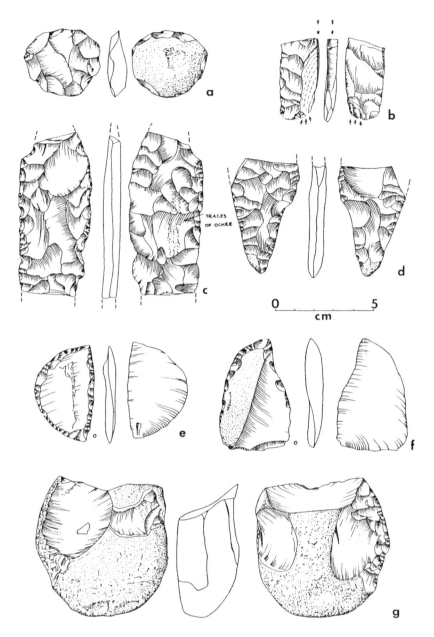

Figure 3.28. Examples of stone tools found at Kom el-Hisn. Drawings b–d are probably fragments of knives or other heavy-duty cutting tools. Drawings e-f are retouched flakes. Drawings a and g are cores that have been prepared for detaching flakes. We found only six cores. *Sources:* Wenke, Buck, et al. 1988. Courtesy of the *Journal of the American Research Center in Egypt.*

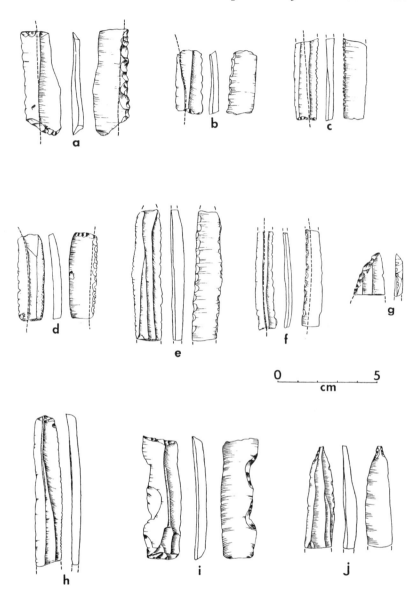

Figure 3.29 Examples of flint blades from Kom el-Hisn. Most of these appear to be fragments of sickle blades. Note the edge damage on drawing i and others, probably as a result of harvesting wheat and barley. *Source:* Wenke, Buck, et al. 1988. Courtesy of the *Journal of the American Research Center in Egypt.*

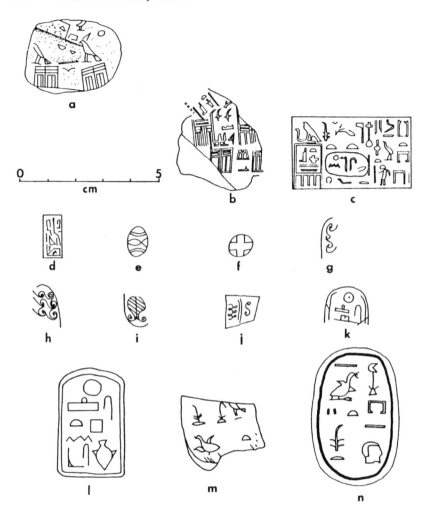

Figure 3.30 Seals and sealings from Kom et-Hisn. Cylinder seals (drawings a, b, and c) often contain the Horus name of the king and the titles of the owner of the seal (but not his name). Stamp seals (d-k) began to replace cylinder seals toward the end of the Old Kingdom, and one of the two examples from Kom el-Hisn seems to be similar to those from Hu and Qua/Badari that have been tentatively dated to the Sixth–Eighth Dynasties. In contrast, the stamp seal in scarab shape from Kom el-Hisn is most similar to those of the First Intermediate Period–Middle Kingdom at Sedment. The geometric designs (linked scrolls or crossed lines) of some of our samples (drawing f) are of styles that appear first in the Old Kingdom but continue with great variability into later eras. Drawing k gives part of the throne name of Ammenmens I (c. 1930 B.C.). *Source:* Wenke, Buck, et al. 1988. Courtesy of the *Journal of the American Research Center in Egypt.*

0 ⊢————————⊣ 5cm
ҺOM EL-HISN

Figure 3.31 A bronze mirror from Kom el-Hisn. We found few "expensive" goods at Kom el-Hisn. This mirror would probably have been a prized possession. It was found with a human burial that was hard to date. It may be of the First Intermediate Period or Middle Kingdom. *Source:* Photograph by Robert J. Wenke.

Figure 3.32 Camp Kom el-Hisn, 1988. *Source:* Photograph by Robert J. Wenke.

4 The Neolithic and Early Predynastic Origins of Dynastic Egyptian Civilization, c. 12,000 BP–4500 BC

Many heroes lived before Agamemnon.

Horace (65–8 BC)

Introduction

The Roman poet Horace inferred that many "heroes" must have lived before Agamemnon, commander of the Greek forces in the Trojan War, the first legendary Greek of whom the Romans had much knowledge. The Romans considered the earlier Greeks to be the source of nearly all things of aesthetic, scientific, and philosophical value, and they wondered about Greece's "Dark Age," during the centuries before Agamemnon.

The glories of pharaonic civilization, too, evolved from an earlier and obscure age, between about 9000 and 4000 BC. It was in this interval that Egyptians first created the socioeconomy that eventually became the foundation of dynastic culture.

We know little about the lives of the Egyptians of this age, in part because they had no written language or elaborate tombs, but also because their archaeological record has been substantially destroyed or deeply buried by alluvia and later settlements, or hidden under desert sands. A few tantalizing traces remain, however, enough to show that by 5000 BC (and probably earlier), Egyptians were farming the crops and herding the animals that later supported the Dynastic state.

These basic economic linkages are relatively simple to demonstrate, but it is far more problematic to connect Egypt's Neolithic peoples with the ideology of the later, dynastic, state. David Wengrow suggested, for example, that "Neolithic social-forms in North-East Africa and South-West Asia were more diverse, distinctive and robust than previously thought, and exerted a lasting influence upon the political development of these regions. There is a temporal continuity...between Neolithic modes of engagement with the social and material worlds, and the modes of self-preservation adopted by dynastic elites" (2006: 8).

136

Understanding Egyptian Agricultural Origins

And the children of Israel . . . wept . . . and said, who shall give us flesh to eat? We remember the fish, which we did eat in Egypt for nought; the cucumbers, and the melons, and the leeks and the onions and the garlic.

(Numbers 11:4–6)

The Egyptian foods the ancient Israelites longed for as they wandered Sinai's deserts (according to the Bible, at least – Egyptian texts make no clear reference to the Israelites) were the produce of one of the world's most fertile agricultural regions. For more than six thousand years, the lush farms of the Nile Valley and Delta sustained not only Egyptians but also foreigners who found refuge in Egypt when famine stalked their homelands. And when the Romans controlled Egypt they converted it into a "bread basket" from which they exported Egyptian wheat, barley, and wine to feed their empire. Even today's expatriate Egyptians are prone to laments much like those of the biblical Israelites, with nostalgic descriptions of fragrant lamb and beef kebabs, garden-fresh vegetables, oven-fresh bread, fresh fried fish, and succulent fruit.

So central was food production to the lives of elite pharaonic Egyptians that, upon dying, they expected to be quizzed by the god Osiris and other divine judges about their agricultural bona fides. The Book of the Dead, for example, requires that the newly deceased elites – most of whose farming experience was probably limited to watching their sharecroppers sweat through long hard days of agricultural toil – answer Osiris's questions about their agricultural virtues by saying: "I have [not] desolated plowed lands, [nor have] I made inroads on fields of other people, [nor] have I driven away the cattle that were upon their pastures . . . [nor] have I cut a [canal] . . . in water running" (after Brewer, Redford, and Redford 1994: 22). The earliest known copies of the Book of The Dead date to after about 1500 BC, long after the period of primary interest in this book, but Egyptian concerns about water and land management go back to the very beginnings of their civilization.

Table 4.1 provides the names and dates of some of the cultural changes and periods that have been applied to the Egyptian past, culminating in the appearance of an agricultural economy. The purpose of this chapter is to use the archaeological evidence from these many periods to understand how and when agriculture began and developed in ancient Egypt.

Establishing a chronology of the cultural transitions that led to pharaonic agriculture is relatively easy; explaining their causes and characteristics is more difficult.

Table 4.1. A Chronology of Paleolithic-Neolithic Egypt

Paleolithic-Epipaleolithic
  Lower Paleolithic c. 700/500,000–250,000 BP*
  Middle Paleolithic c. 250,000–70,000 BP
  Transitional Group c. 70,000–50,000 BP
  Upper Paleolithic c. 50,000–24,000 BP
  Late Paleolithic c. 24,000–10,000 BP
  (End of the Pleistocene Period c. 11,550 BP)
  Epipaleolithic c. 10,000–7000 BP

Saharan Neolithic
  Early Neolithic c. 8800?-6800 BC
  Middle Neolithic c. 6600–5100 BC
  Late Neolithic c. 5100–4700 BC

The Lower Egyptian Neolithic
  Early Neolithic c. 6000–5000 BC
  Late Neolithic c. 5000–4500 BC

---

*BP = Before the Present.
After Shaw 2000: 479.

The "short story" of Egyptian agricultural origins is deceptively simple. It begins hundreds of thousands of years ago, a time when our African ancestors lived only by hunting and foraging. This same adaptation was the basis for human existence for all people until about ten thousand years ago. We suspect that these hunter-foragers spent most of their lives periodically moving, probably in groups of about twenty-five to fifty people, depending on the resources available at different seasons. This hunting-foraging way of life was extraordinarily effective: With little more than crude stone tools and small-group social organization, they colonized most of the Old World, from Scotland to Indonesia. Although these people exploited many diverse plants and animals, there is not the slightest evidence that they interacted with plants or animals in ways that we would consider *domestication* or *agriculture* – terms that are defined in detail later in this chapter.

Soon after about 9000 BC, however, people in Turkey, Syria, Israel, Iran, and elsewhere in Southwest Asia began exploiting and manipulating wild genera of wheat, barley, rye, flax, lentils, peas, sheep, goats, pigs, and cattle in such a way that the gene pools of these plants and animals were radically changed. In fact, they created new populations of these genera that were radically different from their wild cousins in ways that we collectively and loosely call "domestication." The first permanent villages that were occupied for most or all of the year seem to have been established by hunter-foragers in particularly rewarding environments. But soon thereafter people in Turkey, Syria, and elsewhere in the "Fertile Crescent" began living year-round in villages, and they reshaped their daily lives in ways that we call "agriculture": They began sowing, cultivating, and harvesting cereals and other crops, and penning and herding animals, to exploit them for meat, hides, traction, transport, milk products, and other purposes.

Between about 9000 and 6000 BC, some Egyptians began herding domesticated sheep and goats – introduced from Southwest Asia – and intensively exploiting cattle as well. They lived in areas that since 5000 BC have been hyperarid deserts, but which were occasionally grasslands for long periods in the Pleistocene and between about 9000 BC and 5000 BC, as shifts in African and Mediterranean climate patterns brought rain to this region. They apparently established communities that were occupied for long periods of the year, where people subsisted on a combined exploitation of domesticated sheep and goats, as well as cattle, hunting, fishing, and intensive collection of seeds from several species of wild grasses. It is not certain that the cattle were domesticated or that they were native to Africa; they may have been introduced from Southwest Asia.

Domesticated sheep and goats from Southwest Asia appear to have been introduced to Egypt as early as 7000 BC, but it was not until after about 5500 BC that Southwest Asian varieties of domesticated wheat and barley were cultivated in Egypt – the most critical step in the evolution of the pharaonic agricultural economy. The first evidence we have of agriculture based on the cultivation of domesticated cereals in Egypt comes from the Faiyum Oasis (see Figure 1.1) and dates to just before 5000 BC. This evidence is in the form of domesticated grains of wheat and barley found in underground "silos," as well as areas strewn with sickles, grinding stones, and other stone tools. By 4000 BC farming communities had been established in many parts of Egypt, and by about 3500 BC almost every Egyptian lived in a farming village or town.

This reconstruction of Egyptian agricultural origins sounds simple, but the devil is truly in the details of this evolutionary process, and many unanswered questions remain. We can begin with the most general question of all: Why after millions of years of hunting, fishing, and foraging did people in many parts of the world take up farming at about the same time during the past ten thousand – a tiny slice of time in the million or more years of our existence as a genus? Why did the economic adaptation of our highly successful hunter-forager ancestors change so abruptly, in so many parts of the world, and at about the same time?

Recent research has indicated that the answer is much more complex than early theorists thought. Archaeologists have identified at least eight to ten different independent centers of plant and animal domestication, with each region offering a different and independent story of agricultural development (B. Smith 2006; Zeder et al. 2006). As domesticates and agricultural economies spread outward from these independent centers, adjacent regions often selectively adopted some but not all of the domesticates offered by the "donor" culture, and in the process created new agricultural economies that fit well in local social and natural landscapes. As the Near Eastern agricultural system was adopted in Egypt, for example, two crops – barley and emmer wheat – as well as domesticated sheep and goats and, perhaps, cattle, were the focus of the agricultural economy. From at least 3500 BC and throughout dynastic times, cattle became a major element of the economy, and other animals had less (but still significant) importance.

When we consider this broad pattern of worldwide changes to food-producing economies, it seems manifestly evident that domestication and agriculture could not be the result of a few "geniuses" who somehow developed the idea of planting, cultivation, and herding, and then convinced others to become farmers. The origins of farming economies involved scores of *independent* transitions to agriculture, comprising the domestication of hundreds of plant and animal species, and occurring in many cases among people who had no cultural contacts with one another (e.g., Chinese and Mexicans).

A detailed discussion of the many attempts to formulate comprehensive and general explanations of worldwide agricultural origins is beyond the scope of this book. Such explanations usually appeal to some mix of climate changes and population growth or dispersal; none of these "explanations" is particularly persuasive. We know, for example, that the first farming economies occurred after the end of the last "ice age," but there were many expansions and contractions of the world's glaciers that were not followed by the development of agriculture. We also know that human population densities in some areas of the world increased after the end of the last glacial period, but nowhere is there convincing evidence that "population pressure" somehow forced people to become farmers.

There are other, more specific, questions about Egyptian agricultural origins that we can address here, however. We would expect, for example, that the earliest agriculture in Egypt was practiced in the eastern Delta, in areas close to Southwest Asia, from which these first domesticates were introduced. But we have almost no archaeological evidence with which to test this hypothesis. Did Nile floods simply wash away or bury the archaeological record of the Egyptian farmers who lived before about 5000 BC in the Delta? Or were they not in the Delta until after 5000 BC? And by what routes and cultural mechanisms were domesticated genera of cereals and animals introduced to Egypt? Were these introductions via land, or possibly by maritime routes? Were the first Egyptian farmers ethnically Southwest Asians who migrated to Egypt, bringing farming techniques with them? Or were they descendants of Sudanese or eastern Saharan hunter-foragers, who were perhaps forced into the Nile Valley as the African rainfall pattern shifted, and then adopted Southwest Asian domesticates and farming practices?

To answer these questions, we can begin by examining the general characteristics of Neolithic domesticates and economies.

Common Features of Neolithic Economies

Egyptians successfully met six requirements for making a living through preindustrial subsistence agriculture, as did the people of all other early civilizations.

First, they developed a reliable, productive, and storable carbohydrate source. In fact, all ancient civilizations were based on the cultivation of one or more of just six kinds of plants: barley, wheat, a few species of millet, rice, maize, and potatoes. For the Egyptians, bread and beer made from barley and wheat were two of the most important sources of calories and other nutrients in their daily diets.

Second, they procured abundant and reliable sources of proteins and fats from domestic animals, such as cattle, pigs, goats, and sheep, and by fishing the Nile, which swarmed year-round with vast numbers and varieties of fish. They also exploited cattle for milk products and fowl for eggs and meat. Citizens of early states in Mexico and Central America met this protein need primarily by hunting and cultivating legumes, but in all Old World early Neolithic economies, domesticated animals were a key resource.

Third, they developed reliable sources of edible oils. This was significant in part because some foods become more palatable and nutritionally richer than the separate ingredients when fried in oil or combined with it. *Ful mudammis*, for example, an Egyptian staple today, costs just a few cents a serving. It consists mainly of boiled fava beans mixed with vegetable oil, seasoned with garlic, onions, salt, pepper, and other spices. This mixture is often served wrapped in flat bread. For centuries, such humble foods have provided an impressive spectrum of nutrients and calories from cheap, abundant, and storable raw materials.

At least thirty names of oils appear in ancient Egyptian texts, and oil was greatly valued as a food (H. Wilson 1988). Some of the vegetable oils used by ancient Egyptians apparently came from seeds of sesame, lettuce, radishes, balsam tree fruit, and other plants. Ancient Egyptians got some of their cooking oil and dietary fats from rendered animal fat; and they may also have used clarified butter (produced by heating butter and removing the solids), which today remains a staple of western and southern Asian cooking in the form of "ghee."

A *fourth* basic need of agricultural societies that the ancient Egyptians met was a cheap and reliable source for textiles. They made clothing, tents, bags, sandals, and so forth from fibers of flax, papyrus, and other plants, as well as from wool and leather from sheep, goats, and cattle.

A *fifth* basic need was for agricultural containers and tools. In all ancient agricultural economies, containers, for example, were needed for cooking plant and animal foods, as well for protecting stored food from rodents and dampness, and for hand-watering gardens, and so forth. At many sites in what are now Egyptian deserts, and that date to before about 6000 BC, archaeologists have found fragments of shells of ostrich eggs, which had been pierced by people, presumably to serve as canteens. But pottery was, of course, the means by which early farmers across the world independently invented the means to produce unlimited numbers of cheap and varied containers suitable for cooking and storing food. Pottery can be used for making highly nutritious food out of what appear to be unpromising ingredients (e.g., lentils boiled with herbs and a picked-over sheep bone), by cooking them into stews and soups. Early farmers in Southwest Asia managed initial agriculture without pottery ("The Pre-pottery Neolithic Period"), and some hunter-foragers used pottery, but eventually all agricultural societies came to rely on pottery as a primary agricultural tool. All ancient agricultural societies also developed stone tools for harvesting and processing plant foods. In Egypt flint blades were set in wooden sickles and then used to cut cereal plants. Mortars and pestles were made from stone to process harvested plants. Plows, too, were employed in most early Old World states – but never in the New World until European colonization. Basketry was also independently invented around the world, probably long before pottery was, and by people who were hunter-foragers, not farmers. Basketry remained an important element in all preindustrial agricultural societies.

Bryan Pfaffenberger argued that technologies should be viewed as a system, not just of tools but also of related social behaviors and techniques (1988: 241). Although we have little evidence about the social matrix in which Egypt's first agricultural tools were used, we must assume that it was complex. But an important aspect of lithics, pots, baskets, and the other tools of Neolithic economies and of agricultural ancestors of each of the world's earliest states is that people in these diverse times and places invented the *same kinds of tools*. No doubt these people invested these tools with radically varying ideological significance and traded them in a diversity of exchange systems; and they decorated the tools in styles that conveyed complexly varying social significance. Yet in the end, the cold, hard hand of economic cost–benefit calculations produced the same basic technology across the Neolithic world.

A *sixth* basic need of farming folk is shelter. Across the world, as agriculture appeared, several types of architecture were used, but nearly all of the people of the earliest civilizations lived in houses made of mud or mud brick. Early agriculture was usually associated with *permanent settlements*, because the range of activities required by farming would seem best accomplished if people lived in one place for all or most of the year. But in the very earliest stages of agriculture in many parts of the world, the relationship between farming and permanent settlements was somewhat variable.

Another common element of preindustrial agriculture, including that in Egypt, was alcoholic beverages. History has no record of an ancient civilization that did not discover that grain and fruit could be improved out of all proportion through fermentation. This, of course, is not a "need," in an insanely narrow sense of that word, but the Egyptians would probably beg to differ. Beer and wine were important methods of *storing* cereals and fruits. Egyptian beers and wines were more than mild anesthetics; both were important sources of nutrients (see Chapter 2).

In meeting these various requirements of agricultural subsistence, ancient Egyptians and the populations of the other early civilizations constructed an agricultural economy that was not just productive and stable; it was also very healthy. Nutritionist Michael Pollan neatly summed up (2007) what we know about a healthy human diet in just seven words: "Eat food. Not too much. Mainly plants." Polland restricts the term "food" to natural "whole foods," not the highly processed foods that figure so largely in the modern diet. He also recommends that people eat only about 80 percent of what they need to feel satisfied, and he specifies that this food should come mainly from plants, not animals.

The inhabitants of nearly all the world's earliest civilizations had precisely this kind of diet – which, of course, they consumed due to economic forces, not necessarily because they liked it or understood its nutritional virtues.

Domestication, Agriculture, and Sedentary Communities

Cursed is the ground for thy sake,
In sorrow shalt thou eat of it all the days of thy life,
Thorns also and thistles shall it bring forth to thee,
In the sweat of thy brow shalt thou eat bread.

(Genesis 3:17–18)

The Bible depicts the origins of agriculture as a fall from grace, an eviction from an Eden in which one's dietary requirements could be met simply by collecting the profusion of foods available in the natural world. After mankind's original sin, people were forced into a life in exile from Eden, where they had to labor hard just to scratch a daily subsistence out of the soil.

Indeed, various ethnographic studies suggest that subsistence farmers typically work harder for their livelihood than did our hunting-fishing-foraging ancestors. But agriculture produced vastly more food per unit of labor, and much more reliably than did hunting and foraging, which in turn gave agriculture a competitive advantage over other economic forms. Thus, the indignities of stoop labor were no barrier to the worldwide spread of agriculture.

Domestication

A weed is a plant whose uses for humanity have yet to be discovered.

(Attributed to American botanist Luther Burbank [1849–1925])

In the discussion of Egyptian agricultural origins presented previously, the terms "domestication" and "agriculture" were used rather loosely, but we must now precisely define them. An essential aspect of domestication is *mutualism*, the interactions and evolving relationships of biological species. Domestication in this sense often involves changes in the genetic *fitness* of plants and animals, that is, changes in their abilities to survive and reproduce in their native habitats without human intervention.

Undomesticated species of wheat, for example, which can still be found in isolated stands in Southwest Asia, have evolved – through natural selection – certain mechanisms that ensure that they disperse their seeds effectively so that the next generation will germinate and thrive. As the seeds ripen, the stems (*rachises*) holding the seeds to the plant gradually dry and become so brittle that they shatter – progressively, from top to bottom – even when passing birds, people, or other animals brush them, or a light wind blows. This is adaptive, because the seeds must be dispersed somewhat widely; else they would germinate in a clump that would have little chance of producing plants that could, in turn, seed the next generation.

But once people started storing the wheat seeds they harvested and used these stored seeds to plant the fields the next year, it was the plants that could hold their seeds firmly, rather than quickly dispersing them upon ripening, that would contribute the most to the next year's seed stock. Thus, through the simple planting of stored seed stock, humans unintentionally established new rules for success in their fields, rules that favored plants with nonshattering rachises.

The initial genetic changes that eventually resulted in domesticated wheat and barley were just the random mutations all biological organisms continually produce. Unlike the scientists who made genetic manipulations that resulted in our "Frankenfoods" today, however, ancient peoples could not knowingly *produce* the genetic mutations that resulted in such characteristics as tough rachises; they could only *select* them. In the process of wheat domestication, for example, the genetic mutations responsible for relatively tough rachises occur in only about 10 percent of wild wheat plants. Through the process of harvesting, storing, and seeding these crops, people were able to perpetuate that mutation in nearly 100 percent of their crop.

These initial genetic changes reflect an adaptive response on the part of the crops to the new selective pressures imposed by people, a process that biologists call *the adaptive syndrome of domestication*. The basic interactions among people, plants, and animals in ancient farming were set in an elaborate socioeconomic context (Terrell et al. 2003).

Great progress has been made in recent years in tracing the developmental history of different domesticated species, by discovering archaeological evidence of genetic and morphological changes linked to both unintentional and deliberate selection on the part of humans (B. Smith 2006). We assume that many millennia ago our ancestors became aware that the offspring of plants and animals resembled their parents; and that at some point, people began to sow seeds from plants that had desirable characteristics, including a tougher rachis, larger kernels, more rows of kernels on the grain head, greater drought tolerance, and so forth. Nonetheless, many of these beneficial changes may have been accidental, or the result of intentionally selecting for other characteristics that were genetically associated with the characteristics that these early farmers were trying to select. The role of such human "intentionality" in the domestication process remains a controversial issue. Some scholars argue that we need not speculate on the intentions of long-dead people to understand the evolution of the first forms of domestication and agriculture. Some species of ants, for example, have mutualistic relations with mold species that parallel in many ways human–plant mutualism (Rindos 1984). In any case, what ancient people *thought* they were doing while exploiting plants and animals is beyond the reach of an empirical science.

"Domestication," in any sense, is clearly a continuum. Some plant genera have been selectively bred to the point that they little resemble their ancestors, as is the case of hybrid maize, for example, which was domesticated from a wild plant, *teocintli*, that does not closely resemble modern maize. Through mutualistic relationships with people, domesticated varieties of maize have become incapable of reproducing themselves because their kernels – maize's main reproductive organs – have been bred to remain tightly bound to the cob. In contrast, natural and cultural selection has produced many varieties of domesticated wheat, but they all strongly resemble their ancestor, the wild wheat still found in a few areas of Southwest Asia and elsewhere.

We can identify some of the characteristics that made wheat, barley, several species of millet, rice, some species of maize, and potatoes the mainstays of ancient civilizations (Flannery 1972).

First, all are annuals, and thus people can manipulate their genetic structure relatively rapidly, compared, for example, to oak trees – which could also be manipulated genetically but whose manipulated genome would benefit only the distant descendants of the original domesticators.

Second, all offer relatively high returns in useful carbohydrates, proteins, and lipids – the cereals, breads, tortillas, rice, and so forth that still sustain most people today.

Third, all thrive in disturbed habitats of the kinds typically created by human occupations.

Fourth, all are comparatively reliable in terms of annual food production and can tolerate a wide range of environments (e.g., some varieties of maize, a Central American native, have been adapted even to Canada).

Fifth, all can be stored for comparatively long periods.

Sixth, all are easily converted to other products, including bread, soups, and beer, as well as to portable and storable form when fed to cattle, sheep, goats, pigs, and fowl.

Although plants with these characteristics evolved into the primary food sources of ancient peoples, many other plants were domesticated by ancient cultures. Some were extremely important nutritionally, such as lentils, peas, and beans, and many varieties of fruit, and others were more important as flavor enhancers, such as chilies, sage, peppers, and onions (though a few of these also have substantial nutritional benefits).

Box 8. Egyptian Varieties of Barley and Wheat

Barley was probably the main source of human sustenance in ancient Egypt, followed closely by wheat. Today, barley is a major component of animal feeds, but it rarely appears on the modern European or American table, except in the form of beer or as a minor ingredient in soups and breads. But the ancient Egyptians used it to make bread, beer, pancakes, porridge, and other foods, and derived most of their calories from it. Even today it can be found in the Egyptian village cuisine, mainly in a form of *eish baladi*, or "village bread." This bread is notorious for concealing small stones and rodent hairs, but hot out of the oven and slathered with butter and preserves it is not entirely inedible and is quite nutritious. It also provides about as much dietary roughage as cardboard, from which, when stale, it is indistinguishable in taste or texture.

Barley is a highly adaptable and productive grain. Its many types are variations of the ancestral *Hordeum spontaneum*. DNA evidence suggests that the variant of barley that was so central to dynastic agriculture was originally domesticated in the region of Israel-Jordan about ten thousand years ago (Badr et al. 2000). Barley remains have been found in graves and occupational sites of almost every type and period in Egypt. Analyses of the stomach contents of Egyptians buried in Upper Egypt between 4000 and 3000 BC demonstrated that almost all of them had recently eaten barley (Caton-Thompson and Gardner 1934: 46).

A review of the history of wheat in ancient Egypt requires a modest foray into genetics (reviewed in Brewer, Redford, and Redford 1994: 23–30). Today's variants of wheat, of the genus *Triticum*, number in the hundreds. Of these the most important are *T. aestivum*, used mainly to make bread; *T. durum*, a primary source of pasta; and *T. compactum* (club wheat), a softer type used for cake, crackers, cookies, pastries, and flour.

These can be grouped on the basis of their number of chromosomes. The main variants have 14, 28, or 42 chromosomes. Today most people eat the 42-chromosome variety in the form of bread. Most kinds of pasta, however, are made from the 28-chromosome kinds of wheat, mainly the endosperm of *T. durum* (*spaghetti di mare* and many other delights of Italian cuisine would be inconceivable without these "hard" wheats). Wheat with 14 chromosomes was widely used in Southwest Asia, in both the wild and domesticated forms of "einkorn" wheat.

The ancient Egyptians ate mainly the 28-chromosome variety of wheat called *emmer* (*Triticum dicoccon*). The remains of *T. durum* wheat, however, have been found in Predynastic areas of Hierakonpolis (Friedman 2007), and at a few other places as well, and perhaps this form of wheat was eaten more widely than previously supposed. *T. durum* is a free-threshing wheat, which makes it easier to process than emmer wheat because laborious pounding and milling are not needed to free the grain from the hull and chaff. Nevertheless, emmer remained the dominant type of wheat throughout pharaonic history, perhaps because the tough hull made it relatively resistant to damage from pests and fungi during storage (Friedman 2007).

Wheat and barley both provide powerful nutritional packages. "Whole wheat," for example, is about 60–80 percent carbohydrates, which provides a lot of energy. It also includes about 2 percent fat, as well as relatively heavy concentrations of B and E vitamins, and about 15 percent of the flour is a nearly complete protein.

Ancient Egyptians on occasion may have eaten dishes similar to *tabuleh*, or "bulgur wheat." This is made by boiling wheat kernels and mixing them with various condiments, such as lemon, parsley, and oil. Tabuleh is a tasty, cheap, and sustaining preparation eaten widely in the Middle East today.

In sum, if an ancient Egyptian had a meal of lentil soup, barley or wheat bread, a bit of fruit, and a jar or two of beer or wine, he or she would have had most of the nutritional resources necessary to farm fields and build pyramids in his or her spare time.

When we consider general patterns of domestication of animals, we see some similarities to the processes of plant domestication. In the period circa 10,000–6000 BC, for example, the Egyptians exploited several species of wild grasses, and perhaps they had begun changing the gene pools of these plants in a way that might have led to their eventual domestication. But this process, if it occurred, would have been cut short by the introduction of Southwest Asian domesticates. Similarly, Egyptians apparently tried to domesticate the gazelle, but even if they had persisted in this process, gazelles would never have provided the returns of pigs, cattle, sheep, and goats.

A key to the domestication of many animal genera is that they have a strong instinctual sense of social hierarchies. Pack and herd animals are particularly susceptible to human exploitation of these instincts because these animals seem to want to know "who is in charge," and humans can easily usurp that role (Brewer, Redford, and Redford 1994: 77–90). Pack and herd animals also tolerate a degree of closeness and crowding that some other genera will not.

Dogs were probably the first domesticated, from wolves, at least fourteen thousand years ago – and probably much earlier. Southwest Asian varieties of sheep, goats, pigs, and cattle appear to have been domesticated several centuries *before* any plants were. In Southwest Asian sites dating to about ten thousand years ago, archaeologists have found the bones of goats, sheep, and pigs that were probably kept in managed herds. This inference is based on the distinctive age and sex composition of animals as reflected in these samples Legge (1996). These bones closely match the profile of modern livestock herds that have been managed for maximum meat production: They include the bones of many adult females and a few adult males, suggesting that most males were slaughtered just as they reached maturity. Only a few males are needed to continue the reproductive cycle. Soon after these changes appear in the archaeological record, there are indications that people began to select (probably by controlling mating and slaughtering) for other traits that are useful to people. These include increased meat and milk production, greater docility, and traction power in cattle, and thicker fleece and greater temperature tolerance in sheep and goats.

Consider sheep, for example. Domesticated Southwest Asian strains of these animals were introduced into Egypt by about 6000 BC (and probably much earlier), and by dynastic times depictions of sheep in Egyptian art, as well as skeletal remains, indicate that the Egyptians exploited at least two kinds of domesticated sheep. One was probably a descendant of the Asiatic mouflon (*Ovis orientalis*). It was hairy and had a thin tail and twisted horns. The other was a fat-tailed sheep (*Ovis* spp.). Both of these kinds appear to have been introduced to Egypt from Southwest Asia. The fat-tailed sheep may have been introduced much later, however; although these sheep were depicted in Mesopotamian art as early as 3000 BC, they seem to appear in Egyptian art only after about 2000 BC (the evidence is ambiguous). These sheep had tails that were two- to four-kilogram masses of fat (which has led some people to conclude, erroneously, that these animals could not mate without human help). These are the primary variety of sheep in the Middle East today, and the oil rendered from their tails is still used in some areas. (It is very much an acquired taste, especially when rancid and used to fry okra in a dirty skillet – a meal featuring this dish can haunt one's memory for a lifetime.)

The fleece of Egyptian varieties of sheep has been selected by both natural and cultural factors to be thick enough to protect these animals against the ferocious Middle Eastern sun, as well as to provide reasonably good weaving wool. Zoologists have measured the temperature of these sheep at different times and seasons, by taking their temperatures on the outer coat and at the surface of their skin, and by inserting thermometers in their rectums. Accounts of these experiments indicate that sheep share our profound ambivalence about all matters proctological, but, more important, they demonstrate that these animals' fleece provides a degree of insulation that only aluminum siding could rival – these animals frolic in the hottest Middle Eastern summers with no apparent ill effects.

With regard to cattle, genetic and archaeological evidence indicates that *initial* domestication of this genus took place in the natural habitat of wild cattle. People exploited these animals for centuries before they began to change their size and other attributes. But after about 7000 BC people began to change these animals' gene pools. Simply by slowly introducing these animals into the hotter lowlands and breeding the survivors, people of later periods were able to select for the smaller, more heat- and disease-resistant and diet-tolerant cattle that eventually dominated lowland Mesopotamian herds.

The cattle that were so central to dynastic Egypt may have been descendants of these Southwest Asian progenitors, or perhaps they were independently domesticated from African ancestors. The initial focus of selection in the domestication of North African cattle may have been their use as "walking larders," exploited mainly for milk and blood, and only on special occasions for meat. Milk production from North African cattle, however, would have been low, given the heat and poor quality of fodder in their environment, not to mention the demands of calves (Brewer, Redford, and Redford 1994: 85). Pharaonic Egyptians exploited several varieties of domesticated cattle, perhaps distinct species, and it is likely that these were selected for somewhat different characteristics and uses.

Despite the primary role of cattle, sheep, goats, and pigs in Old World civilizations, it is important to note that many animals were domesticated around the world, from yaks to cats, cows to sows, reindeers to rodents, and dogs to ducks. In the New World, only a few species of camelids (e.g., the llama) and some rodents were domesticated. In fact, the Europeans' easy conquest of the New World was in part a result of the absence there of domesticated animals like oxen for plowing and horses for use by armed cavalry, as well as the introduction of "germs, guns, and steel" (Diamond 1999).

As people changed their kinds and degrees of interactions with plants and animals, changes in these plants and animals occurred in many dimensions – and still continue. Today, selectively bred pigs, for example, are "harvested" for parts of heart valves for humans, and as this chapter is being written, there are news reports of sheep that have been bred to have 15 percent human genes – the better to use their internal organs for transplantation in humans. A "brave new world," indeed. These manipulations of other genomes always include risks. Animals engineered for spare parts for humans may allow diseases to cross species boundaries and affect people and the edible animals upon which they depend. And if most of the world becomes dependent on fewer and fewer species of rice, for instance, the evolution of a single new crop disease could catastrophically reduce the world's food supply.

Domestication is never really "over," of course. "Genetically modified" foods, for example, are currently a topic of heated debate. But we humans have been genetically modifying plants and animals for tens of thousands of years, and likely will continue to do so.

Thus, it is encouraging that scientists are currently storing seeds from every species they can find, wild and domesticated, to be preserved as insurance against extinction and disease. Seeds of ancient varieties of wheat and barley were looted from storage at Abu Ghraib, Iraq, during the recent war, but scientists are storing additional samples of seeds from thousands of plants in vaults under the permafrost on the Norwegian island of Spitzbergen and elsewhere. In addition, there are efforts to maintain ancient species of cattle, sheep, pigs, and other animals so that their unique genomes are not forever lost. All biological species are products of millions of years of accumulated evolutionary changes, and we simply do not know which of their genes may be beneficial to people in the long-term future.

Agriculture and Sedentary Communities

I went into farming because it allows me to choose the seventy hours a week that I want to work.

(Old farming joke)

The key element in the concept of "agriculture" is *environmental modification*, in the sense that early farmers engineered "artificial" ecosystems and constructed unique ecological niches. Ice-age hunter-foragers had minimal impact on their landscapes, at least compared to farmers; but ancient Egyptians plowed fields, weeded crops, fashioned scarecrows, penned pigs, caged wild water-fowl, force-fed geese, hand-watered gardens, walled orchards, and in many other ways modified, transformed, and created the environments of their farm plants and animals.

Moreover, to modify the environments of plants and animals effectively enough to be able to depend on them for one's entire livelihood, farmers must live permanently in a single place. Anthropologists use the term *sedentary* to distinguish such groups from *mobile* hunter-foragers – although this is a rather rough partitioning of the rich diversity of the world's ancient economies. Communities along what is now the Pacific Northwest Coast, for example, never became farmers, but they developed sedentary communities and some of the elements of complex societies by exploiting the rich interface of terrestrial and marine environments. Sedentary communities and some elements of socioeconomic ranking require only a relatively high level of food production, not necessarily an agricultural economy.

There are obvious reasons for the close association of sedentary communities and agriculture, however. Crops need constant attention for many months of the year. Farmers have to plant, water, and harvest them, to store the varieties of produce as they ripen at different times, and to reduce losses caused by competing weeds, rodents, birds, and other animals. Also, farming requires tools that are less portable than those used in hunting and gathering, such as pots, stone hoes, sickles, grinding stones, and silos. Sickles, hoes, and grinding stones are particularly important cereal-farming tools and are the most archaeologically visible evidence of the transition to farming.

The Paleolithic–Neolithic Transition in Egypt (c. 9000–4000 BC)

For long periods during the Pleistocene Epoch (c. 1.6 million to twelve thousand years ago), large areas of what is now Egypt's portion of the Sahara Desert received sufficient rain to support grasslands and even lakes. These regions, which are now utter deserts, once offered hunting-foraging people vast herds of wild cattle, gazelles, and other animals, as well as the nutritious seeds of wild grasses and various edible tubers and fruits. The most rewarding ecological niches in Northeast Africa in the late Pleistocene would have been along the Nile and other rivers, where people could combine riverine and terrestrial resources.

If ethnographic studies of recent hunter-foragers are any guide, these people probably lived in groups of about fifteen to thirty members, most of whom were blood relatives. When plant and animals resources were particularly rich, these early Egyptians came together briefly in larger groups of perhaps a hundred or more people. It was on these occasions, we suspect, that they formed sexual relationships, traded small amounts of fine flint and other precious goods, and exchanged information about resources and hostile intruders, among other topics. Debris left by these people over hundreds of millennia litters Egypt's desert margins. Stone hand axes and other stone tools, for example, have been found along buried ancient watercourses that tens of thousands of years ago supported people, plants, and animals in areas that are now hyperarid.

Our earliest direct ancestors, "modern" *Homo sapiens*, probably reached the Nile Valley from central Africa at least a hundred thousand years ago and likely lived there for many generations before their descendants reached the wider Euro-Asian world. One of the earliest known *Homo sapiens* skeletons found in Egypt belonged to a child who lived around forty to eighty thousand years ago. Belgian archaeologists (Vermeersch et al. 1988) found the bones of this eight-to-ten-year-old at Taramsa Hill, near Qena, in southern Egypt. This skeleton was found in a shallow pit, where it apparently had been buried in a sitting position, perhaps so as to be "looking" at the sky. This child lived at a time when Neanderthals probably still roamed much of Europe, but its preserved bones were entirely modern in appearance – "one of us," in other words.

For tens of thousands of years after the death of this child of Taramsa, hunter-forager groups lived in these same areas. Their lives occasionally must have been ones of intense competition, especially when climate fluctuations made resources scarce. Excavations at Jebel Sahaba (in southern Egypt), for example, revealed a cemetery containing the skeletons of fifty-eight people who lived in the period of about 12,000–10,000 BC, many of them children under three years of age. Their remains would arouse the suspicions of any coroner: In the bodies of both adults and children were more than a hundred stone projectile points (probably arrow or spear heads), many in positions in the body that indicate the killing of these people (Figure 4.1) (Wendorf 1968: 959).

At the time the world's glaciers began to retreat, about twelve thousand years ago, the Nile Valley was at times a favored location for hunter-foragers. We know something of the lives of these people from sites in Upper Egypt (e.g., Vermeersch, Paulissen, and van Neer 1989) (see Figure 1.1).

Between about 9000 and 7000 BC, people living in the rich aquatic environment of the Nile, as it flowed through southern Egypt and into Nubia, made a handsome living on fish, hippos, mollusks, wildfowl, and other riverine resources, complemented with terrestrial resources – the animals and plants that thrived in the grasslands and lake shores in what is now the Eastern and Western Deserts. When the Nile was at full flood and its margins under water, these people intensified their exploitation of terrestrial resources (Wetterstrom 1993: 172). They were already intensively exploiting plants and perhaps were changing the gene pools of these

Figure 4.1. Paleolithic conflict. Anyone who thinks that our late Paleolithic (c. 12,000 BP) ancestors were peaceful, gentle folks quietly living out their unremarkable lives in primitive communism should meditate on this picture. Here at Gebel Sahaba, in southern Egypt, a cemetery contained many people who had chert stones embedded in their bodies – marked here by pencils. *Source:* Wendorf 1968; reproduced by permission of Oxford University Press from Shaw 2000; p. 30. © Oxford University Press 2000.

plants in ways that would have eventuated in "domestication," had not southwestern Asian cereals replaced them. Already by this time, some of their flint tools exhibit "sickle sheen" wear patterns, which are glossy patches produced on flint by repeated impact on silica in the plant stalks. Among the native species of flora these people probably exploited is "nut-grass" (*Cyperus rotundus*), as well as the seeds of other seasonal grasses.

The Sahara Neolithic

Human occupations in the Sahara between about 9000 and 5000 BC waxed and waned, in concert with climatic changes (Kuper and Krö-pelin 2006: 803). Soon after about 9000 BC, hunter-foragers in these now desert areas west of the Nile Valley were apparently developing some elements of a food-producing economy. These people may have been immigrants from the Nile Valley (Wendorf, Schild, and Close 1980, 1984a, 1984b; Wendorf 1985). They intensively collected the seeds of wild grasses and other plants, and perhaps herded cattle. In southern Egypt, for example, at Nabta Playa (Wendorf and Schild 1998), rainfall was sufficient to create a lake, which apparently attracted people, as it provided a source of water as well as vegetation for grazing cattle, goats, and sheep. These people obtained water simply by digging through the sand down to the water level, and thus even if the lake shrank and rainfall lessened, they could have lived here for a significant part of the year.

We do not know exactly what plants these people exploited, but they may have been harvesting nondomesticated varieties of millet, sorghum, and other grasses, as well as wild fruits, tubers, and other plants. Many grinding stones have been found in this region, probably reflecting an increased exploitation of wild grasses. Pottery has been found at Nabta Playa, and although it occurs in small numbers, some of it was elaborately decorated with paint; other pottery was painted and then combed or impressed with cords or combs before firing, perhaps to imitate basketry. The people also hunted with arrows tipped with points (Figure 4.2) that are similar stylistically to points found far into the Western Desert, near oases, and later in the earliest Neolithic communities along the Nile (Holmes 1989: 183).

Cattle bones were found in some sites of this time and in this region, and arguments continue about precisely how these animals were exploited. Did the people of Nabta Playa simply hunt them, or did they manage herds of them in some fashion? This may seem a trivial question, but the North African record of cattle exploitation is an integral element in understanding worldwide patterns of animal domestication in general. Fred Wendorf and Romuald Schild, who directed the research at Nabta Playa and similar sites, argue (1998) on the basis of bone measurements, ecological factors, and other evidence that these cattle were domesticated and perhaps were used as "walking larders," as explained earlier in the chapter. As noted, however, the availability of surplus milk from animals browsing on poor fodder in a semiarid environment remains problematic (Wengrow 2006: 48–49).

Between about 6500 and 5100 BC, the human population density in the eastern Saharan borders of the Nile apparently reached a peak. Bir Kiseiba, Nabta Playa, Wadi Kubbaniya, and other epipaleolithic/neolithic transitional sites have been found in the deserts between the Kharga Oasis and the Nile, from Armant to Elephantine (shown on Figure 5.3 in the next chapter). Excavations in these areas (Wendorf, Schild, and Close 1980, 1984a, 1984b, 1989) revealed numerous ground stone tools that were used to grind the seeds of wild grasses, or to process bulbs and other plants. Ground stone tools were produced across the ancient world once agriculture appeared. Mortars and pestles were shaped by chipping stones until they had the desired shapes. Years of use produced finely shaped tools. At Nabta Playa, Wendorf and Schild (1998) also found an

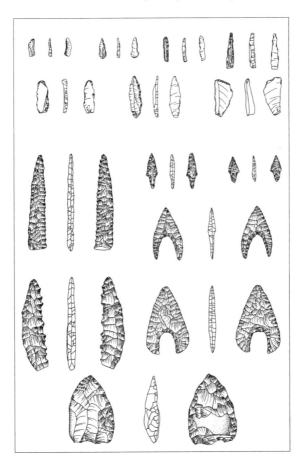

Figure 4.2. Faiyum lithics. The two top rows of this drawing illustrate the epipaleolithic tools found at pre-agricultural ("Qarunian") sites across the Faiyum. The other drawings indicate the great differences that the Neolithic Faiyum represents, as an agricultural subsistence strategy evolved. *Source:* Wenke, Long, and Buck 1988. Reproduced from the *Journal of Field Archaeology* with the permission of the Trustees of Boston University. All rights reserved.

impressive example of relatively large-scale architecture dating to shortly after 6000 BC. The people here lived in huts that were made in part by piling large stones. Some of these structures were arranged in orderly rows, suggesting some formal planning of the community. Near the houses was an alignment of ten large (2×3 m) stone blocks and a circle of smaller blocks set upright that some have suggested was a "calendrical circle" used for astronomical observations. There were also nine piles of stones, and beneath one was the skeleton of a long-horned bull. Others contained disarticulated cattle bones. The radiocarbon dates from one of these burials suggest a date of about 5400 BC. The cattle almost certainly were domesticated, and were perhaps used as a meat and fat source to sustain these people during periods when rainfall decreased.

These cattle remains and associated artifacts have been interpreted as the first evidence of a "cattle-cult" in ancient Egypt, but their links to dynastic cattle-cults are uncertain. Still, some of the earliest agricultural communities in Egypt, such as Hierakonpolis, contained what may have been ritual burials of cattle – although these vary widely in their contents and locations (Flores 2003). Fekri Hassan (1992) has argued that the cattle-cults of pharaonic Egypt had their origins in Saharan pastoralist cultures, and perhaps the evidence from Nabta Playa is an early sign of this (Brass 2007).

Growing aridity after about 5500 BC gradually drove people out of the Sahara and perhaps into the Nile Valley or desert oases. Once these patterns shifted and agriculture evolved in the Nile Valley and Delta, the ancient Saharan Neolithic way of life was doomed to extinction – except as it might have lived on in the genes and cultural repertoire of Egypt's first cereal farmers.

The Lower Egyptian Neolithic Period, c. 6000–4000 BC

The term "Lower Egyptian Neolithic" is used here to distinguish the "Neolithic" Saharan adaptations from those that appeared in and/or closely adjacent to the Nile Valley and the Nile Delta, in Lower Egypt, just before and after 5000 BC. Most of our evidence about this period and adaptation comes from sites in the Faiyum Oasis and Merimde Beni Salama (shown on Figure 5.3 in the next chapter), but several other sites of this age and general type have also been found in Lower Egypt.

Lower Egyptian Neolithic communities differed from their earlier Saharan counterparts in various ways: Most important, they were based on farming strains of wheat and barley that were introduced from Southwest Asia, in contrast to the Saharan economy, which was based on exploitation of nondomesticated plants. Although the Sahara Neolithic and the Faiyum-Merimde Neolithic communities shared some characteristics, it was the Lower Egyptian Neolithic economic system that became the foundation of the dynastic economy.

One would hardly imagine the eventual importance of the Lower Egyptian Neolithic cultures from their remains. Few tourists in Cairo's Egyptian Museum find their way to the galleries near the front of the second floor, where a small collection of artifacts of Egypt's last hunter-foragers and first farmers is displayed. These stone arrowheads, knives, and sickle blades are understandably less a draw to tourists than the gilded furniture from Tutankhamun's tomb just down the hall. But Tutankhamun and all his riches, and all the power and wealth of the other pharaohs, were possible only because of the agricultural economy established by these first Egyptian farmers who toiled three thousand years before Tutankhamun.

This agricultural economy seems to have developed out of several different cultures and economic transitions. One possible source for the Faiyum–Lower Egyptian Neolithic culture is somewhat hypothetical. We know that many of the people who lived in the Nile Valley between about 9000 and 7000 BC, at sites in Upper Egypt (e.g., Vermeersch, Paulissen, and van Neer 1989), focused their attention on the rich resources of the Nile and its banks, and that they also had the luxury of hunting and foraging the verdant plains and ancient wadis that extended far out into what are now the Eastern and Western Sahara (Wetterstrom 1993: 172). But we have little evidence of human occupation of the Nile's immediate environments for the millennium just before domesticated cereals were farmed in Egypt. The people of the Saharan Neolithic may, in fact, have been descendants of these Nile Valley people, but it is likely that people lived in great densities along the Nile between about 6300 and 5300 BC, when the transition to cereal agriculture first began. Were these Nilotic peoples the physical and cultural ancestors of the first farmers in the Faiyum and elsewhere? There is some evidence against this hypothesis. We know, for example, that at about 7000 BC people lived immediately adjacent to the Faiyum Lake, just a few kilometers. from the Nile, but they had no agricultural tools and did not farm domesticated strains of wheat or barley. It is difficult to imagine that these Epipaleolithic hunter-foragers lived nearly side by side with people in the Nile Valley and Delta who had established cereal agriculture and a sedentary settlement pattern.

In any case, if people were living along the Nile's banks between about 7000 and 5000 BC, these sites may have long since been buried or washed away.

Another possible origin of the Lower Egyptian Neolithic culture involved people in what are now Egyptian Nubia and the Sudan. People lived there as hunter-foragers and, perhaps, as farmers all through the period of Egypt's transition to agriculture, and farming in the Sudan is nearly as old as that in Egypt. These people and their culture may have influenced those in Egypt in various ways, but the evidence is not clear. Sorghum and millet, for example, became staple grains in what is now the Sudan, but they were virtually unknown in dynastic Egypt.

Yet another possible ancestor of the Lower Egyptian Neolithic is, obviously, the Southwest Asian people who were farming cereals and herding domesticated stock animals centuries before the Egyptians were. Syro-Palestinian peoples often migrated to Egypt, but it is difficult to imagine that Southwest Asian farmers themselves migrated in great numbers into Egypt.

Perhaps the most likely origin of the *people*, as opposed to the economies, of the Faiyum–Lower Egyptian Neolithic are the Saharan Neolithic peoples, who were likely driven into the Nile Valley and Delta by growing aridity after about 5100 BC, where they adopted the farming way of life.

We do not have enough evidence to evaluate these various ideas about the origins of the Faiyum-Merimde Neolithic, but we do have some relevant data.

Early Farming in the Faiyum

Gertrude Caton-Thomson and Elinor Gardner (1934) were the first to demonstrate the important role that the inhabitants of the Faiyum played in Egyptian agricultural origins. In 1925–1926 these intrepid women excavated many archaeological sites in the Faiyum, and they identified two radically different cultures. They mistakenly believed that the early Faiyum farmers – their "Fayum A" people – had been replaced by a "degenerate" race of hunter-foragers, the "Fayum B" people. In fact, they had simply misinterpreted the lacustrine geology of the Faiyum. Since Caton-Thompson and Gardner's time, the Fayum B label has been replaced by the term "Qarunian" (a reference to the Arabic name of the Faiyum Lake, *Birket Qarun*. The Qarunian period and people are technically known as part of the Egyptian Epipaleolithic. Figure 4.3 illustrates the complex geomorphology of this part of the Faiyum.

These Qarunian people flourished along the margins of the Faiyum Lake between about 8000 and 6000 BC, on the basis of fishing, foraging, and hunting, an adaptation that resembles that of the people broadly distributed over the Sahara at this time. There is no evidence at all of domesticated plants or animals in their archaeological record, nor of ground stone tools, flint sickle blades, or pottery. In fact, these people may have subsisted mainly on fish: Most Qarunian sites contain hundreds of small flint blades scattered amidst myriad fish bones. They apparently lived in the Faiyum in periods or seasons when fishing was particularly easy, perhaps because annual Nile floods left pools of water swarming with fish as they receded. But even rudimentary reed boats would allow them to fish the entire lake. Nearly all their archaeological remains are found adjacent to ancient beaches of the Faiyum Lake. If these people were seasonal migrants to the Faiyum, it is not clear where they would have lived when they were elsewhere.

This Qarunian culture vanished at about 6000 BC. The radiocarbon dates from the Faiyum show an apparent gap in occupations between about 6000 and 5200 BC, which was a period in which the annual floods into the lake were dramatically lower.

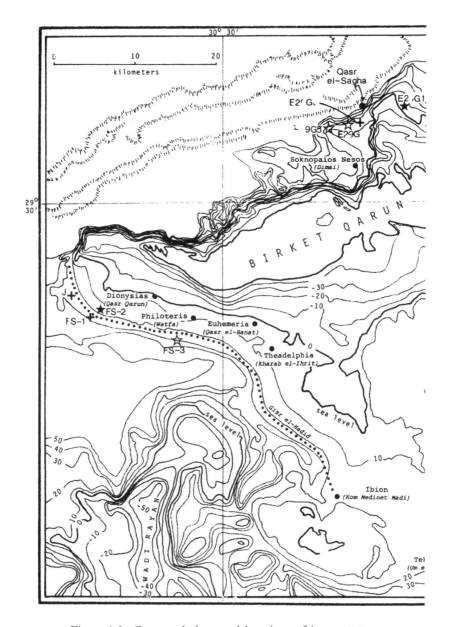

Figure 4.3. Geomorphology and locations of important
archaeological sites in the Faiyum Oasis. The complex
topography surrounding the present lake reflects millennia of
lake level changes. Kom K and Kom W, two primary sites
excavated by Caton-Thompson and Gardner (see text) are on
the northeastern side of the lake. Our surveys and excavations
(see text) at FS-1 and FS-2 are on the southwest side of the

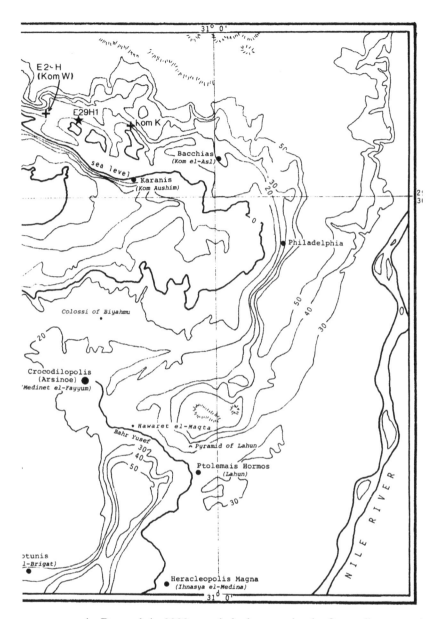

oasis. Research in 2008 revealed what may be the first well-preserved Neolithic settlements found in the Oasis (near Karanis). Note that large "Graeco-Roman" towns between 300 BC and AD 300 encircled the lake. *Source:* Wenke, Long, and Buck 1988. Reproduced from the *Journal of Field Archaeology* with the permission of the Trustees of Boston University. All rights reserved.

In any case, cereal farmers resettled the Faiyum shortly before 5000 BC. It is possible that remnant populations of the Qarunian peoples adapted to agriculture, but it is much more likely that colonizing farmers moved into the Faiyum from the Nile Valley or from the grasslands of what is now the Western Desert. What is manifestly obvious, however, is that the stone tools and other artifacts of the people who lived in the Faiyum after 5000 BC are radically different from those of the Qarunian peoples (Ginter and Kozlowski 1986). Neolithic Faiyum sites contain pottery, grinding stones, sickle blades, and other agricultural tools that are not found in Qarunian sites just a few hundred meters away (Figures 4.3, 4.4).

In sites of these Neolithic peoples, Caton-Thompson and Gardner found the remains of hundreds of hearths surrounded by massive quantities of stone tools, fragments of crude pottery, and other cultural debris. Near the hearths and other artifacts they found the earliest indisputable evidence of cereal farming in Egypt. They located about 165 pits, at least 67 of which were lined with coiled straw "basketry," forming "silos" that contained domesticated wheat and barley (Figure 4.5). These silos averaged one meter in diameter and fifty centimeters in depth; one contained a beautifully preserved sickle of wood and flint. Some contained cereals so well preserved that botanists at the British Museum tried (unsuccessfully) to germinate them – seven thousand years after they were put into the silos. Almost all silos found in the Faiyum contained both wheat and barley, with barley predominating in most. Caton-Thompson suggested that each of these silos would have held about 350 kilograms of grain, which she inferred to represent the production of about two to three acres. These silos lay about a half mile from their supposed owners at Kom K and Kom W (see Figure 4.3),

Figure 4.4. Ground stone tools from the Neolithic Faiyum. One of the clearest archaeological traces of a concentration on plant foods, especially cereals, is dense concentrations of "mortars" and "pestles" such as these. *Source:* Photograph by Robert J. Wenke.

Figure 4.5. Caton-Thompson and Gardner found many grain "silos" while working in the Faiyum area. This one still contained a wood and stone sickle. These silos were found in greatest concentration several kilometers from Kom W, the presumed home or seasonal settlement of these farmers. *Source*: The British Library.

where the largest known concentrations of Faiyum Neolithic artifacts have been found. This seems quite a distance, but there are no major sites of later periods located near these silos. They contained pots and lithics of a style very like those from nearby sites, and radiocarbon dates indicate that they were contemporary with the concentrations of hearths at Kom K and Kom W.

Contemporary researchers have found other silos, and more are probably still buried (Wendrichs and Cappers 2005: 12–15). The sites near these silos contain other evidence of farming, including limestone grinding stones, flint sickle blades, pottery, and the remains of domesticated cattle, pigs, sheep, and goats, as well as fish and other animals.

One expected feature was curiously absent, however. None of the many archaeologists who worked in the Faiyum before about 2007 found any evidence of the kinds of permanent houses that mark early agriculture in much of the rest of the world. A few traces of possible architecture in Faiyum Neolithic occupations have been found on the north side of the lake, in the form of a series of "post-holes" (Dagnon-Ginter et al. 1984), but this is hardly conclusive evidence of the type of agricultural village architecture that appeared in many areas of the Nile Valley after about 4000 BC. The only reasonable conclusion seemed to be that these first farmers in the Faiyum were either seasonal migrants to the area or lived year-round in pole-and-thatch huts that left few archaeological traces.

In early 2008, however, scholars concerned with Egyptian agricultural origins were abuzz with news that an American-Dutch team, directed by Wilike Wendrichs and Rene Cappers had found the first evidence of an intact Neolithic community on the north side of the Faiyum Oasis, near the Roman city of Karanis (see Figure 4.3). Press reports of the find were vague and somewhat contradictory, but apparently several layers of "clay floors" were found intact, with Neolithic tools and faunal remains scattered upon them. It is not clear whether these domestic features suggested pit houses or rectangular mud-brick structures.

Some decorative objects made from shells from Red Sea species of shellfish might suggest that agriculture was introduced by boats plying the Red Sea coast, rather than spread through land routes from Syro-Palestine, across the Delta, and into the Faiyum. Until more evidence is published, the ultimate significance of these recent finds cannot be assessed.

In any case, seasonal agricultural occupation of the Faiyum is somewhat questionable, given that the surrounding deserts were already hyperarid when these cereal farmers lived. The Nile Valley seems the only place they might have gone once the grain harvest had been completed, but it is difficult to imagine that the Faiyum could compete with the Nile Valley in terms of agricultural rewards. It is possible that these early Faiyum farmers were the immediate descendants of pastoralists who herded cattle, sheep, and goats across the Sahara in earlier periods. Perhaps these Faiyum sites and the somewhat later sites along the Valley's and Delta's western margins were predominantly temporary camps of these pastoralists, especially given the evidence in the form of animal dung, bones, and iconography (Midant-Reynes 2000: 39–43).

We know that from 8500 BC onward, people in Syro-Palestinian areas just a short distance from Egypt were growing the kinds of wheat and barley that became the basis for the Faiyum peoples and, eventually, for all of Egypt. Thus, we know of two areas of early agriculture, one in Syro-Palestine and the other in the Faiyum, but what about the expanse between them?

There are some traces of Neolithic occupations in the form of domesticated goats that date to about 6000–5000 BC in Sodmein Cave, near Quseir on the Red Sea Coast (Hendrickx and Vermeersch 2000: 36), but that is somewhat off the most direct land route between Southwest Asia and the Faiyum. Lech Krzyzaniak (1989) had to auger more than six meters near Minshat Abu Omar (shown on Figure 5.3 in the next chapter), on the eastern edge of the Delta and far below the water table, to find the remains that have so far yielded some of the Delta's earliest cultural materials (some dating to between 4000 and 5000 BC). But it may never be feasible to excavate such sites on a large scale.

As noted, we cannot rule out the introduction to Neolithic Egypt of people and domesticates via sea routes. Already by forty thousand years ago, people were able to navigate their way from Asia to Australia, and people with domesticated animals and seaworthy boats settled Cyprus soon after 9000 BC. Thus, it is certainly possible that the sheep and goat herders reflected in the remains at Sodmein Cave made their way there by boat.

We must remember that by the time Southwest Asian domesticates began to appear in Egypt, complex trade routes carrying many commodities, such as obsidian, carnelian, lapis lazuli, copper, gold, and other exotic and expensive goods, had been in operation throughout Anatolia, Mesopotamia, Persia, and Syro-Palestine for many centuries. Egypt was on the periphery of these exchange networks, but by 7000 BC mollusk shells, ostrich egg shells, fine flint, and other goods were already cycling along the Nile Valley and its margins, and deep into Nubia.

The Faiyum Neolithic evidence does not provide a conclusive answer to questions about the cultural and physical origins of these ancient Faiyumis. Some scholars have suggested that, on the basis of artifact styles, both the Faiyum sites and Merimde Beni Salama (see later section), another Neolithic site, near the western Delta, had the same ancestor – the people of the Jordan Valley. Others dispute this possibility. As noted, there are some stylistic similarities between Faiyum Neolithic stone tools and those of the hunter-foragers who had previously roamed what are now Egypt's desert margins, but this is hardly conclusive evidence.

After at least a thousand years of dense Neolithic occupation, the Faiyum seems to have been abandoned soon after about 4300 BC: Only a few small sites can be reliably dated to this period, and these appear to have been seasonal hunting and fishing camps (Wenke and Brewer 1992).

Perhaps once farming of wheat and barley and stock raising became well established in the Faiyum and also in the main Nile Valley, the Faiyum would have been considered a relatively poor place to farm. The main Nile Valley would have been a much more attractive location because the fertility-renewing silts deposited in the main Nile channel were greater than those deposited along the shores of the Faiyum Lake. Also, the farmlands created by the annual floods would have been more predictable and larger in the main Nile channel than those along the shallows of the Faiyum Lake.

Even as early as 4000 BC, societies organized on the basis of different levels of wealth and power for their members were beginning to form along the Nile's course. But the Faiyum seems to have been nearly abandoned during this formative epoch. Indeed, it only reclaimed some of its previous importance after about 1500 BC, and especially in the first few centuries AD, when people reduced the lake's size by damming the channel that brought water to the Faiyum from the Nile. The fertile lake bed made accessible by these water-management techniques made the Faiyum one of the most agriculturally productive regions in all Egypt.

Recent Research in the Faiyum

Since Caton-Thompson and Gardner's research, numerous later scholars have studied this area, but this more recent research has not substantially challenged the central conclusions they reached in the 1920s, except for the sequence of Faiyum A and Faiyum B cultures and the geomorphology and history of the Faiyum Lake. Wendorf and Schild (1976) and Hassan (1986) revised the cultural and lacustrine history of the Faiyum; other scholars have provided a wealth of details about stone tool types and faunal and floral remains of the earliest Faiyum farmers (e.g., Ginter and Kozlowski 1986).

In our own (Wenke, Long, and Buck 1988) research, we addressed several questions: 1) What was the relationship between the Qarunian cultures of the Faiyum and the approximately contemporary cultures at Bir Kiseiba, Nabta Playa, and elsewhere in Northeast Africa, and with the first Faiyum farmers? 2) At what time and by what mechanisms did cereal agriculture appear in the Faiyum? 3) What were the spatial characteristics of the first Faiyum agricultural societies?

Because most previous research on the Faiyum Neolithic had been concentrated on the northern Faiyum shore, we tried to broaden the sample of evidence about this period by focusing on the far southwestern shore (Figures 4.3, 4.6). Also, sites in this area have been much less disturbed by looting than those on the northern perimeter of the lake (personnel associated with the U.S. embassy used to organize weekend trips to the northern shore of the Faiyum to collect "arrowheads").

The slope of the land on the southwestern shore of the Faiyum, however, is much shallower than that on the north. It may have been

Figure 4.6. Western end of the present Faiyum Lake. FS-1 and FS-2 (see text) and other epipaleolithic and Neolithic sites can be found along the fossil beaches south of the southern lakeshore. *Source:* Photograph courtesy of Paul Buck.

quite different from the northern shore in terms of the amount of land covered by the rise and fall of the lake and the extent of swamps. Thus, our results must be compared to the data from northern shore sites, and then combined to reconstruct subsistence and settlement patterns.

We were principally concerned with identifying the spatial associations of large samples of artifacts, animal remains, hearths, geological features, and so forth, so that we could determine the basic economic and occupational characteristics of Faiyum cultures. The Faiyum's ancient shorelines are littered (Figure 4.7) with millions of pottery sherds, limestone grinding stones, and rocks cracked by campfires, as well as innumerable flint sickle blades, arrowheads, and knives. Amidst these artifacts are millions of bones from fish, ducks, crocodiles, hippos, and many other animals. The problem, obviously, was to identify patterns in such a complex mosaic of archaeological remains.

Our sampling design (Figure 4.8) was an attempt to strike a balance, gathering the data necessary to answer the questions posed by our research design within the constraints placed on those aspirations by simple economics: For example, how many people are going to have to work for how long, at such and such a cost, to retrieve the artifacts and analyze them? Our sampling design, like most archaeological sampling, did not meet all the theoretical requirements of optimal statistical inference. It would take millions of dollars and many years of research to sample the Faiyum archaeological record adequately. It is fortunate, thus, that some statistical sampling techniques are very "robust" in that one can strain their assumptions badly and still get reasonable results.

Figure 4.7. Faiyum fossil beaches and artifact distributions. The fossil beaches along the perimeter of the ancient Faiyum Lake are littered with fire-cracked rocks, animal bones, stone tools, and other artifacts such as are found in this area of FS-1 (see text). *Source:* Photograph by Robert J. Wenke.

We made systematic surface collections of artifacts and faunal remains over a large area that contained extensive remains of both the Qarunian and Neolithic periods, and we excavated several small areas where these occupations were relatively well preserved. We collected all artifacts and bones in 1,257 squares of five by five meters each. These were selected on the basis of a sampling design that would allow us to make inferences about more than three square kilometers of Neolithic and Qarunian occupations.

We defined two base lines parallel to and on each side of the fossil beach separating the "Faiyum A" (Neolithic) and "B" (Epipaleolithic) occupations and used a stratified random sampling design to locate forty-eight transect lines perpendicular to these base lines. We then chose collection squares on these transects, also according to a stratified random design. After all artifacts in these squares had been collected, we walked the entire study area, including those areas that were not part of our random samples, and collected all "finished" artifacts, such as "projectile points," "sickle blades," and "grinding stones." We mapped

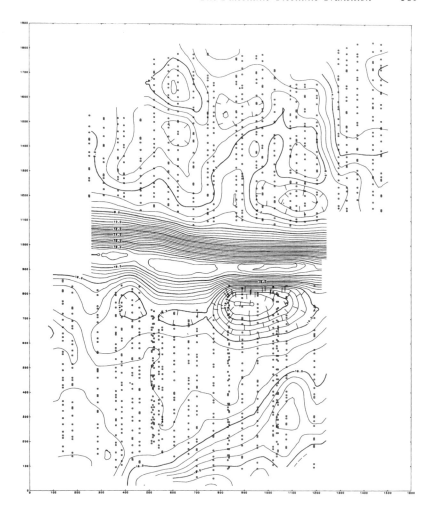

Figure 4.8. Our sampling design at FS-1 and FS-2 (see text). Each small black square represents an area in which we collected all artifacts and faunal remains. Note that the epipaleolithic ("Qarunian") artifacts are found almost exclusively on the north (top) side of the fossilized beaches, while the Neolithic remains are almost entirely limited to the south (bottom) side of these beaches. The total area depicted here is about 1.6 by 1.9 kilometers. *Source:* Wenke, Long, and Buck 1988. Reproduced from the *Journal of Field Archaeology* with the permission of the Trustees of Boston University. All rights reserved.

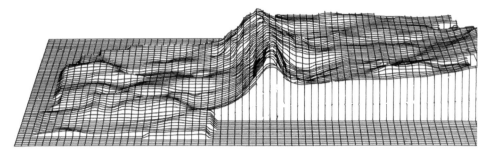

Figure 4.9. Three-dimensional computer reconstruction of the topography of FS-1 (left) and FS-2 (right). The total area depicted here is about 1.6 by 1.9 kilometers. *Source*: Photograph by Robert J. Wenke.

each of these finds so that we had three-dimensional coordinates for each. We collected identifiable animal bones as well. In one ten by ten meter area of the Neolithic occupations, we mapped all artifacts, bones, and other cultural debris with exact point proveniences, in hopes of revealing community structure here (Figures 4.8, 4.9).

Most previous researchers have interpreted the contrasting stone tool styles of the Qarunian and Neolithic periods to indicate that there was no direct cultural relationship between the people who made these different industries, and we found little in our analyses to challenge this supposition – no tools, in other words, that seemed "intermediate" types between Epipaleolithic and Neolithic types.

Another possibility we considered was that the greater agricultural and hunting-gathering potential of the nearby Nile Valley drew Qarunian peoples into that area, and that settlements were only reestablished in the Faiyum by marginal cultivators coming from the Nile Valley long after the Valley had been intensively settled by agriculturists. As with so many questions about early Northeast African agriculture, the evidence with which to confirm or reject such scenarios may be buried beneath the Nile alluvium or destroyed by Nile floods.

Despite intensive examination, we found less evidence than expected of domesticated cereals in the several Neolithic hearths and other deposits we excavated. Indeed, were it not for the "grain silos" that Caton-Thompson and Gardner found, the main basis for inferring the appearance of farmers in the Faiyum would have been the ground stone tools, flint sickle blades, and pottery. The area we surveyed was "deflated," in the sense that over the millennia winds have continuously shifted the sands of the original surfaces on which the stone tools were laid. In some areas clear patches of the lake bed were exposed; in others thick sand layers covered the surface. In sum, the remains of cereals and many other plants have long since blown away.

Perhaps the most useful product of our research was a clearer understanding of the distribution of the activities of the Neolithic farmers. In the area of the Faiyum that we surveyed, we found that grinding slabs and sickle blades were located most frequently within a relatively narrow range of elevation, and seem to be distributed (Figures 4.10, 4.11) mainly in areas of relatively low frequencies of other artifacts and animal bones. It is quite possible that the distribution of these artifacts marks the areas where cereals were grown, but we have no independent evidence for that supposition. Some of the grinding stones may mark areas of grain processing, and the sickle blades may reflect some episodes of blade manufacture and resharpening, as well as harvesting in these areas.

Since the area we studied is at the far end of the lake, it is possible that cereal cultivation was restricted to a fairly narrow topographic range, where the water table was sufficiently high that no artificial irrigation would have been necessary, and where retreating lake waters revealed land fertile enough and sufficiently moist to make the cereals worth the effort of their cultivation.

Our analyses of the Faiyum faunal remains agree with those of other researchers in this area. From one of the sites on the northern shore, Caton-Thompson and Gardner reported the remains of at least five pigs, eight sheep or goats, nine cattle, four hippopotami, and significant numbers of canines, turtles, fish, and crocodiles (1934: 34). But their counts of the non-mammalian fauna were not exact, nor did they publish an extensive analysis of these faunas.

Later research (Wendorf and Schild 1976) in the Faiyum revealed the remains of what appear to have been domesticated sheep, but the identification of the sheep species used in ancient Egypt is a thorny problem. It is difficult to distinguish sheep from goats, if one has only bone fragments to work with. Also, as people domesticated sheep they selected for some traits, such as quality of wool and fattiness of the tail, that are archaeologically invisible. Nonetheless, the sheep/goat remains found in the Faiyum are probably from domesticated animals, given that domesticated sheep, at least, were used in the Sahara Neolithic, thousands of years earlier.

Our own faunal collections from Qarunian and Neolithic sites, as well as from a small Predynastic site in the Faiyum, show a surprisingly low frequency of identifiable sheep/goats and cattle. Animal remains at some settlements on the northern Faiyum shore are dominated by the remains of sheep/goats. Our samples included many unidentified mammals that

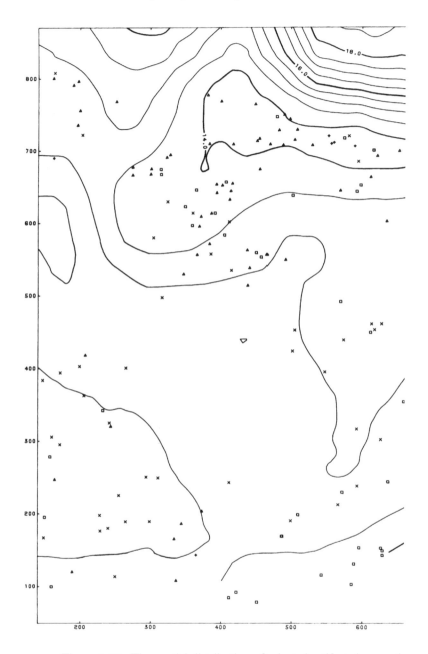

Figure 4.10. The spatial distribution of selected artifacts in a section of FS-1. *Source:* Wenke, Long, and Buck 1988. Reproduced from the

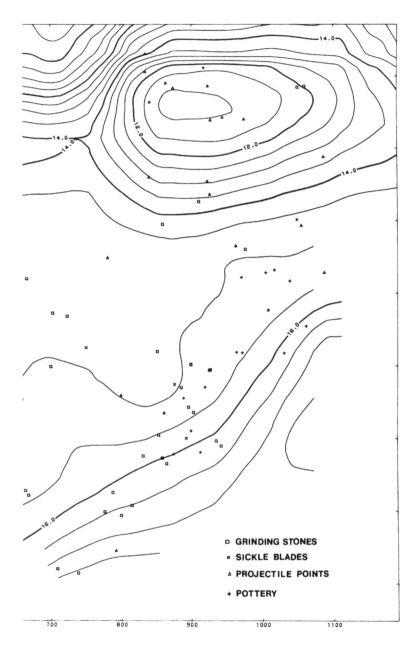

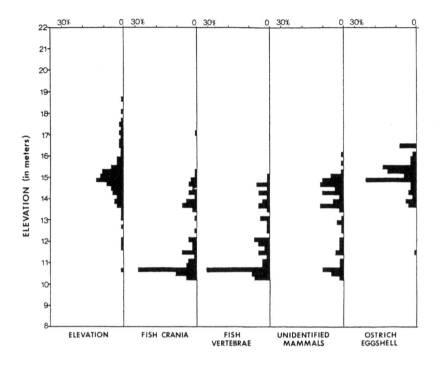

Figure 4.11. Elevation as a factor in artifact distribution in the Neolithic Faiyum. The distribution of selected artifacts and faunal remains in relation to elevation at FS-1 is plotted here. It is not surprising that fish remains are typically found at a lower elevation (i.e., nearer the lakeshore) than, for example ostrich eggshell fragments, which we infer were used as canteens for these farmers. Similarly, the distribution of grinding stones is found at relatively higher elevations, where we assume these farmers processed their cereals. *Source*: Wenke, Long, and Buck 1988. Reproduced from the *Journal of Field Archaeology* with the permission of the Trustees of Boston University. All rights reserved.

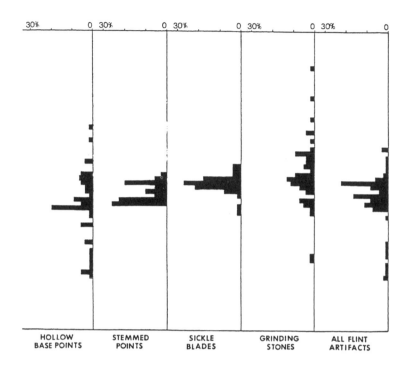

30%	0 30%	0 30%	0 30%	0 30%	0

HOLLOW BASE POINTS	STEMMED POINTS	SICKLE BLADES	GRINDING STONES	ALL FLINT ARTIFACTS

are probably the remains of sheep and goats; thus, the low frequencies of identified sheep/goats that we found may be misleading.

That there were few remains of cattle in our collections is interesting, given that there is evidence that cattle may have been domesticated in the Egyptian Sahara about two thousand years before they appeared in the Faiyum. Cattle remains comprise 42 percent of the identifiable mammal elements at Hierakonpolis, in southern Egypt adjacent to the Nile, in occupations that date to about a thousand years after those in the Faiyum (McArdle 1982: Table V.1) – a percentage that is much greater than is reflected in our own samples. Most of the cattle remains we collected, however, were from the surface, not excavated, and so the high proportion in our sample represented by the category of "unidentified mammal" probably masks the actual use of cattle. Also, we found numerous bones from dogs, jackals, and other canids in the Faiyum samples, and these suggest high rates of bone loss via these scavengers.

Alternatively, it is possible that the rich resources of the Faiyum Lake made cattle raising a relatively unimportant part of the overall adaptation. Presumably the fish, ducks, turtles, and other lake resources were abundant and dependable throughout most periods, and in the absence of a need for a draft animal, cattle may not have been particularly cost-effective.

Fish bones and most other faunal remains in our Faiyum collections were found in a relatively narrow topographic band that may have been close to the edges of pools of water. It is difficult to determine if these remains represent noncultural depositional processes, such as the stranding of fish by receding floods. But many of the bones in these areas exhibit burning and cut marks and lie amidst extensive and dense concentrations of stone tools, potsherds, fire-cracked rocks, and other cultural debris.

If these people lived in villages, as recent evidence from the northern side of the lake suggests, we found no evidence of them. Figure 4.10 illustrates the distribution of pottery and lithics on the Neolithic surface. The relative elevation of these artifacts (see Figure 4.11) demonstrates an obvious point. The fish remains are found at predominately lower elevations, whereas artifacts likely to have been used where the community resided are found at higher levels. As always, however, we must consider oscillations of the lake levels to have been a potent factor as to where various activities occurred.

If we consider the Faiyum Neolithic archaeological record in the much larger context of general models of agricultural origins, the Faiyum data seem somewhat in contradiction to the "Wave of Advance" model described by A. J. Ammerman and L. L. Cavalli-Sforza (1984). In their model, agriculture spread from Southwest Asia into Europe at a rate that seems relatively unaffected by local environmental diversity. But other assessments of the European evidence suggest that the rate of the spread of agriculture there may not have been as gradual and as constant as previously believed. Also, whereas the spread of agriculture into Europe was mainly through environments that had at least some agricultural potential, the barrier posed by the Sinai's deserts to the spread of agriculture into Egypt must be considered.

Early Egyptian Agriculture Beyond the Faiyum

Beyond the Faiyum, one of the earliest Nile Neolithic communities for which we have substantial archaeological information is Merimde Beni Salama on the western edge of the Egyptian Delta (Eiwanger 1982–1992; see Hendrickx and Vermeersch [2000: 37–39] for an excellent English summary of this site).

Today the area around Merimde is desert, but seven thousand years ago a branch of the Nile provided water to areas near this site. Merimde was occupied from about 5000 to 4100 BC, though probably not continuously. At least three distinct cultures appear to be represented at this site. Over centuries of occupation, they created an archaeological record of domestic debris about 2.5 meters thick in the main site area.

The initial community probably consisted of just a few families, related by ties of blood and marriage, who cultivated wheat, barley, lentils, peas, flax, and other crops, and raised sheep, cattle, and pigs. These earliest people at Merimde, much like their contemporaries in the Faiyum, seem to have lived in tiny encampments of mud and reed houses. They made coarse untempered pottery that was only marginally more useful than the Neolithic Faiyum pottery, but the styles of the Merimde pottery and other artifacts may indicate connections to Syro-Palestinian cultures of much earlier date.

After a period of apparent abandonment, Merimde was reoccupied by people who may have been descendants of Saharan cultures. This material culture is intriguingly different from the first culture, and from that of their contemporaries in the Faiyum. In this second phase of occupation, Merimde became a permanent settlement composed of simple oval homes made of wood and reeds. These homes encompassed hearths and clay storage jars set into their floors. No bones of dead Neolithic Faiyum farmers have been found, but the deceased of Merimde's second cultural phase were apparently buried more formally, with the bodies of the dead contracted and buried among the residences. The pottery of this second culture at Merimde was straw-tempered, making it more useful for various purposes than the untempered pottery of the first phase of occupation. Tempering involves adding inelastic materials (e.g., straw, shell) to pottery clay before firing; it makes the ceramic much less susceptible to fracturing when it is fired or heated to cook food.

Some of the stone tools from the second Merimde culture are similar to the "hollow-base" projectile points found in the Faiyum (see Figure 4.2), and several harpoon points were also found. Both suggest that fishing was a major part of the economy. Clay models of boats have been found at Merimde, perhaps indicating that the Nile was already a transportation artery, not just the source of irrigation water.

The third cultural phase at Merimde occurred between about 4600 and 4100 BC. In this interval, Merimde became a large farming village, boasting oval "pit houses," homes made by digging down to a depth of about forty centimeters, erecting walls of straw and plastering them with mud, and then roofing the structures with branches or reeds. These houses contained storage bins, water jars, hearths, and other domestic features. They were even arranged along a main "street."

Some small clay figurines have also been found at Merimde, along with many objects of bone and ivory. Some figurines resemble human beings and are covered with small holes that probably were used to attach hair or feathers to represent head hair and beards (Hendrickx and Vermeersch 2000: 38). These are among the earliest known human representations in Egypt. About fourteen of the figurines have been identified as representations of cattle.

Many burials of this cultural phase have been found, most in shallow pits scattered around the community, in which the bodies were placed in contracted positions. Only a few "grave goods" were found, and most of the burials are of children and adolescents. Thus, it seems likely that adults were buried in a separate area of the community, which has yet to be discovered.

Some of the pottery of this era was highly polished and red or black in color, with few other decorations. It may seem a substantial leap of faith to infer from a few decorated pots, formal burials, figurines, and so forth that Merimde was a more complexly organized community than were their contemporaries in the Faiyum, but it seems a reasonable conclusion. Merimde stands at the divide between the Neolithic and the Predynastic periods, and some of the main elements of the Predynastic seem to have roots in Merimde (see Chapter 5).

Conclusions

In general summary of the origins and development of the first stages of the Egyptian Neolithic, we have some evidence but even more questions. The origins of the peoples who became Egypt's first farmers remain obscure. There are indications that Sudanese, Saharan, and/or Southwest Asian cultures played a role, but Neolithic Egyptian economies and societies cannot be definitively traced directly to a single source. Perhaps there was a fusion of these various cultures, out of which Egypt's first farmers emerged.

Here, too, we must always qualify such inferences by noting that there could be hundreds of large Neolithic Egyptian communities that are deeply buried under later settlements or that have simply been washed away or buried by Nile floods.

Finally, some scholars argue that an accurate and comprehensive understanding of Egypt's Neolithic origins can only be realized by transcending the blunt facts and forces of stone tools, rainfall patterns, plant and animal remains, pottery, and the ambiguous traces of shelters; they concentrate instead on the social and ideological elements they envision in Egypt's Neolithic transformation. Most of these discussions are beyond the scope of this book, but some sense of them has been provided by David Wengrow (2006: 62–71). He argues, for example, that we should abandon such terms as "village," "hamlet," "socializing," and "domesticating"; instead, he suggests, the complexities of cultural changes associated with the Neolithic

. . . [d]emand that human perceptions and uses of plants and animals should either resolve themselves into a dichotomy between "controlled" or "uncontrolled," or align themselves upon a continuum between these or similar values. Animals, as a category, are made to stand either for that which is unclassified, formless, wild, and threatening, or as an abstract matter "waiting to be given shape and context by the mind of man." (2006: 62 [citing Sahlins 1976: 209–210])

Wengrow provides what he terms new "terms of engagement" between humans and the nonhuman world that he postulates were formulated as agricultural economies spread across the western Old World. He argues that this pattern of cultural change cannot be understood in the simple binary constructs of wild/domestic, nature/culture, trust/domination; instead he treats this pattern of as "the unfolding of regionally distinct, and historically interrelated transformations" (2006: 62).

Regarding Neolithic Egypt, Wengrow argues that the emphasis placed by previous scholars on *residences* is misplaced, suggesting instead: "It is the domain of the funerary . . . that provides a window not only on rituals that structured the human lifecycle, but also on the wider range of social practices through which Neolithic communities established their stability in space and their continuity in time. The focus of these practices was not . . . the house, but the bodies of people and animals, which themselves provided generative frameworks for configuring social experience" (2006: 69).

It is unfortunate for Wengrow's analysis that no Neolithic human burials have been found in the Faiyum, and he considers Merimde's graves to be only indirectly relevant for understanding Neolithic Egyptian culture. Instead, he concentrates on the bodies of late Neolithic/early Predynastic sites, such as el-Badari and Hammamieh – sites that are considered in the next chapter of this book. He suggests that the cosmetic palettes and combs found in these sites reflect the importance of skin and hair as "symbolic media." How are we to understand their significance? He concludes that the adoption of the herding lifestyle by the peoples of the Saharan Neolithic, the Faiyum, Merimde, and other sites was associated with the spread of new ritual practices and social classifications that are most visible to us in the contents of graves, not in domestic residential architecture, and he argues that "domestication" is an inappropriate metaphor in this case. The cultural idiom of Neolithic transformation in the Nile valley seems better understood in terms of "incorporation" or "embodiment" (2006: 71).

Some other elements of Wengrow's approach, and similar analyses, are considered in subsequent chapters of this book. These ideas require what for many scholars is a wrenching shift of analytical focus, from the "empirical" to speculative hypotheses about Neolithic societies. But for some of these scholars, this is precisely the virtue of such a revised perspective.

5   Lords of the Two Lands: The Origins of Dynastic Egypt, c. 4500–2700 BC

War is the father of all things.

Heraclitus (c. fifth century BC)

Introduction

The Greek philosopher Heraclitus probably overestimated the power of war as a force in history, but it is difficult to refute him with the evidence from dynastic Egypt. The military exploits of Egyptian kings are recorded in numerous texts (but in exaggerated form, no doubt), and the Egyptians profusely engraved plaques, palettes, maceheads, and temple walls with depictions of violence and power.

Consider, for example, the Narmer Palette (Figures 5.1, 5.2). Found in 1894 at Hierakonpolis (Figure 5.3) in Upper Egypt by British Egyptologists, it probably dates to about 3100–3000 BC – the period in which Upper and Lower Egypt were politically joined to form Egypt's first unified state. Its "functional" significance seems trivial: The intertwined necks of two mythical animals form a depression that presumably contained some kind of pigment for purposes unknown – perhaps an evocation of ancient practices of body decoration. The use of this artifact as a palette for cosmetics was probably its least significant aspect: It is its engraved symbols that command our attention. Even if we knew nothing else about this era, the headless corpses, military-style flags, and ferocious beasts incised on this and other objects, such as the Tjehenu Palette (Figures 5.4, 5.5), would suggest that the ancient Egyptians were no strangers to bloody conflict.

Like all art, of course, the Narmer Palette has no singular "real" meaning; the people who made it and imbued it with meaning have been dead for five thousand years. It is attributed to a legendary king, Menes (perhaps also known as Aha), but then again all ancient civilizations trace their origins to mythical rulers who reigned in a pristine "golden age" long ago. Moreover, the ancient Egyptians apparently saw no need to distinguish, as we do, between "real" historical events and purely

181

Figure 5.1. The
Narmer Palette. See
text for interpretation.
Source: Werner
Forman / Art
Resource, NY.

ritual or magical acts (Shaw 2000: 3–4; Allen 1992). As Donald Redford
suggested (1986a), the palette may be about events and rituals that are
"commemorated," as opposed to "narrated." If so, we cannot distinguish historical fact from fiction in their texts or engraved artifacts. We
know, for example, that ancient Egyptians typically portrayed foreigners
as naked and disheveled, to reinforce the notion of their inferiority to
and suppression by the Egyptian state (Redford 1992: 33–55), but are
these depictions accurate descriptions of these individuals? One can
argue that there can be no "accurate" depiction of such matters – that
these representations are all ambiguous cultural constructions.

Yet the Narmer Palette does convey ideas that we know from later
texts were at the heart of ancient Egyptian state ideology. Note, for
example, the depictions of the king wearing different crowns on the two

Figure 5.2. Reverse side of Narmer Palette. See text for interpretation. *Source:* Werner Forman / Art Resource, NY.

sides of the palette: We infer from texts written centuries after the Narmer Palette was created that the "white crown" (Figure 5.1) symbolized Upper Egypt, and the "red crown" (Figure 5.2) referred to Lower Egypt. And there is evidence that the white crown illustrated the king as an individual historical person, while the red crown was more associated with ritual and eternal kingship. Also, we know that these two crowns were depicted throughout the history of Dynastic Egypt in the context of textual references to the political unity of "the two lands," that is, Upper and Lower Egypt. The Egyptians who made and used the Narmer Palette, however, may not have had a fully functional written language, and so we are unlikely ever to find ancient texts contemporary with the palette that explained what it "meant."

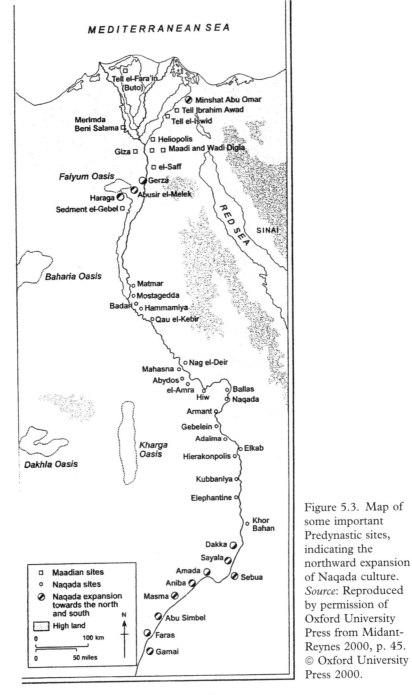

MEDITERRANEAN SEA

Tell el-Fara'in
(Buto)

⊘ Minshat Abu Omar
□ Tell Ibrahim Awad
□ Tell el-Iswid

Merimda
Beni Salama □

□ Heliopolis
□ □ Maadi and Wadi Digla

Giza □

□ el-Saff

Faiyum Oasis

⊘ Gerza
⊘ Abusir el-Melek

Haraga ⊘

Sedment el-Gebel □

RED SEA

SINAI

Baharia Oasis

○ Matmar
○ Mostagedda
Badari ○ ○ Hammamiya
○ Qau el-Kebir

○ Nag el-Deir

Mahasna ○
Abydos ○
el-Amra ○   ○ Ballas
Hiw ○ ○ Naqada
Armant ○

Gebelein ○

Adaïma ○

Kharga
Oasis

Hierakonpolis ○   ○ Elkab

Dakhla Oasis

Kubbaniya ○

Elephantine ○

○ Khor
Bahan

Dakka ⊘
Sayala ⊘
Amada ⊘   ⊘ Sebua
Aniba ⊘
Masma ⊘

⊘ Abu Simbel

⊘ Faras

⊘ Gamai

□ Maadian sites
○ Naqada sites
⊘ Naqada expansion
   towards the north
   and south
▨ High land

N

0   100 km
0   50 miles

Figure 5.3. Map of
some important
Predynastic sites,
indicating the
northward expansion
of Naqada culture.
Source: Reproduced
by permission of
Oxford University
Press from Midant-
Reynes 2000, p. 45.
© Oxford University
Press 2000.

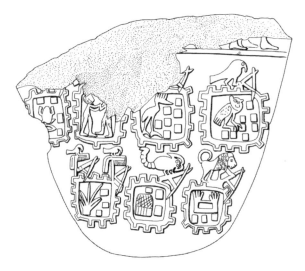

Figure 5.4. The Tjehenu Palette. The illustration suggests a battle scene in which fortified towns are being attacked by animals symbolizing the monarchy. The palette probably commemorates the successful expansion of the Kingdom of Hierakonpolis in the late fourth millennium BC. *Source:* After Kemp 1989, fig. 16 (see his references). Reproduced by permission of Barry J. Kemp.

Figure 5.5. This palette appears to commemorate a battle in which people were killed and left to be eaten by lions and vultures. The opposite side – somewhat paradoxically – illustrates two giraffes eating fruit from date palms. Gray schist, c. 3100 BC. *Source:* © The Trustees of the British Museum.

Although Narmer may have unified Egypt through warfare, other factors no doubt were important. Increasing socioeconomic interactions between Upper and Lower Egypt, for example, may have been potent forces in the emergence of the Egyptian state. We must also assume that many factors other than warfare and trade played a role in the appearance of the first Egyptian states. Scholars have spent many decades trying to identify these variables and measure their interactions, but there appear to have been not only multiple causal variables but also myriad interconnections. Thus, these analyses have been maddeningly inconclusive. One would hope that the artifacts of precisely this era (c. 4000–3000 BC) would provide unambiguous evidence about the factors that produced Egyptian civilization. But not only is the archaeological record of Egypt for this period highly fragmentary; it also seems to offer no clear and conclusive evidence concerning the primary factors that transmuted Neolithic Egyptian agricultural communities into dynastic civilization.

In fact, the archaeological record of Egypt suggests that, in a sense, dynastic civilization was just the "natural" outcome of simple farming in an exceptionally fertile environment. Such an assertion explains nothing. Yet the long search for some more fundamental explanation of how and why the dynastic state – and other ancient states – evolved out of Neolithic farming communities has been largely unsuccessful.

In fact, few contemporary scholars express an interest in the search for a unified powerful explanation of the origins of any ancient state, including Egypt; they consider such a search chimerical, a search for a unicorn – perhaps even a capitalist plot (Shanks and Tilley 1987a). But, again, how are we to understand the strong patterns of similarity found in all ancient states if not in terms of a limited number of factors? And what are we to make of their differences?

In this chapter we consider such questions (and again in Chapter 7). Our analysis begins, however, with just a few artifacts and a minor mystery. The Narmer Palette may mark the first formation of the Egyptian state, but what about the earlier stages of this process? Some clues are found on the Palermo Stone (Figure 5.6). This document was probably inscribed in the middle of the fifth Dynasty of the Old Kingdom, at about 2400 BC, but it apparently refers to kings who lived earlier than Narmer. The inscriptions cover both sides of the stone, and were written in separate "registers," or rows. One register lists the names of kings, the second refers to events in specific years of a king's reign (such as commemorations of festivals and enumerations of the country's wealth), and a third register records the precise height of annual Nile floods in each year. These inscriptions list the names of perhaps mythical kings in the period *before* Narmer, who is thought to have been the last

Figure 5.6. The Palermo Stone. This is a slab of basalt inscribed with hieroglyphs that purport to list the names of kings going backward into semimythological times. The small defined rectangles in which the king's name is found contain mentions of significant events in each king's reign; some events are designated with a hieroglyph meaning "regnal year" (Shaw 2000: 5). *Source:* Erich Lessing / Art Resource, NY.

king of "Dynasty 0," that is, before the First Dynasty. Some of these names also appear on Predynastic tags on vessels in tombs at Abydos.

But who were these kings, if in fact they were actual historical figures? When precisely did they live? And, most important, what processes produced the kingdoms that these putative kings ruled?

As with the Narmer Palette, we can at least consider the question (likely irresolvable) of whether the inscriptions on the Palermo Stone reflect a valid record of kings and events that actually happened in history, or were just another example of the ancient Egyptians' predilection for finding continuity and balance. Even if the continuity and balance were, to our minds at least, imaginary, we suspect that the ancient

Egyptians were generally untroubled by the division between the "real" and the "imaginary" that is so important to us. The ancient Egyptians' long history of accurate record keeping, however, and their notion that such precise record keeping was an essential element in good governance, argues that the inscriptions on the Palermo Stone reflect at least some "real" sequence of events.

Thus, in a sense the Palermo Stone and the Narmer Palette may serve as "bookends" of the last stage of the state-formation processes. But what were these processes, and how far back in history did they extend? And what was the nature and significance of Egypt's evolving state?

The Nature and Significance of Ancient States

I should like to see, and this will be the last and most ardent of my desires, I should like to see the last king strangled with the guts of the last priest.

(J. Messelier, clause in a will, Paris, 1733)

Many citizens of France no doubt shared Messelier's apocalyptic wish during the last period of its oppressive theocratic monarchy – and citizens of many societies, both ancient and modern, have expressed similar sentiments. But the inconvenient truth is that analyses of the origins of ancient states and civilizations are in large part analyses of the evolution of the roles of kings and priests. And nowhere is that generalization truer than in the case of ancient Egypt, where so much of what we know about this culture comes from royal graves and tombs. Unlike Messelier and other French revolutionaries, however, most ancient Egyptians appear to have respected their political rulers and genuinely embraced the religious ideology of which the king was the center.

To analyze the origins of the divine kings and the powerful priests who were the basic framework of the ancient Egyptian state – and the social, economic, and political institutions through which they organized and administered the state – we must "begin at the beginning." At about 4000 BC, evidence suggests, almost all Egyptians were farmers, living in insubstantial houses of mud brick in communities of a few score people. The inhabitants of each village had little to do with other communities, except for intermarriage and modest trade in stone tools and a few other commodities. People in different areas of Egypt at this time made pottery and other artifacts in distinctive and different regional styles, suggesting that the people in Upper and Lower Egypt had little contact with one another. It is even possible that Northerners spoke a dialect of a North African language different from that of Southerners and may have been slightly different genetically (even today, some natives of Upper and Lower Egypt differ somewhat in their physical anthropology and dialects). Neither had a written language. There is no evidence that these villagers cooperated to build massive irrigation systems or monumental buildings, or that there were major differences in the wealth, power, or prestige of individuals within these communities. Every extended family, composed of two or more generations of the same family living and working together, probably produced almost all of the goods and did most of the work necessary for each family's survival. They made crude pottery, bows and arrows, stone hoes and knives, grinding stones, thatched mud-brick huts, and not much else. Their lives probably did not encompass much beyond the ordinary events of subsistence cereal farmers everywhere. Their most dramatic episodes were probably conflicts with neighboring villages or raids by desert tribes. There were no lavish tombs or temples.

By about 2900 BC, however, the Egyptian world had been radically transformed. The great mass of people still lived as illiterate farmers in small villages, but now they were citizens of a national state that extended from the Nubian border in the far south, down the Nile to the Delta, and even into Sinai and Syro-Palestine. Most of them spoke the same language and worshipped the same gods. And all of them were ruled by the king from the capital at Memphis (see Figure 1.1), who acted through myriad provincial and village officials to implement his commands. Although nearly everyone was illiterate, a written language was in everyday use. Every Egyptian citizen paid taxes in goods or labor to the provincial and national governments. Where previously these farming villages were self-governing, now the Egyptian state exercised coercive power over them: A citizen who defaulted on his taxes or failed to appear for military duties, for example, could be swiftly and harshly punished. A rigid class system divided people at birth into the rich and powerful or the poor and weak. The king and other elites were buried in large tombs stocked with the wealth of the nation, while the vast majority of people were interred with a few pots and personal goods. Large volumes of food and other goods flowed along the Nile in exchange networks that linked communities throughout the Nile Valley and Delta. Egyptian ships plied the shores of the Mediterranean; via these ships and trade caravans, turquoise and gold from the Sinai, lapis lazuli from Afghanistan, aromatic oils from Palestine, cedar from Lebanon, and many other expensive goods flowed into the Egyptian state. Military excursions exploited large areas of North Africa and some areas of Syro-Palestine as well, and by 3000 BC Egypt was already enmeshed in the cycles of conflict/cooperation with its eastern Mediterranean neighbors that would continue throughout Egyptian history.

As described in Chapter 1, the term "state formation" has been used to refer to these and other kinds of socioeconomic and political changes that occurred in Egypt between about 4000 and 3000 BC. And the evolution of similar states and civilizations in various areas of the world poses important questions about comparative historical analyses. Various scholars have questioned the usefulness of such terms as state formation and have rejected some of the assumptions on which analyses of these processes have been based; some consider dubious at best the whole enterprise of arranging Egyptian culture in a linear sequence and abstracting from this sequence causes and effects (reviewed in Wengrow 2006).

Yet the stark fact remains: Egyptian culture and history were profoundly and thoroughly transformed between about 4500 and 2000 BC. How are we to understand this transformation?

Chronologies of Egypt: 4000–2575 BC

Analyzing the origins of the ancient Egyptian state is obviously a problem of analyzing *cultural change over time*, and to do that we need a reliable chronology of these changes. Egypt's history between 4000 and 2575 BC has traditionally been divided into the Predynastic Period (c. 4000–2920 BC) and the Early Dynastic Period (c. 2920–2575 BC). But, in fact, the cultural developments of these two periods are just intervals in a single continuum of correlated cultural changes. Even such dramatic developments as the appearance of a written Egyptian language in the late fourth millennium BC can be shown to be the product of centuries of evolving use of signs and symbols, as well as the economic functions they served.

Sir Flinders Petrie and His Predynastic Chronology. Predynastic chronologies are all based in part on the research of Sir William Matthew Flinders Petrie (1853–1942), who is deservedly known as the "Father of Egyptian Prehistory." His reputation stems in part from his brilliant analyses of thousands of Predynastic graves in Upper Egypt (e.g., 1920; Petrie and Quibell 1896).

In excavating graves at several Upper Egyptian sites, Petrie initially thought that the pots found in these graves dated to the First Intermediate Period, that is, 2160–2055 BC, many centuries after they were actually made. He noted, however, that none of the graves contained inscribed materials, and eventually he correctly concluded that these graves must be of Predynastic age. He also found that the graves' contents varied greatly in construction and context. Some were just small holes in the ground containing a corpse wrapped in animal skins or reed mats (Figures 5.7, 5.8). Others were larger and more elaborately constructed and furnished. The larger tombs contained pots of many different sizes, shapes, and decorations (Figure 5.9), as well as a variety of

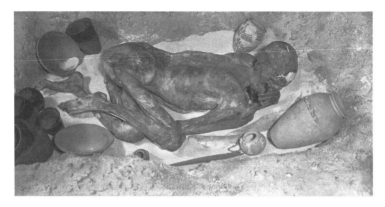

Figure 5.7. "Ginger," the naturally mummified body of a Predynastic (about 3400 BC) man in a reconstructed grave. The pottery styles are typical of this period in Egypt. "Ginger" is a reference to the few reddish hairs on his head. Mummification of bodies by simple inhumation in hot, dry sand may have inspired the Egyptians to develop mummification techniques. *Source:* The Trustees of the British Museum.

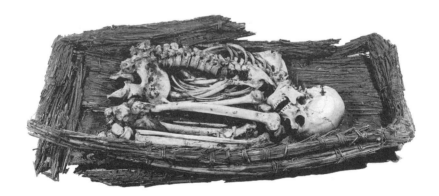

Figure 5.8. Skeleton of a man found in a reed coffin in a mastaba tomb at Tarkhan (c. 3000 BC). *Source:* The Trustees of the British Museum.

Figure 5.9. Predynastic pottery jar. Between about 3500 and 3200 BC, Egyptians in southern towns (e.g., Hierakonpolis, Naqada, and Abydos) began making beautiful pottery that often combined depictions of boats (complete with cabins and a standard), a stick figure of a man, and various animals. These may have been elite goods, used by royalty and noblemen. As discussed in Chapter 6, the replacement of these lavishly decorated pottery types by simple, utilitarian wares is a common feature of several early civilizations. *Source:* Erich Lessing / Art Resource, NY.

"grave goods," including ivory spoons and combs, flint knives, mace-heads, stone engravings of animals, and other objects.

Petrie made precise records and detailed drawings of each grave and its contents. Just this meticulousness alone was a major advance. In Petrie's time, Egypt's rich archaeological record was thoroughly despoiled by supposed "Egyptologists" who were little better than looters. They simply ripped off arbitrary levels of sites in layers of half a meter or more, keeping only museum-quality artifacts. European excavators of this age stocked their national museums with the best artifacts and sold others on the antiquities market.

Petrie, in contrast, carefully analyzed many aspects of the artifacts he retrieved. He began by considering the problem of chronologically seriating these graves; that is, he wanted to order the graves through time, from the earliest grave to the latest, on the basis of the similarity of their construction, location, and contents. He concentrated his analysis on 900 graves at the sites of Hiw and Abadiya, which are near to, and contemporary with, Naqada (see Figure 5.3).

Petrie made several inspired guesses to seriate them. He hypothesized, for example, that a specific type of Predynastic globular jar with a "wavy" handle had gradually over time been replaced by cylindrical vessels with a representation of the wavy handle simply painted on it. This turned out to be the case, and this inference and others like it allowed him to distinguish roughly between earlier and later graves.

But Petrie's genius was most evident in his "sequence dating," a statistical analysis of Predynastic graves that ordered them – and the styles of their artifacts – in time. To do this, Petrie conceptualized a form of mathematics that has come into widespread use only with the invention of modern computers. He envisioned a multidimensional space such that every grave in his sample of 900 could be exactly located in that Euclidean hyperspace of 899 dimensions. He wanted to express each grave's similarity (defined largely in terms of types and numbers of pottery styles and grave goods found) to all other graves in terms of metric distances within this multidimensional space. Petrie reasoned that graves located closest together in this imaginary multidimensional space were also closest together in time; those most dissimilar were farthest apart in time. He envisioned all of these graves as tied to all other graves by metaphorical elastic bands whose relative lengths expressed the similarities among them. From this matrix of similarities he could arrange the pottery styles found on pots in these graves in a chronological sequence.

In today's language, Petrie employed a form of *multidimensional scaling and correspondence analysis*. The calculations involved are an exceedingly

complex and tedious form of matrix algebra. The objective is to reduce
the number of spaces to just one or two (such as "time" or "space" or
"wealth"), without losing too much information about the exact position
of the object (in this case, graves) in the space of 899 dimensions. In the
end, Petrie relied on *ranking* graves in a few dimensions, rather than
working with the exact Euclidean multidimensional locations, but this is
rather unimportant.

Similar scaling methods have been applied to archaeological data,
with mixed results (for an application to Egyptian materials, see Kemp
1982; for a more generalized analysis, see Shennan 1988: 262–352). Yet
Petrie produced a workable seriation, or scaling, simply by shuffling
index cards recorded with information about grave contents and cal-
culating with his trusty slide rule (Drower 1985: 476). Later analyses of
his seriation have resulted in some corrections and additions, but his
basic chronology remains useful today. Petrie's analyses posed many
intriguing statistical and categorical problems that are still of interest.
His calculations conflated both functional and stylistic differences in
pots and other artifacts, and additional research assisted by computers
might further reveal his genius.

Petrie was primarily concerned with chronologically seriating early
Egyptian pottery, and since his time, numerous scholars have greatly
extended our knowledge of the technology that produced these implements and their spatial distribution (e.g., Adams and Friedman 1992;
Friedman 1996). Much research has also been done on the supposed
"meaning" with which these graves and their contents were invested by
their creators (Wengrow 2006: 92–93).

Since Petrie's time, chronologies of Predynastic and Early Dynastic
Egypt have been refined by a century of excavations and analyses, but
problems remain. The chronology of the Late Predynastic and Early
Dynastic Periods used here (Table 5.1), for example, is based in part on
fragmentary and somewhat dubious records of the succession of kings
and the genealogies of royal families – especially for the first part of the
Early Dynastic Period. Even if these royal genealogies have been
accurately reconstructed, the divisions based on them correspond only
roughly to changes in the underlying socioeconomic and political processes of Egyptian state formation – which are the real focus of the
analysis in this book.

Predynastic chronologies frustrate most nonspecialists because they
involve many names of subperiods and sites. Worse, different chronological terms are used for Upper and Lower Egypt before the unification
of the country, at about 3100 BC. Professional archaeologists who study
Egyptian state origins almost universally think of the Predynastic Period

Box 9: Sir William Matthew Flinders Petrie (1853–1942)

Petrie's personal history is as intriguing as his archaeology (see Drower 1985 for an excellent biography). Because he was a sickly child, he was home-schooled by his mother, primarily in ancient languages. He was largely self-taught in mathematics; his father, a civil engineer, helped him map Stonehenge and other antiquities. Like many other Egyptologists, Petrie became fascinated with ancient Egypt at a young age (thirteen), after experiencing an epiphany upon reading a book about Egyptian pyramids.

Petrie's first research in Egypt, in 1881–1913, was to map the pyramids at Giza. With the support of the Egypt Exploration Fund, he excavated many sites (summarized in Petrie 1920). In 1892 he was appointed chair of Egyptology at University College, London, and for the next three decades he excavated numerous sites throughout the Nile Valley and Delta. In 1926 he shifted his attention to southern Palestine, where he excavated several sites on the frontier of Egyptian culture.

As a field director he was somewhat authoritarian and exceedingly frugal. He usually quartered his expeditions in mud-brick hovels (see Figure 3.4) largely because he was always working on a small budget, but also because he himself cared little about material comforts. He could never get used to Egyptian food and lived almost exclusively on canned goods – a diet he also inflicted on his expedition staff. A light sleeper, he was plagued by barking dogs. Unlike Sherlock Holmes's famous dog in "Silver Blaze," which did not bark during a particular night, the dogs around Petrie's camps constantly woke him with their nocturnal howls. After a particularly bad night he told his workers that because of barking dogs he was too tired to work, and he canceled the day's activities – and their day's pay. The villagers soon rounded up the miscreants, and Petrie and his staff finally got a good night's sleep.

He had a rather prickly personality and was occasionally undiplomatically critical of others. He faulted a major British foundation that sponsored research in Egypt because of what he considered its wasteful spending. Yet he treated his Egyptian staff with a courtesy unusual for the times. He trained Egyptian workmen in the finer points of excavation, and the descendants of these workers still work on archaeological projects. As an archaeologist he displayed the energy and focus of true genius in his indefatigable study of Predynastic Egyptian pottery (his Egyptian workers called him *Abu Bagousheh* ("Father of Pots")).

Among his illustrious friends were Karl Pearson, a founding father of statistical analyses, and the great lyric poet A. E. Houseman. He enjoyed a long and happy marriage to his wife, Hilda, who was effectively the codirector of his many projects and coeditor of his hundreds of publications.

Petrie's interpretations were not always correct. For a few years he maintained that a "New Race" – perhaps from Libya – had invaded Egypt and that they were responsible for the "decline" of Egypt in the First Intermediate Period. He recanted, but not before an errata slip had to be placed in the publication *Naqada and Ballas* (Petrie and Quibell 1896 [see Drower 1985: 241])

Still, Petrie spent forty productive years excavating in Egypt and Palestine, leaving a rich legacy of publications and artifacts he donated to various museums, as well his methods of excavation and analysis, which remain key elements of modern Egyptian archaeological techniques.

Petrie retired to Jerusalem and died in 1942. He is buried on Mount Zion. The Petrie Museum of Egyptian Archaeology, at University College, London, is a fitting tribute to his life and works.

in terms of period names and dates applied to Upper Egyptian sites: Badarian, c. 4400–4000 BC, Naqada I (also known as the "Amratian"), c. 4000–3500 BC; Naqada II (also called "Gerzean"), c. 3500–3200 BC; Naqada III, 3200–3000 BC. These Naqada subperiods have been subdivided into even smaller intervals – these have mercifully been omitted from Table 5.1.

The Predynastic record of Lower Egypt, in contrast, has been divided simply into the Merimde, el-Omari, and Buto-Ma'adi sub-periods up to about 3200 BC, when Naqada III styles of pottery replaced the distinctive Lower Egyptian styles.

Table 5.1 is just one version of the many chronologies of this period and doubtless contains errors and incomplete data that will be corrected by future research.

Overview of Early Egyptian State Formation

Egyptologist John Wilson (1951: 36–37) likened the formation of the first Egyptian state to a chemical reaction in which the slow, continual addition of certain chemicals to a solution results in the sudden precipitation of its solids.

Table 5.1. A Chronology of Predynastic and Early Dynastic Egypt

Major Period Names	Estimated Dates BC	Chronological Subdivisions and Cultural Names: Upper Egypt	Chronological Subdivisions and Cultural Names: Lower Egypt	King List	Some Important Sites	Major Developments
Neolithic/ Predynastic Transition	5000–4000	Tasian? (?–4400) Badarian (4400–4000)	Faiyum Neolithic (c. 5500–4000) Merimde–Omari (5000–4350)	None	Faiyum Merimde El Omari	Widespread settlement of Egypt by farmers living in communities made up of circular huts
Predynastic: Naqada I	4000–3500	Naqada I (Amratian)	Ma'adi-Buto (c.?–3200 BC)	None	Hierakonpolis Abydos Hammamieh	Development of basic Egyptian agricultural village socioeconomy
Predynastic: Naqada II	3500–3300	Naqada II (Gerzean)	Ma'adi-Buto (c.3900–3200)	None	Ma'adi Buto Mendes?	
Predynastic: Naqada III	3300–3200	Naqada III	Naqada III	? (see Dreyer 1988)	Gebel Tjauti? Abydos Hierakonpolis Naqada Buto Ma'adi	Earliest forms of Egyptian writing
Early Dynastic I: Dynasties 00? and 0 (also called "Protodynastic")	3200–2920	Early Dynastic I	Early Dynastic	? Iri-Hor? Ka Scorpion II Narmer	Minshat Abu Omar Abydos Saqqara Hierakonpolis	

(continued)

Table 5.1 (*continued*)

Major Period Names	Estimated Dates BC	Chronological Subdivisions and Cultural Names: Upper Egypt	Chronological Subdivisions and Cultural Names: Lower Egypt	King List	Some Important Sites	Major Developments
Early Dynastic II: Dynasty 1	2920–2770	Early Dynastic II	Early Dynastic	Menes Djer Wadj Den Adjib Semerkhet Qa'a	Memphis-Saqqara Hierakonpolis Abydos Mendes	Unification of Egypt and establishment of capital at Memphis
Early Dynastic: Dynasty 2	2770–2575	Early Dynastic II	Early Dynastic	Hetepsekhemwy Ninetjer Kha'ba Huni (?)	Elephantine Abydos Saqqara	

This table includes a number of disputed items. A Tasian Period, for example has been suggested by some scholars, but evidence of it is uncertain. No national "kings" probably existed in Egypt until Dynasty 0, but it's possible there were powerful earlier rulers. Some scholars dispute the historical existence of Iri-Hor and other Dynasty 0 rulers. This period is also called the "Protodynastic" by some. Van den Brink (1992) used the term Dynasty 00 for the elites buried at Abydos. Gunter Dreyer (1988) has reconstructed the succession of kings for the Late Predynastic as follows: Oryx, Standard, Shell, Fish, Elephant, Bull (=Bucranium standard?), Stork, Canid, Bucranium standard (^), Scorpion I, Falcon I, Min standard+plant? Falcon II, Lion, Double Falcon, ?, ?, ?. Their historical existences and lives remain largely undocumented.

The relative "suddenness" of the first Egyptian state's appearance, however, is a matter of dispute. We cannot, of course, identify a single event or a particular year when Egypt first became a "state"; in fact, ancient Egyptian civilization was the product of centuries of cumulative cultural changes, and segmenting this history into Predynastic, Early Dynastic, Old Kingdom, and so forth is a descriptive, not an analytical, enterprise.

Wilson also attempted to apply V. Gordon Childe's (1934) ideas about early urbanism to ancient Egypt, and concluded by damning Childe's model with the faintest of praise: "[O]ne may accept a truth in Childe's [concept of] 'urban revolution' provided that it is understood that with regard to Egypt it was not 'urban' and was not a 'revolution'" (J. Wilson 1951: 34). He argued that Egypt had been instead a nation-state that comprised a "civilization without cities." Wilson probably exaggerated this point, but we still do not know the validity of his observation: The earliest levels of many early Egyptian settlements are so obscured by later occupations and alluvia that we cannot reconstruct their sizes and interior composition with precision.

Nonetheless, despite the imprecise and incomplete evidence about its past, Egypt has played a central role in theories of ancient state formation that extend from Herodotus in the fifth century BC to the present (discussed in Chapter 7). The many scholars who have analyzed ancient Egypt have had to confront not only Egypt's data deficiencies but also the uncongenial fact that analyses of early Egyptian state-formation must be done almost entirely without the aid of textual evidence. Egypt had already been a state and complex civilization a century or more before a written language was in widespread use.

Thus, our primary evidence for understanding Predynastic Egypt must be the bones, stones, graves, pots, houses, and other debris left by these people. To interpret this evidence we must make some awesome leaps of faith. We must infer, for example, the baroque structure of an extinct society's social differences in gender, age, wealth, rank, and prestige from variations in such mundane things as grave contents, settlement patterns, and mud-brick architectural styles. Similarly, conflict and warfare must be inferred from fragmentary town walls and ambiguous signs and symbols, such as the Narmer Palette.

This problem can be illustrated with the concept of *occupational specialization*, which is considered perhaps the most important element in a complex society. Religions, settlement patterns, agricultural systems – all these varied in ancient states, but each and every state was based on a highly differentiated and integrated economy. "Occupational specialization," however, is just a shorthand term for a multidimensional underlying reality. Occupational specialists can be categorized as either full or part time; they can be independent contractors or attached to a particular elite family; they can produce utilitarian (e.g., bread) or nonutilitarian goods (e.g., gold beads); and they can produce on vastly different scales, ranging from the household to factories (Earle 1991). Identifying such variations as they apply to ancient Egypt requires many assumptions and inferences. Moreover, of course, occupational specialization is just one element of "cultural complexity." Similarly, we must assume that the ancient Egyptians valued "grave goods" much differently than we do.

Some archaeologists have argued that instead of trying to build a science of archaeology on the shaky premise that we can accurately infer these abstractions of ancient Egyptian culture, we should attempt to create a science based on the artifacts themselves (e.g., Dunnell 1982). This rather abstruse argument is reviewed in Chapter 7.

Other scholars have rejected most traditional categorizations of the Egyptian past, and the objective of trying to reconstruct the Egyptian past in terms of distinct classes, such as "art," "technology," and so forth. Wengrow, for example, approaches the material remains of the Egyptian past with the objective of interpreting artifacts "as mutually constitutive elements within total, developing forms of social life" (2006: 7). This approach, too, is discussed in Chapter 7.

In sum, our inferences about ancient Egyptian society are not useless, but we must remain alert to the fact that elaborate hypotheses about Egypt's past are based on a rather thin and equivocal database. There is an old joke to the effect that for an archaeologist, a "temple" is the remains of any structure that is big enough for a person to stand up in. One archaeologist's "temple" can be another's mud-brick domestic dwelling. Moreover, debates about the correctness of such varying inferences do not in any way constitute a "science."

A related problem is that although we are forced by the archaeological record to focus on the *material* remains of Predynastic peoples, the evolution of the Egyptian state was fundamentally also an evolution in *ideology*. Ideological elements are more difficult to infer from the archaeological record than, for example, the kinds of plants and animals that ancient Egyptians ate. And by the time the first detailed texts appeared, it is clear that they had long since formulated a state ideology.

Figure 5.10 is an elegant evocation of this ancient ideology – although it was created about a millennium after the first Egyptian state evolved. It depicts how the ancient Egyptians imagined their state in idealized form, and it uses signs and symbols that go back far into the Predynastic Period. The entire range of evidence from Egypt suggests that from the

Figure 5.10. Throne base of Senusret I (c. 1971–1928 BC). The ideological context is the Egyptian idea of the source of political order and stability. The gods Horus (on the left) and Seth (right) are expressing the unity of the two lands by tying together the heraldic plants of Lower and Upper Egypt (the lotus and the papyrus). The stylized trachea (windpipe) connects to the lungs to form the hieroglyph for the term "to unite." On top of this is the oval cartouche that includes one of the king's names. The hieroglyphs above the gods refer to localities with which they were associated. *Source:* After Kemp 1989, fig. 6. Reproduced by permission of Barry J. Kemp.

early Predynastic Period onward, rulers grounded their visions of their polities and their own actions in terms of several ideological elements – which changed over time in their formulations but which were persistent elements of dynastic ideology.

Perhaps the most important element was the *containment of unrule* (Kemp 1989: 46–53). The Narmer Palette and the many other stone engravings of its era make visible the Egyptians' yearning for "order." Kings imposed order in many ways, by uniting Upper and Lower Egypt, conquering foreign enemies, encouraging harmony among the social classes, and so forth. As Kemp notes (1989: 51), harmony did not *necessarily* flow from the reconciliation or balancing of opposites; in some cases there had to be a "winner" and a "loser": Horus's domination of Seth in Egyptian myths is an example. Another foundational ideological element was the use of *architecture as political statement*. The Narmer Palette; the massive mortuary cults at the Predynastic towns of Abydos, Hierakonpolis, and Naqada; the Great Pyramids – all of these and many more remains were intended to project the power of the ruler over all others. These projections of power changed significantly over time: Narmer was the central focus of material manifestations of his power, but by the time the pyramids were built, the king had been sublimated into an expression of the sun god.

The early dynastic state rested on several other ideological foundations, and some of these are discussed in Chapter 6.

A Model of Egyptian State Origins

Barry Kemp (1989: 31–35) has produced a model (Figures 5.11, 5.12) of Egyptian state-formation. It will serve here as an example of various issues and possible factors in analyses of Egyptian state origins.

A "model" is a set of related hypotheses about the variables and variable interactions in a complex system. Such models are intended to explain the evolution over time of a complex system, or the functioning of that system at a particular time. Models are used today for many purposes, such as weather forecasts, predictions of illness outcomes, the probabilities of success in locating retail stores, and for many other applications. Models are useful because they *simplify* complex variable interactions. They are based on the assumption that if one can predict the outcome of complex variations from few factors, one then can explain and in some cases manipulate these causal interactions and results.

As useful as such models are, they are prone to many problems. One of these is *equifinality*; that is, different combinations of variables can often produce the same results. The replacement of Lower Egyptian artifact styles by those of Upper Egypt after about 3300 BC, for example, may have been the result of warfare, but this pattern could also be the product of expanding economic interactions, or some complex combination of these and/or other factors. Also, models intended to

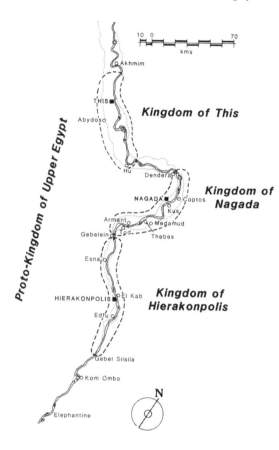

Figure 5.11. Barry Kemp's hypothetical model of the formation of early Egyptian regional kingdoms and proto-states. *Source:* Fig. 8 from *Ancient Egypt: Anatomy of a Civilization*, Barry J. Kemp, Copyright ©1991 Routledge. Reproduced by permission of Taylor & Francis Books UK and Barry J. Kemp.

explain ancient cultural changes are typically much less rigorously defined in mathematical terms than models built for other purposes, and thus their accuracy is more difficult to test. For this reason, archaeological modeling has usually produced hypothetical *descriptions*, not *explanations*.

Kemp's model (Figures 5.11, 5.12) hypothesizes a three-stage developmental process occurring in Egypt between about 4000 and 3000 BC:

At *Stage 1* there were small clusters of agricultural communities in both Upper and Lower Egypt. There is little in Stage 1 communities to suggest that they were complexly organized in terms of occupational specialization or unequal access to wealth, power, or prestige. There was probably little competition for farming lands, because much of the Nile Valley appears to have been only lightly populated.

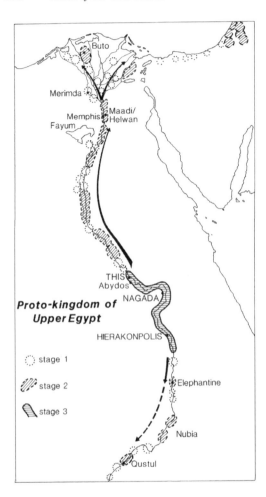

Figure 5.12. Barry Kemp's hypothetical reconstruction of initial Egyptian state-formation. The process is presented as it was in operation on the eve of the formation of a unified state in the First Dynasty (see text for discussion). *Source:* Fig. 13 from *Ancient Egypt: Anatomy of a Civilization,* Barry J. Kemp, Copyright © 1991 Routledge. Reproduced by permission of Taylor & Francis Books UK and Barry J. Kemp.

Stage 2 (see Figure 5.12), however, saw increasing population density and the formation of small socioeconomic polities, perhaps similar to what ethnographers traditionally have called "chiefdoms." These are regionally organized societies with a centralized decision-making hierarchy that coordinates activities among several village communities (Earle 1991). Some chiefdoms are based on hereditary, or *institutionalized,* inequality: If you are the first son of a chief, chances are you will become a chief, no matter how untalented you may be; but if you are able but born a "commoner," your options in life will still be narrowly circumscribed.

These differences in power usually correlate with preferential access to prestige and wealth. Chiefs and their families can claim the best farmlands or fishing places, as well as more food and exotic and expensive items than can commoners. As these communities expanded and intensified their interrelationships, Kemp proposed, some of them became "kingdoms."

The utility of the concept of chiefdoms has been challenged, and some have concluded that it is a sterile conflation of many diverse elements (Kristiansen and Rowlands 1998). Yet the fact remains that at some point in Egypt's past, differential access to wealth, power, and prestige appeared and became institutionalized in dynastic ideology and practice. It is very difficult to document the origins of this fateful transformation archaeologically, but there is evidence that such systems began to form at about 3500 BC in Upper Egypt, at Hierakonpolis, Naqada, and Abydos (e.g., Kaiser 1964, 1985, 1990). In contrast, in Lower Egypt at about 3500 BC, Maadi, Buto, and a few other settlements were flourishing trading and farming communities, but there is little evidence that they were complexly organized in terms of inherited access to wealth, power, and prestige.

Stage 3 (see Figure 5.12) depicts Egypt as it was just before political unification of Upper and Lower Egypt, at about 3200 BC. This was probably an era of intense competition, perhaps sustained warfare between several major towns, culminating in the appearance of "proto-kingdoms," most likely centered at Hierakonpolis, Naqada, and Abydos. These towns probably had populations of several thousand, most of whom were farmers. But about 3–5 percent of the people were likely specialized craftsmen who made pottery, stone tools, boats, beer, and other products, or served as full-time administrators or priests. This proto-kingdom included some monumental architecture, in the form of tombs and funerary enclosures. Stage 3 burials in Upper Egypt suggest significant differences of wealth, rank, and power that were probably based on hereditary inequality.

We could add a *Stage 4* to this model, to encompass the century or two just after Upper and Lower Egypt were joined politically, at about 3100 BC. In this period the earliest pyramids and other monumental architecture were built, and the Egyptian state was centralized at the city of Memphis.

This developmental pattern was in no sense *necessary* in the direction, rate, or form that it took. Not all "chiefdoms," however that term is defined, became "states." Egypt's natural environment and its cultural connections to foreign lands created many diverse opportunities for cultural formation and change. Yet when we contrast Egyptian communities at 4500 BC with those at 2500 BC, we are inevitably led to the conclusion that radical cultural transformations occurred. And we can consider which factors and events were involved in these transformations.

Kemp's model (see also Mortensen 1991) raises various issues in this regard. *First*, what is the evidence that the developmental trend in these four stages was one in which the South incorporated the North, and not vice versa? To begin with, Upper Egyptian pottery and architectural styles entirely replaced Lower Egyptian styles between 3200 and 3000 BC, and the Lower Egyptian styles entirely disappeared. Moreover, well into the First Dynasty, after the Egyptian state had formed, Egyptian kings were buried in the South, at Abydos, long *after* the political and economic center of the state had shifted to Memphis in the North. Also, the signs and symbols that were to become the written Egyptian language were in use in Upper Egypt in the Predynastic Period, but evidently not in Lower Egypt until later.

A *second* issue relevant to the changes over time and space that Kemp's model hypothizes concerns the role of population growth and agricultural potential. While population growth appears to have been slow and very gradual between 4000 and 2700 BC, the overall population of Egypt appears to have more than tripled over this span. We find no evidence, however, that growing populations somehow forced the origins of state institutions, even well after about 2500 BC, when there were many largely unoccupied areas of the Valley and Delta. Population growth appears to be more a *result* than a *cause* of evolving cultural complexity. Nor is there evidence of sustained and labor-intensive efforts to increase agricultural production per unit of farmland: There appear to have been no massive intricate canal systems, for example. Nonetheless, the Nile flood basins in Upper Egypt do appear to have been larger and thus to have offered better returns than those of Middle Egypt.

Third, Kemp's model describes Egypt's cultural evolution, but through what causal processes did these cultural changes occur? The archaeological evidence relevant to this question is at best equivocal. The replacement of Lower Egyptian styles by those of Upper Egypt appears to have been gradual at some sites, abrupt at others. From 4000 BC onward, we see traces of evidence that some towns were walled, perhaps as defenses against a violent world outside. Warfare, however, is difficult to demonstrate on the basis of fragmentary archaeological evidence.

A related issue is the importance of foreign cultures in Egypt's cultural evolution. We must remember that Dynastic Egypt, with its distinctive culture, was just one of the evolving cultures of the contemporary Mediterranean and Southwest Asian worlds. Already by the Predynastic Period, foreign cultural strands were interwoven in Egyptian culture, from the plants and animals that fed Egyptians to the many commodities that circulated into and out of Egypt as foreign trade and political relationships evolved.

Donald Redford notes (personal communication, 1998):

Traditional interpretations of Egypt's history from the Gerzean Period through the 1st Dynasty argue a kind of *Drang nach Norden* [i.e., a forceful march to the north], with the forces of political unification and expansion moving up the Nile Valley, engulfing the Delta, and expanding into Asia, increasing in force as the process proceeded.... There is one element that is particularly difficult to accommodate within this south-north sweep of Egyptian political evolution, and that is the clear evidence in Gerzean [3500–3200 BC] and later sites of artifacts and artifact (and architectural) styles that are Syro-Palestinian and Irano-Mesopotamian in origin [Figure 5.13].

Redford added that "although it is perhaps premature to arrive at conclusions, the evidence for contact with Mesopotamia is more extensive and specific than can be accommodated by a theory of inter-mittent and casual trade. It would seem that besides trade items, a human component of alien origin is to be sought in the Gerzean demography of Egypt" (1992: 22).

We do not have a sufficient sample of human remains from this period to determine if there was a significant influx of Southwest Asians into Egypt, but the possibility is intriguing. In any case, invasions by Southwest Asians are not required to explain these changes; cultural traditions can spread quickly worldwide, as the distribution in today's world of fast-food franchises and the English language clearly show.

If external cultures significantly influenced Egypt during its formative era, it may have been via land and sea routes from Egypt to the Mediterranean world, or perhaps via Red Sea ports linking Egypt to Mesopotamia and beyond. Egyptian artifacts from 2900–3000 BC, including metal and pottery vessels from royal workshops, are found throughout the Negev and southern Syro-Palestine, which had a population at that time of perhaps 150,000 living in walled towns and villages (Redford 1992: 29–35; de Miroschedji et al. 2002). Egypt appears to have been dominant militarily and economically during this period, and Syro-Palestine was probably more influenced by Egypt than vice versa.

In raising the possibility of significant Southwest Asian cultures on Egypt, Redford emphasizes the apparent abruptness of Egyptian state-formation. He notes that "[U]nlike the Tigris-Euphrates Valley, where the temples of Uruk presage the glories of Sumer centuries in advance, Egypt bounced overnight, as it were, out of the Stone Age and into urban culture" (1992: 3).

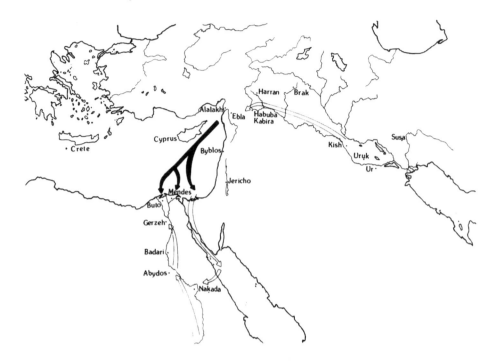

Figure 5.13. Possible Southwest Asian influences on early
Egyptian state-formation. Donald B. Redford stresses the possibility
of Southwest Asian influence on Egypt at the time of initial state-
formation. *Source:* Redford, Donald B; *Egypt, Canaan, and Israel in
Ancient Times.* © 1992 Princeton University Press, 1993 paperback
edition. Reprinted by permission of Princeton University Press and
Donald Redford.

However, some scholars take a contrary view: Dietrich Wildung, for
example, whose excavations of late fourth/early third millennium occupations in the far eastern Delta revealed numerous artifacts of Syro-
Palestinian origins, suggested:

The alleged "cultural explosion" of Egypt in ca. 3100 B.C., with the foundation of the state, the "discovery" of writing, and the canonization of arts
did not take place. In Egypt, too, the "higher culture" developed in a long
organic process of evolution, which already in Naqada II and Naqada III
covered the whole of Egypt, including the Nile Delta, and found its end
several generations before the fictitious unification of the Kingdom. What is
for us historically legible, are the very latest phases of a long-term natural
growth. (1984: 269)

We shall return to the question of the impact of foreign cultures on Egyptian state origins in later sections of this book. But as these contrasting opinions indicate, this issue is far from resolved.

Anthropological Perspectives on the Initial Formation of Cultural Complexity

The distance doesn't matter; it is the first step that is . . . difficult.
>   (Marie Anne de Vichy-Chamrond [1697–1780], when
>   told that a Christian saint had walked two miles with
>   his head in his hands after he was beheaded)

The cultural changes that Predynastic and early Dynastic Egypt underwent are rather easily summarized, but, we must ask, what was the nature of the all-important *first step* toward cultural complexity? Anthropologists have long speculated about the various factors that might have produced the first crucial step, the very beginnings of differences in social rank and access to wealth, power, and prestige.

Marvin Harris (1977, 1989) has proposed a hypothetical scenario that is broadly representative of pre-2000 anthropological approaches to this question. He uses examples primarily from Pacific Island societies, and he ties the appearance of initial power and status differences to the appearance of "big men." These are particularly influential older men whose advice and guidance the community seeks. Village big men act as "nodes" in various socioeconomic and political systems: They can act to intensify production, carry out redistribution of harvest surpluses and trade goods, and use their prestige and position to lead the way in fighting or trading with neighboring villages. Harris suggests that elements of complex societies appeared with the first "intensifier-redistributor-warrior complexes." The more production is intensified, for example, the more there is to redistribute and trade, the larger the population becomes, the more intense the warfare, the more complex and powerful the chiefly sector. "Other things being equal," he writes, "all such systems tend to move from symmetric forms of redistribution (in which the primary producers get back everything they produce) to asymmetric forms (in which the redistributor gets more of what is produced for longer and longer periods). Eventually the retained portion of the harvest surplus provides the chief with the material means for coercing his followers into further intensification" (1977: 92).

We can only speculate as to when, where, how, or even if the first such intensifier-redistributor-warriors appeared in Egypt. Already by about 8000 BC, people living amidst the lakes and grasslands of what is now Egypt's Western Desert may have been organized socially in groups with differential power, wealth, and prestige (see Chapter 4). The extent to which such cultures might have influenced dynastic culture is problematic. In any case, we can assume that the earliest farming communities in the Nile Valley and Delta differed in their basic economic potential. In this era, settlements were concentrated around flood basins, and around these basins the annual floods created productive farming lands, where simple diking and damming could intensify agricultural production. But these basins varied in the amount of agricultural land available to a given community's inhabitants. These settlements also varied in other natural advantages, such as proximity to sources of minerals (e.g., salt, high-quality flint, and other stones such as basalt) and other precious commodities. And although the Nilotic environment was remarkably uniform, some locations were advantageously located near the intersection of ecological zones, such as the additional pastures provided by low-lying erosional channels. We know also that very early in Egyptian history some commodities from Southwest Asia were being traded into Egypt, and favored locations along these trade routes would have benefited some communities.

We must also assume that many other factors differentially affected these agricultural communities: Crop diseases that struck one village's farms more severely than others, the fortunes of local warfare, varying success in devising the tools and tactics of subsistence agriculture – all these and many other factors could have resulted in great differences in the economic and political power of individual people and communities.

Kemp (1989: 32–35) has combined these and other factors to describe the first stage of Egypt's cultural evolution in the terms of *game theory*. He envisions a process in which small differences, in everything from agricultural potential to the personalities of some villagers, upset the equilibrium of the earliest farming villages. Conflicts between villages might have upset this equilibrium by leading to the confiscation of one community's wealth by another. But this equilibrium could also have been upset by a change in social ranking that gave more power to a particular individual who knew how to use it to increase his and his community's wealth and power. Kemp imagines thousands of such "games" being played out and the results being cumulative: Once a community or individual has accumulated sufficient resources to outweigh the threats posed by competing communities or individuals, it or he could have rapidly expanded at the expense of others. The progress of this game would have gone on at different rates throughout Egypt, and the balances of wealth and power would have shifted, but in the end, a powerful state emerged.

Evolving *ideologies* would have been important elements in these transitions (Bard 1992; Hassan 1992; Hassan et al. 1980). Communities that evolved coherent religious traditions and unifying political philosophies would have had a distinct advantage over those that did not. And as Kemp noted, part of the explanation of the Egyptian state origins is in "the creative power of the imagination to fashion a distinctive ideology which through a wealth of symbol and ritual commands widespread respect. The Egyptians early showed a genius for this" (1989: 35).

We must assume that the earliest complexly organized Egyptian societies evolved out of the myriad interactions of these ecological and ideological factors, but it is difficult to document them precisely with Egypt's archaeological record.

Settlements and Settlement Patterns (c. 4500–3000 BC)

The scores of sites dating to this interval that have been excavated are of radically different size, location, and occupational spans (see Figure 5.3). Some communities were occupied for a short time, while others spanned most of this era. Some sites appear to have been continuously occupied for centuries; others were abandoned and then reoccupied. Delta sites continue to be underrepresented in our sample, as some of the most important communities of the fourth millennium BC must be assumed, like Buto (described later in this chapter), to be largely under the water table. Recent excavations in the Delta (e.g., van den Brink and Levy 2002) have revealed that many Delta sites of the early third millennium BC are, in fact, accessible, but we simply do not know how many of these and other sites overlay fourth millennium BC occupations. Our own excavations at Mendes (Wenke and Brewer 1992) illustrate this problem. We found pottery and many other artifacts and some architectural remnants dating to the First and Second Dynasties just above the water table, but our auger samples below this level revealed at least two meters of additional deposits – which must be of Predynastic age – but these are inaccessible. Matthew J. Adams, too (2007), has identified areas that seem to be extensive Predynastic occupations at Mendes.

Most contemporary budgets for archaeological research do not permit the removal of many meters of occupations to reach a site's lowest levels, or long-term voluminous pumping below the water table. The Predynastic sites described in the following sections, thus, are a biased sample of variability in occupational spans and geographic locations.

The Neolithic-Predynastic Transition (c. 5000–3500 BC)

Late Neolithic cultures can be distinguished only vaguely from those of the first part of the early Predynastic, at about 5000–4500 BC, but a demographic shift occurred about 4000 BC, when Egyptians apparently abandoned Neolithic settlements in the Faiyum, Merimde, and other locations where subsistence agriculture yielded relatively low returns. They then began clustering around the most productive flood basins along the Nile, where annual floods made relatively large expanses of land available for farming, and where small canals and dikes could extend the area of cultivation.

Unlike the south-to-north developmental gradient of the Egyptian state, the transition to agriculture appears to have been a north-to-south pattern – as might be expected, given the Southwest Asian origins of some of the domesticated plants and animals on which the dynastic economy was based. No southern Egyptian sites that reveal cereal farming have been found to be as early as those in the Faiyum, Merimde, and Middle Egypt.

Soon after 4000 BC, agricultural villages were established in many areas of the Nile Valley and possibly the Delta. In the southern Egyptian Nile Valley, Naqada, Abydos, Hierakonpolis, and other sites were probably first settled shortly before 4000 BC and were continuously occupied throughout the Predynastic Period, when they became Egypt's largest religious and political centers. Soon thereafter, communities also appeared at Buto, Maadi, and other northern Egyptian sites.

Although the focus of this chapter is the evidence from Predynastic Egypt, it is important to note that soon after Predynastic Egyptians were evolving productive Neolithic economies and the first elements of what would become dynastic culture, people living in what is now Sudan were also making these transitions. Strong cultural connections existed between the Egyptian and Sudanese Nile peoples, and they made many of the transitions to the farming way of life and early cultural complexity in concert.

Hammamieh. A representative site dating to the transition between the Neolithic and the Predynastic is Hammamieh, a "Badarian" community in the terms of the original Predynastic chronologies.

Perhaps only an archaeologist could find Hammamieh's tumbled debris interesting. Here, near the boundary of Middle and Upper Egypt (see Figure 5.3), is an archaeological record of human occupation spanning the period from about 4500 to 3500 BC. It consists mainly of superimposed layers of pit houses, hearths, burials, and other remains – the detritus of a millennium of community life compressed into two meters (Brunton and Caton-Thompson 1928; Holmes and Friedman 1989).

Hammamieh's earliest occupations probably date to between about 5000 and 4500 BC, somewhat later than the nearby Faiyum Neolithic sites (c. 5500–5000 BC). However, the few Faiyum sites that date to the period c. 4500–4000 BC show no evidence of pit houses or other residential architecture (Wenke and Brewer 1992). Neolithic residential architecture discovered on the north side of the Faiyum Oasis (Wendrichs and Cappers 2005) indicates that Neolithic and early Predynastic communities existed, encouraging the search for transitional occupations between the Neolithic and Predynastic. Wendrichs and Cappers (2005) suggest that these domestic occupations have been found, and archaeologists anticipate additional data.

In the late Neolithic and early Predynastic, pit houses were constructed by digging a hole approximately two meters in diameter and to about waist height, and then by driving posts into the ground around the hole, attaching reed mats to these posts and plastering them with mud, and then roofing them with thatched reeds or palm fronds. Residing in small holes in the ground may sound rather unattractive, but such pit houses had many virtues: They were cool in the summer and relatively warm in the winter, and they were easy to build and maintain. Some of the pit houses at Hammamieh included hearths, suggesting that these were residences, while others had concentrations of sheep/goat droppings and may have been tiny animal pens, or just storage areas where dung was collected for fuel or fertilizer. Some were probably occupied year-round, while others appear to have been just temporary shelters, perhaps used seasonally as a base for tending flocks of sheep or other specialized tasks along the Nile's desert margins. If the pit houses found at Hammamieh and contemporary sites were only seasonally occupied, the main residential communities must have been closer to the Nile – and therefore long since buried or washed away.

Compared to the earlier Faiyum Neolithic people who used coarse and crude pottery, the people of Hammamieh used an impressive array of decorated ceramics. Their black-topped pottery jars, for example, link them to contemporaries to their south, probably at Abydos, Naqada, and Hierakonpolis – although only a few traces of occupations dating to before 4000 BC have been found at these Upper Egyptian sites. This kind of decoration persisted throughout the Predynastic in southern and central Egypt. There are even figurines (Figures 5.14, 5.15) that hint at something of a religious life of the Badarian people. The Predynastic lithic tools of Upper Egypt are impressive in their diversity and styles (Holmes 1989).

The highly stylized "hollow-base" stone projectile points from Hammamieh are nearly identical to those from the Faiyum (see Figure 4.2), and these projectile points probably connect the people of Hammamieh to the peoples who lived centuries earlier in the Western Desert, before desertification.

Figure 5.14.
Predynastic statue of a
"bird deity." Precisely
what this statue
represents is a matter
of dispute. *Source:*
Werner Forman / Art
Resource, NY.

Figure 5.15. Neolithic/early
Predynastic (c. 4000 BC) ivory
figurine of a woman. There is
little "art" known from these
early periods, and most is in the
form of decorated pottery or
figurines. *Source:* © The
Trustees of the British Museum.

The people of Hammamieh and other communities of this age
probably lived the short, uncertain lives of subsistence farmers. We tend
to think of the transition to an agricultural economy as a sudden and
comprehensive transformation, but these socioeconomies had to be put

together piece by piece. They no doubt were still experimenting with different combinations of plants and animals, developing tools for specialized tasks, and determining the optimal planting and harvesting schedules. The productive village socioeconomy of dynastic Egypt was the product of centuries of trial and error in adapting to the Nilotic environment and developing the tools and tactics necessary to exploit this environment. Starvation may have been common in the early Predynastic, when people were just beginning to develop the methods of food storage and exchange necessary to level out highs and lows of agricultural production.

Even something as simple as using animal wastes for fuel and fertilizer was a vital element of the village economy and had to be developed. The ancient Egyptians, for example, probably used cattle dung for various purposes, as today's poorer villagers still do. They collect the dung and form it into "cow patties," dry them in the sun, and then use them as fuel (yogurt made from cow or water buffalo milk and heated with dung cakes, for example, has a distinctive, not unpleasant, taste). The inference that cow dung was used in this fashion early in Egyptian history is based on analyses of charred plant remains; these often are composed mainly of meadow and pasture plants – just the kinds of plants that cattle graze upon (Moens and Wetterstrom 1989). Some of this expertise must have been part of the cultural repertoire of the cattle herders in the then-verdant Sahara of ten thousand years ago, but every tool, every technique, had to be adapted to the complexities of Nilotic farming.

At el-Badari, Hammamieh, and their contemporaries, people appear to have been in the process of adapting ancient Saharan hunter-forager economies and technologies to the intersection of the desert and Nile. There were probably few constraints on how they organized their activities in this niche: Population densities were low, resources were almost uniformly distributed along the Nile's banks, and construction materials, in the form of straw, mud, wood poles, reed mats, and so forth, were cheaply obtained and easily moved or replaced. No doubt the Neolithic incentives to concentrate people in sedentary communities amidst their primary areas of exploitation (as described in Chapter 4) still were in force. But the earliest agricultural communities along the Nile had great flexibility in how they arranged themselves and their activities across their lands (Midant-Reynes and Buchez 2002: 38; Wengrow 2006: 79–80). We must also assume that these changed over time and across the area of this evolving adaptation.

The demands of subsistence farming probably left the people of Hammamieh and their contemporaries with little time to contemplate life, death, and the universe, but their putative ancestors in the Sahara had already expressed complex ideological ideas in stone architecture (see Chapter 4). And everything we know about Egypt suggests that dynastic ideology had deep and thick roots in the ideologies of its Neolithic and Predynastic past. Some Badarian sites contain, for example, artifacts in animal forms, such as ivory spoons whose handles are shaped to resemble horned animals. The Badarian peoples sometimes buried animals or representations of animals, including cattle, gazelles, canids, and catfish spines. The significance of these items is obscure: Some were probably personal possessions; others may have been connected to the much later representations of divinities in animal forms. Some social ranking appears to have evolved in the Badarian Period (Anderson 1992), but it is unlikely that it was institutionalized in forms whereby social rank was inherited and provided some individuals with inordinate access to the society's resources.

The Middle and Late Predynastic Periods (Naqada II–III) in Upper and Middle Egypt

In the period 3700–3300 BC, Egyptian cultures were transformed. An early indication of this is presaged in domestic architecture: Upper and Middle Egyptians abandoned the pit houses of their ancestors and began living in mud-brick houses composed of rectangular rooms.

This may seem a rather trivial innovation, but it reflected revolutionary cultural changes. Pit houses are found in many areas of the ancient world, amidst a wide variety of environments and economies, but villages made up of adjacent rectangular buildings that share common walls (Figures 5.16, 5.17) replaced all other residential forms in early states. Why should this be so? It is probably because they offer crucial advantages over compounds of circular huts. As Kent Flannery (1972) noted, in communities of people who live in circular huts – and such communities existed until the very recent past in some areas – granaries and other storage facilities are typically shared by all members of the community. In such communities the basic economic unit seems usually to have been the entire group. In villages composed of rectangular units, however, the basic socioeconomic unit seems to have been the extended family, each of which maintained its own food stores and storage of animals and other goods. This provided greater incentives for intensification of production, which in turn could have produced differences in wealth among these families, all of which may be linked to the complex national economy of early states.

In sum, the rectangular village community structure seems to have rewarded occupational specialization, wealth differentials, and other aspects of complex societies. Such communities have other minor advantages. They are more easily enlarged than compounds of circular huts because rooms can simply be added on, whereas increasing the number of circular residences rapidly increases the diameter of the settlement and adds to the cost of moving goods and people around the community, and of defending it.

Architecture, of course, does not *cause* the evolution of complex social and economic organizations; it simply *reflects* these processes. Different architectural forms offer different cost–benefit ratios for people in varying socioeconomic and political contexts. Some architectural arrangements are more efficient than others for specific kinds of social and political organizations, and for the different environments in which these organizations are located. But the subtle interplay between cultural considerations and architectural "facts on the ground" is not easy to unravel.

We can also assume that the replacement of communities of pit houses by mud-brick villages occasioned dramatic shifts in ideology other than those associated with the emergence of the extended family as the primary economic unit. Ancient Egyptians, Mexicans, Chinese, Anatolians, and others made this same transition, and the ideologies of these different communities must have been somewhat different; but in the end they all converged into unified state ideologies.

In Egypt, compounds of circular huts were the basic residential community in the north at sites like Merimde at about 5000 BC, and still at about 3300 BC at Maadi, and perhaps even later at Delta sites (van den Brink 1992). But at about 3400 BC the standard village form of rectangular rooms and buildings was evident at several sites in Upper Egypt, and by about 3100 BC this village pattern apparently replaced communities of pit houses in most of Egypt.

Hierakonpolis. More than a century of excavations at Hierakonpolis – Greek for "City of the Hawk" – has provided a wealth of evidence about the cultural transformation of Egypt throughout the Predynastic Period (Kaiser 1958; Quibell and Green 1902; Kemp 1963; Hoffman 1982; B. Adams 1974; Fairservis 1981, 1986; B. Adams and Friedman 1992; Friedman 1996, 2007; Friedman et al. 1999: 1–35).

Today the archaeological remains of Hierakonpolis (see Figure 5.3), located on the Nile's west bank about a hundred kilometers south of modern Luxor, are surrounded by agricultural lands, but in ancient times the community sprawled onto adjacent low desert hills and plains. Today the central area of the archaeological site is called Kom el-Ahmar – "The Red Mound" in Arabic. It is marked by a large mud-brick "fort" (probably not a fort but a ritual center) built in the early Dynastic Period

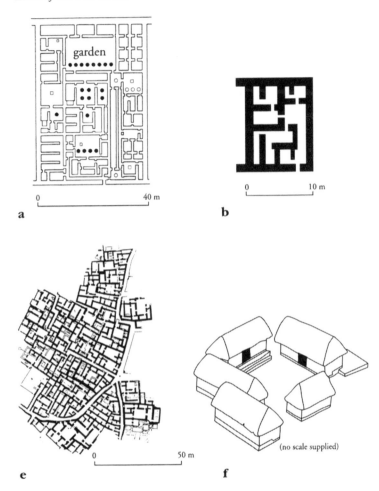

Figure 5.16. Various house types in early civilizations. These are examples of domestic structures in early states. These reconstructions, as illustrated by Bruce Trigger, are: (a) plan of a large (and expensive) Middle Kingdom Egyptian residence at Kahun; (b) an ordinary lower-class home at Kahun; (c) plan and elevation view of a Mesopotamian private home, at Ur, from about 2000 BC; (d) reconstruction of such a house; (e) street plan of a small area of Ur at about 1750 BC; (f) lower-class classic Maya (c. AD 500) house group; (g) plan of upper-class

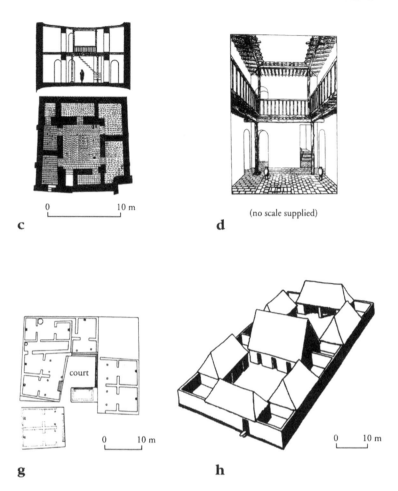

0   10 m

c

(no scale supplied)

d

court

0   10 m

g

0   10 m

h

house in the Valley of Mexico at about AD 1000; (h) a residential
enclosure (probably built by the Inca government at about AD 1500),
but it is not certain what family units lived in such structures. As
discussed in the text, rectangular houses occupied by extended families
are a key feature in early state origins. Communities of such houses
are economically efficient in preindustrial states. *Source:* Reprinted with
the permission of Cambridge University Press from Trigger 2003,
pp. 170–171 (see his references). © Cambridge University Press 2003.

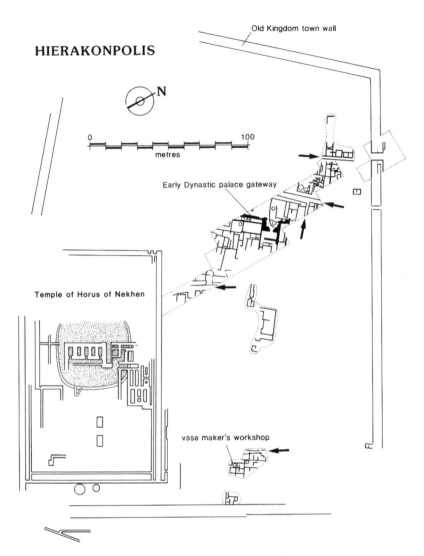

HIERAKONPOLIS

Old Kingdom town wall

N

0   100
metres

Early Dynastic palace gateway

Temple of Horus of Nekhen

vase maker's workshop

Figure 5.17. Urban layout at Hierakonpolis. Hierakonpolis was perhaps the largest and most important site for much of the Predynastic Period, and it continued as a large town into the early Dynastic and Old Kingdom Periods. This map, by Barry Kemp – based on the work of many other archaeologists – indicates that the central area of the town was encircled by an impressive mud-brick wall in Old Kingdom times. The arrows point to probable streets. The earliest Predynastic community is probably deep under the water table (except for the hundreds of Predynastic graves on higher levels above the residential architecture illustrated here) and covered by early Dynastic and Old Kingdom remains. *Source:* After Kemp 1989, fig. 48. Reproduced by permission of Barry J. Kemp.

near a wadi close to the site. Estimating the size of the community at Hierakonpolis at any point in the span of 4000–3000 BC is difficult, but at times it was probably at least thirty hectares in extent. We can infer that it was probably much larger, when we consider how much of the site is buried under later occupations, as well as the subsidiary activities that took place far into the two main wadis that bracket the site.

The late Michael Hoffman, who excavated this site for many years, concluded that Hierakonpolis was initially settled at about 4000 BC by colonists from more northern parts of Upper Egypt. Hoffman exposed the remains of a building, dating to about 3700–3500 BC, which appears to have been burnt and thus is relatively well preserved. It is among the earliest examples of the standard rectangular buildings that eventually became the main architectural element in all dynastic Egyptian communities. Although this building measured only about 4.0 by 3.5 meters, it was large compared to other mud-brick structures that appeared at other sites at about this time. An oven and a pot were set in its floor. Traces of mud brick near its entrance suggest the construction methods of later periods, but there are also post-holes, and so its walls could have been simple reed mats plastered with straw-tempered mud.

In the Predynastic age, the region around Hierakonpolis was one of rich ecological diversity and exceptional agricultural potential. As a result, Hoffman concluded, Hierakonpolis experienced a "population explosion" between 3800 and 3400 BC, reaching a population of five to ten thousand people in the central area of the site during the latter stages of this period. If so, Hierakonpolis was huge in comparison to most other Predynastic settlements.

Estimates of ancient population sizes, however, are inherently suspect when the remains of only part of the community have been revealed. Also, in Egypt the Nile provides a direct connection between widely separated communities along the river, and thus the immediate environs of a site such as Hierakonpolis were not the only factor dictating its population size. The Nile allowed food supplies to be shipped to these settlements to support the many priests, administrators, and craft specialists who did not grow their own food.

In all early states, moreover, a settlement's political and religious importance, its proximity to trade routes, and other nonagricultural factors determined its population size. In our own era, for example, the population sizes of cities such as New York, London, and Tokyo have almost nothing to do with the agricultural productivity of their surroundings. In ancient Egypt, Hierakonpolis, Abydos, Memphis, and other settlements, too, achieved populations greater than just their regional agricultural productivity would predict.

Hierakonpolis was probably divided into different zones of occupational specialists by about 3500 BC. It seems to have been a major producer of pottery, beer, stone vases, maceheads, palettes, and other commodities, not just for its own people but for other Upper Egypt communities as well. Pots from Hierakonpolis and other sites with the characteristic boat motifs (see Figure 5.9), for example, are both beautifully rendered and quite uniform in design, suggesting that they were made by a small number of specialists. Excavators have found pottery kilns and other remains that suggest large-volume production by specialists working within fairly strict canons of style (Friedman 1996). In one area, which has been interpreted as a "temple workshop," there is evidence that craftsmen produced large numbers of highly stylized flint tools, which were then traded in an exchange network that linked Upper Egypt to Nubia and perhaps even Syro-Palestine. Hierakonpolis also boasted a large brewery, probably to supply the town and surrounding communities with beer (Geller 1992).

Artifacts found at Hierakonpolis and other Predynastic Egyptian sites suggest – somewhat counterintuitively – that many of the first specialized commodities made in Egypt were, in a sense, luxury goods. The highly stylized flint knives, for example, are useless for sustained cutting, but they probably played an important ideological role by distinguishing elites from commoners. In any case, economic terms such as "luxury good" do not reflect the critical role such items played in the complex symbolic system used by ancient Egyptians.

Among the thousands of graves and tombs at Hierakonpolis, dating to 3700–3300 BC, are some that were relatively large (up to 2.5 by 1.8 m) and contained beautiful goods, such as decorated stone maceheads – probably the possessions of powerful elites. Some of these graves also contained pottery vessels decorated not only with paintings of boats but also of animals – mainly of Nile wildlife, such as hippos and crocodiles, and also of gazelles, cattle, scorpions, and lizards. Representations of people on these pots are typically in the form of hunting scenes or what are usually interpreted as depictions of victorious warriors after a battle.

In one area of Hierakonpolis, a few kilometers up a large erosional channel, excavators found several tombs, each with about twenty-three square meters of interior space, all dating to about 3200–3100 BC. All were looted but still contained beads in carnelian, turquoise, gold, silver, and other precious materials. Fragments of other artifacts in obsidian, lapis lazuli, ivory, and crystal were also recovered, along with the remains of a wooden bed with feet in the traditional shape of carved bull's hooves.

Another primary evidence of social differentiation at Hierakonpolis is Tomb 100, the "painted tomb," which dates to about 3200–3100 BC. It is the only painted tomb known for mid-Predynastic Egypt. Painted on its walls, in red, black, and white, are representations of people, animals, and boats, perhaps as they participated in battle or possibly as they transported a ruler's corpse in the single black boat in the composition (Midant-Reynes 2000: 52–55). Tomb 100's internal architecture was complex, with mud-brick walls dividing the area into "rooms." We do not know if the tomb was prepared well in advance of the death of a powerful individual or was executed at the time of his death. Earlier scholars saw similarities between the tomb's motifs and those of Saharan rock art, but these supposed similarities are ambiguous (Wengrow 2006: 115). Tomb 100 was apparently the focal point of a large group of elaborate contemporary mud-brick tombs, but these were poorly preserved and little is known about them.

There are other rather intriguing developments in mortuary practices at Predynastic Hierakonpolis. Renée Friedman, who directed excavations of 260 burials there that date to about 3600 BC, found several bodies – all of women – that appear to have been partially and artificially mummified. The heads and hands of some of these erstwhile citizens were wrapped in linen pads. This would be among the earliest known examples of this mortuary technique.

Because of the impressive size and rich contents of some tombs at Hierakonpolis during this era, Hoffman suggested that this varied and integrated economy operated in the context of significant social ranking. Between about 3400 and 3200 BC, the people of Hierakonpolis built a large cobblestone foundation that Hoffman interpreted as the remains of a "fortified palace, temple, or administrative center" (1980b, 1982). They also built a thick mud-brick wall around part or all of the settlement and constructed some large mud-brick tombs for apparently privileged members of the society. These constructions at Hierakonpolis also appear to illustrate the persistence into dynastic times of architectural motifs of simple Predynastic structures. Until large stone buildings began to be built after about 2700 BC, all Egyptian architecture was built with mud-brick, or *pisé*, constructions in which the walls were reeds and logs plastered with mud. Papyrus marshes could have supplied the raw materials for supporting columns, if many of them were bound tightly together. Papyrus reeds could even be bent into curved archways. With the advent of stone buildings, these Egyptian architectural elements from the Predynastic were replicated in stone in the forms of cornices, screen walls, false doors, and columns that suggest poles, thatch, and reeds (Dieter Arnold 1991: 3).

Hoffman concluded that at about 3200 BC, Hierakonpolis was a nome capital and had become the capital of a southern Egyptian state.

He also argued that the pottery and architectural styles at Hierakonpolis indicate that the development of Egyptian civilization was essentially an internal and uninterrupted process, a process that was not primarily a result of contacts with foreign cultures.

Naqada and Adaïma. As rich and powerful as Hierakonpolis was in the middle of the fourth millennium BC, there were other important centers. By Naqada II times (c. 3500–3200 BC), the community at Naqada may have been as populous and powerful as Hierakonpolis. At the "South Town" area of Naqada, Claudio Barocas and others (Barocas, Fattovich, and Tosi 1989: 301) found what they call "state authority devices," such as clay sealings that were widely used to "lock" containers and room doors. They concluded that these sealings and other evidence indicate that the South Town area of Naqada was part of an incipient Egyptian state.

As Béatrix Midant-Reynes notes (2000: 53), this was an era of expansion, as Naqada II cultures moved northward, reaching even the far eastern edge of the Delta, at Minshat Abu Omar (Kroeper and Wildung 1985), and southward into Nubia. Yet Naqada seems to have lost some of its importance shortly after about 3200 BC, perhaps because Hierakonpolis and Abydos emerged as preeminent communities.

Much of our evidence from the Naqada II Period comes from mortuary remains. A French team working at Adaïma, near Hierakonpolis, found both a settlement and two cemeteries containing hundreds of burials dating to circa 3500–3100 BC (Midant-Reynes et al. 1990, 1991). The settlement area is today a large expanse of sand whose surface is cluttered with potsherds, flint flakes, fragments of grinding stones, bones, and other artifacts. In one area, excavators uncovered the remains of three quadrangular constructions that probably once were subterranean pit houses made with walls and roofs of perishable materials, such as wood and reeds. Elsewhere on the site the excavators found layers of occupational debris. A third area yielded a series of pits and clay constructions, such as silos.

The most ancient tomb, in the western necropolis, contained the remains of five infants and an adult who were buried together at the bottom of a hearth. In the eastern necropolis, many undisturbed graves were found, and the bodies in them were all of relatively young people, from fetuses to late adolescents. Few grave goods were found with these bodies, but some showed patterns of dismemberment. Burials of dismembered individuals have been found at several Upper Egyptian Predynastic sites (reviewed in Wengrow 2006: 118–119). Some funerary rituals of this period apparently involved the dismemberment of the bones of corpses and the reburial of several individuals in the same tomb. Also, the remains of a few unfortunates at Adaïma suggest that their throats had been cut and that they then were decapitated. Adaïma's remains and the evidence from early Dynastic Abydos are the primary evidence that human sacrifice was an early part of Egypt's late Predynastic ideology.

Hierakonpolis, Naqada, Adaïma, and other Upper Egyptian sites of the mid–fourth millennium BC reflect a new order of life, one dominated by large political and socioeconomic centers for many smaller nearby communities, as well as religious centers boasting shrines dedicated to various gods and goddesses (Hassan 1988: 162). David Wengrow has termed the emergence of these cult centers the "urbanization of the dead" (2006: 82–83)

The Middle and Late Predynastic Periods (Buto-Maadi Culture and Naqada II–III Culture) in Lower Egypt

Maadi. The only known Lower Egypt communities that were contemporary with the evolving Upper Egyptian socioeconomic and political centers at Middle Predynastic Hierakonpolis, Abydos, and Naqada were at Maadi and some nearby communities, such as Abusir el-Melek (close to the entrance to the Faiyum), as well as el-Omari, just south of Cairo, and Buto, in the north-central Delta (Debono 1956).

One of the saddest sights for an archaeologist is a precious site that has been looted or destroyed. The site of Ma'adi, which is now almost entirely buried under a southern suburb of Cairo, is particularly heartbreaking. This, the largest and most diverse mid–fourth millennium BC site known in all of Lower Egypt, has now been obliterated.

But at about 3400 BC, Maadi was a thriving village, covering about fifteen hectares. Centuries of continued and repeated occupation left layers of superimposed debris two meters thick in some places. The site was partially excavated in the 1950s, and a few remaining areas were excavated in the 1980s (Caneva, Frangipane, and Palmieri 1987). Finds from earlier excavations have been comprehensively reanalyzed (Rizkana and Seeher 1989; also see Hartung et al. 2003).

Maadi's destruction is particularly lamentable because a large area of its settlement, not just its graveyards, was preserved (at least until the 1950s). Hundreds of Predynastic graves have been found at the site, but Maadi also offered a rich opportunity to study how the people of this time actually lived, not just how they died and were buried.

Radiocarbon dates indicate that Maadi was first settled at about 3650 BC and that it was continually occupied for at least several centuries thereafter. Predynastic Maadi comprised several different types of architecture. In one style, which is reminiscent of the communities in southern Syro-Palestine, oval holes about three by five meters in area and up to three meters in depth were cut into the bedrock and used for living quarters, storage, and other activities. Another settlement type at Maadi was similar to the pit houses at many Predynastic sites in Egypt: clusters of circular semisubterranean pit houses covered by thatch roofs supported by poles – but sometimes incorporating stone blocks. Maadi also contained numerous post-holes spaced in round or oval patterns, which probably reflect the buildings' uses as residences, storage areas, animal pens, and so forth.

Most of the animal bones found at the site are from domesticated pigs, sheep, goats, cattle, and donkeys. Fish bones, too, were found in abundance. The plant remains reflect the core of the Predynastic economy: domesticated species of wheat and barley, as well as lentils and peas, supplemented by other vegetables and fruits.

The styles of pottery and other artifacts from middle Predynastic Maadi contrast sharply with those from Upper Egyptian communities in this age (Hartung et. al. 2003). Pottery in the earliest levels of the site, for example, includes vessels in the distinctive styles of Lower Egypt, as well as some pots of Syro-Palestinian origin or style, and even some that resemble Saharan and Sudanese styles. Only in the last occupations of the Maadi were there significant numbers of pots in Upper Egyptian styles. Inferring degrees of cultural interactions from similarities of artifact styles is an inherently questionable enterprise, but early Maadi's distinctive artifact styles suggest only loose cultural connections with Upper Egypt.

Maadi's stone tool styles suggest a wide network of communication and trade that included parts of the Levant and northern Syria (Caneva et al. 1987). Hassan (1988: 160) argued that Maadi shows unequivocal evidence of organized trade, not just informal, occasional transactions, and that it included a "commercial" zone, reflected in the separation of the stores and magazines from the dwellings (see Wengrow 2006: 86–87 for a contrary view). In this area, excavators found many pots that were made either in Syro-Palestine or at Maadi in the styles of that area. They also found jars of grain, animal and fish bones, some vases, beads, and lumps of imported asphalt. In another area of the site were large pottery jars, some 1–1.2 meters high and .60–1 meter in diameter, containing such items as grain, fish bones, cooked mutton, resins, flint tools, spindle whorls, pots, and wood. It is easy to imagine the people of Maadi, 5500 years ago, busily crafting the goods they exported locally and regionally. They could, for example, net vast quantities of fish from the Nile and then dry or pickle them, to be shipped off to other towns in

Egypt or Syro-Palestine. The cost to the Egyptians of preserved fish was probably negligible, except for transport.

Boats are one of the most common motifs on pots and other artifacts of Predynastic age, and the Nile and its Delta branches connected all of Egypt to the Mediterranean world. But Predynastic Egyptians also used land routes along the Delta's southern edge and across the Sinai, into Syro-Palestine. The remains of apparently domesticated donkeys have been found at Maadi (Bokonyi 1985), and these beasts of burden (whose pitiful progeny are still common sights on the streets of modern Cairo) probably carried wine, honey, aromatic and edible oils, fruit, dried fish, and many manufactured commodities to Maadi's foreign neighbors.

Maadi is located near known copper workshops in southern Syro-Palestine and the Sinai, and some copper implements have been found at Maadi. Communities in Beersheva Valley of Syro-Palestine were occupied at the same time as Maadi, and Maadi's flourishing import and export business apparently gave rise to entrepreneurial centers in Syro-Palestine.

We tend to associate systematic and varied trade relationships with wealth, and thus it is surprising that Maadi's buildings and its approximately six hundred graves reflect only minor differences in social ranking and wealth differentials – certainly nothing approaching that of contemporary sites in the south, such as Hierakonpolis. Despite its considerable wealth, Maadi apparently never saw a voracious elite emerge to exploit it.

Maadi also demonstrates that although communities consisting of rectangular mud-brick houses, clustered in villages, may have certain hypothetical advantages over compounds of pit houses, socioeconomic organizations based on pit houses could be nonetheless diverse and highly productive. Still, rectangular ground-level building foundations have been found at the site, and we will never know exactly how the community was arranged in terms of the functions of different structures.

Buto. The history of research concerning Buto comes about as close as archaeology gets to the "Indiana Jones" vision of the discipline. And it is not very close. The "story" does start, however, with mysterious mentions in ancient texts of a fabled and unknown city. Some of Egypt's most ancient texts refer to a city in the north, "Per Wadiit," the home of the cobra-goddess, Wadjet. The ancient Egyptians saw Per Wadiit as the northern balance to the southern city of Hierakonpolis, a part of which was known as "Nekhen," named for the vulture-goddess Nekhbet. For millennia, however, the location of Per Wadiit, or Buto, remained unknown. Some scholars speculated that it was imaginary – just another expression of ancient Egypt's predilection for counterbalancing dualities. Sir Flinders Petrie, however, was convinced that Tell el-Fara'in, in the northern Delta, was the site of Buto, but his excavations in 1903 revealed that the Predynastic levels of the site were largely beneath the water table, and thus he could not excavate them.

Finally, beginning in the 1980s, German scholars reached the site's Predynastic levels (Von der Way 1988, 1989, 1992), and they concluded that Tell el-Fara'in was indeed Buto (see Figure 5.3). Subsequent excavations (Faltings 1996, 1998a, 1998b; Köhler and Faltings 1996) have shown that a substantial community existed here in the northern Delta from the mid- to the late Predynastic and perhaps earlier. The scale of excavations of Buto has been greatly limited by the high water table: Large diesel-powered pumps have had to be run continuously for days to lower the water table below the Predynastic levels, and thus only a few hundred square meters of early occupations have been revealed.

The earliest levels of Buto found so far date to about 3500 BC. Excavators found clay cones, pottery, and other artifacts that originally were thought to reflect contacts with Southwest Asian states. Recent reanalyses, however, raise doubts about a Syro-Palestinian or Mesopotamian connection. The cones do resemble those made in Mesopotamia between about 3500 and 3100 BC, where they were used as elements in mosaics on temple walls. But the Buto examples were found mainly in trash pits, not in association with temples. Similar pieces have been found at other Egyptian sites, and they may have been nothing more than game pieces. Also, some pottery sherds that originally were interpreted as similar to Uruk styles (c. 3500–3100 BC) of Mesopotamian pottery appear to be more similar to Syro-Palestinian styles, and there seems to be a strong Canaanite presence or influence at Buto in the later fourth millennium BC (Faltings 1998b).

The architecture and functional complexity of Predynastic Buto are largely unknown, although the Syro-Palestinian styles of pottery suggest that Buto, like Maadi, was a node in exchange networks linking Egypt to foreign cultures. Also, what appear to have been a small early Dynastic administrative building and perhaps a temple's remnants have been found.

Pottery at Buto suggests that the replacement of local styles by those of Upper Egypt was relatively gradual. The earliest known levels contain pottery in the distinctive Lower Egyptian styles found at Maadi and several sites; these styles were gradually replaced by pottery in the Naqada III tradition of Upper Egypt. Buto, thus, supports the idea that the rise of the first Egyptian states was a process of gradual integration of the Valley and Delta cultures, perhaps by way of evolving socioeconomic relations, not by violent conquest. This issue remains unresolved, however, as this transition was markedly abrupt at other sites.

In general, Predynastic Lower Egyptian communities appear to have been prosperous and stable, as well as important nodes in trade routes linking them to the outside world, but none matched the size, wealth, and power of southern towns at Hierakonpolis, Abydos, and Naqada.

The Origins of Written Egyptian Language

One of the most important developments of the mid- and late Predynastic Period is the origin of written Egyptian language. The earliest known examples of written Egyptian language date to the early Dynastic Period, but their origins are in the late Predynastic Period.

Ancient written Egyptian is classed as a member of the Afro-Asiatic language family, which also includes Hebrew, Arabic, the Akkadian form of cuneiform in ancient Southwest Asia, and several African languages. The early spoken forms of these languages probably began to diverge between about 8000 and 6000 BC. This divergence occurred perhaps in part because of oscillating climatic changes across Southwest Asia and Northeast Africa that alternately drew people into what are now deserts as rainfall at times increased, and then forced them back into river basins and wetter areas in more arid periods.

The earliest known example of Egyptian writing may be the "King Scorpion Tableau" (Figure 5.18), an eighteen by twenty inch (46 × 51 cm) scene carved into a limestone cliff at Gebel Tjauti, about twenty-five miles north of Luxor. This carving, in fact, may be one of the oldest known documents in human history, dating to perhaps 3250 BC (Darnell 2002). The symbols used in the carving resemble later hieroglyphs.

It is not clear from this carving, however, that the Egyptians had made the most critical step in developing a written language – the use of symbols that could be read as sounds in the spoken speech, as opposed to just the intrinsic meaning of the symbols. But the Gebel Tjauti carving does seem to tell a story. Its discoverers, John and Deborah Darnell, interpret it as a depiction of a triumphal procession of King Scorpion, after he and his troops had conquered the rival king and town of Naqada. One of the most significant elements in the carving is the image of a falcon incised above the image of a scorpion. Throughout dynastic Egyptian history, the falcon was used as a symbol of the god Horus, and all Egyptian kings were considered to be manifestations of Horus. Moreover, the concept of a god-king, or "divine kingship," is the primary element in Egyptian state ideology.

Figure 5.18. Section of rock carving at Gebel Tjauti. John and Deborah Darnell found a rock carving in the hills near Abydos. This is just one section of a larger engraving. The Darnells suggest that the whole composition is a record of the king of Abydos leading the king of Naqada off to public execution, after a battle sometime in the late fourth millennium BC. Some of the symbols also appear in the earliest Egyptian writing found in tombs at Abydos. *Source:* Courtesy of John Coleman Darnell and Deborah Darnell, Theban Desert Road Survey and Yale Egyptological Institute in Egypt.

The other elements in the tableau are familiar from the iconography of later Egyptian history. The Darnells note the image of what appears to be a bound captive, who is perhaps the king of Naqada being led off to public execution. The whole composition, they suggest, is an illustration meant to convey the metaphysical idea of the triumph of order over chaos.

Many ambiguities exist, however, about the transition between the Gebel Tjauti carving and the first inscriptions that faithfully express the spoken language, which date to the late Second or early Third Dynasties. The Darnells argue that because the styles of the elements in the carving are so similar to those in Tomb U-j at Abydos, this may have been the tomb of King Scorpion. Tomb U-j is part of a set of mud-brick rectangular tombs that appear to link Egypt's late Predynastic with its early Dynastic Period (Figures 5.19, 5.20). It has been dated with radiocarbon analyses and the archaeological context to c. 3300–3100 BC. In Abydos's vast cemeteries, German archaeologists (Kaiser and Dreyer 1982; Dreyer 1988, 1992) and others have found objects bearing the names of apparent rulers about whom we know almost nothing. Scholars dispute the relationships between Kings Scorpion, Menes, Narmer, and Aha. There are many opinions. Narmer or Aha may have been the same person; else they could have inherited a united kingdom from Scorpion or Menes. Our current evidence cannot resolve these and similar disputes. Some of the tombs included objects marked with the names of Narmer/Aha (see Table 5.1) – kings who likely were actual historical individuals. Their tombs are carefully constructed and have the many small side rooms for the equipment that the king (for example, King Qa'a, c. 2900 BC) needed in the afterlife. In Tomb U-j and contemporary structures, German researchers also found about 150 "tags" made of bone or ivory, on which various symbols had been engraved and then filled with paint (Figure 5.21). These symbols are often representations of animals or abstract symbols, but they also include some *serekhs* – a symbol of kingship. These tags were originally attached to pots and other containers in tombs that are presumed to have contained goods, such as wine and cloth. At least a hundred pots have been found whose surfaces had been painted with cursive symbols suggestive of writing.

Hundreds of ceramic "bottles" were also found in Tomb U-j. Their alien form suggests that they were imported, perhaps from the Levant, and that they once contained wine flavored with figs and resin (Hartung 2000). But other scholars dispute this contention (Wengrow 2006:203). Other early writing at Abydos is in the form of seal impressions bearing symbols. Some of the apparent written names on the mud sealings of pottery vessels were made with "cylinder seals." Primarily small limestone cylinders carved with stylized fish and abstract designs, they were rolled over wet clay to produce impressions. The earliest forms of these seals come from northern Mesopotamia from deposits dated to circa 7000–6000 BC, but the Egyptian examples – which were probably inspired by these Mesopotamian forms – date to soon after 3500 BC. At around this time, the Egyptians rolled the seals over balls of clay that were perforated so that they could be attached to goods by means of a string. But between 3500 and 3000 BC, the Egyptians simplified this process by rolling the seal over mud stoppers molded over the rims of vessels (Hartung 1998a; Wengrow 2006: 187–188). These impressions seem to have been both for decorative effect and for identifying the name of the ruler associated with various commodities – probably cloth, in many instances.

Gunter Dreyer (1988) has correlated the inscriptions in Tomb U-j with other early inscriptions and has identified at least fifteen rulers who may have lived before Iri-Hor (see Table 5.1). But there is only scanty evidence that these "kings" existed.

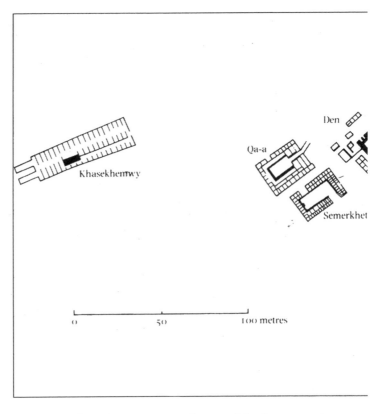

Figure 5.19. Spatial arrangement of some of the known tombs of Egyptian kings of the late Predynastic and early Dynastic Periods, at Abydos. *Source:* Reproduced by permission of Oxford University Press from Shaw 2000, p. 71. © Oxford University Press 2000.

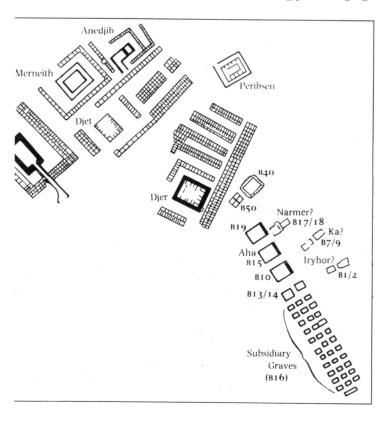

Figure 5.20. The First Dynasty tomb of Qa'a at Abydos.
c. 2900 BC. *Source:* Delimont, Herbig & Assoc.

Figure 5.21. Labels from Tomb U-j at Abydos. These date to about 3050 BC and are among the earliest known examples of Egyptian writing. Less than two centuries after these labels were made, the basic hieroglyphic writing system had been developed. The labels, usually made of clay, wood, or ivory, were probably used to tie and mark containers of commodities. *Source:* Deutsches Archäologisches Institut, Kairo.

Nonetheless, the materials from Abydos suggest that by at least 3100 BC, written Egyptian included both symbols that stood for a complete word (a "logogram") and those that represented individual sounds in the spoken language, or pairs of such sounds ("phonemes") (Baines 2000: 883).

It is possible that the *idea* of writing was imported to Egypt from Southwest Asia and simply adapted to Egyptian forms. And the argument that Mesopotamian writing influenced the development of written Egyptian is not without support. Egypt, Syro-Palestine, and Mesopotamia were in relatively close cultural contact between 3300 and 3000 BC – precisely the time when written Egyptian appeared. Also, the "niched" style used in the construction of monumental mud-brick "funerary enclosures" at Hierakonpolis, Abydos, and other sites has parallels in Mesopotamian architecture (Figure 5.22) (although niching may be more functional than stylistic). Other evidence includes the use in both Mesopotamia and Egypt of cylinder seals to inscribe containers and other "documents," the appearance in both Mesopotamia and Egypt of decorations featuring intertwined imaginary feline animals, and the style used in both Egypt and Mesopotamia for the depictions of kings' regalia. Furthermore, the spread of these styles was all one way: No traces of unique Egyptian styles have been found at Mesopotamian sites in this period.

Nonetheless, Egyptian writing seems to have been an independent and indigenous development. The earliest stages of the written language, for example, perhaps were reflected in the various markings on artifacts from Abydos, but people living in many other late Predynastic/Early Dynastic communities were also using similar signs to decorate pottery and other artifacts. These images of plants, animals, religious symbols, and other elements were gradually stylized into forms that became the characters in written Egyptian. These characters, as well as the methods of writing them, are so different from those of Mesopotamia that it is difficult to believe that they have a close common ancestor. Many of the "characters" of written Egyptian are images of wild animals native to Egypt, or are represented by such traditional Egyptian goods as papyrus and rolls of linen.

Whatever its ultimate origins, Egyptian writing does not seem to have been invented primarily to record "history." Rather, writing was used initially both for administration, such as labeling goods with the names of kings, like the tags and pottery from Abydos, and simply to display the kings' names. The king's name on tags that were affixed to commodity containers may represent the government's share of production; they record the quantity and geographic origin of particular commodities. Older

Figure 5.22 Early Dynastic royal architecture at Abydos. This
illustration of "niching" of mud-brick walls is from the funerary
palace of King Khasekhemui, Second Dynasty (c. 2640 BC), and may
reflect Mesopotamian styles, but it is more likely an independent
invention of the structural advantages of niching and the aesthetic
appeal of manipulating sunlight and shadow. *Source:* Pl. 2 from *Ancient
Egypt: Anatomy of a Civilization*, Barry J. Kemp, Copyright © 1989
Routledge. Reproduced by permission of Taylor & Francis Books UK
and Barry J. Kemp.

clay-seal impressions and ink inscriptions also seem to be economic
devices, used to indicate the origins or ownership of different commodities.

We not know if writing before the First Dynasty could express the
entire spoken language, but soon after this time, it probably could
express even fine nuances of the spoken language, and it was used in two
forms, hieroglyphs and hieratic.

The Early Dynastic Period: The First and Second Dynasties (c. 3100–2686 BC)

Nearly all of the elements of Egyptian culture in the early Dynastic Period have clear antecedents in the Predynastic, but it was in the first phase of the early Dynastic that the culture of what we now think of as "ancient Egyptian civilization" appeared.

With the early Dynastic Period we move into the *historical* era, in the sense that from about 3000 BC onward, we have at least a few texts to aid us in interpreting archaeological data. These earliest texts may record as much legendary information as "real" events. But in the latter early Dynastic we begin to see documentation of ordinary life, such as records of economic transactions, legal documents, "biographies" of individuals displayed in tomb inscriptions, the names of mothers and wives, and so forth. And to complement these documents, we have spectacular archaeological data.

Early Dynastic State Ideologies

The intellectual foundations of the ancient Egyptian state were formulated in the Predynastic Period, but it is in the early Dynastic era that we find substantial evidence of how these ideas were expressed. In hieroglyphic texts, stamp and cylinder sealings, and other artifacts of the Predynastic and early Dynastic Periods, we see glimpses of the formative processes that produced the Egyptian state ideologies of later times.

Central to these ideologies were *cult centers*. The few fragmentary traces of *shrines* found at Hierakonpolis, for example, mark the emergence of the stylistic elements that permeate Egyptian religion and architecture thereafter. Representations of shrines depict them as simple constructions, made from reed mats attached to a wooden framework, such as the traces of shrines found at Hierakonpolis (Friedman 1996; Friedman et al. 1999). As unlikely as it may seem to connect these flimsy buildings to the massive rich temples of later periods, they were like them in an essential way: They were considered the actual house of a god. A simple mud-brick wall encircled the shrine – as was the case in all Egyptian temples – to signal that this was indeed a house, and to separate the sacred from the profane. We assume that a statue of the god was placed inside the shrine, making it his "home" in every important sense of that term. Several poles were erected in the courtyard of the shrine and near its entrance, and to some of them were attached flags; the pole and its flag became the hieroglyphic symbol meaning "god" or "divine."

On the basis of later texts we assume that initially only the king and his priests could enter these shrines and commune there with the god. The statue of the god would have been "washed" and "fed" in various ritualized ways. Later texts suggest that these earliest statues of deities were paraded through the community on special days. It is also likely that shrines were built in many different places to honor different local deities. Indeed, a recurrent theme in all dynastic religion was the rearrangement of the multiplicity of gods, with some elevated over others, and others fused with different gods (Hornung 1999), as dynastic families changed over time and the power of families and their home territories changed over space.

For reasons we will probably never understand, the Egyptians – beginning in the Predynastic Period but extending throughout dynastic times – envisioned some of their gods in animal forms, animals that were understood as real, living incarnations of the gods. By the Second Dynasty, some of these gods were illustrated as humans with the heads of animals, and eventually some gods were depicted in fully human form. But in the latter part of the early Dynastic, the Egyptians worshipped gods who were portrayed variously as fully human, animal-human hybrids, or in animal forms. The Egyptians chose animals for association with divine beings in an interesting way. The wild cows of the Egyptian marshes, for example, were considered dangerous, but the Egyptians observed that they were also fiercely protective of their young, and thus they associated these cows with the protective inclinations of all mothers, as in the form of the goddess Hathor (T. Wilkinson 1999: 262).

Early Dynastic religion is fairly well documented in the archaeological records of Abydos, Saqqara, and other sites, and also from some texts of that period and from later times (T. Wilkinson 1999: 261–320). This religion was based on *cults* dedicated to various gods. These cults consisted of the beliefs and rituals that facilitated the peoples' interactions with the gods, as well as with the cult centers, the physical constructions that were the venues for these interactions. We know the names of some of these gods as they are recorded in religious texts, such as Nekhbet, "She of the Nekheb," referring to the town of El Kab.

Often Egyptians also attached a god's name to a child's name, in somewhat the same way that "Jesus" became a popular name in contemporary Hispanic culture. From these names we infer the names of gods that are not well documented in other texts.

Because Egypt first became a unified state in the late Predynastic and early Dynastic Periods, we can consider whether changes in Egyptian religion reflected this political transformation. And indeed there was an apotheosis of some local gods into even greater divinities who were recognized throughout Egypt, while other gods remained associated primarily with the communities where they originated. This transition may have been the result of the forces of socioeconomic and political integration, whether by virtue of the king's astute political calculations or as the predictable result of underlying and largely unrecognized economic forces. Participation in a national ideology would have tied all Egyptians, from Gaza to Aswan, into a powerful, unified, and stable cultural system. By maintaining local gods and cults, the national state could allow the free expression of regional religious notions and yet dampen any tendencies toward civil wars stimulated by these regional differences.

Such *functionalist* explanations, however, are inherently suspect. Their limitations are discussed in Chapter 7.

The nature of early Dynastic cultic *practices* remains obscure. Texts suggest that the supplicants prayed in some form, but we do not know the words used; they also sacrificed animals, but we do not know in detail who or what was sacrificed or how. Votive offerings at various sites frequently involved stone or faience representations of animals, such as scorpions, or of hybrid animal-humans, sometimes in the form of a plaque depicting human-hedgehog hybrids (T. Wilkinson 1999: 269–272). We assume that by offering these representations in shrines and temples, people somehow connected themselves to deities. But we do not know if only rulers could offer these votive figurines, or if common people could make these divine associations as well. We know that there were special classes of priests associated with cults, but we do not know if these were full-time professionals. Somehow the king maintained a relationship with deities that worked to connect him to the gods and the gods to him.

There is much evidence that the creation myths and other ideologies that were central to the Dynastic state were already well developed in early Dynastic times, but documentation of them is difficult. Dynastic ideology is discussed in Chapter 6, in the context of the much better documentation of the Old Kingdom Period.

A Brief Political and Archaeological History of the First and Second Dynasties

The first dynasties of the early Dynastic Period appeared at around 3100 BC with the rise to power of a succession of kings, about whom we know comparatively little. The Second Dynasty ends at about 2686 BC with the death of Khasekhemy, a king who ruled a unified Egypt and whose history and deeds are comparatively well documented in both texts and archaeological evidence.

Despite gaps in texts and archaeological evidence, we can at least outline the main dimensions of early Dynastic political history (Grimal 1992: 49–59; T. Wilkinson 1999) and its administrative structure. Some scholars consider the Third Dynasty (2686–2613 BC) to be part of the early Dynastic Period, but it is included here as part of the Old Kingdom Period (Chapter 6) because its architecture, socioeconomy, and religious and political institutions most closely resemble those of the Old Kingdom.

Ancient documents mention the names of several individuals who are thought to have been rulers in the centuries just before 3100 BC, a period some call the "00 Dynasty," or "Protodynastic Period." Tombs thought to belong to the last pharaohs of Dynasty 0, Iri-Hor, Ka, and Narmer, have been found in the Royal Cemetery at Abydos, but some scholars dispute the historical existence of these kings or their identities.

Two names are particularly important in this transitional period: Scorpion and Narmer. These may refer to different individuals or to the same person – or perhaps to two kings named "Scorpion." Whoever "Scorpion" and "Narmer" may have been as individuals, the Egypt of their putative reigns was a powerful polity. Sites of Dynasties 00 and 0 have been found throughout the Valley and Delta, and it is an indication of the power of the Dynasty 0 state in particular that scores of sites of this age have been found in the Sinai and southern Palestine. Most of these settlements were probably stations on the overland trade routes that linked Egypt with neighboring cultures, or were military outposts established to protect Egyptian communities and trade routes in this region. The "Byblos run," by ship up the Mediterranean coast, had probably become important in the late Predynastic, and by early Dynastic times it supplied Egyptian elites with lumber from coniferous trees for use in coffins, boats, and other expensive constructions.

In the early Dynastic Period, Egypt's relationship with its early Bronze Age neighbors in Syro-Palestine was multifaceted, including the exchange of products, diplomatic ties, and sporadic military skirmishes. Southern Canaan remained an important source for copper, but the geographical focus of Egyptian commodity acquisition broadened north, to the Galilee and the region of northern Canaan and Mount Hermon. Excavations (de Miroschedji et al. 2002) of the Dynasty 0 Egyptian settlement at Tell es-Sakan (near Gaza City) indicate that this town was surrounded by a city wall, which is among the earliest known constructions of this kind, and the internal architecture of the settlement is typically Egyptian. A large proportion of the pottery vessels found in the earliest occupation are Egyptian wine jars, seal impressions, and other artifacts that suggest Tell es-Sakan was an important community on this periphery of the Egyptian state.

In the south, too, Egypt was expanding its powers. The Egyptians fortified the island of Elephantine, near Aswan and the Egypt/Sudan border, and used it as a base to oversee their contacts with cultures to the south. The remains of a small Early Dynastic shrine have been found at Elephantine, as well as votive figures and a small statue of a seated king that appears to have been inscribed with the name of King Djer, who ruled in the First Dynasty. South of Elephantine, up the Nile into Nubia, excavations of a cemetery at Qustul revealed burials dating to just before 3000 BC. These graves contained Egyptian pottery and other goods, as well as artifacts in the distinctive local style, known as the *A-Group culture*. Some tombs were the final resting places of local rulers who apparently ruled at the same time as the earliest pharaohs (Williams 1986).

Texts and other evidence suggest that First Dynasty Egypt was ruled by at least eight different pharaohs. Aha was the apparent founder of the First Dynasty. He may have been the same person known as "Menes," whom the Egyptian priest Manetho credited with establishing Memphis as the capital of Egypt.

Memphis at about 3000 BC appears to have become the first true Egyptian city, in the sense of a large populous community that included not just a national administrative center but also workshops to produce many different goods for both regional distribution and international trade.

Only a few areas of early Dynastic Memphis have been excavated, largely because it is buried many meters beneath the debris of later occupations and the present water table. In fact, even the extent of Memphis is unknown, although it may have been centered near the modern village of Abusir, on the west bank of the Nile, between King Djoser's Step-Pyramid and the pyramids at Giza.

We know that later Dynastic Egyptians thought of their country as balanced like a scale, with Memphis as the center point. Indeed, the province in which Memphis was situated was known in some periods as *Mekhattawy*, "Balance of the Two Lands."

While Memphis's archaeological record remains largely unknown, excavations of early Dynastic graves and tombs at Saqqara, as well as at Helwan just south of modern Cairo, reflect the riches of Egypt at this time. These graves contained engraved stelae, hundreds of fine ceramics, jewelry, metal tools and vessels, stone tools and vessels, cylinder seals, textiles, and ivory objects.

Aha is credited with establishing the cults of the crocodile-god Sobek (of the Faiyum) and the Apis-bull (of Memphis) as major religious institutions. The Egyptians saw no conflict in a profusion of different gods or the combination of the attributes of several gods in one, and, as mentioned, they often promoted local gods into nationally worshipped figures.

If the fragmentary texts – and some inventive speculations based on these texts – are to be believed, Aha furthered the socioeconomic and political integration of the Delta and Valley by marrying Neithhotep, the daughter of Delta royalty. Aha also sent military expeditions to Nubia and Libya, while expanding trade with Syro-Palestine. Aha's political strategy thus was in some ways a model for every subsequent king. To legitimize his rule and unite the country, he associated himself with gods and invoked their powers and blessings; he used strategic marriage as a political tactic to maintain national solidarity; he also confronted his neighbors with both the threat of military might and the inducements of economic relationships – and in that way enriched his state, deterred possible invasions, and brought glory to himself.

Gaps in ancient king lists after Aha's death (at about 2900 BC) may reflect struggles in the line of succession. We know little about Aha's immediate successors, but there is solid evidence for a king named Djer. His daughter Merneith was the wife of Wadjit, his successor. Djer built a tomb at Abydos and possibly a temple at Memphis, perhaps to express in architecture the principle of the integration of the Two Lands.

It was also during Djer's reign that we see evidence of the development of a crucial element in Egyptian history: In this period we find the first evidence that elites, not just the king, could aspire to a rich eternal afterlife. They would thus have had a personal stake in the pharaoh's fortunes, and also in amassing wealth and remaining faithful to the ancient gods. Some of the elites of Djer's time were buried in relatively rich and elaborate tombs, perhaps reflecting the first formal recognition of the nobility's aspirations for eternal life.

We know little about Djet, who followed Djer. Djet's successor, Den, however, had a glorious reign of about fifty years, during which he seems to have dealt successfully with Egypt's administrative problems. He tried to limit the power of subordinate elites in outlying nomes, and he created the post of "Chancellor of the King of Lower Egypt" to help him maintain the unity of the state. The tomb of this official, named "Hemaka," was large and lavishly furnished – a sign of the growing importance of bureaucrats in the Egyptian state, and their aspirations for a life after death. Den also used a tactic that was employed by most pharaohs, that of promoting the national religion by building temples and celebrating public rituals to honor various gods. Early in his rule, Den invaded Syro-Palestine and brought back, among other spoils of war, many women to stock his harem. An ivory plaque found at Abydos shows King Den striking an Asiatic-looking enemy on the head with a mace (Figure 5.23), a composition entitled "The first occasion of the smiting of the east."

Den may well have had good tactical motives for his battles in Syro-Palestine. If later Egyptian history is any guide, Syro-Palestinians, Nubians, Libyans, and groups continually encroached on Egypt's frontiers, probably in small hit-and-run attacks aimed at looting rather than open warfare, or by simply taking up residence on Egyptian territory. Egypt did not have a large permanent standing army until late in its history, and so foreigners along the border could overpower local defenses, especially when the power of the central Egyptian government weakened. The adage that "the best defense is a good offense" was particularly true in Egypt's early dynasties: Egyptian military expeditions spared the country much grief by periodically invading its neighbors, keeping them off guard, and dispersing enemy troop concentrations.

Figure 5.23. This ivory plaque from Abydos is entitled "The first occasion of the smiting of the east." It dates to about 2950 BC. The cartouche names King Den, and the hairstyle and other characteristics of the man being assaulted suggest he was from Syro-Palestine. It's difficult to believe that this plaque records the first battle between Egypt and its neighbors, as there are indications of warfare predating this example. *Source:* © The Trustees of the British Museum.

In ancient Egypt, as well as in most other states, military excursions were primary tools of economic expansion. But the Egyptians probably did not conceive of economic expansion in the same terms that we do. Early Dynastic and Old Kingdom texts record the wealth received in trade or though warfare in the form of leopard and panther skins, ebony, cedar, turquoise, giraffes, monkeys, ostrich eggs, ivory, incense, gold, copper, and other goods that were highly valued but had little to do with economic needs. These early Dynastic Egyptians did not live in a capitalist, money-based economy, of course, and thus seemingly "worthless" exotic goods had enormous intrinsic value in that they validated the power of the pharaoh and helped distinguish the elites from the hoi polloi. But these early texts also recount the confiscation of cattle and other "real" economic commodities.

Similarly, the capture of foreign women to stock a pharaoh's harem seems to have been a common military theme; yet it is hard to believe that there was a shortage of Egyptian women such that captured foreign women were needed to replace them. Rape and forced concubinage, as always, seem to have been expressions of power as well as simple lust.

Regardless of the personal motives of Den and his successors, it was during their rules that Egypt expanded its powers into foreign cultures. Expansionism is an excellent evolutionary strategy for any organism, whether it is a biological population or sociopolitical organization.

Anedjib, Den's successor, apparently reigned only briefly, but he is the first pharaoh we know of to use the title "Lord of the Two Lands," in the sense of uniting the Valley and Delta and their associated cultures and ideologies. Horus and Seth (see Figure 5.10) were also seen as balanced, if not reconciled. Horus's association was with order and Seth's with disorder, and their resolution in the person of the pharaoh was a basic element in Egyptian religious and political philosophies. "Disorder" was not necessarily and intrinsically "bad," especially if it could be visited upon Egypt's enemies. We have little evidence about the disorder expressed in actual violent confrontation between the Delta and the Valley cultures, but from Aha onward, kings took names that expressed the unity of the Two Lands. This title meant "He of the Two Ladies" – a reference to the protection of the king by the cobra-goddess Wadjet of the community at Buto and Lower Egypt and the vulture-goddess Nekhbet of Hierakonpolis and Upper Egypt.

Another iconic expression of royal power was in the form of *serekhs* (Figure 5.6). These stylized rectangles contained the Horus name of the king (each king had five different royal names). In some of these, Horus, protector of the king, was depicted as a falcon placed over the representation of a palace courtyard. Some of the kings of the Second Dynasty included a representation of Seth, god of disorder, in their serekhs, either in place of Horus or next to him. In later periods the king's names were placed in elongated ovals called *cartouches* in French.

Manetho reported a change of the ruling dynastic families in the Second Dynasty. Apparently during the reigns of the Second Dynasty's first kings, the political relationship between Upper and Lower Egypt had deteriorated. A ruler named Peribsen rose to power at about 3000 BC, but he may have controlled only Upper Egypt: he appointed a "Chancellor of the King of Upper Egypt," and seals bearing Peribsen's name have been found as far south as Elephantine.

Peribsen's successor, Khasekhem, was born at Hierakonpolis. At the time of his coronation he ordered that stone statues of himself and stone vessels be inscribed with texts that commemorated his victories over northern Egypt. These texts were accompanied in some cases by carvings depicting dead and dismembered bodies – presumably those of rebels. He placed representations of both Horus and Seth over his serekhs. At the same time he chose a name ("Khasekhemwy"), which means roughly "The Two Powers Have Risen and the Two Lords Are Satisfied [with] Him." Khasekhemwy retained a primary interest in southern Egypt, where he built large tombs, temples, and funerary enclosures at El-Kab, Abydos, and Hierakonpolis.

By the end of the Second Dynasty, Egypt's internal geography was organized in terms of several settlement types – types that persisted far into the Old Kingdom and later periods. We have a sense of early Dynastic administrative structure, but we no doubt are missing some elements (Figure 5.24).

Religious and Political Centers. Despite the apparent political unification of the Nile Valley and Delta and the establishment of the capital at Memphis, Aha and most of the First Dynasty pharaohs appear to have been buried at Abydos, which remained the country's religious center. Religious and political centers such as Memphis and Abydos were probably combinations of important cult centers and necropolises that were situated near large residential communities, where some of the state's political and economic business was transacted.

Most major early Dynastic Upper Egyptian settlements seem to have been walled communities made up of tightly packed mud-brick houses and some common storage areas and "ceremonial" buildings and areas. The substantial enclosure walls at many early Dynastic sites may imply some central planning and design, but most of them are not precise rectangles or squares; they have long, straight sections that sometimes

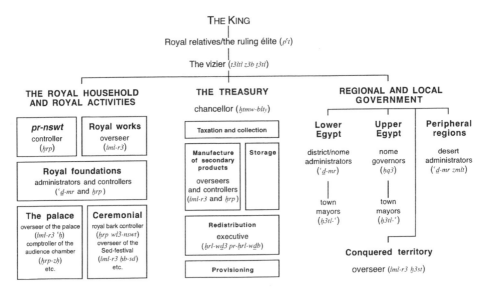

Figure 5.24 T. Wilkinson's reconstruction of an early Dynastic administrative structure. This structure became much more elaborate in later periods. *Source:* Fig. 4.6 from *Early Dynastic Egypt*, Toby A. H. Wilkinson, Copyright © 1999 Routledge. Reproduced by permission of Taylor & Francis Books UK.

form curvilinear patterns. So, perhaps this lack of uniformity indicates that they were built on a local initiative, not under the direction of the central government (Kemp 1989: 138).

Most residential areas of Abydos, Hierakonpolis, Memphis, and many other early Dynastic settlements are buried beneath later occupations or alluvia, and so it is from their mortuary complexes that we find most of the evidence about life in this era. Even these tombs and temples, however, are only a dim reflection of the riches of the early Dynastic age. All the tombs were looted in antiquity; some were burned, and most were excavated in the nineteenth century before sophisticated archaeological techniques were practiced.

Nonetheless, the tombs at Abydos provide many details about life and death in this era. At the center of these tombs were wooden shrines that contained the corpse of the ruler. Around these shrines, the Egyptians built complex mud-brick structures whose interiors were subdivided into chambers of various sizes.

Khasekhemwy's tomb at Abydos contained the earliest known bronze vessels in Egypt. The appearance of bronze has been used as a major mark of cultural development. The term "Bronze Age" describes an era in Old World antiquity in which bronze manufacturing and use spread across Europe, Asia, and parts of Africa. Bronze manufacturing and use appeared at different times in places within this vast area, and so Bronze Age is more a technological term than a chronological reference. In Predynastic and early Dynastic Egypt, bronze was used for arrowheads, chisels and other tools, decorative hairpins and bracelets, and many other items, but its use for tools and other artifacts may not have had a revolutionary impact on most local economies. Flint knives and sickles continued to be the primary agricultural tools until late in Dynastic history.

The structural plan of the tombs at Abydos evolved throughout the early Dynastic Period. By the middle of the First Dynasty, staircases in the interior of the tombs facilitated the excavation of the tomb itself and then the furnishing of it with the king's corpse and grave goods. These tombs were probably roofed with poles covered with thatched reeds or palm leaves.

The largest early Dynastic structures at Abydos, and at Hierakonpolis as well, are mud-brick "funerary enclosures," which were identified as "forts" by the first archaeologists to excavate these sites. This architectural form persisted in several places during the first three dynasties, and these tombs may have been places where priests could perform the rites and rituals necessary for the king's perpetual happy existence after death.

Among Abydos's many funerary remains are large buried boats (Figure 5.25). David O'Connor (1995) and a team from the University of Pennsylvania discovered and excavated the buried remains of fourteen First Dynasty wooden boats that were probably early examples of what in the Old Kingdom have been named "solar boats" (Figures 5.26, 5.27). We do not know precisely when these early Dynastic boats were buried or in what sequence or in "honor" of which ruler, but they appear to have been deposited in the second half of the First Dynasty (T. Wilkinson 2004).

The Egyptians made the sensible inference that the sun-god Ra traveled by boat through the sky by day and the netherworld by night, in cycles that regenerated him forever. Thus, boats were buried near a king's tomb so that in death he, too, could achieve endless renewal. It is a measure of how literal the Egyptians sometimes were in their beliefs that these solar boats were fully functional. Seams were carefully joined with mortises and tenons and then caulked with grass. Oars, masts, ropes, and the other equipment needed to propel and navigate the boats were placed in them. It is estimated that thirty rowers would have been necessary to propel the boats at Abydos.

Figure 5.25. Remains of early Dynastic "solar boats" at Abydos. See text for discussion. *Source:* Delimont, Herbig & Assoc.

Figure 5.26. Petroglyphs in Wadi Hammamat. The ship in this rock carving is similar to boats painted on pottery in the period 3400–3050 BC. Oars are visible, as is a prominent representation of a female figure with her arms raised above her head. Depictions of boats very much like this one have been found in tomb paintings and pottery at Hierakonpolis. *Source:* Redford, Donald B; *Egypt, Canaan, and Israel in Ancient Times.* © 1992 Princeton University Press, 1993 paperback edition. Reprinted by permission of Princeton University Press and Donald Redford.

Figure 5.27 The solar boat of King Khufu. This boat was found buried in an airtight pit near Khufu's Pyramid. It is probably a representation of the same idea that motivated early Dynastic kings to bury similar boats near their tombs. *Source:* Erich Lessing / Art Resource, NY.

The canny Egyptians of later periods simply included models of boats in the tombs of pharaohs. This spared them the cost of making these vessels – on the principle that a model or painting of a boat was just as effective in the afterlife as what we, in our ignorance, would consider the "real" thing.

Earlier representations of boats, such as those painted on Predynastic pots and the wall of Tomb 100 at Hierakonpolis, suggest that some of these crafts were made out of reeds, but by the early Dynastic Period some were made of wood. One of the boats at Abydos measured about twenty-three meters in length – which is small compared to the forty-four meters of the reconstructed Old Kingdom "solar boat" at Giza (see Figure 5.27). The Egyptians had many different kinds of boats from the Predynastic onward.

Human Sacrifice in Early Dynastic Egypt. Human sacrifice was widely practiced throughout the ancient world and for many different reasons. The Spanish *conquistadors* of the New World observed, for example, that untold multitudes of people were sacrificed to propitiate the gods and that these bodies were cannibalized. Anthropologist Marvin Harris (1977) suggested that these practices were in part a way of meeting protein shortages resulting from the absence of domesticated animals – although even he did not suggest that the Aztecs recognized the economic basis of their ideological calculations. "Long pig" was a name given to a repast of human flesh by some Pacific Islanders. Early Celts were apparently sacrificed as a means of divination. The death pits at Ur and other Mesopotamian sites are well known, and there is even informed speculation that China's Great Wall incorporates the remains of many sacrificed people. Ancient North Americans at about AD 1000 stocked one burial mound near modern St. Louis with the remains of about 250 people, some of them missing hands, feet, or heads, suggesting that they were not just the victims of old age, farming accidents, or lightning bolts.

Human sacrifice is horrifying to the modern mind, but we must remember that ancient peoples were struggling to deal with a universe that they understood even less than we do. It made sense to them that a powerful ruler in life needed servants and assistants after he died, and that that could be accomplished by burying his staff with him. Also, human sacrifice could be a shrewd political calculation: If a king's doctors, bodyguards, cooks, and other personnel knew that their lives depended on the king's continued good health, they would have ferociously protected him. Yet it is also possible that sacrificed retainers viewed it as a great honor to serve the king in the afterlife.

We know little about what was going on in the minds of people around the world as they sacrificed other people and, in some cases, ate the deceased, but from what we do know it seems evident that all of these practices were imbued with profound religious feelings. Even the cannibals of the recent past (and some of our own contemporary serial killers) have reported that one of the reasons they eat human flesh is to further a sense of intimacy with the dead, to keep them with them, in a sense.

The early Dynastic tombs at Abydos and other data provide compelling evidence (Figure 5.28) of human sacrifice (T. Wilkinson 1999: 109–149; Bard 2000: 71–72; Wengrow 2006: 245–249). Near the alluvial border of the ancient site, the Egyptians built several large (the largest is 130 × 70 m) rectangular mud-brick enclosures whose purposes remain enigmatic. These enclosures and the graves associated with them have been attributed to various kings of the First and Second Dynasties. The enclosures did not contain human burials, but several hundred graves thought to be contemporary with Djer and other kings indicate human sacrifice: They were precisely spaced and had been covered with uninterrupted wooden roofing – which means that the burials had to have been made at the same time. And although the graves near the tomb of King Aha were individually separated, they were roofed with wooden planks that

Figure 5.28 Iconographic evidence of human sacrifice. (1) This fragmentary label from the tomb of Aha from Abydos shows a bound prisoner being sacrificed. An individual plunges a dagger into the chest of the prisoner, while a bowl stands between them to collect the blood. (2) This is a wooden label from the time of Djer, from Saqqara, showing a scene similar to (1) in the upper right-hand corner. *Source:* From *Early Dynastic Egypt*, Toby A. H. Wilkinson, Copyright © 1999 Routledge. Reproduced by permission of Taylor & Francis Books UK.

were covered by a continuous layer of mud plaster, which had been applied at about the same time that an adjacent mortuary ritual structure had been built. It is likely that all of these people under these structures died and were buried at the same time. Whether these unfortunates were dispatched through strangulation, poison, or some other means is unclear.

There are even some rather vague references to cannibalism in the Pyramid Texts – written many centuries after these apparent human sacrifices at Abydos.

Compared to the execution of hundreds of people to provide tomb "furnishings," as occurred in Mesopotamia, China, and Mexico, Egypt's rituals of this kind were apparently infrequent and persisted for only a short time. Eventually Egyptians came to believe that a deceased ruler could just as well be served in the afterlife by figurines of members of his staff, or by illustrations of servants, craftsmen, and others in tomb paintings.

Human lives were not the only expensive commodities "wasted" at the early Dynastic tombs at Abydos. One of the commodities that flowed into Abydos was aromatic oil, perhaps from Syro-Palestine,

Nubia, or other regions of Egypt. These oils were probably made from tree resins or some other vegetable source, and were no doubt very expensive, because of both collecting and distilling the resins and also transporting them long distances. Sir Flinders Petrie found that the entrance ramp to Semerkhet's tomb at Abydos was so saturated with oil that he could still smell it, five thousand years later (cited in Bard 2000: 72–73).

Abydos is the richest known site of the early Dynastic Period, but elaborate tombs of this period have also been found in Lower Egypt. Some of the best-preserved tombs of this era are at Saqqara, just south of Memphis. Probably all of the First Dynasty kings were buried at Abydos, but some of the Second Dynasty kings may have been buried at Saqqara. South of the Step-Pyramid at Saqqara, archaeologists have found two large galleries (each more than 100 m in length) that contained seal impressions of the first three kings of the Second Dynasty. Other early Dynastic galleries and tombs have been found within the Saqqara complex, and there is compelling evidence that some structures of early Dynastic tombs had to be removed when Djoser built the Step-Pyramid, at about 2650 BC. To the north of the Step-Pyramid complex are the tombs of early Dynastic elites.

Small Provincial Villages and Towns. The early Dynastic socioeconomic landscape was largely one of small towns and villages. Their internal architecture was probably similar to that of Egyptian villages of the recent past. Settlements of all kinds are basically about feeding people and distributing goods and services. In rural ancient Egypt, life revolved around the village, but occasionally one had to consult the provincial governor to argue a tax case, or participate in religious rites, or purchase goods only available at larger settlements. Every Egyptian village had a town nearby where people could go to use these services.

Recent excavations have revealed several early Dynastic settlements in the Egyptian Delta, at Tell Iswid, Tell Ibrahim Awad, and elsewhere. In later periods the Delta was famed for its vineyards, and these communities may have specialized in growing grapes for wine and herding cattle. This may have reduced the demand for wines from southern Syro-Palestine.

In general, early Dynastic towns and villages were very much like such communities throughout Egypt's dynastic history. Some pit houses appear to have persisted in the Delta, but the majority of communities throughout Egypt were composed of densely packed rectangular mud-brick buildings. Many communities also had small shrines. Most indicate at least some artifact manufacturing, ranging from pottery kilns to flint-tool workshops.

Box 10. Early Dynastic Tombs at North Saqqara

They say the Lion and the Lizard keep
The Courts where Jamshyd gloried and drank deep:
Bahram, that great Hunter – the Wild Ass
Stamps o'er his head, and he lies fast asleep.

(Edward Fitzgerald [1809–1883], *The Rubaiyat of Omar Khayyám*)

Omar Khayyám and many other poets have meditated on the contrast between the glories of imperial courts in life and the solitary, decaying remains of the same kings in death. The early Dynastic tombs at Saqqara provoke similar thoughts. Some of the most powerful and wealthiest people who lived in Egypt between about 2920 and 2575 BC were entombed along this desert ridge, which runs along the Nile's western bank northeast of Djoser's Step-Pyramid at Saqqara. Artifacts bearing the names of First and Second Dynasty kings have been found in tombs at Saqqara, but these are more likely "cenotaphs" – monuments honoring an individual whose remains lie elsewhere – than actual tombs of these kings (their bodies were probably buried at Abydos).

It is a lovely place to spend eternity – although the corporeal remains of few, if any, of the occupants of these tombs survived centuries of looting and excavations. To the east, a few hundred meters below the ridge on which the tombs were built, green fields and orchards stretch to the Nile; beyond that, many kilometers away, are the first low outcrops of the mountains of the Eastern Desert. To the west – land of the dead – the desert extends to the horizon. The elites buried along this ridge at Saqqara probably spent their lives at Memphis, the capital city, a few kilometers to the northeast.

Walter B. Emery (1967) began systematic excavations of these tombs at Saqqara in 1935. Many of the archaeologists of his time simply directed their workmen to rip tombs open with adzes, and then loaded tomb contents on mule carts and sent them off to museums and antiquities dealers. Emery tried to understand how these tombs had been built, and he kept careful accounts of their contents. He found that some of the larger tombs were partially subterranean structures in which the rooms below ground level were chambers that held the body and massive quantities of wealth.

The deceased of Saqqara were supplied in death with many of the things they enjoyed in life. They were buried in their elaborate tombs in wooden sarcophagi, near which were rooms stocked with games and bottles of wine with which to while away eternity, as well as a last meal. These last meals included soup, ribs of beef, pigeon, and other meats, as well as fruit, bread, and cakes (Figure 5.29). Various compartments within the tombs held metal weapons, cloth, and other goods.

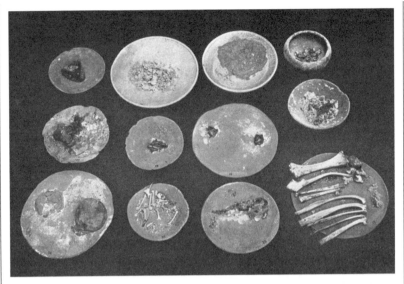

Figure 5.29 Remains of a funerary meal found in an early Dynastic tomb at Saqqara. The bottom image shows the meal as it was found in an intact tomb. The top view shows the elements of the meal laid out on stone and pottery plates. *Source:* Egyptian Museum.

The Roman poet Horace reminds us that "pale death knocks with impartial foot at poor men's hovels and king's palaces," but the dead elites at Saqqara fervently hoped that death was not the end of their luxurious existence.

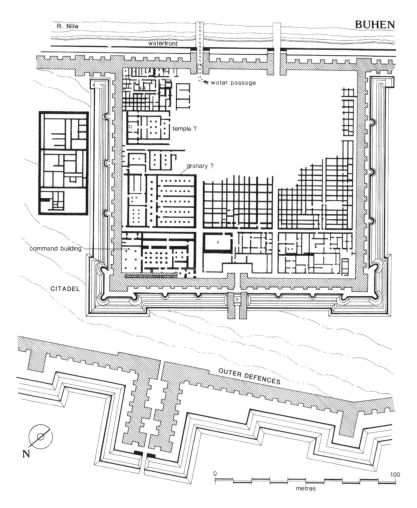

Figure 5.30 Barry Kemp's reconstruction of Buhen in the Middle Kingdom. Early Dynastic structures have been found on this site, and it probably played a role as a port and defensive installation on the Nubian border throughout Dynastic times. *Source:* After Kemp 1989, fig. 60. Reproduced by permission of Barry J. Kemp.

Forts and Trading Entrepôts. Elephantine, near Aswan, is a good example of such settlements. It served as a trading center and a fortress in the latter early Dynastic Period, serving as a conduit for many of Egypt's interactions with Nubia – and via Nubia to the other peoples of northeast and central Africa. Similar outposts were built further south, at Buhen (see Figures 1.1, 5.30) in Lower Nubia, near the Libyan border (e.g., in Dakhla Oasis), the northern Delta (e.g., Mendes), and on the Syro-Palestinian frontier. Communities on the Syro-Palestinian frontier were especially important. Egypt's relationship with people in the early Dynastic Period appears to have been one of almost continuous trade, punctuated by wars.

In summary, by the end of the Second Dynasty, at 2575 BC, Egyptian civilization had realized much of the promise of its Predynastic past. The Old Kingdom Period that followed (Chapter 6) was in many ways an elaboration on early Dynastic cultural themes (T. Wilkinson 1999, 2000, 2004), but Egyptian culture never froze in place and character – changes over time were many and some were profound.

6 The Pharaonic State in Early Maturity (2686–2160 BC)

Introduction

Weni, an official in the administration of the Old Kingdom Pharaoh Merenre (c. 2287–2278 BC), celebrated his accomplishments in pyramid construction in the prideful terms typical of such texts:

His majesty [the pharaoh (Merenre)] sent me to Ibhat to bring the sarcophagus . . . together with its lid, and the costly august pyramidion [i.e., capstone]. . . . His majesty sent me to [Elephantine] to bring a granite false door and its libation stones for the upper chamber of the pyramid. . . . I traveled north with them to the pyramid . . . in six barges and three two-boats of eight ribs. . . . His majesty sent me to Hatnub [a quarry] . . . [to build] . . . a barge of acacia wood of sixty cubits in length and thirty cubits in width. Assembled in seventeen days, in the third month of summer, when there was no water on the sandbanks, it landed at the pyramid . . . in safety.   (After Lichtheim 1973: 21–22)

Weni was just one of the thousands of people whose labors created the splendors of Egypt's Old Kingdom, its great "Pyramid Age." The marvels of this epoch are perhaps best appreciated from the top of the Great Pyramid of Khufu (see Figure 1.4) – a long, hard climb but well worth the detour, as they say. To the east, one can look down on the Sphinx and the simple beauty of adjacent temples and causeways, and to the west – the direction of death in the Egyptian mind – are scores of tombs of the elites, as near to the pharaoh in death as they were associated with him in life. On a clear day, looking south from the top of Khufu's pyramid, one can see a stately sequence of pyramids arcing along the sharp divide of farm fields and desert. Khafre's beautiful pyramid is just a few hundred meters away, its highest levels still clad in a limestone sheath of the kind that once graced all of the pyramids. Menkaure's pyramid stands just south of Khafre's, and from Khufu one can also see the pyramids at Abu Sir. Beyond them are the pyramids at Dahshur and the jagged outlines of Djoser's Step-Pyramid at Saqqara. Lost in the distance to the south on most days are the pyramids at Dahshur and beyond (Figure 6.1)

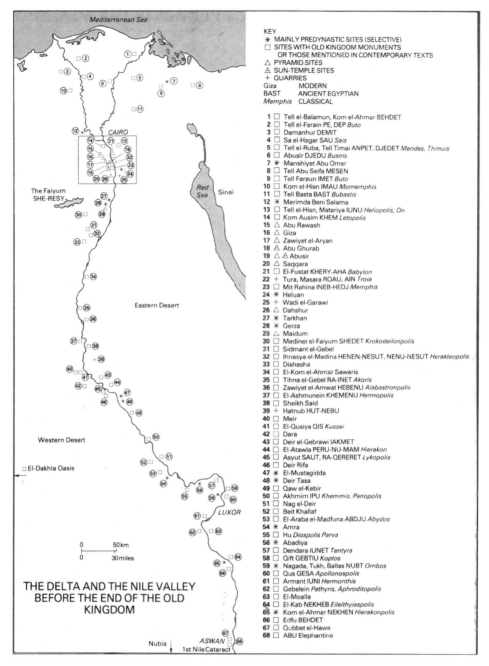

KEY
* MAINLY PREDYNASTIC SITES (SELECTIVE)
□ SITES WITH OLD KINGDOM MONUMENTS
  OR THOSE MENTIONED IN CONTEMPORARY TEXTS
△ PYRAMID SITES
▲ SUN-TEMPLE SITES
+ QUARRIES
Giza   MODERN
BAST   ANCIENT EGYPTIAN
Memphis   CLASSICAL

1 □ Tell el-Balamun, Kom el-Ahmar BEHDET
2 □ Tell el-Farain PE, DEP Buto
3 □ Damanhur DEMIT
4 □ Sa el-Hagar SAU Sais
5 □ Tell el-Ruba, Tell Timai ANPET, DJEDET Mendes, Thmuis
6 □ Abusir DJEDU Busiris
7 * Manshiyet Abu Omar
8 □ Tell Abu Seifa MESEN
9 □ Tell Faraun IMET Buto
10 □ Kom el-Hisn IMAU Momemphis
11 □ Tell Basta BAST Bubastis
12 * Merimda Beni Salama
13 □ Tell el-Hisn, Matariya IUNU Heliopolis, On
14 □ Kom Ausim KHEM Letopolis
15 △ Abu Rawash
16 △ Giza
17 △ Zawiyet el-Aryan
18 ▲ Abu Ghurab
19 △ ▲ Abusir
20 △ Saqqara
21 □ El-Fustat KHERY-AHA Babylon
22 + Tura, Masara ROAU, AIN Troia
23 □ Mit Rahina INEB-HEDJ Memphis
24 * Heluan
25 + Wadi el-Garawi
26 △ Dahshur
27 * Tarkhan
28 * Gerza
29 △ Maidum
30 □ Medinet el-Faiyum SHEDET Krokodeilonpolis
31 □ Sidmant el-Gebel
32 □ Ihnasya el-Medina HENEN-NESUT, NENU-NESUT Herakleopolis
33 □ Dishasha
34 □ El-Kom el-Ahmar Sawaris
35 □ Tihna el-Gebel RA-INET Akoris
36 □ Zawiyet el-Amwat HEBENU Alabastronpolis
37 □ El-Ashmunein KHEMENU Hermopolis
38 □ Sheikh Said
39 + Hatnub HUT-NEBU
40 □ Meir
41 □ El-Qusiya QIS Kussai
42 □ Dara
43 □ Deir el-Gebrawi IAKMET
44 □ El-Atawla PERU-NU-MAM Hierakon
45 □ Asyut SAUT, RA-QERERET Lykopolis
46 □ Deir Rifa
47 * El-Mustagidda
48 * Deir Tasa
49 □ Qaw el-Kebir
50 □ Akhmim IPU Khemmis, Panopolis
51 □ Nag el-Deir
52 □ Beit Khallaf
53 □ El-Araba el-Madfuna ABDJU Abydos
54 * Amra
55 □ Hu Diospolis Parva
56 * Abadiya
57 □ Dendara IUNET Tentyra
58 □ Qift GEBTIU Koptos
59 * Nagada, Tukh, Ballas NUBT Ombos
60 □ Qus GESA Apollonospolis
61 □ Armant IUNI Hermonthis
62 □ Gebelein Pathyris, Aphroditopolis
63 □ El-Moalla
64 □ El-Kab NEKHEB Eileithyiaspolis
65 * Kom el-Ahmar NEKHEN Hierakonpolis
66 □ Edfu BEHDET
67 □ Qubbet el-Hawa
68 □ ABU Elephantine

THE DELTA AND THE NILE VALLEY
BEFORE THE END OF THE OLD
KINGDOM

Figure 6.1. Map illustrating many of the most important Old Kingdom
settlements, pyramids, sun temples, quarries, and other features. Some
important Predynastic sites are also listed. *Source:* Reproduced by permission
of Little, Brown Book Group from Malek and Foreman 1986.

As beautiful as this panorama is today, it is only a pale reflection of what the ancient Egyptians would have seen, for they viewed the pyramids still clad in their gleaming limestone sheaths, and set in their massive original context of temples, causeways, and necropolises. We delight in the apparent Spartan simplicity of Egyptian monumental constructions, but Egyptians painted many elements of them in red, metallic green, and the other colors they loved. One is tempted to see an overall design to these monuments at Giza (Figure 6.2), perhaps a design that was laid out before the first temple, tomb, or pyramid was built there.

This contrast in aesthetics is a superficial reflection of an important analytical point: We cannot entirely understand all aspects of pharaonic civilization in our own terms and values, not even the lively Old Kingdom world about which we seem to know so much. The pyramids are only the proverbial tips of the iceberg, in the sense that they protrude literally and figuratively from the more massive but largely submerged remains of the Old Kingdom state. Today, for example, most of the Old Kingdom capital city of Memphis, home to the dynastic elites whose tombs and pyramids dominate the western bank of the Nile, lies buried under the accumulated silts of millennia of floods and the ruins of later settlements. Hundreds of other Old Kingdom towns and villages, from the Nubian border to the frontier of Syro-Palestine, have been similarly obscured or destroyed.

But we have enough archaeological and textual evidence to glimpse some elements of this brilliant age (Kemp 1983, 1989; Malek 2000)

A Chronology of the Old Kingdom

Compared to earlier periods, the chronology of the Old Kingdom period is relatively well established (Table 6.1). It is based on many texts, as well as archaeological evidence, and although arguments continue about details of this chronology, royal sequence and dates in Table 6.1 are probably close approximations to the actual chronology. Some scholars consider the Third Dynasty to belong to the early Dynastic Period, but it is treated here as part of the Old Kingdom Period because many of the cultural changes associated with the Old Kingdom (e.g., monumental architecture) clearly were elements of the Third Dynasty as well.

Political Geography of the Old Kingdom State. Precise border definition and defense are hallmarks of powerful states, and thus it is significant that the Old Kingdom state occupied almost exactly the same territory as the Predynastic state (and the current one), except for minor border adjustments. Old Kingdom outposts on the Nubian frontier, in the

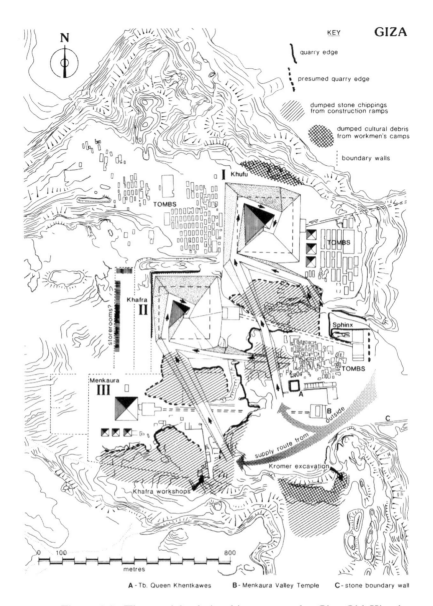

KEY **GIZA**

⎰ quarry edge

⁝ presumed quarry edge

▨ dumped stone chippings
    from construction ramps

▨ dumped cultural debris
    from workmen's camps

⁝ boundary walls

I Khufu

TOMBS

TOMBS

Khafra
II

Sphinx

storerooms?

TOMBS

Menkaura
III

A

B
outside

C

supply route from

Kromer excavation

Khafra workshops

0   100   800

metres

A - Tb. Queen Khentkawes   B - Menkaura Valley Temple   C - stone boundary wall

Figure 6.2. The spatial relationships among the Giza Old Kingdom
monuments. Scholars have long debated whether there is an overall
design or some "meaning" in how these many units were located
relative to one another. This figure shows spiral ramps that may have
been used in the construction of the pyramids. *Source:* Kemp 1989,
fig. 45, after an original drawing by Mark Lehner (1985: figs. 46, 50, 51).
Reproduced by permission of Barry J. Kemp, the Institute of
Orientalistik, and Press Berger & Sons.

260

Table 6.1. A Chronology of Old Kingdom Kings

Third Dynasty (2686–2613)
Nebka 2686–2667
Djoser (Netjerikhet) 2667–2648
Sekhemkhet 2648–2640
Khaba 2640–2637
Sanakht? (uncertain)
Huni 2637–2613

Fourth Dynasty (2613–2494)
Sneferu 2613–2589
Khufu (Cheops) 2589–2566
Djedfra (Radjedef) 2566–2558
Khafre (Chephren) 2558–2532
Menkaura (Mycerinus) 2532–2503
Shepseskaf 2503–2498

Fifth Dynasty (2494–2345)
Userkaf 2494–2487
Sahura 2487–2475
Neferirkara 2475–2455
Shepsekara 2455–2448
Raneferef 2448–2445
Nyuserra 2445–2421
Menkauhor 2421–2414
Djedkara 2414–2375
Unas 2375–2345

Sixth Dynasty (2345–2181)
Teti 2345–2323
Userkara [a usurper?] 2323–2321
Pepy I (Meryra) 2321–2287
Merenre 2287–2278
Pepy II (Neferkara) 2278–2184
Nitiqret 2184–2181

Seventh and Eight Dynasties (2181–2160)
(Names of pharaohs and their dates are uncertain.)

First Intermediate Period c. 2160–2055 BC

After Shaw 2000: 479–480. All dates BC.

western oases (e.g., Dakhla), at the Libyan border, and in the Sinai were physical expressions of the range of power of the central government and its protection of Egypt. Texts indicate that Old Kingdom Egyptians even viewed parts of southwestern Asia as belonging to the pharaoh, although they did not refer to these lands with the vocabulary of colonial administration that was used in later periods (Redford 1986b: 48–53).

Old Kingdom Egypt's *internal* political geography was shaped by the traditional *nome* structure – that is, the provincial sociopolitical entities that were established in the late Predynastic and early Dynastic Periods. Also, the political center of Egypt had been established at Memphis already by about 3000 BC, and in the Old Kingdom the socioeconomic and political center of the country shifted even more toward Lower Egypt. Scores of Old Kingdom communities were established in the Delta, including large towns and cult centers, as well as scores of small farming communities. In many cases these Old Kingdom communities were simply continuations and expansions of settlements that had been established in the early Dynastic Period or earlier, but the Old Kingdom state expanded the Delta's population size and economic importance. The Delta's land routes and sea routes to the outside world also increased its importance in Old Kingdom times.

At the same time that the Old Kingdom Egyptian state was developing, similar polities were evolving in nearby Mesopotamia and the Mediterranean world. Land and sea trade routes linked Egypt to these foreign states, and Egypt was a powerful player in a complex network of international trade.

Ideological Foundations of the Old Kingdom State

It was a wise man who invented God.

(Plato [c. 428–348 BC])

It is useful to begin an analysis of the Old Kingdom state by examining its intellectual foundations because they are the keys to an understanding not only of the rest of the archaeological record but also of the entire culture. We know relatively little about Predynastic religion, for example, but the combination of early Dynastic and Old Kingdom texts gives us sufficient evidence to reconstruct an outline of the main ideological elements of this era.

Ideologies in general are the doctrines and beliefs that form the basis of a polity's social, political, and economic systems; ideologies are the means by which people conceptualize their lives, experiences, and culture in terms of a set of shared assumptions. Pharaonic ideology, like that of most others, was based on assumptions that were largely unexamined; indeed, like modern religions, it was considered largely beyond the reach of empirical analyses. Yet it was on the basis of Egypt's ideological system that Egyptians invested their world with meaning.

Barry Kemp has identified (1989: 20) three particularly important elements in the ideological foundations of the Egyptian state: 1) Pharaohs put great value on their role in ensuring cultural continuity between Egypt's present and its past; 2) Egyptians believed that they had a god-given territorial claim of unity over the land's geographical and political subdivisions; and 3) pharaohs were expected to ensure stability and prosperity through wise and pious government.

Kemp suggests (1989: 107) that ancient Egyptian ideology is a primary example of how ancient states developed and perpetuated state ideologies, how these ideologies expanded at the expense of local religious and political traditions, and how they achieved balanced conceptualizations of the past and the present. He stresses the significance of *myths* in states. He notes, for example, that myth is not necessarily a narrative form of expression; myth statements do not require speech or writing, in that they can be powerfully conveyed through art and architecture. Kemp argues that myths provide a distinctive dimension to the "assault on the senses" that lies at the heart of state ideologies. Egypt's many massive pyramid and temple constructions, for example, were a powerful way to express the pharaohs' relationship to the rest of the population, and to the gods.

But why did ancient Egyptians – and the citizens of other early states – express their state ideologies so relentlessly and pervasively in religious terms, instead of, for example, the largely nonreligious principles underlying American, British, and other contemporary democracies?

The origins of the profound religious consciousness of most people of many cultures remain something of a mystery, but most sociological analyses of human religious consciousness appeal to *functional* arguments. One of the tenets of traditional Marxism, for example, was the idea that a society's socioeconomic base determined the nature of its religion and other forms of ideology, and that, in general, religion was merely the "opiate of the masses." From this perspective, the specific elements in a particular religion are not their most important aspects. It does not matter if you believe that your only comfort in life or death is your Lord and Savior, Jesus Christ, or that you *know* with utter certainty that we are all the progeny of the sun-god Atum-Ra, as the Egyptians believed. All that matters, so far as state origins and functioning are concerned, is that one shares with many others a compelling national theology and political philosophy, as well as adherence to rules and regulations as to how one should live one's life. And from this perspective, the competitive advantage was with cultures that developed belief systems that motivate people in specific, "efficient" directions – as is well illustrated in centuries past, for example, by the link between capitalism and Calvinism.

Religious beliefs are powerful forces that can motivate people to pay confiscatory taxes, fight and die in futile wars, and perform other inherently disagreeable actions simply because they are "moral" and "right," as defined by religions. In this way state religions obviate the necessity of maintaining a massive and expensive police force to coerce the majority into doing what's needed to perpetuate the state. Egyptian religion, with its improbable myths, may seem primitive to us, but it "got the job done." Marx thought that organized religion would disappear with the advent of true communism and social equality, and only the future will tell if he was right. The sharp decline in religious affiliations and observation in much of Western Europe during the past century suggests he may have been prescient.

In any case, ancient Egyptian religion is rather entertaining in its cast of characters and supposed events. It was never set down in a compendium, such as the Bible or the Koran. Siegfried Morenz classified (1992) ancient Egyptian religion as *cultic*, to differentiate it from Judaism, Islam, and Christianity, which he considers *scriptural* religions. Instead, Egyptian religion was a farrago of myths, rituals, and architectural statements.

A thorough review of ancient Egyptian religion is far beyond the scope of this book, but some central ideas are discussed here. Our earliest sources for understanding Egyptian religion come mainly from Old Kingdom texts in tombs and on coffins; we know least about the personal beliefs and practices of ordinary people. It is easy to become lost in the myriad names of gods and goddess, the rituals and rites, and the religious complexities reflected in temple and tomb architecture. And Egyptian religion was a dynamic institution that changed markedly over time and in different areas. But the central *objective* of Egyptian state religion, as ancient Egyptians conceived of it, is starkly clear: It was to counteract the forces of chaos, disorder, and death, and to perpetuate the cosmos in proper order.

Elements of Egyptian Religion

Our birth is but a sleep and a forgetting:
The Soul that rises with us, our life's Star,
Hath had elsewhere its setting,
And cometh from afar:
Not in entire forgetfulness,
And not in utter nakedness,
But trailing clouds of glory do we come
From God, who is our home;
Heaven lies about us in our infancy!
    (William Wordsworth [1770–1850], "Intimations of Immortality . . . ")

The ancient Egyptians would have agreed with Wordsworth's sentiments – at least insofar as the king was concerned, for they believed that the king was indeed a god, a divine reincarnation who came to earth "trailing clouds of glory" from his heavenly home.

In the ancient Egyptian belief, the cosmos began as an undifferentiated ocean. According to creation myths, Atum somehow created himself or was a child of a preexisting god, and he rose out of the ocean, to stand on the primeval mound. The Egyptians would have been reminded of this event every year, when mounds emerged as the Nile floods receded. But there was a sense in Egyptian religion that the first moment of creation is irretrievable, a "big bang," in effect, that will echo for all time throughout creation. The Egyptians represented this event in the form of the *benben*, a miniature replica of the mound of creation, housed in a sacred shrine of the sun at Heliopolis – traces of this site have survived the obliterating effects of modern Cairo. At his principal home, Heliopolis, the sun-god was called Atum, "the All," referring to his preeminence in the pantheon of gods and his connection to all the material cosmos. The Egyptians kept a pyramid-shaped stone at Heliopolis that they believed was the actual stone on which Atum first stood at the moment of creation, and replicas of this stone were elements in many temples and pyramids in the later Old Kingdom.

In later periods, obelisks (Greek for "needles"), too, were commemorations of the first moment of creation. Hewn from single stones, they were placed in pairs in front of some temples. Their form perhaps originated from the Egyptians' observations of "sun pillars," formed when atmospheric ice crystals create an illusion in which the morning or evening sun seems to be a single beam shining directly downward.

At some point in Egyptian religious history and in some theological concepts, Ra and Atum were fused into a single deity, "Atum-ra." Atum proceeded to separate light and darkness and to introduce order and structure in chaos so that this world and all its elements came into being. It was in this creative act that Atum first expressed the principle of *maat*: He replaced chaos with order.

Many ancient religions incorporated sun worship in the state religion. Sun worship was particularly important in the Egyptians' concept of the connection between pharaohs and the sun-god. Every day they saw the sun set, with the sun becoming only a pale reflection of its brilliant noonday self, and then they saw it rise every day with its strength renewed. This observation led directly to the concept of renewal and regeneration.

By masturbating or possibly by sneezing or spitting (the texts are ambiguous), Ra brought two children into the universe, the gods Shu (associated with the preserving effects of light and air) and Tefenet (associated with the corrosive effects of moisture). These in turn created Geb and Nut, the earth and the sky. Shu and Tefnut became the atmosphere. They stood on Geb, who became the earth, and raised up Nut, who became the sky. Geb and Nut later had two sons, Seth and Osiris, and two daughters, Isis and Nephthys. The first nine gods, from the creator Atum through Isis and Nephthys, constituted the *Ennead*, or "The Nine of Heliopolis."

Osiris succeeded Ra as king of the earth, helped by Isis, his sister-wife. Seth, however, hated his brother and killed him. Isis then embalmed her husband's body with the help of the god Anubis, who thus became the god of embalming. Isis resurrected Osiris, who became king of the netherworld, the land of the dead. Horus, who was the son of Osiris and Isis, became king of the earth.

The relationship of Seth and Osiris is a good example of the complexity of the gods and events that the Egyptians believed produced and operated their universe. When Osiris became king of the world, for example, his brother Seth was jealous and plotted his revenge. In post–Old Kingdom interpretations of this myth, Seth held a banquet for Osiris and other gods, at which time he showed them an exquisite coffin that any right-thinking Egyptian would want for his own funeral. Seth promised it to the god who best fit inside the coffin. Osiris fitted it perfectly and lay down inside it. Seth suddenly slammed the lid shut and eventually threw it in the river. Isis searched everywhere for Osiris's body, eventually locating it at Byblos, in Syro-Palestine. Isis revived Osiris, but then Seth butchered him into many pieces and threw them into the Nile, where they were dispersed throughout the Valley and Delta. Isis managed to collect most of the gory bits and, with the aid of Nephthys, reassembled Osiris until he had sufficient life to inseminate Isis with a son, Horus. Osiris became king of the underworld, leaving Horus and his mother to deal with Seth. When Horus became a man he was locked into continual struggle with Seth for dominion over the world. Finally, a tribunal of gods, weary of the wrangling, hit upon a happy compromise: Horus would rule over the agricultural lands of Egypt, and Seth would rule over the deserts.

Egyptian gods could split into two gods, to represent two different aspects of the same underlying divinity, and different gods could be fused into a single entity. A key to understanding the multiplicities of deities and their baroque interactions is various kinds of *creative force*, or potency. To fashion the cosmos from the original void, Atum used *Heka*, a form of magic that protected him, the cosmos, and other people from the forces of annihilation. The act of creating something material was accomplished by using the force *Hu*, "the divine word."

Old Kingdom texts tell us much about the formation of deities but surprisingly little about the creation of people and the human world, as well as our place and purpose in the whole scheme of things. Egyptians seem to have believed that people derived from the tears of Ra – perhaps tears of joy. They also believed that the god Khnum fashioned people (and other animals) out of clay on his potter's wheel and put them in their mother's womb. There is some suggestion that the gods considered people to be the "cattle of Ra," and that the world was created for people. But there is some sense in these religious texts that the gods created people to do the heavy lifting for the gods – to provide the gods with food and rituals necessary for their perpetuation (Mathieu 1986: 499–509).

The Egyptians celebrated male sexual potency, worshipping Min, a god pictured with an erect penis. Women's sexuality was also celebrated, in the form of the goddess Hathor. This goddess, worshipped throughout Egypt, was represented as a cow tending her calf when the Egyptians wanted to express her attribute of motherly love. When they wanted Hathor to represent women's sexuality, they pictured her as a beautiful woman.

As noted in Chapter 5, various Egyptian gods were represented in different forms, sometimes as animals, other times as human torsos with animal heads, and on occasion as fully human. The characteristics of the god Ra, for example, were expressed in the form of the head of a hawk, which was sacred to him because of its swift flight across the sky. Hathor, the goddess of love and laughter, was given the head of a cow. Anubis sported the head of a jackal because these animals ravaged the desert graves in ancient times. Gods associated with death were Mu, depicted as vulture-headed, and Thoth, who was portrayed with the head of an ibis. Because of the gods to whom they were attached, the sacred animals were venerated and the sacrifices of these animals were intended to carry messages to the gods. Ibises and baboons, for example, were thought to report to Thoth, cats to the goddess Bastet, and so on.

Concepts of the Soul

For God, our God is a gallant foe that playeth behind the veil.
Whom God deigns not to overthrow hath need of triple mail.

(Ezra Pound [1885–1972])

To most of us the universe can be ultimately unknowable, and even a frightening concept. Here we are, and to all evidence very much alone. Modern astrophysics is a beautiful science that explains so much about the cosmos, but it gives few clues as to what it all means and strategies as to how we can confront the infinity of time and space within which we live so briefly.

Unlike the ancient Egyptians, most of us may have lost our fear of ghosts and goblins, but the loss of faith in such myths and mysteries comes at a price: Unlike the ancient Egyptians, many of us do not have a comforting faith in the notion that we are in a constant but winnable war between order and disorder, heaven or hell. The ancient Egyptians also had to face life's existential burden, and some concluded with the same sentiment that the Roman poet Horace expressed as *Carpe diem, quam minimum credula postero*, "Seize the day, put no trust in tomorrow." But as much as they enjoyed life, they were concerned with doing good works and trusting the gods to give them a happy afterlife.

Most ancient Egyptians were convinced of the power of prayer and ritual. They made offerings, for example, to Hapy, god of floods, in hopes of a good annual inundation, and to many other gods as well. Some of their texts express doubts, worry, and dark broodings that the gods might judge them too sinful for eternal life and thus damned to an eternity as a *mut*, a dead, virtually nonexistent person. Thus, many wore and were buried with amulets to ward off the manifold evils of this world.

Pharaonic Egyptians believed that death was a dismal process in which one's life force was disrupted, but death also *liberated* a person, in a sense. By shuffling off this mortal coil, they believed, elements of one's soul were set free. Again, most of our evidence about Egyptian religion comes from New Kingdom times, but Egypt had great cultural continuity, and Egyptian royalty and some elites were assumed to have souls by Old Kingdom times. We do not know when or if the concept emerged that all people have a soul.

The god Khnum was thought to manufacture each person's *Ka*, a form of one's soul, at the same time that he manufactured the actual person out of clay on his potter's wheel. The Ka was one's life force or personal genius. Although it was created at the same time as one's physical body, it had no separate existence until the time came to "go to one's Ka," as physical death was sometimes described (Allen 2000: 79–81). The Ka could not exist without the body, and so every effort had to be made to preserve the corpse. After death the Ka could inhabit the statue of the deceased in the tomb and could move about the tomb and pass through the "false door" to "eat" the offerings that were regularly placed there.

In addition, wood or stone replicas of the body were put into the tomb, presumably to provide a habitable body in the event that the mummy was destroyed. Thus, the more statue duplicates in his or her tomb, the more chances the dead person had of eternal life.

Each person also had a spirit/soul called the *Ba*, which seems to have been an expression of a person's individual personality and distinctive mentality. The Ba could assume any form it wished and move anywhere in the cosmos – so long as it eventually returned to the person's corpse. The Ba could visit the "real" world of the living and bring back food and other provisions for the corpse of the person the Ba belonged to. It could also communicate with the living through dreams and visions, and it was the means by which a dead male could experience sexual orgasm via his mummified penis.

One's Ba and Ka eventually were reunited. One's Ba was associated with one's *Akh*, a soul/spirit that severed all connections with one's physical body at death and lived in celestial isolation. Another common symbol concerning life and death is the *ankh*, the meaning of which is unclear – although it seems to refer generally to some life force.

After leaving the tomb, the souls of the dead were beset by innumerable dangers, and the tombs were therefore furnished with instructions for how to pass the foreseeable eternity. From at least New Kingdom times onward, these instructions were in the form of the Book of the Dead – which was derived largely from Old Kingdom coffin and tomb texts and other documents. But the earliest known copies of the Book of the Dead date to several centuries after the end of the Old Kingdom, and we don't know how much of its contents is relevant to Old Kingdom religion. This guidebook consisted of charms designed to overcome dangers. After arriving in the kingdom of the dead, the Ka was judged by Osiris, the king of the dead, assisted by various other divinities. The Book of the Dead also contained instructions for proper conduct before these judges. If the judges decided the deceased had been a sinner, the Ka was condemned to hunger and thirst or to be torn to pieces by executioners. If the decision was favorable, the Ka went to a paradise where grain grew high, and where existence was a glorified version of life on earth. All the necessities for this paradisiacal existence, from furniture to food, were therefore put into the tombs. As a payment for the afterlife and his benevolent protection, Osiris required the dead to perform tasks for him, such as working in the heavenly grain fields. Even this obligation could, however, be obviated by placing small statuettes, *ushabtis*, into the tomb to serve as substitutes for the deceased.

Another benefit of the Egyptians' sense of dying as a "good career move" was that after death, individuals had the unalloyed pleasure of wreaking vengeance on those who had mistreated them in life, and also of interceding with the gods on behalf of living people whom the deceased liked. Living people could write to the deceased by leaving letters at the tomb, asking them what problems they were experiencing. The deceased understandably found it difficult to write in return, but they could express troubles and anxieties by stimulating dreams in the living.

All in all, the Egyptians viewed death as a depressing and highly inconvenient interruption of one's earthly life, but they had ways of mitigating death and even enjoying some of its after-effects.

To place Egyptian religion in a larger context, Shmuel Eisenstadt (1986) divides antiquity into eras defined in terms of the relationship of the *sacred* and *mundane*. In early Egypt, for example, the national religion included many mundane elements: The gods were imagined in semihuman forms, and each had many human characteristics and engaged in many of the same routine activities as people, such as quarreling, marrying, and giving birth. Only in later religions, such as Christianity, Judaism, and Islam, were the transcendental and mundane characteristics of gods and people radically separated. In the Christian concept of God, for example, the supreme deity is assumed not to engage in the prosaic activities of the living.

Still, some traces of the mundane remain in most religions. The God of the Old Testament, for example, seems to have been – or perhaps is – rather irascible and vindictive. He is recorded as having sent bears to eat forty-two children who had mocked his prophet Elisha's baldness (II Kings:2) – which seems harsh punishment for simply shouting "Go up, old bald-head." And in the Old Testament books of Leviticus and Deuteronomy, God commands his faithful to stone to death people whose "crimes" range from being a "stubborn" son to homosexuality.

The monotheism of the Judeo-Christian and Islamic religions has been considered an "advance" by some scholars, in the sense that all three converged on what they suppose to be the central truth of a single, invisible, omniscient, and omnipotent divinity. Eisenstadt describes the period in which a civilization's religion made the transition from a mundane focus to a sacred one as an "axial age."

Measuring "progress" in religions, however, is a somewhat dubious undertaking. As A. Bernard Knapp (1988: 102–108) and others have noted, the flexible polytheistic religion of pharaonic Egypt had many functional virtues, in that it enmeshed Egyptians in a supportive ideology that gave them a sense of being able to mitigate the world's ills, and later to enjoy a pleasant afterlife.

Relentlessly functional interpretation of religions reduces their richness and significance to cost–benefit equations, and obviously, no religion can be accurately and entirely understood as a set of dependent variables that only *reflect* underlying, causal, "independent" variables, such as environmental, technological, and socioeconomic factors. Religions can be strong causal agents, at least in a proximate sense, of cultures and their histories. It was on the basis of his religious convictions, for example, that King Akhenaten reformulated Egyptian ideology and settlement patterns (c. 1352 BC). Such major transformations are difficult to explain adequately in terms of ecology, demography, economy, or technology.

Divine Kingship, Incest, and Maat

And that inverted Bowl we call the Sky,
Where under crawling coop't we live and die,
Lift not thy hands to *It* for help – for it
Rolls impotently on as Thou or I.
            (Edward Fitzgerald, [1809–1883] *The Rubaiyat of Omar Khayyám*

No ideological principle was more fundamental to ancient Egyptian society than that of *divine kingship*. The ancient Egyptians thought of the king as the holder of a divine office, and that – at least by the Fifth Dynasty – he was considered to be the embodiment of the god Horus, a direct descendant of the god Ra. Our main textual sources for trying to understand the concept of "divine kingship," however, are ambiguous about the relationship of the king to the gods. It appears that the ancient Egyptians had no trouble distinguishing between the divinity of the office – the job the king did – and the entirely human character of the pharaoh himself. At least in the later periods, the ancient Egyptians certainly knew that the kings were not omniscient. But these texts do not stress the fallibility of kings, and every king apparently felt compelled to assure his subjects repeatedly of his divinity by taking names such as "Son of Ra." By the end of the Fifth Dynasty, each king had five great names: his Horus name; the appellations meaning "Two Ladies" (a reference to the titular deities of Upper and Lower Egypt); a Golden Horus name; a prenomen (taken at the time of accession to the throne and the name that was inscribed in cartouches); and a nomen. In artistic representations, the king was typically shown as he was at vigorous young or middle age, and equipped with a flail, crook, striped headdress, Double Crown, and other royal regalia. In accession to the throne, strict primogeniture was the ideal, but this principle could be adjusted to the absence of a first son of the chief wife and other exigencies.

Not only did the concept of divine kingship confer power and privilege on the pharaoh; it also obligated him to act justly and in accordance with the will of the gods. Central to this idea is the concept of *maat* (Teeter 1997). Maat was associated with the goddess Maat, the daughter of Ra. The meaning of maat for ancient Egyptians seems to have been an amalgam of the ideas that we express as "duty," "truth," "order," "justice," "right dealing," "propriety," and so forth. Maat as an ethical concept goes back at least to the Third Dynasty, and probably centuries earlier. It is associated with the idea of the world and universe in an ideal state. The king's primary responsibility was to further maat throughout his realm. He could compel citizens to pay taxes, labor on pyramids, or die in battle, but in turn he was expected to fund the construction of temples and religious rituals, to root out corruption, right wrongs, repel invasions, enrich Egypt by invading foreign lands, prevent suffering and starvation, and, in general, maintain this world in an imitation of the balance and order of the eternal world of the gods.

In sum, being pharaoh was no sinecure. The king had the burdensome duty of intervening with the gods to make sure that the Nile's annual floods were conducive to productive farming, that the seasons followed one another in timely fashion, and that his people lived in peace and harmony, untroubled by revolts, invaders, and pestilence.

Among the names assumed by various Old Kingdom rulers was Iry-ma'at, meaning something like "Performer of maat" and "He who puts maat into practice" (Kemp 1983: 76). And an Old Kingdom text, *Instructions for Kagemni*, orders that one do "maat for the king [for] maat is what the god loves. Speak maat to the king [for] maat is what the god loves" (Teeter 1999: 411–413). Also, an Old Kingdom ruler recorded that "I was . . . one beloved of his father, praised by his mother, loved by all his brethren. I gave bread to the hungry, clothing to the naked. . . . I was one that said what is good and repeated what is desirable; never did I make any evil accusations to one in authority against any persons, [for] I desired it to go well with me with the great god" (quoted in Brewer, Redford, and Redford 1994: 13)

The ordinary Egyptian, too, was expected to live in harmony with the precepts of maat. It was the principle that allowed petitioners to expect legal justice, widows and orphans to expect provision by the wealthy, and other people to look for fair treatment in ordinary commerce. Egyptians believed that the cosmos was especially threatened by disorder at three times: sunset, the low point of the annual cycle of the Nile flood, and the death of a pharaoh (Trigger 1993: 91). The pharaoh was the primary guardian of the cosmic order, but it was everyone's responsibility to help by behaving in accordance with maat, especially at these times.

Not everyone adhered to the principles of maat at all times, of course, and there were numerous codified punishments for the guilty. For example, one text states: "As for any commander of the [local] fortress, and scribe of the fortress, any inspector belonging to the fortress who shall board a boat belonging to the Temple and shall take [ivory, ebony?], leopard and other animal skins . . . punishment shall be meted out to him in the form of one hundred blows, and he shall be fined . . . in terms of the value of the goods at the rate of eighty to one" (after Kemp 1989: 238).

The notions of divine kingship and maat were bound to the idea of royal blood. One of the first duties of the pharaoh was to perform burial rituals for his predecessor, for only in that way could he validate his claim to the throne (Shafer 1997). Many ancient societies in which power was concentrated in a single person considered the lineage of the royal family as something to be kept "pure." Thus, many societies developed degrees of intermarriage that in our day are considered unhealthy and even criminal. Incest was practiced by some of the elites in ancient Egypt, Hawaii, and elsewhere, but it was specifically banned by Hammurabi's famous code of laws for ancient Babylon. And an ancient Greek dramatist largely viewed it as an evil that had tragic consequences. Incest, by our standards, may not have occurred in the Old Kingdom – the earliest known mentions of it are from later periods. If it was practiced in the Old Kingdom, it was probably in the form of brother-sister marriage among royalty, and perhaps father-daughter relationships. Incest is, in fact, an extreme form of endogamy (marriage within defined social or familial groups), and one traditional anthropological explanation of endogamous marriage is that it protects the socioeconomic and political interests of elites in class-based societies. The Egyptians may have seen royal incest in terms of a parallel to the incestuous divine marriages they ascribed to various gods and goddesses.

A Brief Political History of the Old Kingdom

The following historical synopsis does not do justice to a dramatic and impressive age (see Grimal 1992 and Malek 2000 for overviews). Every Old Kingdom pharaoh who managed to rule for a significant period probably saw at least a few bloody battles, some won and some lost. He and his subjects would have lived through both years of rich harvests, and the associated sense of being blessed by the gods, and years of poor harvests, and the attendant implication that something was wrong with his relationship to the deities. And Old Kingdom court intrigues probably rivaled those of medieval Italy, as the pharaoh's various families maneuvered to become the favored lineage from which the next pharaoh would be selected, and various sons jostled in line to succeed the king.

John Wilson noted that Old Kingdom Egypt's written language had no words for "government" or "state" as impersonal terms, conceived apart from the pharaoh: "[T]he Egyptian 'theory of government' was that the king was everywhere and did everything. . . . The fiction of direct delegation of duty and of a direct report to the king was impossible to maintain in practice; but in the theory of government it was no fiction, it was a working reality" (1951: 79).

Some pharaohs, nonetheless, actively participated in the administration of the state. For example, some directed the establishment of new communities in Egypt, and they did so for a variety of secular motives, including consolidating royal power, producing wealth to underwrite the expenses of mortuary cults, stimulating economic development, and defending the frontiers. A pharaoh of the First Intermediate Period, for example, forcefully recommended building towns as a means to counteract political fragmentation and inefficient organization in the eastern Delta, which, he lamented, was being subdivided into rival provinces and towns (Badawy 1967: 105). It is likely, however, that Old Kingdom kings concentrated their administrative efforts on religious affairs and delegated most other responsibilities to a vizier (who was sometimes a king's son not in line to inherit the throne).

The Third Dynasty

Djoser, a Third Dynasty king, is famous even in our age because of his association with the Step-Pyramid at Saqqara (Figure 6.3). The design of this – the first great stone building known in human history – is usually attributed to his vizier, Imhotep, whose reputation as a scholar, community leader, and priest increased over the centuries after his death. He was thought to have had the power to mediate between gods and people, particularly with regard to medical problems.

Pyramid building, simply in the sense of stacking stone blocks on one another, is not a particularly brilliant leap of aesthetic creativity. But when one places the pyramids in their cultural context and considers their evolution, they are, indeed, impressive. The great size and stunning architecture of the Step-Pyramid, for example, reflects the relationship

Figure 6.3. King Djoser's Step-Pyramid at Saqqara. This is the
first known monumental stone building in the world. Its design appears
to have evolved out of the context of stacking "mastabas" – the
rectangular tombs of the late Predynastic and early Dynastic – on top
of one another. *Source:* Photograph by Robert J. Wenke.

of pharaoh and state to subjects: It is one of the first and most vivid
indications of the permanent and preeminent role of kingship in Egyptian society. Any commoner who saw the pyramid and its many massive
associated structures could not help but sense his or her minuscule
personal significance in relation to the great wealth and power of the
king, and to be intimidated by this disparity.

The design of the Step-Pyramid changed several times as it was
being built, and it and its many associated structures were built over
tombs and other buildings of the early Dynastic Period. When finally
completed, it had six steps, or levels, and measured 140 by 118 by 60
meters.

The pyramid was set in a rectangular enclosure wall measuring 545 by
277 meters. As is the case with so much of Egyptian architecture, the
detailed designs of buildings and other elements within the enclosure
wall at Saqqara are nearly unintelligible without knowing their various
meanings and purposes. There is still much we do not know about
the Step-Pyramid complex, but some elements seem significant. The

Step-Pyramid's design reflects its origins in mastaba tomb constructions, such as those found at Early Dynastic Abydos. This design suggests that it was built to appear as if six successively smaller mastabas were built, one on top of the other.

The courtyard is marked at intervals with cairns, or stone markers, that were probably used to mark off a course that the king had to run during the *Sed*-festival, to demonstrate his continued strength and vitality. The *Sed*-festival was apparently celebrated after thirty years of a pharaoh's reign, and after that at three-year intervals (authorities differ on this point). The theme of this ceremony appears to have been the king's regeneration: He symbolically died and was reborn during these festivities. Within the enclosure walls, on the eastern side of the complex, is a series of beautiful stone buildings arranged along both sides of the court. Like movie sets, these "buildings" are just facades (Figure 6.4). They are decorated with renderings in stone of timber, reed matting, and other perishable materials that were probably used in the construction of

Figure 6.4. The enclosure wall around Djoser's Step-Pyramid featuring "facade" buildings. Their "doors" don't open. Some stylistic elements in this photograph illustrate the architectural continuation of using stone replicas of palm logs and reeds to evoke the first Egyptian temples. *Source:* Photograph by Robert J. Wenke.

the earliest Egyptian temples – an example of the many architectural elements that were meant to express the connection of the present to the past that is so important in Egyptian ideology. At one end of the courtyard at Saqqara is an elevated stone "throne." One can imagine the king sitting on this throne, under a canopy, participating in the pageantry of the Sed-festival. It is unclear, however, where this festival was celebrated in the Old Kingdom Periods; perhaps it was celebrated at Memphis and the constructions at Saqqara were simply symbolic representations of these events

The Fourth Dynasty

One of the signs of change in the transition from the Third to the Fourth Dynasty was the shift of the royal necropolis from Saqqara to Meidum and Dahshur (see Figure 6.1). This may reflect the ascendancy of a pharaonic family different in origin from the preceding dynastic line.

In the initial phases of the Old Kingdom, the state government appears to have grown progressively stronger and more centralized. The royal family of the Fourth Dynasty was probably actively involved not just in its theoretical political and religious institutions but also in the practical administration of the state.

The first ruler of the Fourth Dynasty appears to have been Sneferu (also known as "Snofru"), one of the greatest builders in Egyptian antiquity. In his long reign Sneferu seems to have been everything an Egyptian pharaoh should be, at least according to the descriptions of him preserved in later texts. These (probably romanticized) sources describe him as immensely popular with his people. He is depicted as genial, a virtue the ancient Egyptians would consider in no way diminished by the fact that he apparently sent rapacious military expeditions into Nubia, Libya, and Sinai, killing many people and taking thousands of prisoners, many herds of cattle, and other riches. These military raids were powerful expressions of the pharaoh's power and his ability to ensure the continual flow into Egypt of both exotic and ordinary goods. Giraffes and monkeys imported from Nubia, for example, were particularly popular in Old Kingdom Egypt (for display rather than for culinary purposes, one hopes), as were ostrich eggs, panther skins, ebony, ivory, and incense. Sneferu ordered his tomb to be built in a pyramid at Meidum, and he ordered the construction of several other pyramids and monumental works.

Sneferu's successor was Khufu (the Greeks knew him as "Cheops"), whose pyramid at Giza is the largest of them all. Herodotus related a (rather dubious) story told to him by Egyptians that Khufu drove his people to an "extremity of misery" by the forced labor he inflicted on them in order to build his pyramid:

But to such a pitch of wickedness did [Khufu] come that, when in need of money, he sent his own daughter to take her place in a brothel, instructing her to charge a certain sum – the amount they did not mention. The girl did what her father told her, but she also got the idea of leaving some memorial of her own; and so she asked each man that came to her to make a present of one stone . . . and from these stones, they say, a pyramid was built mid-most of the three, in front of the great pyramid. Each side of it measures one hundred and fifty feet.   (*Histories II* [trans. Grene 1987: 185–187])

This pyramid still stands, but whether or not it was paid for with the wages of sin is unknown.

Other texts, in contrast, suggest that Khufu was a traditional oriental monarch but good-natured and amiable toward his inferiors. One text recounts that Khufu was so impressed by the powers of a magician named Djedi that he ordered a prisoner to be decapitated so that he could have the pleasure of watching Djedi magically reattach the head and revive the man. Djedi wisely suggested that it would be irreligious to do such a thing (Grimal 1992: 70–71).

At least two of Khufu's sons, Djedfra and Khafre, reigned after him. Khafre's pyramid complex is the second largest at Giza. He was followed by his son, Menkaura ("Mycerinus" to the Greeks), who is commemorated by the third pyramid at Giza. Menkaura appears to have been followed by Shepseskaf, the last Fourth Dynasty king. He broke with tradition by not building a pyramid; rather, his tomb is a huge ($100 \times 72 \times 19$ m) sarcophagus-shaped structure.

The texts that describe the later pharaohs of the Fourth Dynasty hint at some dynastic struggles and continuing concerns with the theological ideas at the foundation of the state. The shifting of the royal necropolises between several sites, including Abu Roash, may reflect attempts to break with the past or to express divergent religious views. Successive pharaohs may also have had fewer resources at their control; after Kahfre the general trend in the Old Kingdom was toward smaller pyramids, some of which were never finished.

The Fifth Dynasty

The Fifth Dynasty apparently began with King Userkaf, scion of a branch of the royal family different from that of the Fourth Dynasty. Userkaf built his pyramid at Saqqara, east of the Step-Pyramid, but on a much smaller scale than Third and Fourth Dynasty kings. Egyptian artifacts dating to Userkaf's reign have been found at various sites in the Aegean area, and other evidence reflects voluminous trade between Egypt and this region.

Userkaf was followed by Sahura, who expanded Egypt's trade with its neighbors both in the Mediterranean world and in Nubia and "Punt," which was probably located in what is now eastern Sudan and Eritrea. Products of tropical Africa, such as myrrh, gold, ivory, ebony, resins, and leopard skins, were imported in large quantities during the Fifth Dynasty.

Under Sahura's successors, some elites appear to have grown richer and more powerful, probably at the expense of the central government. The elaborate tomb built at Saqqara by a late Fifth Dynasty court official named Ti, for example, would have been beyond the means of anyone but members of the royal family in the Fourth Dynasty. Ti was a hairdresser to the royalty, as well as controller of the farms and stock that belonged to them. His wife was related to the royal family; thus he, too, was no doubt rich.

Bruce Trigger (1983) suggests that a slow but continuous expansion and elaboration of society and economy in the Old Kingdom may have been accompanied by the growing complexity and power of provincial administrative institutions. In this context it is interesting that until the late Fifth Dynasty, we find only meager evidence of writing in provincial tombs and towns. Although writing was just one element in the functioning of the Egyptian bureaucracy, the apparent unimportance of writing in the provinces at this time is interesting. It suggests that the full power of the central state was not applied to these areas, at least in the form of administration by literate officials, until after the Fourth Dynasty. Perhaps, however, the relative scarcity of writing in provincial tombs was primarily due to the fact that few provincial elites could afford lavishly decorated tombs, and the fact that their correspondence, though possibly voluminous, was in the form of hieratic documents on papyrus, most of which would have long since decayed.

The Sixth Dynasty

There is some evidence in the Sixth Dynasty of growing competition and even tension between the central government and the provincial rulers. King Teti chose as one of his names Sehetep-tawy, meaning "He Who Pacifies the Two Lands," which was typically assumed by kings who reunified the country after disruptions. Manetho records that Teti was assassinated, perhaps by his successor, Userkara, but the evidence is – typically – ambiguous. Teti apparently tried to solidify the loyalty of the nobles by marrying his daughter to Mereruka, his vizier, and by permitting a broader distribution of power and wealth.

Userkara's successor, Pepy I, is reported to have married two noble-women of Abydos in what may have been an attempt to foster the unity of Upper and Lower Egypt. Pepy I's successor, Merenre, continued his father's policies and appears to have successfully expanded Egypt's power in Southwest Asia and Nubia. In his autobiography, which was inscribed on his tomb's walls, Weni (mentioned at the start of this chapter), a high official in the administration of the first kings of the Sixth Dynasty, recounted that King Merenre appointed him to lead an army of many tens of thousands of soldiers to fight the "Asiatic sand-dwellers." He records that his army invaded five times, landing by ship behind the enemy lines, and killed tens of thousands, took many prisoners, burned villages and towns, and cut down orchards and vineyards.

Other texts record that Merenre established vassals in Nubia and supported them militarily to protect the caravan routes that brought sub-Saharan Africa's riches to Egypt. Harkhuf, governor of Aswan, recorded his trips into the "Land of Yam," and, of one expedition, said that he returned home with "three hundred donkeys laden with incense, ebony . . . oil . . . grain, panther skins, elephants tusks, throw sticks, and all sorts of good products" (Lichtheim 1973: 25–26).

The next ruler was Pepy II – the king with which this book began (Chapter 1). Someone in Pepy II's court wrote a letter to the leader of a royal expedition that had reported that it was returning with a "pygmy" from central Africa, in which Pepy II had taken a strong and rather bizarre interest:

> You have said . . . that you have brought a pygmy . . . from the land of the horizon-dwellers. . . . Come north to the residence at once! Hurry and bring with you this pygmy . . . alive, [hale], and healthy . . . to delight the heart of the king Neferkare who lives forever! When he goes down with you into the ship, get worthy men to be around him on deck, lest he fall into the water! When he lies down at night, get worthy men to lie around him in his tent. Inspect ten times at night! My majesty desires to see this pygmy more than the gifts of . . . Punt. [If] you arrive at the residence and this pygmy is with you live, hale and hearty, my majesty will do great things for you.   (After Lichtheim 1973: 26–27)

Before Pepy II, provincial rulers and elites had decorated their tomb walls with texts that celebrated their connections to the royal family and the central government; but after the sclerotic Pepy II's last years came a loss of equilibrium between a powerful court and the aspirations of provincial elites. Texts suggest that provincial elites began to stress their own accomplishments in their tombs of this period; other documents suggest that the centralized government at Memphis, which had ruled Egypt as a united country for a thousand years, was apparently weakened at this time and that rival kings ruled from Middle and Upper Egypt. The Old Kingdom period ended with the Seventh and Eighth Dynasties (c. 2150–2134), a time in which there were several kings, about whom we know little. It seems clear, however, that they were not able to manage the entire state, as Pepy II did, however ineffectually.

The First Intermediate Period (c. 2156–2055)

Turning and turning in the widening gyre
The falcon cannot hear the falconer;
Things fall apart; the center cannot hold;
. . .
The ceremony of innocence is drowned;
The best lack all conviction, while the worst
Are full of passionate intensity.
Surely some revelation is at hand;
Surely the Second Coming is at hand.
The Second Coming! Hardly are those words out
When a vast image out of *Spiritus Mundi*
Troubles my sight: somewhere in sands of the desert
A shape with lion body and the head of a man,
A gaze blank and pitiless as the sun,
Is moving its slow thighs, while all about it
Reel shadows of the indignant desert birds.
The darkness drops again; but now I know
That twenty centuries of stony sleep
Were vexed to nightmare by a rocking cradle,
And what rough beast, its hour come round at last,
Slouches towards Bethlehem to be born?

       (William Butler Yeats [1865–1939], "The Second Coming")

Yeats must have been referring to the Sphinx in this passage, and he used the imagery to convey a sense of decline and eventual rebirth of a different world- and lifeview (some scholars believe he was bemoaning the waning of Christianity).

At about 2160 BC, Egypt seems to have entered about a century of political fragmentation and conflict known as the First Intermediate Period. Textual evidence from this period is sparse, but Manetho (writing in the third century BC) hyperbolically described dynastic succession in the First Intermediate Period as "seventy kings in seventy days."

Ipuwer, an Egyptian official of this period, lamented the chaos of the times in similar sentiments, remarking that "see now, things are done that never were done before. The King has been robbed by beggars. . . . What the pyramid hid is empty."

We know, too, that pyramid construction almost ceased toward the end of the Old Kingdom and in the First Intermediate Period, reappearing in the Middle Kingdom on a much-reduced scale. Nonetheless, in some areas of Upper Egypt, at least, the First Intermediate Period involved no apparent change in the richness of the tombs (Seidlmayer 1987). Moreover, Naguib Kanawati's assessment (1977) of texts and tombs is that they show little evidence of a decline in royal power in the late Old Kingdom. And Matthew D. Adams's research (2005) on the First Intermediate Period town at Abydos suggests that the basic economy and social organization of this community remained much the same as in the Old Kingdom communities, even in the apparent absence of a powerful central government.

So, perhaps the "breakdown" of the First Intermediate Period affected only parts of the country and mainly in the form of conflicts over royal succession. Nonetheless, there seems to have been a decline in the richness of mortuary cults at that time, and perhaps in the amount of land directly controlled by the crown that supported these cults.

From the perspective of historical analysis, periods of cultural breakdown are as interesting as periods of cultural "evolution." In our own age we have seen periods of prosperity interrupted by wars and economic depressions. Why do "things fall apart"? In the case of Egypt, the First Intermediate Period "breakdown" – if that was what it was – probably was the result of a complex interaction of many factors. Complex political systems usually collapse because of a coincidence in time and space of malign factors, not just single events. Throughout its history, dynastic Egypt, for example, periodically experienced low Nile floods, epidemics, crop diseases, inept leadership, bureaucratic inefficiencies, unsuccessful military campaigns, ruinous struggles for power that verged on civil war, and other ills. Occasionally these setbacks coincided in sufficient intensity and combinations to throw the whole state and country into turmoil.

Thus, for example, if Pepy II's reign was close to its reputed fifty to ninety years, corruption may have become deeply entrenched among the bureaucracy, and Pepy's leadership may have declined in his long senescence. But other problems may have been well beyond his control. There is evidence of climatic changes in the North African and Mediterranean area a few centuries before and after 2000 BC. Shifts of the monsoon rains in central and east Africa in this period may have greatly affected Nile flows, and thus Egypt's prosperity. Also, it is possible that reduced rainfall could have forced people on Egypt's borders to migrate into the Valley and the Delta, resulting in social conflict and economic stresses. Karl Butzer (1976: 17; also see Hassan 1988) estimates a 30 percent decline in Nile discharge during the late Old Kingdom and links this to the collapse of the political order after Pepy II's death.

Another factor may have been the accumulating expenses of maintaining and supplying mortuary cults for dead pharaohs (Kemp 1989: 143). This continual financial hemorrhaging may explain in part why pyramid construction slowed and eventually ceased.

But perhaps the most important factor was the competition between provincial authorities and the pharaoh and his state apparatus. Even in preindustrial societies such as Old Kingdom Egypt, the cost–benefit calculations of balancing the state's interests against those of the provincial powers were complex and always in a state of flux. On the one hand, the "mayor" of an Old Kingdom village in the Delta, for example, would have been in a better position to make important socioeconomic decisions for his village than a bureaucrat living at Memphis. The mayor would likely have been a lifelong resident of his community and thus have had great experience in determining how much land could be cultivated on the basis of that year's flood level, which crops did best in which specific plots, and so forth. On the other hand, a bureaucrat in the administrative center at Memphis would have been in a better position to know, on the basis of tax receipts and other documents, which crops were likely to be in short supply for the country as a whole, which crops had the best market value in international trade, and the like. Thus, local, provincial, and national socioeconomic concerns and functions had to be balanced and integrated.

Highly centralized states that attempt to administer directly the whole country are in danger of creating a bureaucracy so large that ever-greater taxes are needed to support it. Such states lose some of the efficiencies of local decision making based on rational economic perceptions and incentives (as the late, unlamented Soviet Union and China's "Great Leap Forward" so definitively demonstrated). But if a state is too decentralized and does not suppress competing provincial powers, it is in constant danger of disintegrating into competing groups or provinces (e.g., the former Yugoslavia and contemporary Iraq).

In a perfectly designed state, the people with the best information and incentives to make local decisions would be left to do so. But their decisions would be constrained by a provincial and national administrative bureaucracy that could monitor and manage the whole system in order to meet long-term national needs that might not be evident or important at the village level.

At some point in Egyptian history, the position of *nomarch* (the governor of a nome) became hereditary. This created a situation in which the provincial authorities had incentives to amass wealth for both the king and themselves. The king appointed an administrator on the condition that he prove to be competent and be able to return to the state a share of the wealth produced. At the same time the provincial governor could become a feudal lord of sorts. But this relationship was inherently unstable, in that the central government and provincial rulers continually competed with each other for wealth and power.

The First Intermediate Period "breakdown," then, may have been a period of administrative breakdown and social ills, but in the long term it may have been a period of constructive reformulation of state administrative structures, as the administrative and economic relationships between the central government and provincial elites evolved in efficiency – as evidenced in the Middle Kingdom and New Kingdom resurgences.

Whatever the ultimate causes of the First Intermediate Period's cultural changes, by about 2055 BC Egypt was once again united, and, although there were other subsequent "Intermediate Periods" of great cultural change, the basic organizational elements of pharaonic civilization persisted until they were transformed by the forces of Christianity and then Islam.

Aspects of the Old Kingdom State

Old Kingdom texts and its archaeological record provide much information about the nature of Egyptian civilization in this period, but we must remember that Egypt changed greatly over the course of the Old Kingdom, particularly in investments in massive pyramid constructions.

Economic Institutions

The Old Kingdom government was divided into five major departments – treasury, agriculture, royal archives, works, and justice – all under the direction of the vizier. The main business of the treasury, which the Egyptians called the "Double Granary" (a reference to Upper and Lower Egypt), was to collect taxes. The taxation system was apparently thorough and efficient: As Kemp notes, revenues could be assessed even on "canals, lakes, wells, waterbags, and trees. . . . [One] must imagine a network of government agencies spread throughout the country, attempting by bureaucratic methods total assessment and management of resources" (1983: 80).

The department of agriculture was divided into two sections, one mainly concerned with livestock, the other with crops. Within these agencies were many administrators, scribes, and other officials. The royal archives' main responsibility was the collection and cataloging of deeds of land ownership, contracts, wills, and royal decrees. The justice department was concerned with the interpretation and application of royal decrees and judgments.

In complex societies, such as Old Kingdom Egypt, there is an inherent economic efficiency in a system in which some people spend much of their time learning complex skills and then performing them well. But it works only if nonspecialists, such as farmers, can supply these occupational specialists with food and other goods and services.

In today's world, for example, surgeons, computer scientists, and even Egyptologists need to spend so many years learning their specialties and then practicing them that they have relatively little time to explore in detail other aspects of human knowledge and other professions. Such extreme occupational specialization comes at a significant cost to the liberal education of these specialists. Nonetheless, if one were to undergo, for example, brain surgery, most people would prefer a surgeon who has spent most of his or her life preparing for and practicing such a procedure, despite the costs to that surgeon's command of French or knowledge of nineteenth-century English art and literature. In most contemporary industrialized societies, an increasing amount of the food and other basic resources needed to support occupational specialists is produced by a decreasing number of farmers, miners, and others in similar occupations.

A list of Old Kingdom occupational specialists would have included, among others, doctors, scribes, potters, soldiers, musicians, stone masons, architects, sculptors, painters, metalsmiths, fishermen, taxmen, priests, judges, and accountants, as well as the many bureaucrats who were required to coordinate and integrate the activities of all these specialists. If functional specialization and integration are such potent mechanisms of cultural evolution, we must ask, why? Throughout the past some cultures persisted and dominated their worlds, while others did not. Why did some cultures succeed and other groups fail? A key requirement for deriving benefit from occupational specialization and functional interdependence is administrative integration. Considerable advantages can be found in a system in which expert administrators are able to match the supply of commodities to demand, and to organize specialists to attend to those tasks that no one individual can perform. The defense of a state's frontiers, for example, requires not only a large military force but also administrators who can position troops, collect intelligence, plan strategy, and provision the troops.

All this might sound like a sermon in praise of capitalism and theocratic oligarchies, but it is not. We must recognize the excesses of greed that seem to drive market economies and the sacrifices that individuals must make to become highly skilled professionals. But occupational specialization and markets are powerful things. Markets, in both the ancient Egyptian and modern sense, work at a basic level because they efficiently match the supply of goods and services to the demand for them. Markets also remove obsolescence (as anyone with a two-year-old computer can attest) and offer incentives for radical changes of many kinds. China's impressive current economic growth rate is a striking example of the power of markets and capitalism, even in an inhospitable ideological environment.

Old Kingdom Egypt had only primitive forms of markets and other capitalist features, but they were sufficient to create one of the ancient world's richest preindustrial states. Various theories of history, including those of Karl Marx and his apostles, suggest that to understand a society and an historical epoch, we should begin by analyzing the goods and services that are produced and how they are controlled and distributed – or as the Latin phrase expresses it, *cui bono* ("to whom the benefit?").

Numerous documents provide information on such matters as the variety and ranks of Old Kingdom central government administrators (Baer 1960; Strudwick 1985) and tax levies on farms and craftsmen. However, we do not have the rich troves of ancient economic texts from Egypt (Strudwick 2005) like those we have from Mesopotamia, and thus many details of the Egyptian economic system remain unclear. Archaeological as well as textual evidence for most of the rural Old Kingdom economy is still sparse (Figure 6.5).

Western capitalist economic principles and concepts are not generally appropriate for studying preindustrial cultures and epochs, such as Old Kingdom Egypt. Before about 300 BC, for example, Egyptians did not circulate "money" in the sense we know it. Moreover, all wealth belonged in theory to the pharaoh. Thus, Egyptian economic activities took place in a religious and political context very different from our own. Still, the Egyptians were not free of the basic constraints of economic factors, and much of what they did economically looks familiar to us. Individuals schemed to maximize their personal wealth by various means, including evasion of taxes.

Money, in our sense, is just a convenient mechanism for exchanging goods and services. The Egyptians bartered goods and services directly, without the use of money per se, but they did use standard weights of gold, silver, copper, bronze, and other goods in exchanges in ways that are not completely different from a monetary system. Values for some goods were closely computed and often standardized, so that if one wanted to exchange, for example, flint sickle blades for a pair of sandals,

Figure 6.5. An Old Kingdom (Sixth Dynasty) tomb relief in the tomb of Mereruka, Saqqara. A line of farm managers is rendering accounts. On the left are two seated scribes. The power of the state in economic transactions is evident in the kneeling posture of the managers and the man forcing them into it. *Source:* Werner Forman / Art Resource, NY.

the parties to the exchange knew the value of each in terms of other commodities – and in terms of equivalent weights of precious metals. The value of weights of silver, bronze, and copper fluctuated somewhat in response to supply and demand, indicating aspects of the Egyptian economy that approached a monetary system. Price lists indicate that the price of labor, too, was rather precisely calculated. The price of the materials to make a bed, linen tunic, or other item was, of course, less than the finished articles – an early expression of the "value added" tax in the terms of modern European economies.

"Wealth," then, in ancient Egypt, as in all societies, consisted of the ability to command goods and services. Marxian and various other kinds of analyses begin with the simple question: Who owns the means of production and the goods and services produced? So much of the wealth of Old Kingdom Egypt was agricultural that among the first questions we must ask is who owned the land, and – more important – who owned its agricultural produce? There were at least three kinds of Old Kingdom agricultural land ownership: estates directly owned by the crown; estates that belonged to pious foundations – that is, land or other resources used to produce wealth that went to support maintenance of temples, tombs, and mortuary cults, or to the central government; and estates held by private individuals and subject to taxation. Kemp notes that in ancient Egyptian texts we see no references to "self-made men of trade or of manufacture, no merchants or money lenders, or makers of other people's tombs" (1983: 82). Yet texts indicate that individuals could, in fact, rise in status and wealth through loyalty to the state and by virtue of special talents.

One incentive for accumulating wealth was to afford rich private burials. In ancient Egypt not only could you "take it with you"; you had to, in fact, if you really wanted to enjoy eternity. Personal accumulation of wealth was also necessary for dowries for one's children, to ensure that they made advantageous marriages (another example of the intricate socioeconomic calculus that Jane Austen described in her wonderful novels). Wealth could be inherited within families, and so a person could help provide for his or her children; throughout history this in itself has been a powerful stimulus for wealth accumulation.

One could also enjoy wealth in the usual ways: elaborate clothes, rich foods, beautiful houses, a life unclouded by the need to work, and several wives. (Even wealthy women, however, did not have the option of several husbands – at least at the same time.) And personal wealth was also important in gaining the favor of the gods through donations to temples and other religious institutions.

Even in a preindustrial economy, such as ancient Egypt's, there were financial rewards to foreign trade – most of which appears to have been monopolized by the state. Egypt probably imported more than it exported, at least in "luxury goods." In the Mediterranean world some of the best lumber came from Lebanon; the most productive farmlands and fisheries were in Egypt; the best pistachios and other nuts were in Anatolia, Iran, and Syria; concentrations of gold, silver, and other metals were in several specific areas; and there were many other concentrations of foods and industrial resources. Thus, a "common market" including Egypt and its neighbors could and did benefit everyone, and during the long history of the preindustrial Mediterranean world there was a long-term increase in trade and cultural interaction – although this long-term evolutionary trend was often punctuated and reversed by wars.

Egypt's participation in foreign-exchange networks is marked most clearly by the many exotic goods we find in tombs. But we have little evidence about the exchange of cereals, oils, wines, dried fish, pickled meat, and other basic goods that were traded but are less visible to us because they did not preserve well. Egypt's contributions to international trade were probably mainly in the form of linen, preserved fish, cereals, wine, beer, and other perishable commodities, and perhaps gold from the Sinai mines.

We know little about the extent to which the state government actually managed the economy – as opposed to expropriating profits from it and regulating commercial exchange. The state government could affect the national economy by creating settlements in the Delta, sending expeditions into Nubia, Libya, and so forth, and periodically reassessing the tax rolls. Later pharaonic texts indicate that the state monopolized trade in certain commodities, such as natron, the naturally occurring chemical salts used in mummification. And the state could also affect prices by periodically releasing commodities, such as grain, from government warehouses. But in general it does not seem as if the state rigidly set prices or strictly regulated commodity production.

Kemp notes (1989: 257) that New Kingdom texts refer to men with the title of *shuty*, which apparently means "trader" or a commercial agent of some kind, some of whom sailed the Nile or coastal waters in boats, buying and selling many different goods. Whether most of them operated on their own or as agents for wealthy estates or other institutions is unclear. Their status was low, but they performed a vital task, and some doubtless got wealthy – or at least made their sponsors wealthy. Whether or not the same kind of bartering took place in the Old Kingdom is uncertain but seems probable.

In many ancient societies, slavery was an important source of wealth. But slavery in Egypt seems to have been rare until New Kingdom times, and even then almost all slaves appear to have been foreigners, some of whom were captured in battle, and even they appear to have had certain basic rights and privileges.

Old Kingdom Settlement Patterns

The economic structures and functions described previously were reflected in Egypt's settlement patterns – the relative sizes and spatial distribution of communities.

Cities, Towns, and States. Bruce Trigger (1993) labeled Old Kingdom Egypt a "territorial state," a term he used to distinguish it from the "city-states" of Mesopotamia and elsewhere. "City" has been defined in many different terms, but generally it is used in reference to communities that are not only relatively large but also functionally complex, in the sense that many different socioeconomic and political functions occur there (Sjoberg 1965).

The idea of Egypt as a large state but one with few large cities has a long history (J. Wilson 1951), but recent evidence suggests that this concept must now be reassessed. The traditional view is that Old Kingdom Egypt had only one large city, Memphis, with the rest of the population distributed throughout hundreds of villages and small towns.

But Mark Lehner and Zahi Hawass (Hawass, Lehner, and Wetterstrom 2006) have directed excavations of the town associated with the construction of Menkaura's pyramid at Giza. It seems evident that at least twenty thousand people lived there for all or much of the year (Figure 6.6) (note that here, too, we must assume that the soccer field and modern houses overlie hundreds of hectares of Old Kingdom occupations). Few or no cities in Southwest Asia could match that number. And there is substantial evidence of similar towns at Abusir, Dahshur, and elsewhere. The population of these communities might have been partly seasonal, but there was likely also a large permanent group of administrators, artisans, and others. Preliminary excavations revealed many small bakeries and other features that seem to be the remains of facilities for preparing food for large groups of people. Along the desert edge of this community are scores of small stone and mudbrick tombs that appear to constitute the community's cemetery.

Is the estimated population of twenty thousand at Menkaura significant within debates about the concept of "urbanism"? Cahokia in Illinois, for example, is estimated to have had a population of tens of thousands clustered around a huge earthen pyramid, with a lavish burial inside. But the evidence indicates that more than 95 percent of these people were just subsistence farmers. The point is that as large as Cahokia was, it did not incorporate the many functions of an ancient state, in craft production, occupational specialization, a powerful centralized bureaucracy, and so forth. In contrast, the town at the base of Menkaura's pyramid included most or all of the elements of a city, complete with hundreds of workshops, many commodities imported from elsewhere in Egypt or other countries, administrative documents in the form of clay sealings and other texts, and a cemetery stratified by degrees of wealth. Surely some of the Menkaura pyramid city's population was seasonal. There seems no reason to doubt that much of the construction was done when the annual floods covered croplands. But Menkaura's pyramid community seems to have been a complex functioning city throughout the years.

Evidence about the degree of urbanization in major Old Kingdom communities in general is fragmentary and ambiguous. Memphis, for example, has long been considered Old Kingdom Egypt's socio-economic and political center, and its largest and most functionally diverse settlement. Old Kingdom texts refer to *Inebhedi*, or "white wall" – perhaps a reference to Memphis's fortifications. Many ancient Egyptian cities were protected by stone or mud-brick walls, and Memphis may have been protected by limestone fortifications that looked like massive white walls to anyone approaching by land or river. Texts also allude to

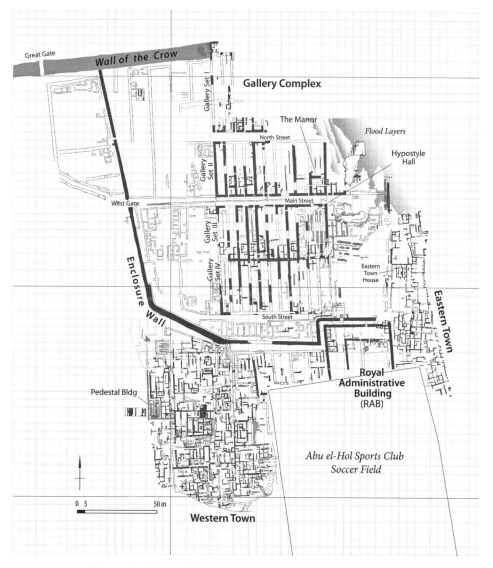

Figure 6.6. Part of the settlement near Menkaura's pyramid. Considering how much of the site is buried beneath the sports complex and the contemporary village, it is clear that tens of thousands of people must have lived here. There are barracks, temples, cemeteries, workshops, kitchens, and many other activity centers. Until excavations began in the 1980s, almost every ancient structure evident here was buried beneath deep layers of sand. Mark Lehner, Wilma Wetterstrom, and others on the Giza Plateau Mapping Project have produced evidence that has forced scholars to reexamine the idea of Ancient Egyptian urbanism. *Source:* Courtesy of Mark Lehner.

Hutnub, or "gold site," at Memphis, possibly a reference to royal workshops that produced gold artifacts there, and to an area of the city called *Pernefer,* which probably referred to the dockyards. Memphis probably incorporated large areas along the river where ships moored and their cargoes were loaded, unloaded, and warehoused. And many palatial residences for the nobility may lie under the silts and modern structures that now cover Old Kingdom Memphis. There is every reason to believe that Old Kingdom Memphis was very much like the extension of this city that Lehner and Hawass have unveiled, but many times larger.

Here, too, data deficiencies greatly restrict our inferences (Jeffreys 1985). We know very little about the size and functional complexities of what we presume were the largest Old Kingdom communities – those at Memphis, Abydos, Mendes, and Hierakonpolis, for example. If Old Kingdom Egypt's degree of urbanization actually did contrast with most other early states, it was probably for simple ecological reasons, and particularly the Nile Valley's ecological uniformity and the Nile's transport potential. Memphis, according to legend, was established by imperial fiat, but its location could be predicted by any locational geographer: It lies at the juncture of the Nile Valley and the Delta, the best place in the country from which to administer the state. With the transfer of governmental institutions and power to Lower Egypt in the early Dynastic and Old Kingdom Periods, Memphis probably became the largest settlement in the whole country – if one includes subsidiary communities that were built alongside many of the pyramids

Hierakonpolis is an example of the larger towns in Upper Old Kingdom Egypt. It seems to have been a walled complex of tightly packed mud-brick houses and other structures. Hierakonpolis was one of the most important communities in all of Egypt in the Predynastic and early Dynastic Periods, and it remained a major town in the Old Kingdom, although it probably began to lose importance and population as the balance of power shifted from Upper to Lower Egypt. Only a small fraction of the Old Kingdom settlement at Hierakonpolis has been excavated, and much more of the Old Kingdom occupations is buried under alluvia and later structures. The huge enclosure walls may have contained a temple community, with the main areas of the town unwalled or encircled by simple mud-brick walls. Hierakonpolis and other Old Kingdom sites imply some degree of central planning and design, but most of these communities were not precisely laid out on rectangular or square plans.

Comparable to Hierakonpolis in size and importance in the Old Kingdom is the Delta site of Mendes (see Figure 1.1). It was a large and diverse town throughout the Old Kingdom Period, boasting a major cult center, hundreds of residences of various sizes, and a large cemetery for priests (Hansen 1967; Wenke and Brewer 1992; Redford 2004; Matthew J. Adams 2007). Mendes was once situated on a large branch of the Nile and no doubt played an important role in Egypt's internal and foreign economy. In ancient Egypt the most "efficient" settlement pattern – in socioeconomic and political terms at least – was one in which about 90 percent of the people, including mainly farmers, fishermen, and herdsmen, lived in widely dispersed small villages, and the other 10 percent of the people, including the government administrators, scribes, priests, generals, goldsmiths, and other specialists, were concentrated in larger towns on the Nile or on the Nile's Delta branches, so that they were directly connected to the central government at Memphis and to the larger world of the Mediterranean.

To cultivate land profitably, a farmer in a preindustrial economy could not regularly walk or travel by means of pack animals more than about five to ten kilometers to his fields, else the energy expended in traveling to them and farming these areas would surpass the energy repaid in the way of produce. But in northern Mesopotamia, available farmlands extended for many kilometers away from the rivers, and in southern Mesopotamia, canals brought water to large areas of land that received too little rainfall to be farmed successfully. Thus, Mesopotamian communities could grow in population simply by extending the area of cultivation and by importing grain and other commodities from the towns and villages that surrounded them.

In the Nile Valley, in contrast, areas suitable for farming were narrowly constrained by the Nile floodplain, and even in the Delta, Egyptians had to build canals to extend the area of farming beyond the narrow areas along the main Nile branches. Thus, efficient farming in the Nile Valley was best accomplished by people living in small villages spaced roughly equally along the river and along the Delta's main Nile branches.

In both the Nile Valley and Mesopotamia, at least some towns were necessary as central administrative points for tax collectors, garrisons for soldiers, and other specialized economic and political activities. But Egypt had less need of such centers, since it had such an effective transport network in the form of the Nile, along which goods, services, and information could easily and cheaply be transported. Also, Egypt's riverine environment was highly similar throughout the country, making local exchange of food and products less important than was the case in Mesopotamia. Egypt had few concentrations of natural resources, except in the form of premium farming land in the largest flood basins along the river, basalt and other stone outcrops, and other minerals and metals from the deserts.

As noted previously, however, we simply cannot ignore the impact of ideological forces on ancient Egyptian settlement patterns (Hassan 1992; Wengrow 2006). Hierakonpolis, Abydos, and other settlements were large and important communities for centuries after the political capital was moved to Memphis and the focus of Egypt's economy and political calculations moved, through the Delta, onward to the Mediterranean and Southwest Asian worlds. These Upper Egyptian towns remained important in part because of their ancient connections to Egyptian religious ideas.

We must also remember that ancient Egyptian settlement patterns changed over time. Many new villages, for example, were established in the Delta during the Old Kingdom, some as "pious foundations" – estates whose agricultural production was sent to Memphis or other religious centers to support the maintenance of cult centers. These could be for gods, kings, or private individuals, and in theory, the proceeds from them were used for this purpose forever. One must assume, however, that as the memory of the individual supported by the pious foundation faded, or as economic circumstances changed, the revenues from these foundations were diverted to living individuals or to cult centers favored by the living.

In sum, Old Kingdom Egypt may have fit Trigger's notion of a "territorial state," but this argument cannot be confirmed by excavated residential areas. And most explanations of why Egypt's settlement patterns may have differed from Mesopotamian and other city-states are based on simple functionalist arguments grounded in ecology (see Chapter 7).

As for other communities, Donald Redford notes (1992: 8) that in early hieroglyphic writings, the Egyptians used at least five terms to describe settlements: 1) a word usually translated as "city," whose root meaning is a collection of reed huts surrounded by a protective wall; 2) a word translated as "town," which actually means "to touch" and refers to locations on the riverbank where boats landed; 3) a word for "mound" that implies a settlement on a rise above the floodplain; 4) a word referring to "clan" or "family" that describes small hamlets of kin groups; and 5) a word meaning "seat" or "abode" of a god, which may imply some kind of temple within a community.

Small Provincial Towns and Villages. Recent archaeological research at Kom el-Hisn was reviewed in Chapter 3. Kom el-Hisn lies in the western Delta (see Figure 3.15), about ninety kilometers from the present Mediterranean coastline. In antiquity the site would have been near a branch of the Nile, and the coastline may have been much closer. Kom el-Hisn is thought to have been the ancient locality "Im3w," mentioned in texts since the Fifth Dynasty (Zibelius 1978: 35–36; Moens and Wetterstrom 1989). (The archaelogical evidence from Kom el-Hisn is summarized in Chapter 3.)

Hundreds – probably thousands – of small towns and temples were part of Old Kingdom Egypt's settlement patterns, and examples of these have been excavated from Dakhla Oasis to Elephantine, from Hierakonpolis to Memphis, and throughout the Delta and into the Sinai.

Frontier Towns and Entrepôts: Elephantine and Buhen. Elephantine, an Old Kingdom community on an island in the Nile near Aswan, was located in one of the most beautiful areas of Egypt. Even today the Nile here is a limpid blue, lined by luxuriant palm groves and bracketed by high stone cliffs. Elephantine, which was named for its role as a center for trade in elephant tusk ivory, functioned throughout its long history mainly as a fortress and a commercial center for the First Upper Egyptian Nome, or province, which bordered Nubia. It was first permanently occupied, apparently, soon after about 3000 BC, perhaps because at about that time the Egyptian state formed and began to define its frontiers precisely and defend them. Just south of Elephantine is the First "Cataract," a stretch of rapids that acted as a buffer between Egypt and Nubia. Throughout the dynastic era there was extensive trade between Egypt and Nubia, but the First Cataract marks the point at which this trade was no longer possible via ships. Old Kingdom Elephantine boasted a substantial community that included a temple and shrine (Kaiser et al. 1988). Some of the local Old Kingdom nobles were buried in tombs on the cliffs across from Elephantine, along the western shore of the Nile.

Deep into Lower Nubia lies the fort at Buhen (see Figure 1.1). Small areas of Old Kingdom Buhen have been excavated, but most of what we know of the site comes from the Middle Kingdom, and some Old Kingdom materials probably underlie these later structures. Buhen may have played some role in the reconstruction of the Egyptian state after its contraction in the First Intermediate Period (Kemp 1989: 169–172).

Old Kingdom Pyramid Complexes

The boast of heraldry, the pomp of pow'r,
And all that beauty, all that wealth e'er gave,

Awaits alike th' inevitable hour,
The paths of glory lead but to the grave.

(Thomas Gray [1716–1771])

The most dramatic evidence of the power and wealth of the Old Kingdom socioeconomy is the awesome remains of mortuary cults – the pyramids, temples, and tombs of Egypt's elites.

After the epiphany one usually experiences upon first seeing the pyramids, the visitor typically begins to wonder why they were built, the means by which they were built, how much time was required to build them, and their cost. How and why they were built remains quite unclear, and we have only tangential evidence about how much time was required to construct each of these monuments, but as to questions about their costs the answer is "lots."

From the typical photographs of the three pyramids of Giza, one might think they stand in splendid isolation, but in reality there are twenty-one large pyramids on the west bank of the Nile within a twenty kilometer span between Giza and Dahshur (see Figure 6.1). They vary greatly in size and cost.

All lie amidst many temples and tombs. Almost all are encircled by modern towns and villages. Much of the meaning with which the ancient Egyptians invested these monuments is lost because no ancient texts have been found that clearly tell us how or why pyramid complexes were built. Hieroglyphic texts painted on tombs of kings and queens, the *Pyramid Texts*, and on coffins, however, tell us at least something about the lives and thoughts of the people entombed inside them. One inscription in a tomb chapel states: "As for anyone who shall lay a finger on this pyramid and this temple, which belong to me . . . he will be judged by the [nine deities], and he will be nowhere, and his house will be nowhere. He will be one who is proscribed, one who eats himself" (after Lehner 1997: 31). Mark Lehner, John Nolan, Melissa Hartwig, Herbert Haas, and I faced this unhappy prospect because we sampled so much of the Old Kingdom archaeological record for datable Carbon-14 samples (see Chapter 3)

The lack of explicit texts that tell us why and how the pyramids were built has resulted in a great profusion of ideas on this subject – many of them strange (e.g., Tompkins 1971). Anyone who has ever published a book or article about the pyramids quickly learns that the world is full of "pyramidiots" – people who have bizarre ideas about them, such as those who attribute the construction of the pyramids to aliens from outer space, or know for a fact that a worldwide conspiracy has suppressed the secrets of libraries that lie under the Sphinx.

A convincing assortment of evidence of all kinds suggests, however, that the pyramid complexes were intended mainly as machines to convey dead kings safely into the afterlife and to ensure them a comfortable life there. They must also have played a complex and vital role in expressing the power of the state in visual terms that the lower classes could appreciate. Also, the arrangement of the pyramids, their associated cemeteries, the capital city of Memphis, and other elements of the Egyptian state in the Giza-Saqqara area reflect a real, functioning society, but of the dead, not the living. If one carefully considers the whole pyramid complex at Giza, for example, one can see what appear to be realizations in stone and mud brick of a complex view of the cosmos and the nature of human existence.

There are some textual references to procuring the raw materials for the pyramids, but not much else in the way of documents about them. As a result, reconstructing the methods by which the pyramids were built and inferring their precise meaning to the ancient Egyptians remain open questions. The following discussion, thus, is simply a compilation of informed speculation. We must also remember that what to many scholars are bizarre ideas about the pyramids simply are not testable, given the current research climate.

Why Did the Egyptians Build Pyramids?

The mighty pyramids of stone
That wedge-like cleave the desert airs,
When nearer seen, and better known,
Are but gigantic flights of stairs.
      (Henry W. Longfellow [1807–1882], "The Ladder of St. Augustine")

As noted elsewhere in this book, the Egyptians believed that a happy eternal life after death depended to some extent on the physical preservation of the deceased's body and its store of goods to sustain him or her in the afterlife. So the kings' motivations in building pyramids likely had as much to do with their aspirations for eternity as their desire to leave a lasting monument to their greatness. Later pharaohs saw that not even the greatest pyramid could provide protection from looters, and this probably explains why they had their tombs carved out of the heart of mountains, with entrances that were hidden after their entombment.

But why did the Egyptians build pyramids for these tombs and not some other structure? Various mystics have suggested that the pyramid shape focuses cosmic energy, and thereby helps preserve organic materials, improve sexual experiences, clarify mental functions, and so forth. A more compelling but utterly mundane explanation, alas, can be found in engineering principles. To begin with, the huge pyramids built not only in Egypt but also in Mesopotamia, China, Mexico, North America, and elsewhere do not reflect transatlantic contact or touristic forays of "ancient astronauts." Rather, given preindustrial materials and construction techniques, a pyramid is one of the few shapes by which monuments could be built to great height and sustain their own weight. Some of the earliest Egyptian pyramids were rebuilt after initial attempts failed, indicating that it took the Egyptians some years of experimentation with proportions and techniques before they developed a stable form that could be built on a massive scale.

The Egyptians could and did build large structures in forms other than pyramids. The Old Kingdom Pharaoh Shepseskaf, for example, built a tomb in the form of a giant rectangular-shaped structure measuring an impressive 100 by 75 by 19 meters. The Egyptians could have built a great wall, like that of ancient China, with labor and material costs equivalent to the pyramid building, or Stonehenge-like structures like those of the early Britons (who built Stonehenge at nearly the same time that Khufu's pyramid was constructed); so the answer to the question of why they chose the pyramid form is not just that it was an obvious solution to an engineering problem. We can attempt to combine ideological and practical considerations to explain the pyramid shape, but here too there are difficulties. Ancient Mexicans, Mississippians, Chinese, and others all built pyramids, and there is little in their ideologies to suggest that they employed the pyramid shape because it represented the primeval mound of creation or a stairway to heaven.

For the Egyptians, however, the pyramid shape may symbolize the mound of earth the Egyptians believed was the first land to emerge as the primordial floods receded at the dawn of creation – a theme deeply interwoven in Egyptian theology and philosophy. Or the pyramids might have been seen as an artificial horizon – "mountains" against the sky – through which the sun would seem to pass as it set on certain days of the year, when viewed from the temples east of the pyramids. Similarly, not only was the pyramid's angle of inclination (most are between 50° and 60°) structurally sound; it may have been intended as a functional "stairway," as various scholars (e.g. Edwards 1961) propose, for the deceased king to ascend, to be transformed into a celestial deity.

The dimensions of the pyramids accord with mathematical relationships that the Egyptians may have regarded as aesthetically appealing. Later texts suggest that the Egyptians had calculated an approximation to the mathematical value of pi (π), and the height of Khufu's pyramid (perhaps the most geometrically perfect of them all) is equal to the perimeter of its base divided by 2π. One can find this ratio in many constructions in ancient Egypt, but it is not certain that Old Kingdom Egyptians ever related it to their aesthetics; this ratio may have been an accidental result of their measuring techniques and the mechanics of building.

In addition to the *conscious* decisions that motivated the Egyptians to build, their construction also had profound effects on the Egyptian socioeconomy. Some scholars (White 1949), considered pyramids and similar monuments to have served important functions as "make-work" projects that kept the labor force organized, disciplined, and less inclined to political revolt. Similarly, Barry Kemp has suggested that Egyptian pyramid building provided "the economic stimulus broadly equivalent to 'built-in obsolescence' in modern technological societies" (1983: 87).

The important point here is that there may be sound economic and political explanations for episodes of pyramid construction in different cultures in terms other than just the unique ambitions of particular rulers and productive economic systems. This issue is discussed in Chapter 7.

Why Did the Egyptians Build the Pyramids Where They Did?

The pyramids were royal tombs, and most of them were built close to the place where the royalty lived, at the capital city of Memphis and at other places along the Nile. They were constructed on the Nile's west bank rather than the east because the Egyptians associated the west and the setting sun with death. Also, the western edge of the Nile Valley comprises several enormous limestone formations perfect for pyramid construction. The limestone there is relatively soft and easy to quarry and yet strong enough to support the great weight of these structures; and this limestone formation dips down toward the river, providing easy access by boat to the construction site. The Nile provided a means for transporting the southern granites (used in the temples associated with the pyramids and in the burial chambers) and the fine-quality limestone from Tura, on the east bank of the Nile, just a few kilometers south of present-day Cairo. Recent construction in the area of the Giza pyramids has revealed what may have been quays and other port facilities along what would have been the river's western bank in the Old Kingdom.

Individual pharaohs probably selected sites for their pyramids on the basis of a variety of religious and/or political motives. Ra'djedef's unfinished pyramid at Abu Roash, about ten kilometers north of the Giza group, for example, may have been built there because it was across the river from the great religious center at Heliopolis. The pyramids also cluster somewhat according to dynasty and royal family.

How Did the Egyptians Orient Pyramids and Build Them on a Nearly Perfect Level Plane?

One simple way of orienting the pyramids would have been to chart the rising and setting of stars. Ancient architects could have created an artificial level horizon by building a level mud-brick wall. Then they could have looked through an aperture of some kind (such as a forked stick) that was oriented vertically with a plumb bob to plot the rising and setting of an appropriate star. Simply bisecting this arc would have given them reasonably accurate indications of the cardinal points.

The largest pyramid of all, that of Khufu, was built on limestone leveled to a horizontal plane with an accuracy of about 18 millimeters, and each of its sides is within 25 centimeters of 230 meters. Some have suggested that this precision was achieved by excavating a shallow ditch around the pyramid and filling it with water. If the Egyptians placed stakes in a series of holes in this ditch and then cut the stakes off at water level, they would have achieved a near-perfect reference for a horizontal plane. Herodotus, in fact, claimed that Khufu's pyramid was built on a stone island created by channeling water from the Nile around the construction site. One problem with this reconstruction concerns the means by which the Egyptians might have brought large volumes of water to the perimeter of the pyramids, since the Nile would have been many meters lower than the pyramids (Lehner 1983a, 1983b).

To create a square and level base for a pyramid, the Egyptians may have used some approximation to the Pythagorean theorem, which specifies the mathematical relationship of the length of the hypotenuse to the length of the sides of right triangles. But this would only work if the pyramid was being built on level ground and the measuring lines were held very close to level. However, the Egyptians apparently left a rather large mound of uncut native limestone in the heart of Khufu's pyramid, perhaps to save labor and materials, or, as Nicholas Grimal suggests, "to perpetuate the idea of the primeval mound covering the burial chamber" (1992: 112). Thus, the Egyptians could not have measured the hypotenuse with level ropes. Getting the sides of the pyramid nearly equal in that case could have been done with plumb bobs and "tape measures" in the form of ropes, but it probably required many successive measurements and then averaging of the results – given the inaccuracies of this method.

Where Did Egyptians Get the Raw Materials for the Pyramids?

Analyses of pyramid blocks clearly show intact stratigraphic sequences of microfossils, reflecting the millions of years of limestone formation on ancient seabeds. (Thus, these blocks could not have been cast from pulverized stone, as some lunatics have suggested.) Ancient quarrying marks show how the limestone blocks were cut from these strata. Khufu's pyramid may have been built of blocks quarried from the area now occupied by the Sphinx and its associated temples. Mark Lehner (1997) and others have suggested that the quarry for some of the Giza pyramids was a large area a few kilometers south of the three main pyramids. This large area is now filled with sand and debris – perhaps from ramps used to construct the pyramids. Granite and basalt were used as decorative elements in some of the pyramids and in their associated temples. Quarries have been found in Upper Egypt that indicate how the Egyptians hammered out the sides of large rectangular blocks and then pried them up, ready for shipment down the Nile.

The method by which the pyramids were sheathed in fine limestone is evident at only a few pyramids. Sneferu's "Bent Pyramid" (Figures 6.7, 6.8) retains much of its veneer. If one stands at the base and looks up the incline, one can see a smooth, fine limestone surface. It is possible that the pyramid was bent in this shape because it was unfinished at the time of

Figure 6.7. Sneferu's "Bent Pyramid" is still covered with much of its original limestone sheath, Fourth Dynasty. It may have been constructed in this odd way because of impending structural failure, or simply to reduce the cost of completing it. *Source:* Photograph by Robert J. Wenke.

Figure 6.8. The precise fitting of the limestone sheath on the "Bent Pyramid." The gaps and holes are from later damage. There is good evidence that most Old Kingdom pyramids were sheathed similarly. *Source:* Photograph by Robert J. Wenke.

Sneferu's death and his successor wanted to save the resources that would be needed to complete it. But it is just as likely that the pyramid's architects discovered a design flaw and "bent" it to keep it stable.

How Did the Egyptians Construct the Pyramids?

There are several more or less plausible hypotheses about pyramid construction. Probably a combination of methods was used. Perhaps the most likely is that the vast majority of blocks were hauled up "spiral ramps" by teams of men pulling on ropes and prying the blocks. This might have been a sand and gravel causeway that ran along each tier of stones, the pavement made slick with water. But we will probably never know because these ramps would have been dismantled and removed after construction, and there are no scenes of ramps, log rollers, or other mechanisms in Egyptian art relating to the Old Kingdom pyramids. There are some traces of a ramp on one pylon at the huge New Kingdom ceremonial center at Karnak, near modern Luxor, as well as a Middle Kingdom scene of people moving a stone colossus on a sled, but we don't know if similar techniques were used to build the pyramids. And even if we were able to show that a particular method was most efficient in engineering terms, there is no assurance that the Egyptians would have actually used that method.

Herodotus was told that the Egyptians built the pyramids in steps, and that stones were pried or levered into position with short wooden planks – but he was a tourist, and tourists in Egypt are told many lies. A lever system would have required intricate and expensive wooden machinery that the Egyptians probably did not possess.

To level and bind the blocks that made up the pyramids, a kind of "concrete" was used in the Fourth to Sixth Dynasties. The Egyptians made it by burning gypsum (found in large amounts in natural formations in the desert) and then mixing it with water, sand, and other materials (pottery sherds and other cultural materials are often found in this mixture). Djoser's Third Dynasty Step-Pyramid, in contrast, appears to have been constructed using relatively pure sand and gravel as a matrix in which to set the stone blocks.

The beautiful white limestone used to sheath the pyramids was probably made of stone from quarries near Tura, across the river and a few kilometers south of the Giza pyramids. Pieces of casing stones were apparently held together by various means, including "butterfly cramps," which were bow-tie-shaped objects of wood or metal that could be placed in incised receptacles on adjoining blocks to hold them together. Most of the blocks of the limestone sheathing were probably cut so that they could hang securely on the blocks of the core body.

How Long Did It Take to Build Each Pyramid?

Much of the work on pyramids was probably done during the annual period of three months or more when farmlands would have been flooded and farmers idle. Masons' marks, however, suggest that some of the work was more than just seasonal. Herodotus was told that a hundred thousand men worked to build Khafre's pyramid, in shifts, and that it took ten years just to build the causeway up which the stone blocks were hauled, and that the pyramid itself required twenty years to build – but we have no reliable information on this point.

Radiocarbon dates and ancient king lists suggest that all of the stone pyramid complexes of the Third through the Sixth Dynasties were built between about 2686 and 2152 BC. If so, the average time for each had to have been less than sixty to a hundred years. It is not even clear that most of the pyramids were built during the reign of the pharaoh for whom they were intended. If a pyramid were begun for an individual as soon as he was born or designated the heir to the pharaoh, some pharaohs would have died well before the completion date of their private pyramids. This may explain some of the "unfinished" pyramids that

Box 11: The Great Sphinx

The Great Sphinx at Giza (Figure 6.9), like Stonehenge and other monuments whose builders left no clear record of their purpose, has excited the fantasies of many people. We have no sure and certain knowledge about when it was built or why it was built or what it "means."

We have, however, some clues to the answers of these questions (Zivie-Coche 2002; Lehner 1997). Royal sphinxes were primarily a Fourth Dynasty motif, having apparently been introduced by Khafre's predecessor, Djedfra. We can assume that the Great Sphinx represents a king because the head is covered with a representation of the *nemes* headdress, which was a folded scarf-like cloth worn exclusively by kings. The Sphinx's location and form strongly suggest that it was made as a representation of one of the Fourth Dynasty pharaohs, perhaps Khafre. Khafre's pyramid is located in close proximity to the Sphinx and to the "Sphinx Temple" just to the south, and its positioning amidst these other monuments suggests to some that the Sphinx, Khafre's pyramid, and other constructions were part of an overall design (Lehner 1983a, 1983b, 1997).

Figure 6.9. Face of the Great Sphinx at Giza. *Source:* Photograph by Robert J. Wenke.

Also, some see similarities between the face of the Sphinx and statues thought to be of Khafre. Others have suggested that the Sphinx represents Khufu (Stadelmann 2003)

Grimal suggests that the "position of the Great Sphinx at the foot of the necropolis . . . demonstrated the king's double significance as the *shesep ankh* of Atum, both in his living form and in the afterworld when his transfiguration has been accomplished" (1992: 74). Also, the Egyptian term *shesep ankh*, meaning "living image," was sometimes written with a determinative in the form of a hieroglyph representing a reclining sphinx.

The Sphinx was carved out of a bed of limestone of variable hardness, and the Egyptians appear to have purposefully carved the face out of the hardest stratum of stone (Lehner 1997). Moreover, the Sphinx seems to be set in the complex of constructions at Giza in such a way that one gets a sense of an overall design and arrangement of the Sphinx, pyramids, and temples on the Giza plateau – although evidence of a grand design remains problematic.

Against these scholarly interpretations are scores of other speculations. American mystic Edgar Cayce, for example, said that he had the good fortune of having been an ancient Egyptian priest named "Ra Ta" in an earlier life. He dreamed that refugees from the lost continent of Atlantis built the Sphinx some ten thousand years ago, and that there was a vast library carved out of the stone beneath it.

Perhaps the most interesting thing about such ideas is not their ultimate validity but the fact that many thousands of people readily believe them. Robert Schoch, a geologist, has argued (2005) that the ten-thousand-year-old date for the Sphinx is approximately correct: He claims that the Sphinx exhibits "precipitation-induced weathering" rather than "wind-induced weathering." Because rains capable of producing this kind of weathering last fell in Egypt about seven thousand years ago, he concludes that the Sphinx must have been carved before then.

Why do almost all professional scholars consider such ideas to be preposterous? To begin with, competent geologists who have worked on the Sphinx have concluded that the weathering on the Sphinx is not the result of rain but rather of wind-weathering and rising groundwater. Water is absorbed from the ground by the Sphinx, resulting in the formation of salt crystals in pores in the stone, which in turn results in hydrostatic pressure that causes small pieces of rock to fall off. Even if some of the weathering of the Sphinx were a result of rain, why was this rain-induced weathering not obliterated because of weathering by wind-borne sand (see this book's cover) and salt-induced exfoliation in the ten thousand years since Egypt last regularly received heavy seasonal rain?

In any case, several centuries of archaeology have shown that before about eight thousand years ago, the people living in Egypt were hunter-foragers who had no supreme rulers to commemorate in stone. If these people or the putative citizens of Atlantis made the Sphinx, there is no evidence that they did so. Moreover, there is not one shred of evidence that the *nemes* headdress and reclining lion motifs that the Sphinx embodies were ever used in the millennia that separate the last period of heavy rains in Egypt and the Old Kingdom.

As for the supposed library under the Sphinx, Mark Lehner and I found a promising shaft on the west end of the Sphinx. We explored and found that it was about a meter deep, and under the sand we found an old – but modern – boot on the bedrock. Who knows, though? The library might be there, and if it were, it would likely change many of our beliefs about Old Kingdom Egypt.

have been found, for some later pharaohs might have been loath to keep building for their dead predecessors.

Old Kingdom Tombs and Temples

Hundreds of Old Kingdom tombs have been identified, and many have been excavated (e.g., Roth 1995a, 1995b, 2003). These span the entire Nile Valley and Delta and all of Old Kingdom history. The Old Kingdom tombs at Giza (Schmitz ed. 1985), in particular, provided not only mummies of elites of this age but also a wealth of information about the art and architecture of mortuary cults. A detailed review of this treasure trove of information is beyond the scope of this book (see Shafer 1997; R. Wilkinson 2000), but some elements are described in other segments of this chapter.

Egyptian temples (Figures 6.10, 6.11) were indispensable components in the mortuary "machine" that not only transported pharaohs to a celestial paradise but also maintained the Egyptian state in good order and functioning well. Old Kingdom Egyptians believed that in performing the appropriate rituals in properly designed temples, not only could they manipulate the cosmos and history but they were also

Figure 6.10. The Sphinx in its temple enclosure, in front of
Khafre's pyramid. *Source:* Werner Foreman / Art Resource, NY.

required by the gods to do so. The Egyptians believed that their temples
were houses of gods – not in the sense that a church or mosque is thought
by Christians or Muslims to be a place where one can commune with
God, but in the literal sense of a house of residence. For the believing
Christian, the church may often be considered "The House of the
Lord," but he or she does not believe that God physically lives in that
particular building as opposed to some other place – God is omni-
present, inhabiting the whole of the cosmos (R. Wilkinson 2000). For
the ancient Egyptian, the temple was indeed the physical house of the
god, not merely a place for people to meditate. The sense of the temple
as a house of a god is evident in various ways, such as the mud-brick
wall that was usually built around temples: The ancient Egyptians
typically lived in villages with mud-brick houses and mud-brick walls,
and so they assumed that a proper home of a god should also have one.

The first Egyptian temples were probably simple mud-brick and reed
structures, but throughout the dynastic era their designs became more
varied and complicated. Some Old Kingdom temples, such as those at
Giza, are relatively well preserved, but the "meaning" of their designs is

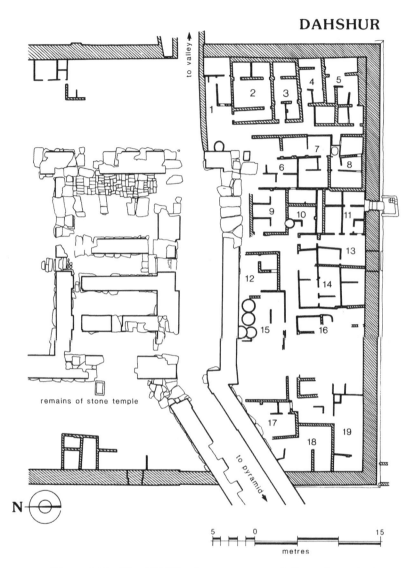

Figure 6.11. The Old Kingdom mortuary cult "town" attached to the Valley Temple of King Sneferu at Dahshur. House number 15 appears to contain at least four granaries. *Source:* After Kemp 1989, fig. 52. Reproduced by permission of Barry J. Kemp.

Figure 6.12. Tomb-chapel of Ptah-Shepses at Abusir, showing the pillared court. He rose to become a vizier in the Fifth Dynasty, in the reigns of Nyuserra and Neferirkara, whose pyramids are in the background. Note that they hardly compare with the Fourth Dynasty pyramids in size or stability. *Source:* Werner Forman / Art Resource, NY.

not well understood, except by dubious extrapolations based on later, mainly New Kingdom examples.

Among the best-known Old Kingdom temples are the "sun temples," "valley temples," and "mortuary temples" associated with the pyramid complexes (Figure 6.12). The valley and mortuary temples are assumed to have been used during the rites associated with the entombment of the king. The cult of the deified king was mainly centered at the mortuary temples, some interiors of which were decorated with scenes of food offerings and other representations of things that appear to have been intended to provide for the king in the life after death. *Sun temples* seem to be a feature mainly of the Old Kingdom. Most of the Fifth Dynasty kings built monumental stone sun temples that stood apart from the mortuary temples, although only a few sun temples have been identified. They appear to have been closely identified with Ra, the sun-god, but exactly what this relationship was is unclear. Perhaps they were meant as literal houses of the god. No sun temples are known for the period after the Fifth Dynasty

Egyptian temples changed over time in form and function. Barry Kemp (1989: 51) has documented what he calls the "villagization" of Menkaura's Valley Temple (Figure 6.13). The original was built in the Fourth Dynasty from mud brick, at about 2500 BC, but by the death of

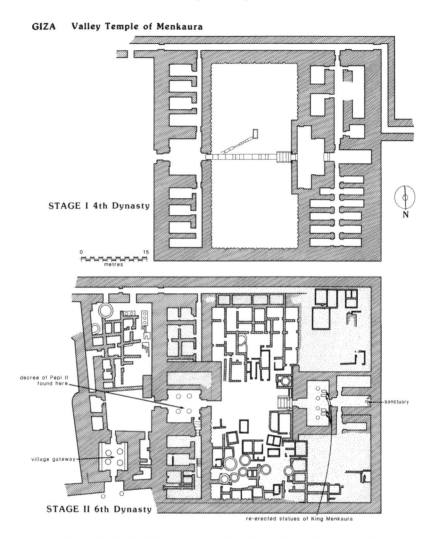

Figure 6.13. In this reconstruction, Barry Kemp illustrates the
"villagization" of the Valley Temple of King Menkaura at Giza. At
Stage I, Fourth Dynasty, it was a simple temple built on a common
plan. But by Stage II, the Sixth Dynasty, at the time of King Pepy II,
the priestly community had moved in and built granaries and expanded
its size by building massive enclosure walls, making it in effect a
fortified village. *Source:* After Kemp 1989, fig. 51. Reproduced by
permission of Barry J. Kemp.

Pepy II of the Sixth Dynasty (c. 2180), it had become a large fortified village – although texts found at the site indicate that in Pepy II's time it was still considered a pyramid town of Menkaura. Its interior structure is simple and represents royal themes mainly in its arrangement of elements around the central court. But by the Sixth Dynasty, the (presumably) priestly community had converted it into something like a fortified village, with granaries and houses. It is possible that by the Sixth Dynasty the priestly community at this temple was directly involved in obtaining and redistributing state revenues and that the priests both lived and worked in the temple.

Still, we know little about Old Kingdom temple rituals and thus must depend on evidence from later periods. In general many Egyptian temples seem to have been intended as replicas of the universe at the moment of creation, a moment that was relived every day as the sun lit the exterior of the temple and eventually penetrated into the internal sanctuaries. Thus, most of the temples were aligned so that each morning the rising sun, the god Ra, would shine through the double pylon gate found at many entrances, representing two mountains, perhaps, and penetrate the innermost chamber of the temple to illuminate the statue of the god. In the New Kingdom, to enter a temple and proceed through it was itself an act of worship. As Nicholas Grimal explains (1992: 264–265):

The approach [to the temple] consisted of a gradual movement from light to shadow, achieving total darkness in the holy of holies where the god dwelt. At the same time the ground slowly rose, achieving its highest point under the naos [a large carved stone cubicle], which was thus located on the primeval mound emerging from Nun, the lake of chaos. Out of this aqueous environment rose the stems of the papyrus columns, their architraves holding up the sky, which . . . was usually represented on the ceiling. In order to achieve this effect, the temple had to consist of at least three elements: a courtyard, a colonnade, and a pylon entrance.

In making the full passage into and through the temple, an individual would have made at least four transitions that had great symbolic religious importance: from east to west, to follow the sun's course; from impure to pure, as one gradually moved closer to the god; from light to dark; and from lower to higher, as one approached the highest point of the temple – which represented the *benben*, the representation of the primeval mound of creation, on which was the *naos*, the shrine enclosing the figure of the god.

Old Kingdom Society and Daily Life

Only a few elements of the rich panoply of Old Kingdom life are discussed here – the reader is directed to the bibliography for many other sources. Much of what we offer about the fabric of Old Kingdom life and

Box 12: Death and Mummification

The bodies (e.g., see Figure 1.9) in the "mummy room" of Cairo's Egyptian Museum are just the gutted and dried remains of demonstrably mortal men. But here – no matter how partially – are some of the people who directed Egyptian armies against Syro-Palestinians in epic conflicts, ordered the construction of beautiful tombs, temples, and other monuments that are still enjoyed by millions today, and in every other way lived the exalted lives of kings.

The practice of mummification was perfected over many centuries. These mummies and other relics of funerary cults may suggest that the ancient Egyptians were obsessed with death, but the reverse is true: They raged against the dying of the light. They desperately wanted to defeat death by perpetuating life beyond it.

We know from Egyptian corpses that were buried as early as five thousand years ago that simply interring the body in the desert's sand without any other treatment desiccates it so well that even skin and hair are often preserved. But the ancient Egyptians no doubt observed that simple graves did not protect the body from disturbances by burrowing rodents and other animals, or from looters, rising water tables, and new constructions. Mummification was a solution to these preservation problems, and its techniques evolved over the course of pharaonic history. No Egyptian texts precisely describing the mummification process in detail have been found; so what we know of these matters comes mainly from modern scientific examinations, partial Egyptian textual accounts, and several secondhand accounts by Greek and Roman tourists who visited Egypt circa 500 BC to AD 300. If we conflate the evidence relating to the mummification process as it was practiced for more than three thousand years, we can get a general sense of what was involved.

The embalmers were probably given a corpse soon after that person's death. Herodotus reported that the bodies of particularly beautiful women were not given to the embalmers for a few days after death, to prevent carnal violation. Some bodies must have been exposed for some time after evisceration, because beetles and maggots have been found in body cavities and embedded in the resin used to cover the corpse.

An essential first step in developing mummification techniques was to dry the corpse with chemical salts to the point that there was insufficient water (we are, of course, mainly water) to sustain the microorganisms of decay. Then the mummy had to be protected from reabsorbing water from the atmosphere or ground, and from insects and animals that will devour even human "jerky."

Removing most of the body's organs was necessary to dehydrate it. The embalmers scooped the brain out through the nose with a metal spoon, and then sliced open the abdomen and removed most of the internal organs. The abdomen and chest cavity were washed in wine and the body was packed in natron crystals (hydrated sodium carbonate and other chemicals found along the ancient lakeshores of the Wadi Natrun) to desiccate it further for, perhaps, forty days. Genesis 50:2–3 records that Joseph commanded the Egyptian physicians "to embalm his father [i.e., Jacob]. . . . And forty days were fulfilled for him for so are fulfilled the days of embalming." In some periods the liver, lungs, stomach, and intestinal viscera were also "pickled" in natron, and then placed separately in four "canopic" jars, to be guarded over by four different deities. Herodotus reports that in cheaper methods of mummification, a corrosive solution, such as turpentine, was injected through the anus, which was then corked until the solution dissolved the internal organs. After that the body was drained.

In more costly mummifications, the cheeks were restored to lifelike dimensions with rag stuffing; the incised abdomen was sewn up and covered with an "embalming plate" of leather or metal, and inscribed with an amulet depicting the protecting eye of Horus. The hair and complexion were usually touched up with paint. Most bodies were stuffed with sand, sawdust, linen, or straw to give them more lifelike contours. The entire body was usually protected with a coating of resin and then wrapped in linen bandages, with amulets placed at selected locations on the body to ward off evil forces. The process began with separate wrapping of the limbs, fingers, and penis, and concluded with larger wrappings of the torso and then the covering of the entire body in a shroudlike piece of cloth, which was often coated with plaster. In some later periods in pharaonic history, a mask representing the person's face (usually of linen or paper covered with plaster, but in gold or other precious materials if the person was royalty) was placed over the head.

After the mummy was placed in a coffin, libations of various kinds were poured over it. Some of these were plant resins that darkened with age, and, in fact, the word "mummy" comes from the Arabic word for bitumen – for which the Arabs mistook these discolored resins. Eventually the body, as well as the embalming refuse and coffin, was carried to the west bank of the Nile for entombment. (Every putrid rag used in the embalming process and the smallest hair and body parts of the deceased had to be buried with him for his use and to prevent these from being used to cast evil spells on the deceased.) At the tomb, the priest would incant the encouraging words, "You live again, you revive always, you have become young again and forever."

The Egyptians mummified many kinds of animals, ranging from crocodiles to lizards. At Saqqara, for example, a major cult site just south of modern Cairo, are huge underground tombs containing thousands of mummified cattle, cats, ibises, and other animals. The ancient Egyptians believed that the gods manifested themselves on earth in the form of animals; thus, offerings to various gods were frequently made in the form of a mummified animal.

the arts and crafts of this age is based on inferences from materials from later periods. Here, too, the inference is that Egypt after the Old Kingdom greatly resembled that of the New Kingdom.

Gender, Sex, and Marriage in the Old Kingdom

Like all known early civilizations, dynastic Egypt was dominated by men. Only a man could truly be king, although at least three women (including Hatshepsut [c. 1473–1458 BC]) achieved nearly all the powers of a king. Among the lower classes, both men and women did much of the hard labor of subsistence farming. Almost all women were illiterate, as were most men. Still, it is probably significant that all representations of professional scribes are male. The many lists of powerful officials name few women, except as priestesses or queens. And yet ancient Egyptian women appear to have been honored and respected, and they had considerable legal power. A wife was entitled to a third of her deceased husband's estate, the remainder going to their children. Elder sons inherited a disproportionate share of wealth from their parents, but patterns of inheritance varied greatly. Wives brought wealth to the marriage, and they had some legal rights to its disposition in the event of death or divorce.

Many tomb scenes show a husband and his wife (or the tomb-owner's mother) together accepting lavish offerings, with the woman in elegant dress and presented as the apparent equal of her husband or son. Whereas men were pictured seemingly realistically in some media, women rarely were. Elite women were often represented in whitish yellow tones, perhaps to distinguish them from suntanned men; it is interesting that bureaucratic officials, too, are pictured sometimes in the same skin tones as women, perhaps to emphasize the fact that they did not toil in the sun.

Box 13. Plato's View of Egypt's Cultural Conservatism

The history of Western philosophy is . . . no more than a series of footnotes to Plato's philosophy.

(Attributed to A. N. Whitehead [1861–1947])

At about 360 BC, Plato wrote one his greatest works, *Laws*, and in it he used ancient Egypt to express his ideas about politics, virtues, and aesthetics, as the following "dialogue" illustrates. It also demonstrates how Egyptian cultural conservatism was world-famous even in Plato's era – although his assertion that Egyptians had been using the same aesthetic forms for ten thousand years was an exaggeration (sometimes even Plato was wrong).

In these dialogues Plato was attempting to stipulate precisely how an ideal state should be organized and operated, even specifying the forms of music, dance, painting, and so forth that should be allowed.

Plato typically used pseudonyms, such as "The Athenian Stranger," to express his own opinions, and he usually presented his ideas in the form of imagined conversations between friends as they strolled the Greek countryside.

CLEINIAS: And what are the laws about music and dancing in Egypt?

ATHENIAN STRANGER: You will wonder when I tell you: Long ago they appear to have recognized the very principle of which we are now speaking – that their young citizens must be habituated to forms and strains of virtue. These they fixed, and exhibited the patterns of them in their temples; and no painter or artist is allowed to innovate upon them, or to leave the traditional forms and invent new ones. To this day, no alteration is allowed either in these arts, or in music at all. And you will find that their works of art are painted or moulded in the same forms which they had ten thousand years ago. . . . [T]his is literally true and no exaggeration – their ancient paintings and sculptures are not a whit better or worse than the work of today, but are made with just the same skill.

CLEINIAS: How extraordinary!

ATHENIAN STRANGER: I should rather say, how statesmanlike, how worthy of a legislator! I know that other things in Egypt are not so well. But what I am telling you about music is true and deserving of consideration, because [it shows] that a lawgiver may institute melodies which have a natural truth and correctness without any fear of failure. To do this, however, must be the work of God, or of a divine person; in Egypt they have a tradition that their ancient chants, which have been preserved for so many ages, are the compositions of the Goddess Isis. And therefore, as I was saying, if a person can only find in any way the natural melodies, he may confidently embody them in a fixed and legal form. For the love of novelty, which arises out of pleasure in the new and weariness of the old, has not strength enough to corrupt the consecrated song and dance, under the plea that they have become antiquated. At any rate, they are far from being corrupted in Egypt.

(Plato [c. 428–348 BC], *Laws*, Book V, adapted from the translation [1871(2006)] by Benjamin Jowett [1817–1893])

The ancient Egyptians married early, boys usually between sixteen and seventeen, girls between twelve and fourteen. In contemporary Egyptian villages, girls still often marry at this age, but the men tend to be much older, as they have to accumulate enough wealth for the dowry. The common practice in ancient Egypt was for the newly married couple to establish a new house, instead of living with parents. If we generalize from tomb scenes and clay models, many women worked hard, spinning, weaving, sieving grain, and performing other domestic tasks. They appear to have been spared some of the most laborious work and the more dangerous occupations, but women could become stewards, overseers, physicians, and other specialists (Trigger 2003: 185).

Many scenes in tomb art celebrate the erotic appeal of female dancers and musicians. These scenes presumably reflect a male view of the world (James, Davies, and Davies 1985), but it is likely that they are somewhat accurate. Most Egyptian women appear to have lived in monogamous marriages – although the king and perhaps other elites had more than one wife on occasion (though only one "great royal wife"). Marriage does not appear to have been either a religious or a social contract. It appears to have been recognized once two people began having sex and living together.

Our knowledge of the sex life of ancient Egyptians is limited to analogies with our own. Unlike the Moche of ancient Peru, for example, whose diverse sexual activities were realistically depicted in pottery, similar representations rarely, if ever, appeared in formal Egyptian art. Some explicit scenes of sexual intercourse drawn on papyrus have been found, however, and this type of art may have been charms to aid potency and fertility. Crude clay figurines of men with enormous penises have been found, as well as figurines illustrating female genitals.

Sexual congress may seem unsuitably classed as a form of "entertainment," but illiterate and physically active people without the modern world's diversions probably had recreational sex more often than people in our world. Egyptian adolescents apparently could enjoy premarital sex, beginning soon after the girl's first menses and the boy's circumcision, without imputations of guilt or sin and without a necessary commitment to eventual marriage.

The loss of virginity in ancient Egypt was apparently considered a minor vice if it occurred outside marriage; but adultery, which threatened the stability of families, was viewed more seriously. A few royal corpses seem to be of uncircumcised men, but male circumcision was apparently such a normal practice that instead of saying "When I was a boy" to refer to one's prepubescence, a man could say "before my foreskin was removed from me" (Brewer and Teeter 1999: 98). There are only a few ambiguous references to female circumcision (surgical removal of all or parts of the clitoris and labia), and these all date to later pharaonic Egypt (C. Reeves 1992: 30–31), and so it is likely that few or no Old Kingdom women experienced this evil.

Brothels (whose entrances were subtly advertised by representations of erect penises over the doorways) were common in Egypt in later periods, and prostitution was probably practiced throughout the dynastic era.

Most Egyptians viewed homosexuality with distaste, but it was known and practiced (Trigger 2003: 191). Some tomb inscriptions, for example, recount that the tomb owner did not have sex with men, listing it as one of his virtues (Reeder 2000). The modern inference that homosexuality is primarily a function of genes is supported by the fact that it appears at about the same frequency in every culture for which we have good records.

Egyptians understood some of the biology of human reproduction: A Late Period story relates that "[s]he lay down beside her husband. She received [the fluid] of conception from him" (Brewer and Teeter 1999: 97). But they seem to have been confused about the physiology of pregnancy. One test for fertility was to place a clove of garlic in a woman's vagina; if the woman tasted garlic in her mouth she was presumed fertile.

In sum, by our standards, ancient Egypt was a male-dominated, sexist society, and a repressive one with regard to homosexuality – but there is a certain idiocy in imposing our moral values on ancient cultures. Still, we can consider why almost all known societies of every age have been dominated by men. Some scholars argue that this difference is genetically based – the result of millions of years of natural selection. Certainly some significant aspects of human personality and sexual behavior are "hard-wired" in one's genes. Human sexual behavior and family structures are the products of many millions of years of Darwinian evolution, and thus it is not surprising that so many societies are similar in these respects. Still, there are economic and social determinants of gender roles. In modern Western cultures, for example, attitudes about the occupations suitable for women have changed radically in just the past few decades – perhaps because restricting the opportunities and undervaluing the talents of half of the population (i.e., women) greatly reduces a society's competitiveness in the global economy.

In economies like that of dynastic Egypt, however, there does not appear to have been any great socioeconomic "cost" to a patriarchal system – and several "benefits" to it. Limiting women's opportunities to become viziers in the Old Kingdom, for instance, did not result in a disastrous shortage of viziers – there were more than enough eligible men for this profession. Also, a woman's labors at child raising, managing the household of an extended family, and performing many other activities were valued and integral parts of dynastic culture. Moreover, marriage in most preindustrial societies was much more a matter of an economic and social alliance between extended families than just an expression of the attraction between two people. Marriage rules, the reckoning of descent, and inheritance laws all seem linked to economic calculations. Ancient customs and laws often were devised to prevent the inheritance of farmlands by simple division among all children, generation after generation, because in a very short time such an inheritance pattern would produce plots of land so small that they could not support a single individual.

In short, in a preindustrial economy such as Old Kingdom Egypt, gender differences in all aspects of the society were institutionalized, making one's roles and responsibilities predictable. And there were clear economic advantages to this predictability and to the integration of socioeconomic activities.

The elaboration and uses of peoples' names are often an indication of socioeconomic roles (Lustig 1994), but whereas many other cultures had special words for relatives and ancestors going back several generations, the Egyptians distinguished only three. The ancient Egyptians appear to have simply used the term "brother" and "sister" in referring to aunts and uncles, and "father" and "mother" to grandparents. Like all people, the Egyptians had terms of endearment, using "goose" and "pigeon," for example, as (presumably) affectionate nicknames (Brewer and Teeter 1999: 120). Some common names in the New Kingdom were Paser, Mose, Ptahmose, Ramose, Qenna, and Neferhotep; these were probably used throughout the dynastic era. Other common names, such as Ptahirrdisu and Ankhnesneferibre, cry out for nicknames.

Formal schooling was probably limited to elites and was mainly concerned with learning to read, write, and understand simple mathematics. Many ancient "practice" texts, written on stones or potsherds ("ostraca"), have been found, some with the invigilating scribe's corrections of the student's efforts. Most arts and crafts were learned through apprenticeships, and some of them probably took many years of training before the student was regarded as proficient.

Dress and Cosmetics

Nearly every Egyptian would have dressed in linen. Linen can be woven into fabrics of varying density, from canvas to a gossamer delicacy. If tomb paintings are a reliable guide, on at least some occasions Egyptian women dressed in ways that would be considered quite erotic today, with form-fitting dresses that partially covered the breasts but with a deep décolletage.

For men, a kilt-like linen garment seems to have been standard for most classes, with farmers wearing little more than a loincloth, but the richer folk sporting fine, pleated kilts. Reed sandals were the common footwear of the poorer classes, but richer people had the option of leather sandals. Leather caps and gloves were found in Tutankhamun's tomb and probably were in use from the beginning of dynastic civilization.

Both men and women commonly used eye shadow, perfumes, and other cosmetics. If you were a man in ancient Egypt, you would not have even thought of growing a long beard – an emblem of rank reserved for the king (who wore a wig-like false beard), although you may have had a short beard and mustache if you were one of the elites.

Recreation and Entertainment

Egyptian elites enjoyed banquets, with formal flower arrangements, elaborate menus, and dancing girls and musicians as entertainment.

They also played several popular board games similar to checkers. Even the poorest farmers probably enjoyed wrestling, boxing, dancing, swimming, archery, fishing, and hunting. Today, even the poorest Egyptian villagers revel on occasion in dances and music, particularly at weddings and on holidays. Since 95 percent or more of the populace was illiterate, Old Kingdom Egyptians could not resort to books for edification or relaxation, but there were professional storytellers to entertain the general public, and most people probably knew by heart their favorite songs and poems. One must remember, too, that the conversational arts were in some ways much more important in preindustrial ages than they are today. Jane Austen – one of the greatest English novelists – described in detail the richly textured conversational lives of people in early-nineteenth-century England, and still today in rural Egyptian traditional villages, long hours are spent chatting over tea or coffee. Ancient Egyptians no doubt enjoyed this pastime as well.

Egyptian music (Manniche 1991) involved many instruments. From tomb paintings and archaeological remains, we recognize various wind instruments, including flutes and pipes. Of these, the flute is the oldest and is depicted on a Predynastic sherd and on a slate palette from Hierakonpolis. Hence, the instrument could possibly have been invented in Egypt. Even today, Arab musicians use flutes in the forms of the *nay* and *uffafa*. Ancient string instruments consisted of lyres, lutes, and harps. During the Old Kingdom, a full musical group probably included singers, hand clappers, harpists, a flautist, and others. An Old Kingdom song – as illustrated in a tomb painting – appears to have been sung antiphonally by two groups, one group asking a question and the second group answering it. As Lisa Manniche summarizes (1991): The first group called out the question, "Oh, Western Goddess! Where is the shepherd?" The second group then responded, "The shepherd is in the water beneath the fish. He talks to the catfish and greets the mormry-fish." The song concluded with the call, "Oh shepherd of the Western Goddess."

This song sounds somewhat bizarre to us, but it was probably familiar in words and themes to all Old Kingdom elites. Its date, circa 2200 BC, makes it one of the oldest known in all of literature and music.

As for the general sound of Egyptian music, it probably resembled "Oriental" music as we know it today, including Chinese, Indian, and Middle Eastern varieties. These are often composed of percussion rhythms and solitary melodic lines marked by a "drone" effect, that is, a single pitch or "tonic" that sounds continuously as the melody is produced above it. If we could hear ancient Egyptian music, it would probably remind us of the traditional music one can still hear at provincial Egyptian weddings and other village celebrations.

The music of Eastern cultures can sound "discordant" to people in the West, because Westerners are habituated to "harmony," the simultaneous combining of pitches to produce chords. Harmony in music apparently was first developed in Europe in the ninth century but seems to have been unknown elsewhere at that time and virtually unknown anywhere before that time. Scholars debate the possibility that harmony appeals to something intrinsic to the human mind. This may seem unlikely, but it is curious that much of the repertory of contemporary orchestras, from Chicago to Vladivostok, from Tokyo to Timbuktu, is the richly harmonious music composed in Europe in the seventeenth to twentieth centuries. Some historians of music suggest that this simply reflects the sociopolitical power of the West in this period, but others dispute this opinion.

It is likely that no system of musical notation was used by the Egyptians – or by any other ancients. There are some scraps of evidence that notation was used in some cultures before the ninth century AD. It was in the period of about AD 1100–1300, however, that a system of pitch and rhythm notation evolved, facilitating the spread of music to different cultures.

Old Kingdom Arts and Crafts

An ancient Egyptian miraculously revived and set down in one of the great art museums of our day would probably admire the "realistic" sculpture of the ancient Greeks, Michelangelo, or Rodin, and the figurative paintings of the European tradition. Like many moderns, however, the ancient Egyptians probably would be puzzled and unmoved by the paintings and sculpture of Picasso, Klee, Moore, Calder, and similar artists. For the ancient Egyptians, "accurate" representation was essential in all art.

But what did they consider accurate representation? To begin with, Douglas Brewer and Egyptologist Emily Teeter observed that "Egyptian civilization lasted for more than 3000 years, yet art from any period during that long time span can instantly be identified as being from Egypt" (1999: 169). This conservatism and distinctiveness is largely a result of the Egyptians' conception of all art as a *tool*, a religious implement, in fact. Old Kingdom art seems quite "approachable" to most people, in the sense that one seems to get an immediate and clear sense of what the artist was trying to "say." But this easy interpretability is something of an illusion, for Old Kingdom art was produced for reasons quite different from art in the Western tradition (Baines 1994). Old Kingdom artists, for instance, apparently worked in groups and their art is largely anonymous. Most compositions were probably the work of several artists who rendered different elements of them. More important, there appears to have been little "art for art's sake," in the sense of just a free-form expression of whim and whimsy. Egyptian sculptors did not, for example, make gigantic stone replicas of papyrus plants as columns for temples because of simple personal aesthetic preference; they did so because these temples represented the "marsh of creation," and marshes have papyrus plants in them. Everything had a symbolic purpose. Egyptian architecture was intended to "work" in a profound sense. The ancient Egyptians viewed sculpture and statuary in general as being for the purpose of giving people and objects a certain form of existence.

To make these objects effective in this sense, one had to capture the "most characteristic aspects" of the subjects. To do this, the Egyptians employed various techniques (Davies 1989). To the Western eye, one of the most distinctive aspects of ancient Egyptian art is its treatment of "perspective." Old Kingdom wood and stone sculptures (Figure 6.14) show not only that the Egyptians could produce realistic three-dimensional representations; they excelled at it. But the paintings on tomb walls did not primarily involve the use of perspective to give a three-dimensional effect. It is possible the Egyptians simply did not know how to achieve this effect in painting on two-dimensional surfaces – after all, it became a standard feature of Western art only after many centuries of development. More likely, however, the idea of representing objects in three-dimensional perspective in tomb and temple paintings and reliefs did not interest the Egyptians: They were trying to present things as they "should be," not as they might appear to someone viewing the objects in real life. In any case, they used almost no foreshortening to achieve perspective, nor did they try to present a single unified viewpoint for an entire composition. Rectilinear forms, such as boxes, were often presented in front and side views together. They also used "false transparency" to show the contents of containers or a basket by illustrating them in or above the basket.

They viewed color as essential to representation. Simple colors predominated: black (which is not really a color), white, red, yellow, green, and blue, with little mixing.

Throughout ancient Egyptian art, idealization is pervasive: Things are represented as they should be, not as they are – although in most periods, there were at least a few "realistic" representations of people, warts and all. During the Old Kingdom, too, there are representations that we might consider extremely realistic and not particularly complimentary, such as a rather fat man represented in a wood carving (Figure 6.14).

As driven as Egyptian artists were by the need for a particular form of vivid realism, they did have techniques that allowed them to invest

Figure 6.14. Wood statue of village headman. In the Old Kingdom, statues of individuals were common and many were well executed. This life-sized wood sculpture is often referred to as "sheik el-Beled," which means headman of the village. In rural Egyptian villages this term is still in use. The village headman reported to the provincial government, but he probably made minor decisions on behalf of his villagers. This sculpture is of a man named "Ka-Aper," of the Fourth Dynasty, found at Saqqara. *Source:* Bridgeman-Giraudon / Art Resource, NY.

representations with sociopolitical concepts. They illustrated the pharaoh as much larger than other people, for example. Figures of people were often presented as facing right, and if a figure is presented facing left, the arms are pictured to show the left–right orientation. Even cattle were usually presented as seen from their right side, and their horns were differently represented to show that they were on the left side. Women were often presented with their right breasts exposed. If a different orientation was required, women could be depicted with both breasts exposed. Furniture was difficult to depict in a two-dimensional space without using perspective, but the Egyptians had various means for showing such items in their most characteristic aspects (Baines and Malek 1980: 60).

Painting was a common form of tomb decoration, but reliefs were often used as well. Relief was more "expensive" than painting, in terms of labor costs; painting could be used when the stone was not homogenous or hard enough for sculpting into reliefs, or as a cheaper substitute for relief in poorer tombs. Raised relief was generally used indoors, while sunken relief was used outdoors, to make use of the effects of different levels and angles of light and the distance of the viewer. In painting and reliefs, too, there was no use of foreshortening to achieve perspective, and no unified viewpoint from which to see the entire composition. The term "register" refers to rows of separate inscriptions that were related to some specific theme. These could be long term, such as in the Palermo Stone (see Figure 5.6). Others were used to show the sequence of specific activities. Some registers illustrated short-term activities, such as wheat cropping, from planting to harvest.

Egyptian "Science"

Let no one unversed in geometry enter here.

(Sign over the gate of Plato's Academy)

"Science," in our sense, is necessarily mathematical, and mathematics as we know it today has some of its roots in South Asian and Middle Eastern cultures, but it is largely a product of Western culture. Its origins are mainly in ancient Greek concepts, and developed primarily in Europe and North America during the past four centuries – although in the past century, mathematicians from India, Japan, and many other countries have made seminal contributions.

Greek mathematicians, however, almost certainly learned some of their mathematics from the Egyptians. Though an ethnic Greek, Euclid lived in Alexandria, Egypt, in the fourth century BC, where he invented many elements of modern geometry.

The number 1.618... (the "golden ratio," or "divine proportion"), which meant so much to medieval European artists, may have been derived by the Greeks from the Egyptians. In fact, the Greeks appear to have invested the practical and workable Egyptian mathematical system with religious ideas about the "magic" of certain numbers. But Greek and Egyptian mathematics differed greatly in general perspective. Despite their tendencies toward magic, the Greeks were the first "pure" mathematicians, in the sense that they abstracted mathematical ideas from particular sets of data and tried to generalize mathematical principles and ground them in the nature of the universe. The ancient Egyptians could compute land areas and volumes of vessels, add complex fractions, and do other kinds of basic arithmetic and geometry, but they seem to have had limited interest in generalizing their mathematics to form a body of theoretical principles.

The Rhind Papyrus, for example, states that the area of a circle equals that of the square of 8/9 of its diameter, which means that the Egyptians had estimated the value of pi at 3.16049 – not bad, given that its correct value is an irrational, almost deranged, transcendental number the first six digits of which are 3.14159 (it is an infinite decimal expansion that apparently does not repeat). With their approximation to pi, the Egyptians could estimate areas and volumes accurately enough to estimate the amount of grain in a silo and do similar calculations. But they seem to have been concerned mainly with the practical application of the concept. Their astronomy, though extremely precise, was set in a profoundly religious context as well.

In sum, theoretical mathematics incorporated some elements of ancient Egyptian, Indian, and other cultures, but as it exists today, its primary concepts are in Greek philosophy, as transformed by European scholars after about AD 1400.

7 Egypt and General Analyses of State Origins

Myself when young did eagerly frequent
Doctor and Saint and heard great argument
About it and about; but evermore
Came out by the Door wherein I went.
                Edward Fitzgerald (1809–1883), *The Rubaiyat of Omar Khayyám*

Introduction

Having reviewed in previous chapters some of the evidence concerning the origins and character of the ancient Egyptian state, we must now return to larger and more difficult questions. Why, for example, did this civilization evolve when and in the form it did, and what can Egypt tell us when we examine it in the context of the world's other early states?

Egypt's great ancient state, and early states elsewhere, have stimulated generations of scholars, from Plato to Marx to the present day, to seek some deeper, more comprehensive understanding of the history and dynamics of civilizations (Table 7.1). Indeed, it is difficult to think of a major theory of history that has *not* been applied to ancient Egypt, including such marginalia as a Jungian analysis (Rice 1990) and a racial/ethnic interpretation (Bernal 1987, 2006). All have failed to a greater or lesser extent. Thus, some scholars might question my devoting a chapter of this short book to what many consider a chimerical, if not preposterous and futile, search for some comprehensive and *general* understanding of ancient states. But even failed theories can raise interesting questions, some of which are discussed here.

As distant as some of these "models" of history are from us in time, many of them directly or indirectly influence contemporary approaches. Table 7.2 presents just some of the major ideas currently being applied to archaeological analyses. The scholars listed there have in no sense achieved the revolutionary insights and historical influence of Marx, Darwin, and others in terms of their worldwide influence on so many disciplines. But they are included in order to reflect some of the ideas

Table 7.1. Some Early Influential Ideas about Historical Analyses

Theorists	Model	Major Premise	References
The Bible (2000 BC–AD 200	Linear progress	We live in an inherently evil world but can hope for eventual atonement and salvation.	Isaiah 13; John 3
Plato (427–347 BC)	Cyclical progress	Civilizations evolve but are periodically destroyed (e.g., Atlantis).	*The Republic, The Apology, Laws, Parmenides*
Lucretius (c. 96–55 BC)	Cyclical progress	Everything in the world is made of atoms and eventually reverts to atoms, but there is an evolutionary trajectory.	*De Rerum Natura* (see Book 6 especially)
Condorcet (1743–1794)	Linear progress	In the evolution of human reason, history moves through eight evolutionary stages, to culminate in a world of peace, reason, and love.	*Sketch for a Historical Picture of the Progress of the Human Mind*
Hegel (1820–1830)	Linear progress	History moves through dialectical interplay to eventual human freedom in a just state.	*Phenomenology of Mind; Science of Logic*
Marx (1848–1867)	Linear progress	History evolves through dialectical processes taking the forms of economic production. Successive class struggles usher in freedom and justice.	*Communist Manifesto; Das Kapital*
Darwin (1871)	Linear progress	Humankind and cultures improve through struggle and selection.	*Descent of Man; Selection in Relation to Sex*
Toynbee (1934–1955)	Cyclical progress	Civilizations grow like organisms in response to external and internal stresses until, like organisms, their spirit leaves them and they die.	*Study of History*

After Barzun and Graff 1970: Table 7.

Table 7.2. Some Recent and Current Theoretical Approaches to Analyses of the Past

Theorists	Model	Major Premise	References
L. White, J. Steward, L. Binford (in part), and many others	Linear progress?	Civilizations arose and evolved by progressively greater energy capture through technology; but the process is neither necessary nor irreversible.	White (1949), Steward (1949), Binford and Binford (1968)
R. Dunnell, R. Lyman, M. O'Brien, et al.	Darwinian evolution	Human history can only be understood as a Darwinian evolutionary sequence, but with no necessary "progress."	Dunnell (1982), Cavalli-Sforza and Feldman (1981), Boyd and Richerson (1985), Lyman and O'Brien (2000)
M. Shanks, C. Tilley, R. McGuire	No "Science of History," in the traditional sense of "science," is possible.	The idea of progress is chimerical. All ideas about evolutionary "progress" and a focus on early states reflect contemporary political ideologies and economics; some archaeological analyses are inherently futile and racist.	Shanks and Tilley (1987a, 1987b)
B. Trigger, K. Flannery, and many others	Holistic archaeology and archaeology as anthropology	Archaeologists must use many elements of different theoretical approaches to address the nature and significance of ancient societies; archaeology is anthropology and remains heavily dependent on anthropological theories.	Trigger (2003), Flannery (2006)
S. Wolfram	A science of all complex systems is possible, but it will not be like the linear or cyclical models of the past.	Evolutionary processes can produce great complexity or simplicity through complex interactions. Complex systems are fundamentally alike and must be understood as evolutionary algorithms.	Wolfram (2002)

current in historical/archaeological analyses, which are discussed in the following sections.

As noted in Chapter 1, Bruce Trigger asserted a powerful hypothesis in stating that the "most important issue confronting the social sciences is the extent to which human behaviour is shaped by factors that operate cross-culturally, as opposed to factors that are unique to particular cultures" (2003: 3). If Trigger's statement is true, attempts to understand the Egyptian past confront us with the same fundamental theoretical problems that are issues in sociology, history, political science, and various other disciplines.

It is little comfort, however, to recognize that archaeology is in the same impoverished theoretical state as these other disciplines. *None* of the social and historical sciences has produced a powerful explanatory theory of its subject matter. Some Marxists and Darwinian evolutionists might disagree, but even these powerful paradigms have produced far more debate than results – especially when applied to the similarities and differences of ancient civilizations.

Even those few scholars who still pursue powerful unified analyses of the human past diverge radically in their perspectives. Some argue that such explanations must be in complex terms and principles that are wholly different from the easily accessible terms and concepts of anthropology (Dunnell 1982; Lyman and O'Brien 2000). Others have proposed explanations in what many consider to be ultimately unsatisfying mathematical concepts and expressions (Lumsden and Wilson 1981; Boyd and Richerson 1985; Neiman 1995). Still others look to recent developments in the abstruse mathematical terms and concepts of chaos and complexity theory (Wolfram 2002), or in interpretations of symbols and symbolic representations and meanings that range far beyond traditional archaeology (Wengrow 2006). We cannot dismiss even the remote possibility that part of "the answer" to questions about human history may be in the truly unsettling concepts of quantum theory.

Even a modest foray into these difficult concepts and computations is usually enough to send archaeologists retreating to the easy embrace of anthropological reconstructions of how ancient civilizations might have evolved and how and why they all were fundamentally similar and yet differed in many characteristics. There is nothing inherently wrong with anthropological explanations of the human past, and some are impressive in their scope and rigor (e.g., Trigger 2003).

As productive and persuasive as traditional explanations have been, it is nonetheless legitimate to consider alternative approaches. This book, unfortunately, does not conclude with a novel and full-fledged explanatory analysis of the human past. No such science exists – at least not in developed form. Instead, the goal of this chapter is simply to review the few limited attempts to arrive at an understanding of the Egyptian past that seem to go beyond the recounting of names, dates, and events of traditional interpretations of ancient Egypt, and also to relate these ideas to ancient civilizations in general.

Essential Issues in Analyses of Human History

Nan-in, a Japanese master, received a university professor who came to inquire about Zen. Nan-in served tea. He poured his visitor's cup full, and then kept on pouring. The professor watched the overflow until he no longer could restrain himself. "It is overfull. No more will go in!" "Like this cup," Nan-in said, "you are full of your own opinions and speculations. How can I show you Zen unless you first empty your cup?"

(Traditional Zen parable)

Unlike the professor in this parable, many scholars today would happily abandon their preconceptions about analyses of history – but if and only if there were a Zen master who could replace their discarded ideas with a better understanding of the human past. Yet there is little evidence in the current scholarly literature to suggest that we are on the verge of such a revolutionary understanding of our past.

At this stage in the development of theories in archaeology, many contemporary scholars would agree with the American essayist James Thurber, who noted that in some cases, it "is better to know some of the questions rather than all of the answers."

Do We Have Enough Data for Comprehensive Historical Analyses?

The aspiration for a powerful general understanding of the human past can be questioned on many grounds, but not because of a lack of data. There are huge gaps in our knowledge about ancient cultures, of course, but archaeologists and other scholars have studied many aspects of our past three million years, and in every part of the world. It is this great time depth and geographical and cultural range that constitute the primary database on which any unified analysis of history must be built. If a true science of the past is ever to be formulated, it is unlikely to simply and suddenly appear as we accumulate more archaeological data. The history of biology and paleontology provides an instructive example here: People all over the world had been collecting and categorizing plants and animals for millennia before Mendel, Darwin, and Wallace developed the few simple principles of biology and evolutionary theory that suddenly and comprehensibly made "sense" of all these biological data.

Similarly, even if we had a complete record of everything the ancient Egyptians ever wrote, we would be no closer to a science of history. We lack the theories to understand the data, not sufficient data.

Is There a Genetic Basis to the Evolution of Human Civilizations?

All efforts to understand the human past must begin with a fundamental question: How much of human history can be explained in terms of our genes?

This question may seem unimportant. Even if a "gene" is somehow linked to the traits exhibited by people in early states, some scholars would consider that to be the least interesting thing about them. From some perspectives, the real focus of analysis must be on how different states *culturally constructed* their worlds. It is the differences between Aztec and Egyptian conceptions of the state and the cosmos, for example, that present the kinds of comparisons that are of primary interest to many scholars.

Also, if there is some genetic basis for social hierarchies, economic exploitation, and the other characteristics of early civilizations, then it must be nearly universal in human populations of the past, for state societies appeared all over the world. Moreover, the genetic differences between peoples around the world today and in the past few thousands of years are minor; thus, it is unlikely that the profusion of variability in some aspects of ancient states can be explained genetically. Even the differences between human and chimpanzee DNA are seemingly minor – but if chimps ever constructed a simian civilization, it has yet to be discovered. Chimpanzees exhibit degrees of empathy, altruism, self-awareness, and cooperation in problem solving that we used to associate only with ourselves, but – to use Leslie White's test (1949) – chimpanzees do not have the capacity to cast a meaningful vote in elections or to transmit much learning – apart from how to get food – from generation to generation.

Nonetheless, the close genetic similarity of chimps and people underscores the somewhat uncomfortable truth that tiny variations in genetic structures can have radical results. Many physiological ills, such as breast cancer and Down syndrome, for example, have been linked to minor mutations in just one or a few parts of genes. Consider also the "African Eve" hypothesis, which suggests that we are all descended from one individual African, or a small group, who lived about 120,000 years ago. Some proponents of this hypothesis argue that because of minor genetic mutations, our African ancestors had some slight competitive advantage (perhaps greater language skills) over other humans, and that this advantage allowed them to drive into extinction all other subspecies of hominids. Among the interesting implications of this notion is that we must admit the possibility at least that the same thing could happen again. Yet the world today is a very different place from what it was 150,000 years ago, as are human mating patterns and gene flow; and the notion that a slight genetic advantage perpetuated in certain groups could lead them to world domination borders on science fantasy.

But what about the fundamental similarities of early civilizations? Is there possibly a genetic basis to this similarity? Though unlikely, this possibility cannot be dismissed a priori (Salzman 1999). Trigger identified (1993: 110) the one *constant* of early states as the production of surpluses that the upper classes appropriated through a tributary relationship. This raises the possibility that people are genetically hard-wired to live in hierarchically arranged societies – if and only if there is sufficient food production to support these societies. Trigger identified (2003) many variations in early states. He noted, for example, that the evolution of a state religion was indeed part of every early state, but that these religions differed in such important matters as their conceptions of the king's ties to the gods. He argued that the objective of any science of history must be to explain *both* these similarities and differences.

Yet the similarities are so fundamental, so invariant. How can we explain them? Is it possible that any of these general similarities are primarily determined by our genes? We saw, for instance, in Chapter 4 that the most useful animals domesticated by people are those with a genetically imprinted sense of group hierarchy. Sheep proverbially follow the leader, as do cattle and other animals whose group hierarchies people can manipulate and subvert to their own uses. "Herding cats," in contrast, has become a common metaphor for trying to get animals with highly egocentric perspectives (e.g., university faculty) to act in a coordinated fashion. Even chimpanzees seem to be genetically wired for living in hierarchical groups, headed by dominant males and females, with their juniors kept on the periphery. Is it possible that people are similarly genetically imprinted with a sense of hierarchy, and that that explains why socioeconomic and political hierarchies appeared in every early state? Some scholars (e.g., Mithen 1996) have considered this idea in plausible terms.

In this context it is important to remember that the human mind was largely forged in the crucible of the millions of years that our ancestors spent in hunting-foraging societies, not in the comparatively brief time we have lived in civilizations. Thus, Darwinian selection acting on groups of Paleolithic hunter-foragers must be assumed to have shaped almost all of our own intellects – including any inherent tendencies to social hierarchies. But it is difficult to disentangle the many factors in our biological and cultural evolution. Vital to our survival as a genus, for example, has been the evolution of our powerful abilities to reason *inductively*. Our ancestors of the past two or three million years constantly had to make crucial inferences from such mundane things as the properties of particular kinds of stones to others that look like them, or from observations of a few deer's behavior to all deer behavior, among others. In fact, natural selection has shaped our minds in such a way that we are masters at making accurate inferences from only shreds and patches of the relevant evidence. Thus, it is even possible that our search for a comprehensible explanation of our past is simply an expression of Darwinian equations our ancestors were exposed to in their many millennia as hunter-foragers. These forces shaped our intellects in such a way that we seem doomed to try unceasingly to reduce the cosmos to cause-and-effect equations. If there is a way to view the world except through the prism of causes and effects, we will never know about it. We can accept intellectually, for example, that our universe is infinite and just the latest result of a series of cosmic "Big Bangs." But our Paleolithic brains make it difficult to accept these cosmological inferences without trying to reduce them to causes and effects, and to reduce the incomprehensible to the comprehensible. It has even been argued that our search for "God" is a necessary and predictable result of these Darwinian forces.

The skeptical reader with some mathematical expertise is invited to enter the term "double-slit experiment" in his or her computer's search engine. Quantum theory illustrates how limited we are in trying to understand a universe in which, for example, a particle may possibly be in two places at the same time and influence another without evident connections between them.

Is there anything in specific about the origins of ancient civilizations that we can hope to link to genetic imperatives? The drive to accumulate personal wealth, for example, so vividly illustrated by ancient Egypt, is found in every early state. Is this basic drive for material goods hardwired in our genes, just "waiting," as it were, for a sufficiently productive economy to manifest the greed inherent in class hierarchies? It seems possible, if not necessary. Darwinian evolutionary theory suggests a powerful natural selection for this kind of behavior. One's chances of surviving, having offspring, and bringing them to their own reproductive age – the gold standard of evolutionary "fitness" – would seem to be increased if one competed successfully for as much food and other resources as possible. Conversely, there would seem to be a major reduction in genetic "fitness" if an individual sacrifices personal interest by working for the common good (Trigger 2003: 680). The true loser in this evolutionary equation would be a man or woman who invests resources and efforts in children who are not their genetic progeny. But mothers regularly sacrifice their lives for their children in fires and floods – how could Darwinian processes select for such behavior?

All such behaviors, some scholars suggest, can be understood in terms of subliminal genetic calculations (reviewed in Godfrey and Lewontin 1993). Some explanations for the persistence of male homosexuality – which would seem to have such dire consequences for the individual homosexual in terms of his reproductive "success" – are based on this premise: A homosexual uncle may not produce children at the same rate as heterosexuals, but he can provide nieces and nephews with many advantages that, in the long run, would improve the reproductive success of his close genetic relatives – and thus his own genes.

Another possibility is that the focus and units of selection changed once people began living in hierarchical and socioeconomically complex societies. Perhaps Darwinian selection operated on the group, rather than just the individual.

The strongest evidence *against* the idea that we have a genetically imprinted sense of social hierarchy is perhaps that our ancestors lived for millions of years as hunter-foragers in small groups that we suspect had virtually no hierarchical structure – just modest distinctions based on age, sex, and individual abilities. Nonetheless, hierarchies appeared in every culture that had a sufficiently productive economic base to support them. In any case, human behavior is obviously the product of both genes and environment. We probably have genes that require certain environmental factors to be fully expressed. But no genetic basis for building monumental architecture, warfare, national religious cults, occupational specialization, and the many other attributes of complex civilizations has ever been identified – or is likely to be.

In the absence of such evidence, it seems appropriate to assume that people are born with great behavioral plasticity, and that it is mainly external factors that determine the kinds of socioeconomic and political structures that define their lives. In fact, the premise of a science of culture and history teeters on the assumption that what we can learn from early civilizations has much to do with cultural and historical processes and almost nothing to do with genes.

Some contemporary scholars have tried to resolve the relationship of genes and cultures in determining human history by promoting a "coevolutionary" approach, in which genes and culture are considered indispensable elements in the explanation of historical and cultural change (Lumsden and Wilson 1981). Much research remains to be done in this area, but preliminary studies have yet to produce powerful and comprehensive explanations.

What Is It, Exactly, about Ancient States That We Are Trying to Explain?

Trigger's massive *Understanding Ancient Civilizations* (2003), for one, addresses this question by analyzing everything from gender roles to warfare in many ancient states.

We shall use here just one example, *settlement patterns* – a topic that has been considered in this book with regard to Egyptian occupations between around 4500 and 2000 BC. Much can be learned about any sociopolitical entity by considering how its component elements – its cities, towns, and villages – are arranged across the space of the polity and how they are socially, functionally, and politically integrated. For instance, developing countries such as contemporary Egypt and Mexico often have one or a few huge cities, such as Cairo and Mexico City, in which a relatively large percentage of the nation's population lives and works, and where the widest range of goods and services is available. In such a "primate" settlement pattern, other communities are relatively small and offer only a small fraction of the goods and services available in the largest city. In contrast, "developed countries," such as the United States and Japan, typically have many large cities and large and small towns, all of which are highly integrated into the national economy and government, such that every city and large town provides most of the goods and services required by their populations.

We can analyze ancient Egypt in somewhat similar terms. In earlier chapters of this book we encountered the categories of *city-states* and *territorial* states, and we can now examine them in more detail. Trigger identified (2003: 110–113) several characteristics that he thought distinguished territorial states, such as Egypt, from city-states, such as those of Mesopotamia:

1. The total area controlled by territorial states tended to be larger than those occupied by city-states.
2. The cities of territorial states were much less populous than those of city-states.
3. The rulers of territorial states had at their disposal much larger surpluses than did those of city-states. Egypt was exceptional in this

regard, and the pyramids represent the most massive construction complexes in the preindustrial world.

4. In territorial states, the exercise of royal power required the maintenance of a considerable degree of centralized control over the economy.

5. There was more continuity in agricultural life in territorial states than in city-states.

Each of these five points can be broken down to ever-finer distinctions that have some applicability to the Egyptian past. Some scholars have argued, for example, that all of the early states began as territorial states, some of which broke apart to form city-states; others suggest that early territorial states evolved into city-states. Eventually some of these evolved into territorial states, and then finally into empires (reviewed in Trigger 2003; Feinman and Marcus 1998).

In Chapter 5 we reviewed evidence that raises questions about the accuracy and utility of the distinction Trigger makes between territorial states and city-states relative to ancient Egypt. Fekri Hassan, for one, has argued that in the Predynastic period and even in Early Dynastic times, Egypt's settlement pattern was one in which there were many large towns, not just a single great metropolis at Memphis, and that the overall pattern of site sizes and locations indicates a high degree of socioeconomic and political integration (1988: 162). Hassan interprets this pattern as principally a reflection of the constraints of the Nile Valley's geography. He suggests that towns in early dynastic Egypt were differentiated on the basis of their administrative, economic, and religious importance, and that in some periods, towns in Egypt were deliberately located to maximize control over specific areas – not simply in response to the forces of local economies.

Nonetheless, many scholars have concluded that Egypt never approached the degree of urbanization characteristic of early states in Mesopotamia. There were spectacular exceptions in the Egyptian pattern. If the population of the "pyramid town" at Giza (see Chapter 6) really reached twenty thousand, as has been estimated, it was far larger than almost every other city in the Middle East, including Thebes and some other settlements during both the New Kingdom and Late Periods that were massive urban centers.

If we define "urbanism" in terms not only of large relative size but also of highly differentiated and coordinated functions, then there seems to be little mystery about Egypt's settlement patterns, given the ecological similarity of environments along the Nile Valley and into the Delta, as well as the rich concentrations of most important raw materials within

Egypt's borders and the transport link provided by the Nile. Extreme urbanism, by this definition, would seem to have few advantages in Egypt – except in special circumstances, such as assembling all the people required to build pyramids and other monuments. Unlike Mesopotamia, where regional and national political and economic factors were powerful determinants of settlement location, Egyptian settlement location for much of the dynastic era seems to have been largely determined by local ecological factors. The overall sameness of the agricultural niche throughout Egypt made for very predictable and largely functionally redundant local economies. The nome, or provincial, structure of the country was largely defined by natural flood basins and river channels. Even the location of Memphis, probably the largest settlement through most of the early dynastic (including the Old Kingdom), is at the juncture of Egypt's two primary ecological zones, the Valley and the Delta.

We cannot discount the impact on settlement patterns of unique events and idiosyncratic rulers. Akhenaten recorded that he wanted a place for his capital that was uncontaminated by the worship of other gods. At el-Amarna he found an unpolluted landscape where the view toward the sharp level edge of the mountain range to the east resembled a horizon, thereby expressing the name of the city, which meant "The Horizon of the Sun Disk." Nonetheless, el-Amarna's history was very brief, and it was abandoned perhaps as much because of its comparatively poor ecological and strategic setting as for the rejection of Akhenaten's radical religious revisionism.

With regard to assessing the significance of Egypt's unique settlement patterns and socioeconomic and political history, many scholars have also argued for the creative role of urban life in shaping the character of a citizenry. Urban centers are effective in fostering innovations and accelerating cultural change – as well as producing feelings of alienation and class conflicts. Egypt's settlement pattern may have been a causal factor in the relatively static, uniform, and ritualized qualities of Egyptian literature, arts, religion, and so forth, rather than just a reflection of these ideologies.

Some scholars have examined cities as mechanisms for encouraging innovation and efficient systems of information processing, storage, and control (H. Wright and G. Johnson 1975; G. Johnson 1987). Here, too, the easy transport links provided by the Nile must be considered

Others have noted the efficiency of cities in terms of "trait transmission": Ancient craftsmen had to learn their crafts, and administrators, scribes, soldiers, and other specialists had to be trained to meet the needs of these ancient states. Cities provide effective venues for these and other functions. All commodities, even information, are subject to transport costs, and these are minimized in cities – provided, of course, that these urban populations can be efficiently supported by resources that are not necessarily produced locally.

In sum, the early Egyptian state was able to do everything essential to create an advanced preindustrial civilization, without the rise of many competing city-states.

In addition, it is important to note at this point that although Trigger stressed techno-environmental factors in his explanation of settlement patterns, he recognized that these were insufficient: There "is no sector of early civilizations that did not display a significant combination of cultural idiosyncrasies and cross-cultural regularities. Such findings do not correspond with the expectations of either neoevolutionists or cultural determinists" (2003: 674).

A measure of the difficulty of analyzing ancient civilizations is the fact that the determinants of the settlement patterns discussed here are just a small part of the overall puzzle of the evolution of early states.

Are Traditional Explanations of the Origins and Functioning of Ancient States Adequate?

The "explanations" of Egypt's settlement patterns proposed in the proceeding section are, in the opinion of many contemporary scholars, either entirely misconceived or of extremely limited use. These critics see such explanations as too focused on ecological and technological variables, at the expense of a consideration of social, political, or other ideological variables (reviewed in Yoffee 2005; Wengrow 2006). They also criticize the use in traditional explanations of such abstractions as "city," "civilization," "occupational specialization," and "class hierarchy," none of which is an analytical unit derived from any theory, and each of which is at best a simple and static description of what is in fact a multidimensional and continuous underlying reality.

They also note that these attempts at explanation are usually formulated in terms of "functionalist" arguments with little explanatory power. Functionalist explanations attempt to explain some phenomena in terms of the functions they served or the needs they met. A classic example of a functionalist explanation is to account for the evolution of the mammalian heart by considering the purpose it serves: circulating blood. Philosophers have long recognized that identifying what function something serves does not constitute an ultimate explanation of its origins. There is no necessary reason why organisms had to evolve with hearts, for example, rather than with some other mechanism to circulate fluids – or to evolve any kind of circulatory system at all. Similarly, there appears to be no necessary reason why early state institutions appeared; many societies did not evolve similar institutions. It is worth noting that Charles Darwin himself had a difficult time explaining the evolution of the eye and the capacity for sight in many life forms, since the elements of such an organ had to be "selected for" in more primitive organisms for eons before the function of the organ was realized. Darwin and current biologists have provided persuasive answers to this question, but it remains a staple "argument" in "creationist" circles.

Another problem with functionalist arguments is that of *equifinality*: In biological and cultural systems a particular result (i.e., a state political organization) can be explained by many different combinations of causal variables. Interactions between nomads and farmers, for example, seem to have been important elements in the evolution of early states in China and Mesopotamia (Trigger 2003; R. Adams 1966), but nomads played almost no role in the evolution of the early Egyptian state.

Despite these and other limitations, functionalist explanations based on causal ecological, demographic, and technological variables have a long history in studies of early states. If you knew nothing about the archaeological evidence of early states, chances are you would be struck by the same facts that so forcefully impressed many theorists of state origins: Most of these cultures developed in similar physical environments and were based on similar agricultural economies. The earliest states and empires arose for the most part in semiarid or more temperate environments that were close enough to the equator to receive intense solar radiation that permitted productive agriculture. But they also arose in environments where crops like wheat, barley, maize, and so forth could be grown without having to plow thick grasslands or suppress competing vegetation, such as one finds in jungles and dense forests.

These simple environmental factors probably explain many of the reasons why civilizations first appeared in places like Egypt, Peru, the Indus Valley, Mesopotamia, and China, and not in Germany, Brazil, the Congo, or Canada.

But how precisely can these blunt forces of latitude and ecology have produced ancient civilizations? Kathryn Bard and Robert Carneiro (1989) developed a detailed model of how this might have happened in Egypt. In their reconstruction, people established Predynastic farming communities in those areas of southern Egypt where the natural flood basins of the Nile offered the easiest and most productive agriculture. These fertile riverine areas were initially sparsely occupied by small villages that had few political and economic interactions. As these populations increased, villages tended to divide because of internal conflicts and the need to find additional farmlands. By the fissioning of these villages and the emigration of part of their populations, the best agricultural areas of the Nile Valley were populated. Eventually, however, given slow but constant population growth and the proliferation of agricultural villages, all the land that could be irrigated and exploited easily became occupied, and the expanding population began to strain available food supplies. The deserts that circumscribed both banks of the Nile were absolute barriers to expansion, and so the population movement had to be northward and southward. Because of the cataracts in the south, the narrow floodplains in Nubia, and the importance of Egypt's cultural interactions with the Mediterranean world, the main direction of the expansion was northward.

As plausible as this reconstruction may be, it is difficult to test. (Note that in later publications [e.g., 1992] Bard puts more emphasis on ideological factors in the formation of the ancient Egyptian state.)

We do not know if there were ever food shortages in the Predynastic that forced people to turn to warfare and expropriation of their neighbors' food as a way to meet such crises, but there is evidence of food shortages at various times in pharaonic history. Nor do we know if the conquest of northern Egypt by Southerners was in any way stimulated by food scarcities in the South, but it is possible. In his general model of early state formation (focused on Peru), Carneiro suggested that war captives stimulated the formation of socioeconomic classes because captives were forced to become slaves or menial workers, and because the conquerors imposed extortionate taxes on weaker states. These factors also encouraged the formation of an institutionalized bureaucracy to administer the taxes and slaves, and the establishment of the bureaucracy in turn intensified wealth and status differentials, as the most successful military leaders were given the administrative posts.

We do not have, and perhaps never will have, adequate data to measure precisely how much population growth, circumscribed environments, and warfare were dynamics in the formation of the early Egyptian state. Many models similar to Carneiro's have been proposed, some stressing the effects of irrigation agriculture (Wittfogel 1957) or simple population growth, others the effects of nomads on agricultural societies – particularly in regard to Mesopotamia and China (R. Adams 1966; Trigger 2003).

All of these models have been faulted on the grounds that 1) they are not truly explanations, just hypothetical and simple descriptions that account for the evolution of state institutions in terms of the functions they served; 2) they cannot be precisely quantified and therefore tested; 3) they consider most aspects of society, arts, religion, and other

Box 14. Function vis-à-vis Ideology: The Pig Taboo

If pigs had a religion, it is pretty easy to guess which species they would designate as unclean.

(Agronomist Eric P. Hoberg, commenting on his research indicating
that pigs were initially infected with tapeworms by people)

Debates about the relative importance of ideological and techno-environmental factors in shaping cultures are, oddly, illustrated well by the pig taboo found in several religions. Thirty years ago some of anthropology's most prestigious publications (e.g., *Current Anthropology*) devoted a lot of print space to arguments about the pig taboo.

That diets are partly shaped by the unique preferences and resources of peoples of different cultures is not surprising. Some Asians, for instance, relish dogs, cats, snakes, and other foods that are unlikely ever to be featured in North American fast food franchises. But basic economic realities and general evolutionary processes have shaped diets throughout history and the world. Consider the humble pig. Pig bones are found in large numbers at most major Egyptian sites occupied after about 5500 BC. In fact, pig bones are among the most common animal remains at Egyptian sites, no matter how small or large (Hecker 1982). Yet there are only a few references to swine in texts or representations of them in tomb paintings. And pork was rarely – perhaps never – included in tomb offerings (Brewer, Redford, and Redford 1994: 96).

Yet pigs were eaten for millennia in the very areas of the world where they eventually became stigmatized as disgusting and taboo animals. Why did these cultural perceptions and subsistence practices change so radically? This is not a trivial question. Pigs are one of the most efficient converters of garbage, animal wastes, and other materials discarded by farmers – better in many respects than goats, sheep, or cows (Harris 1977: 131, 1989). Moreover, pigs have large litters once or twice a year, and so they have the potential to supply much of the animal protein for a subsistence farmer. Why, then, was pork slighted in Egyptian ideology and later tabooed by the Jewish and Islamic faiths, and banned (along with other animals) by Hindus?

Religious taboos about eating such apparently economically efficient animals set many scholars into intellectual conflict. Some believe that such religious prohibitions and every other aspect of cultural behavior can be understood fundamentally in terms of technological, ecological, and demographic variables. Others think it is futile to try to explain adequately such things as religious food prohibitions, and religious and social behavior generally, mainly in terms of technology, ecology, and demography.

Marvin Harris (1977) has forcefully argued that the ultimate causes of many food taboos and preferences are largely to be found in economic factors. He dismisses the notion that the pig prohibition has anything to do with the common infection of pigs with trichinae –parasites that can kill people: Pigs raised in hot climates seldom transmit this disease; moreover, Egyptian and Southwest Asian farmers ate cattle, which carry anthrax, brucellosis, and other diseases that are more deadly than anything pigs can transmit. Some people might be put off pork because of pigs' rather untidy habits, but this prejudice somehow never appeared in Europe, Hawaii, China, and many other places. Why?

Harris notes that pigs are native to woodlands and swamps and do not tolerate direct sunlight and arid environments well. Thus, the clearing of land coincident with the spread of agriculture in Egypt and Southwest Asia greatly reduced the habitat and natural foods available to pigs, and, increasingly, pigs had to be fed on grain, which brought them into competition with people. Pigs can make edible pork out of everything, ranging from feces to truffles, but to do so they require a diet rich in protein and carbohydrates. They also need lots of water, and shade, and they are smart enough not to pull plows, nor can they be sheared or ridden; cheese or yogurt made from pig's milk has yet to succeed in any major markets.

In short, in some environments pigs lost their cost-effectiveness relative to sheep, goats (which can live on food people can't eat, and supply meat, milk, and wool), and cattle (which supply meat, milk, and traction power). So the proscription of pigs made excellent economic sense. Harris extends his argument to many other animals, in particular the sacred cow of India and the animals proscribed by the Old Testament (e.g., eagles, donkeys, dogs, etc.). In every case he tries to show that when one considers the economic conditions in which these prohibitions arose, one can see that there was at least some minor overall advantage to be gained. Thus, he notes that the Old Testament forbids eating any insects other than locusts, which just happen to be the only ones that have much caloric value in relation to the cost of capturing them (and they are crop pests as well). And the sacred cows of India provide milk, as well as fertilizer for an agricultural economy that has great population densities and few funds to spend on meat or "artificial" fertilizers.

Against Harris and his supporters are many people who believe that he is propagating a bastardized version of Marxist theory. Marvin Sahlins, for example, points to the United States, where millions of cattle are slaughtered every year, and yet millions of horses live in relative luxury and enjoy considerable affection. Why, Sahlins asks (1976), do most Americans arbitrarily proscribe horsemeat and yet eat beef? He answers his own question, arguing that it is because every culture creates its own belief systems from its unique blend of economy, society, and ideology. The essential point, Sahlins says, is that *material rationality exists for people not as a fact of nature but as a construct of culture* (emphasis added). He adds that insofar as natural selection shapes ideas like food taboos, these ideas act only as negative constraints – they set limits on functional possibilities, but they leave great latitude in how a particular culture creates its ideology and economy. Moreover, he says, one can never read directly from material circumstances to cultural order as from cause to effect. It is not that techno-environmental variables have no effect, he asserts, but that everything depends on the way these properties are culturally mediated – that is, given meaningful organization by a mode of cultural organization.

Why, for example, didn't Judaism and Islam simply permit a few pigs, as marginal foods, instead of dictating a total taboo? Some would argue that it is because great religions must bind people together with a set of strict rules of behavior, to foster group unity and a sense of separateness and specialness.

All this is rather far from your basic pig, but the point is an important one. For if archaeologists must seek the causes of changes in the archaeological record (like the succession of pig bones by sheep and goat bones in the levels of an archaeological site) in the cultural mediation of "the mode of cultural organization," they will have to apply techniques of analysis currently somewhat beyond them.

Harris argues that one can show by the relative susceptibility to disease, dietary requirements, and other economic and historical factors that it makes economic "sense" to eat cattle and not horses in contemporary America. He does not insist that all human behaviors have such a delicate economic rationality or that religion and other ideologies have no causal impact on cultures. He says only that in the long run, if one is trying to understand something like these different uses of animals, one should look first at the economics of the situation.

This entire debate might be irrelevant if the pig taboos in different cultures were *homologies*, not *analogies*. That is, what if the pig taboo in Orthodox Judaism was not an independent development but was in fact a product of cultural borrowings? The Israelites might have adopted this proscription through cultural contact with Egypt, not as an independent idea. And Islam adopted many ideas from the "People of The Book," both Jewish and Christian.

Such are the complexities of understanding human interactions with just one of God's creatures.

ideological elements to be *dependent* variables – that is, the products of *independent* causal variables, most of which are associated with ecology, demography, and technology; and 4) even if we could assure ourselves that they accurately describe the general processes of early state formation, they would have little to do with the most significant and important aspects of these states, specifically, the unique ways in which these ancient people cognized their worlds and gave meaning to them and to their cultures.

Barry Kemp expressed a primary reason why Egyptologists have been unimpressed by techno-ecological explanations of early states (1989: 7):

It is a feature of many modern treatments of the origin of early states to work, as it were, from the bottom upwards, starting with a group of standard topics: population pressure, agricultural improvements, the appearance of urbanism, the importance of trade and information exchange. The state, by this view, arises autonomously from, or with broad anonymous interrelations between, groups of people and their environment, both the natural and the socioeconomic. States are, however, built on the urge to rule and on visions of order. Although they have to work within the constraints of their lands and people they generate forces, initiate changes, and generally interfere. In looking at the state, therefore, we should keep to the forefront of our minds this generative power that works from the top downwards and from the center outwards.

Examples of Contemporary Analyses of Early Civilizations

Fall down seven times, get up eight.

(Proverbial Japanese advice on dealing with adversity and a lack of progress)

"I can't believe *that!*" said Alice. "Can't you?" the Queen said. . . . "Try again: draw a long breath, and shut your eyes." Alice laughed. "There's no use trying," she said: "one *can't* believe impossible things." "I daresay you haven't had much practice," said the Queen. "When I was your age, I always did it for half-an-hour a day. Why, sometimes I've believed as many as six impossible things before breakfast."

(Lewis Carroll, *Alice in Wonderland*)

In the several decades since the widespread loss of faith in general explanatory models of ancient states and civilizations based mainly on ecological and technological variables, many alternative models have been proposed. The details of most of these are beyond the scope of this book, but some examples are outlined in the following sections.

Holistic Models and Anthropological Archaeology

Bruce Trigger proposed (1984, 2003) that the future of archaeology lies not in replacing the ecological determinism of "processual" archaeology with the "historical particularism" that currently appears to be attracting many archaeologists, but rather in effecting a synthesis of these seemingly opposed positions. He suggested that archaeologists try to investigate as many of the factors that constrain human behavior as possible, not just the external factors of technology and ecology but also the intricacies and idiosyncratic cultural traditions of ancient peoples.

This approach is not particularly controversial. Even scholars closely identified with the historical particularism that Trigger mentioned, such as Ian Hodder (1991), have made a similar argument. The processual archaeology that Trigger refers to was the dominant paradigm in the 1960s and 1970s. It involved attempting to recast archaeology as a positivist science, in the sense of trying to test hypotheses and establish causal connections among environmental, ecological, demographic, and technological variables, and social, political, and ideological attributes of a given culture. Karl Butzer's analysis of ancient Egypt from this perspective (1976) is an elegant example of this approach. The historical particularism Trigger refers to is the shift of focus in much contemporary archaeology to the role of ideological and other factors that produced the many differences among ancient cultures.

How can we apply a "holistic" approach, to use Trigger's term?

Fekri Hassan's Model. Fekri Hassan has proposed a model (1988) of Egyptian state origins that deftly blends techno-environmental factors with ideological elements. He hypothesizes some of the sociopolitical relationships that, in conjunction with ecological factors, were important in Egyptian state origins. He suggests that the processes that led to dynastic civilization were "set in motion by factors inherent in the socioecology of agricultural production" (1988: 165). Hassan argues that as Egyptian villagers became increasingly dependent for food on their crops and domestic animals, they had to adapt to risks inherent in this way of life. Every year agricultural production could be greatly affected by poor Nile floods, loss of soil fertility, diseases of agricultural plants and animals, and other factors.

Hassan notes that the ancient Egyptians probably tried to solve their periodic food shortages and other crises in at least three ways. First, they began to integrate their economies with those of neighboring communities so that food could be shared in hard times. Because of the many variations in the size and shape of local flood basins along the Nile and other factors, one community may have had a prosperous agricultural year while a nearby community did not. Economic links among the economies of even a few villages helped equalize these disparities. Second, they increased the area of cultivation. Third, they gradually improved their agricultural yields per unit of farmland by damming and channeling water, and they improved their crops and domestic animals by selective breeding, intensified weeding and pest control, and other methods. Hassan notes that there is no evidence of government-controlled large-scale irrigation in Egypt until many centuries after the first Egyptian states had formed; thus, the administrative requirements of irrigation agriculture do not seem to have been an important stimulus to initial state formation.

This archaeologist suggests that there was an increase in intra-Nilotic contacts of people along the river as the farming way of life spread and that social and economic interactions among communities would thus have increased. Small farming communities in many cultures and times practiced exogamy, in which a person marries someone from a neighboring community, not someone from one's own small hamlet. Marriage is used in most preindustrial societies as a way to reinforce social and economic relationships that benefit the spouses' extended families and the two communities as well.

Hassan also suggests that boats were plying the Nile throughout the Egyptian Predynastic Period, and that these boats, along with the domestication of the donkey (by about 3600 BC), made it possible to move commodities and people rapidly and efficiently among Egyptian communities. Most of these communities remained largely self-sufficient even during the later pharaonic era, but there were at least a few incentives to trade agricultural products, pottery, stone tools, and other goods and services. As Egyptian communities became larger and more complexly organized during the later Predynastic, the goods exchanged among communities also included elaborately decorated pottery, finely worked stone tools, and other goods that were probably used to indicate ethnicity, status, and power. Hassan notes that already by circa 3900–3600 BC, three "cultural provinces" in the main Upper Nile Valley were each marked by different styles of pottery, stone tools, or other objects. He argues that the increased social and economic interactions among Egyptians in the middle Predynastic led to a more systematic form of trade in the late Predynastic, and this change was "linked to sociopolitical developments and was associated with the emergence of craft specialization" (1988: 159). At some point, kings and priests emerged, and differences in power, wealth, and prestige among individuals and families were legitimized by religion and custom.

We have some tantalizing hints as to how all of these elements of later dynastic civilization may have evolved. There is some evidence of disastrously low flood levels toward the end of the Predynastic Period, for example, and we can speculate that food shortages resulted in regional warfare. The militaristic style of maceheads, knife handles, slate palettes, and other representations during this time may reflect these conflicts.

Hassan points to Maadi as evidence of *trade*, which he distinguishes from informal, occasional individual transactions of goods or gifts. As noted in Chapter 5, Maadi seems to have been a community with strong trade ties in various commodities with Syro-Palestine. In the "commercial" area of ancient Maadi, excavators found pottery in Syro-Palestinian styles, jars of grain, animal and fish bones, some vases, beads, and lumps of imported asphalt. Hassan suggests that although there appear to have been few new communities in the late Predynastic, existing communities seem to have begun the process of "nucleation": the differentiation of Maadi into separate areas where different kinds of activities were conducted and into socially differentiated communities. In early farming villages in Egypt, most of the houses are about the same size and have approximately the same contents. If the archaeological remains of such communities are excavated, one tends to find the same kinds of remains throughout the community no matter where one digs – just houses, stables, garbage pits, and a few other features. Nucleated communities are more complexly organized, however, and usually larger.

Hassan also sees evidence of nucleation at ancient Hierakonpolis. He estimates that the late Predynastic community population there may have been as much as twenty-five hundred, and although that may not sound very large, it was probably larger than other communities in Egypt at this time. But nucleation is more than just an increase in the size of communities. Whether one town has two hundred people and another has two thousand is not particularly significant, in a sense, if the communities have the same sociopolitical organization and economic basis. These kinds of population size differences among peasant agricultural communities can simply be a factor of how much arable land lies within a reasonable walk of the community. By about 3600 BC, however, there were not only substantial differences in sizes of communities but also evidence that managerial elites were emerging. Hassan calculates that at least fifty people's labor would have been necessary to support just one "nonfood producer."

In a sense, it is the basic cleavage of society into those who produce food and those who do not that seems to set into motion the factors that produced civilizations. Thus, kings and priests were valuable economic producers, too, even if they did not grow food, herd livestock, or in other ways directly produce food; kings and priests, in one sense, make everyone richer if they can integrate and administer the economy. Yet there is a fateful quality to that initial break in history, from a time when every extended family directly produced its own (or the community's) food and performed about the same services, to a time in which most people labored in the fields while a relatively few others did not – and those who did not farm got a larger, unequal share of the produce. An early sign of such changes was found at El-Omari, just south of modern Cairo. Here, as Hassan notes, in occupations that may date as early as about 4100 BC, the skeleton of a man was found clutching a well-made wooden staff that looks something like the staffs carried by later Egyptian kings. Some people here appeared to have been buried with many more "luxury" goods, such as pendants, necklaces, ostrich eggshells, and hard stones, than others.

Hassan stresses the importance of the evolution of religion as part of the general processes that eventuated in the emergence of the Egyptian state. Hassan and many other scholars have suggested that Egypt and Mesopotamia differed in the fundamentals of their religious foundations because of the relative stability of Nile floods, and therefore of food. But as rich and stable as Egypt was, comparatively speaking, Nile flood fluctuations did have some effect on political stability. Similarly, the contrast between Egypt's concept of a king who was a god, compared to the Mesopotamian notion that the king was a human intercessor between his subjects and the gods, has been given considerable significance (e.g., Frankfort 1956); but its ultimate importance is unclear. Some changes in some features of Egyptian religion do seem directly to reflect political changes, such as variations in the relative rank of various gods in the pantheon. When Memphis became the preeminent settlement in Egypt, for example, its local god, Ptah, rose to the status of a state god, but he was later eclipsed by Ra, as the power of the community at Heliopolis grew.

Hassan's general model is detailed and makes plausible correlations between environmental and technological determinants, on the one hand, and the socioeconomy and ideological institutions, on the other. One may argue that Hassan's analysis does not escape the criticisms of functional arguments discussed earlier, but it is possible that no "explanation" of the Egyptian past can escape these criticisms. Hassan specifically rejects "functionalism" as a basis for his analyses (e.g, 1988, 1992), and he has adopted a focus on ideological factors in Egypt's evolution. He emphasizes the power of myth/religion as primary evidence with which to understand cultural changes in ancient Egypt. He has appealed to cognitive and sociological forms of analyses. One might question Hassan's interpretations of specifics (e.g., Wengrow 2006: 84–86), but his model stands or falls on its *epistemology* – the manner in which he specifies the crucial issues and arranges elements in causal sequences to explain cultural changes.

Structuralist, Cognitive, and Sociological Perspectives

One never reads the same book twice.

(Variously attributed)

Like the ancient adage that one can never step into the same river twice, because the river you first stepped into has flowed away, the idea that no one can read the same book twice implies that one's circumstances are constantly in flux, and one's interpretation of a book can never be the same with each rereading. This concept has permeated contemporary archaeology.

Almost all scholars who attempt some larger understanding of the Egyptian past – one that transcends simply correlating the Nilotic ecology and demography with Egyptian cultural forms – incorporate elements that have been variously derived from "structuralism," "cognitive analysis," and sociology. But scholars of these different persuasions differ radically in their implementation of these ideas. "Cognitive archaeology" is perhaps the most common theoretical thread in contemporary archaeological theory. Cognitive archaeology focuses on the role that *ideology* had in ancient societies, and how ancient people's cognitive structures and abstract ideas are expressed in the archaeological record. Some of the basic ideas underlying cognitive archaeology come from semiotics and psychology.

Some scholars argue that empirical scientific epistemologies are fundamentally inappropriate for understanding the human past. Archaeologists Michael Shanks and Christopher Tilley, for example, drawing on the work of Jacques Derrida (e.g., 1978), Michel Foucault (1986) Claude Lévi-Straus (1963), Pierre Bourdieu (1977), and other French sociological concepts, have argued that just as one cannot assign a definitive single meaning to a particular novel, poem, or any other text, or even understand precisely what the author of that text was trying to "say," one cannot assign a definitive interpretation to the archaeological record. We create the past, they argue, and our interpretations of the past are limited by, and arise out of, our own cultural context. One cannot help but invent a past that is a reflection of one's socioeconomic and political heritage and context: Shanks and Tilley (1987a, 1989) argue that much of traditional archaeology has been done on the mistaken assumption that it was a nineteenth/twentieth-century kind of "positivist science," in the same sense that general physical laws and analytical techniques mean that a Canadian physicist and a Chinese physicist work with the same Table of Elements.

So, if we cannot aspire to an empirical science of the past, what should archaeologists do? Shanks and Tilley state that "[f]or the subjective idealism of scientistic archaeology we substitute a view of the discipline [of archaeology] as an hermeneutically informed dialectical science of past and present unremittingly embracing and attempting to understand the polyvalent qualities of the socially constructed world of the past and the world in which we live" (1987a: 243).

Exactly what they mean by this statement is far, far beyond the scope of this book, but there are several core elements to the kinds of analyses they and like-minded scholars envision. One element is the conviction that archaeology should be done with *explicit political purposes*. They argue that archaeology should be an attempt to achieve radical political goals, to resist what they see as economic inequalities, racism, and imperialism. Archaeology and all studies of the past, they argue, are necessarily done with sociopolitical motives, whether these motives are explicit or not. So the archaeologist should make explicit his or her motives.

Another common element in some versions of contemporary archaeology is *relativism*. It seems to follow necessarily that if the past is to be read as any other text, that if it contains no ultimate "truth," and if positivist science cannot be applied to the past, then any person's "reading" of the past is as good as anyone else's. This kind of relativism may sound nonsensical to the traditional scholar, but it has had some impact in archaeology. In the United States, for example, disputes about the disposition of Native American remains are entangled in legal proceedings in which one issue concerns whose interpretation of the past has the power of law. For more than two centuries, scientists have amassed evidence that convinces them beyond any doubt that the New World was colonized from Asia and, perhaps, Europe between about 40,000 and 12,000 BC. Many Native Americans, however, insist that their ancestors have "always" been in the New World. So there are two "truths" here. Who is right? Or take "Kennewick Man," a skeleton found in Washington State and dated to about 7600 BC, that has been the subject of many court disputes. The cranial features of the skull bear little similarity to Native American groups that have lived in this area for many centuries. Yet these Native American groups have claimed him as one of their own and sued for possession of the bones. Whose "truth" should have legal standing in such a case? (The courts eventually gave jurisdiction to the state.)

Similarly, as noted in Chapter 3, some people truly believe that the Great Sphinx at Giza was created at about 10,000 BC. It was not, but intellectual relativism would seem to require that equal weight be given to radiocarbon dates, geological analyses, and all the other trappings of the arts and sciences of traditional empirical analysis and the "dreams" of mystics such as Edgar Cayce – that no attempt be made here to discover who is "right," because there is no right or wrong answer. It must be stressed, however, that not all critics of explanatory archaeology adopt this extreme form of relativism.

Another element in many modern archaeological perspectives is *Marxism*. Despite the recent collapse of some Marxist states and the interweaving of Marx's economic analysis with a dubious political polemic, there is no denying the tremendous influence his contributions have had on the social and historical disciplines. Almost any attempt to sum up Marx's theories about the origins of cultural complexity and the dynamics of history necessarily involves great oversimplification and arguable interpretations. One of the most famous statements of Marx's basic ideas, which for pure concentrated insight and powerful explanatory potential is unrivaled in the historical sciences, is the following:

In the social production of their subsistence men enter into determined and necessary relations with each other which are independent of their wills – production-relations which correspond to a definite stage of development of their material productive forces. The sum total of these production-relations forms the economic structure of society, the real basis, upon which a juridical and political superstructure arises, and to which definite forms of social consciousness correspond. The mode of production of material subsistence conditions the social, political and spiritual life-process in general. *It is not the consciousness of men which determines their existence but on the contrary it is their social existence that determines their consciousness.*   (Quoted in Cohen 1978: viii–ix; my emphasis added)

At first glance, this statement would seem to suggest, for example, that much of the panoply of Egyptian laws, manners, customs, and religion was just part of the "superstructure," determined by the underlying economic factors. Contemporary archaeologists who employ Marxist ideas in their analyses, however, would violently object to such a reading. They question the notion that the techno-ecological models of the origins of the state, as discussed earlier in this chapter, are in any way "Marxist," despite their emphasis on ecological and economic determinants. Others scholars have rejected Marxist ideas about economic determinism on the grounds that they fail to accommodate the power of individuals to impose their cultural, often symbolic, perceptions on their world (Bourdieu 1977)

The truth, alas, is that nothing about Marx's famous statement – or interpretations of it – is simple or obvious. After studying the uses to which the French "Marxists" of his time put his ideas, Marx famously said, "All I know is that I am not a Marxist." He himself had very little to say specifically about the origins of complex societies like pharaonic Egypt. His primary focus was detailing the problems of capitalism and the dynamics of the transition from feudalism to capitalist societies, and thence to socialist and communist societies.

Most Marxists, however, still focus on the means by which wealth is produced, how wealth is expropriated by elites, how socioeconomic classes form and relate to one another, and why cultures change over time. A key idea in Marxism is the notion of forces of production, which traditionally has been interpreted to mean all forms of technology, all utilized resources, advances in scientific knowledge and applications, and so forth. The term "relations of production," as used by many Marxists, refers to the ways in which people relate with one another to utilize the forces of production to produce and distribute goods. Thus, if we want to understand ancient Egyptian ideas about inheritance laws, family relationships, religion, architecture, and so forth, we should first identify and examine the forces and relations of production. But these notions of cause and effect in modern Marxism are complex. One cannot just infer, for instance, that the development of productive agriculture in the Nile Valley directly and simply caused the first Egyptian states to appear. Technological changes, such as agriculture, bronze sickles, and irrigation systems, bring about social and political changes, but they themselves are products of specific social and political contexts that "determine," in a sense, what technological changes will occur.

A crucial concept in most Marxist analyses – and one that is still a major concept in some current philosophies of archaeology – is that of "dialectical" historical change. Marx believed that the history of human societies is one in which primitive communist societies of Stone Age hunter-foragers gave way to a variety of clan-based societies, then to the "slave" societies like those of classical Greece and Rome and the "Asiatic" societies like that of ancient Egypt, then to the feudal societies exemplified by medieval Europe, then to "capitalist" economies like those of much of our age, and that these will be succeeded first by socialist societies and finally by communist societies.

The critical question is, why this sequence – why any change at all? Marx – and many of his contemporary proponents – believed that all societies contain within themselves the seeds of their own destruction and of their present state, as well as the embryonic elements of their future condition. The force for change is in the "contradictions," the dialectical oppositions in societal elements. (Some blame Hegel's notion of triadic change, *thesis, and antithesis,* followed by *synthesis,* for Marx's idea of the dialectic.) From the Marxist perspective, therefore, the great disparities between the wealth of Old Kingdom elites and the poverty of the populace could be viewed as an antagonism, a contradiction, that had to be resolved eventually. From this perspective, one might conclude that the pharaonic state apparatus – especially its state religion – developed because it was the mechanism by which the elites could exploit the populace, through laws, police, taxes, and so forth.

There have been few overtly and extended Marxist analyses of ancient Egypt. Jacques Janssen's study (1978) of the economics of a New Kingdom village at Deir el-Medina reveals many interesting aspects of how the ordinary Egyptian viewed prices and other monetary concepts, in relation to the social inequalities of the times. In the absence of a written language and comprehensive documentation, however, how are we to know if, let's say, overt or institutionalized class conflict, or the subordination of women, or other social behaviors and concepts were part of the origins of the first states in Egypt? Testability with archaeological data cannot, of course, be taken as the ultimate criterion of the validity of social theory. Marxist theory might be largely valid but untestable with regard to some periods of the past and some cultures.

But many of the categories and constructs of Marxist theory seem imprecise when applied to ancient Egypt. Ancient Egyptians were so enveloped in the bonds of religion and kinship, and power was so centralized and "legitimized" in the person of the divine pharaoh, that the kinds of class conflict that were important to Marxian analyses of, for example, feudal Europe do not seem directly applicable to Egypt. And dynastic civilization was also so stable in its core elements for so long that Marx's ideas about social revolution and the necessity of historical change seem somewhat dubious. When Marx stated that "religion is the opiate of the masses," he had in mind his assumption that religion functioned to keep the proletariat in capitalist societies docile, even as they were being grievously exploited by the ruthless industrial capitalism of his time. Ancient Egyptian religion may have had something of a similar role, but dynastic religion was interwoven in the culture in a profoundly different manner.

A detailed discussion of the applications of Marxist ideas to the institutionalization of wealth and power differences in early states is beyond the scope of this book, but it seems likely that these idea will inform analyses of early states for many years to come.

Some scholars have proposed models that, while incorporating criticisms of traditional explanatory models of ancient states, draw much of their inspiration from the terms and ideas of French philosophy and sociology. David Wengrow (2006), for one, has comprehensively analyzed Egypt's social transformations as they occurred between 10,000 and 2650 BC. His analysis is not easily summarized, and only a few elements of it can be described here.

Wengrow argues for a "world archaeology," by which he means comparisons that include a large geographical area and time span (he focuses on Egypt and Southwest Asia). Also, he suggests, a world archaeology must address questions of "general anthropological significance." He specifically rejects placing ancient Egypt in the context of comparative studies of "archaic states," "early civilizations," and so forth because he considers that these labels put unnecessary constraints and assumptions on analyses of social change in Egypt, among other reasons. He aspires to thick descriptions of pre–Old Kingdom Egyptian cultures. "Thick description" is a term derived from the work of anthropologist Clifford Geertz and others, who suggest that because human behavior is so complex, the analysis of a culture should provide a detailed description of the complexities of the social and ideological contexts for a set of activities, not just the materials and production techniques used in these activities.

Wengrow, for instance, focuses the relationship between the living and the dead as it is "sustained, negotiated and altered through ritual activity" (2006: 7). He specifically examines how the bodies of ancient Egyptians were decorated, wrapped, and placed in ritual contexts. One of his objectives is to consider how this link between the living and the dead, and all the rituals and materials associated with it, can be related to the ancient Egyptian socioeconomy. He considers that the totality of ancient Egyptian ritual practices, as they formed over thousands of years, constitute a historical reality that cannot be reduced to the conscious intentions of the people who created these tombs and other structures, and that cannot be restricted to forces beyond their control. He argues that these ideas can be related to empirical evidence and thus have some possibility for general analysis.

An example of Wengrow's approach is badly needed at this point, and so here is part of his analysis of tombs at Abydos and Saqqara (2006: 258):

By establishing a tension between presence and absence – the invisible and visible aspects of the deceased's persona – the mortuary complexes at Abydos and Saqqara conform . . . to the dynastic construction of death. . . . Both expressed the idea that death and sacrifice give rise to a new physical structure that dominates the world of the living. In this sense, and also in aspects of physical appearance, the mortuary enclosure was analogous to the mastaba superstructure, just as correspondence existed between their associated subterranean parts. Such relationships should not blind us, however, to the contrasting features of these monuments and their complementary roles within an evolving ritual landscape that encompassed much of the state. Unlike mastaba platforms, mortuary enclosures were hollow spaces, physically separated form the site of burial and provided with real entrances and exits. Their role within the royal mortuary cult went beyond the visual domination of space to encompass embodied performances – movements in time that extended to the generative power of death into rhythms of ongoing life, and constituted the body politic as a container of potentially limitless capacity.

Traditional archaeologists might question the empirical basis of Wengrow's approach, in the sense that he sees in these monuments expressions of meaning and significance that are difficult to tie directly and unequivocally to pyramids, bones, stones, pots, mummies, and the other *things* of which the Egyptian archaeological record is composed. But Wengrow's approach is in its own way highly empirical.

Evolutionary Theory

As the beaver said to the jack rabbit as they looked at the awesome size of Hoover Dam: "No, I didn't build it myself, but it's based on an idea of mine."

(Attributed to Charles Townes, an inventor of the laser)

If Charles Darwin could see the many uses to which his ideas have been put in modern scholarship, he would no doubt echo Charles Townes's remark. The continuing power of Darwin's simple ideas to inform disciplines as divergent as paleontology and genetics is impressive.

Applications of Darwinian theory to the human past, however, have suffered from a century of misuse and conflation with the nineteenth-century sociological ideas of Herbert Spencer and others. Neither human groups nor cultural elements are analogous to biological genes or genera, and "natural selection" cannot be crudely applied to the human past. Darwin himself had doubts about analyzing human history with evolutionary theory, asking, who "would trust the conclusions of a monkey mind?"

Yet Darwin's ideas still have considerable currency in contemporary archaeology (e.g., Lyman and O'Brien 2000), and many consider that Darwinian ideas have great potential in this regard – especially given the unquestionable productivity of these ideas in a broad range of contemporary sciences. But how can we apply Darwinian constructs to the archaeological record?

Some evolutionists argue that archaeology can never be a true science of behavior, because "behavior" does not exist in the archaeological record. Behavior exists only in the form of inferences about it, and these inferences can never rise above the level of analogy and simple and dubious descriptions and reconstructions of the past.

Evolutionists believe that our analyses and understanding of a historical sequence like that of ancient Egypt will always be in a different form from that of our knowledge of physics, chemistry, and mathematics. These disciplines concern phenomena that are universal and (in a limited sense) timeless. Evolutionary theory, however, concerns phenomena on this particular planet and its unique history.

Contemporary thought in Darwinian evolutionary theory, as applied to both cultural and biological systems, emphasizes the uniqueness and essential unpredictability of evolutionary trajectories. Stephen Jay Gould's influential *Wonderful Life* (1989), for example, argues that the eventual appearance of human beings was utterly unpredictable from the nature of life on earth millions of years prior to our appearance as a genus; he concludes that human life would never have evolved if not for random conjunctions of long-term processes and unique events, such as asteroid impacts that killed off many genera that would have competed with our mammalian ancestors. Similarly, evolutionists who analyze culture histories also reject the application to the human past of scientific forms of analysis and explanation based on static, deterministic theories like those of physics (Dunnell 1982).

The kind of evolutionary theory modern scholars propose, however, differs greatly from nineteenth- and early-twentieth-century ideas about *cultural* evolution (e.g., reviewed in Dunnell 1982; Hart and Terrell 2002; Maschner 1996; Shennan 2004). In fact, there is a widening gap between evolutionary archaeology and most other variants of the discipline (Kristiansen 2004).

Evolutionary theory in its most basic sense addresses the transmission of traits through time and space. Population genetics and evolutionary biology – especially DNA analyses – offer powerful mathematical models of how biological species have evolved through time and changed in their distribution in the world. How might we apply these sciences to the archaeology of ancient Egypt?

Many scholars have argued that the fundamental difference between biological and cultural methods of trait transmission necessarily invalidates the application of evolutionary ideas to cultural phenomena. But others have rejected that conclusion: Cultural traits are also transmitted through time and space, and just because these transmission mechanisms are not genetic does not necessarily mean that we cannot analyze them.

The supposed cultural unification of the Nile Delta and Valley cultures at circa 3200–3000 BC provides a useful example here. This pivotal event in Egyptian history apparently involved a process in which the cultural repertoire of the Valley largely replaced that of the Delta. We know that shortly after about 3200 BC, the distinctive artifact and architectural styles of the Delta disappeared. How are we to understand such a process of trait transmission? And, at a higher level, how are we to understand similar processes in other early civilizations? In explaining the lack of variation in early states in such elements as the rise of exploitative elites, Trigger appeals (1993) to the apparent "efficiency" that this feature must have conferred on their individual cultures. If we accept that supposition, the analytical problem then becomes one of understanding and measuring the relative efficiency of various mechanisms of social forms and phenomena, and the kinds of selection that operate on variability, and how that variability is generated in the first place. If evolutionary theory has any application to the analysis of ancient and modern cultures, it would seem to be precisely with regard to these questions of cultural change.

Many scholars have explored these issues, but the development of evolutionary theory as applied to archaeological data remains at a relatively elementary level. As an illustration of how these ideas about evolutionary theory might be applied to the Egyptian archaeological record, consider monumental architecture. There is little analytical value to explaining the pyramids simply in terms of availability of labor and resources and a human penchant for grandiosity. A distinguishing characteristic of early civilizations in Egypt, Mesopotamia, Mexico, Europe, and other areas is that each of them invested vast amounts of resources in pyramids, tombs, or other monumental constructions. Why should such elaborately "wasteful" structures appear in these rather primitive and fragile state economies? And why should they appear at about the same point in the developmental trajectory of these states? And why did they disappear from the architectural repertoire of Egypt and other civilizations? And why did some of the largest early states (e.g., the Harappan civilization of the Indus Valley) not build pyramids?

Trigger (1989) interpreted these constructions in terms of their role in validating religious and political hierarchies. Robert Dunnell (personal communication; 1982), Leslie White (1949), and others have attempted to explain variations in the rate of monumental architecture construction and their geographic distribution in terms of factors of functional efficiency (Trigger 1989). Dunnell (1982; personal communication) has drawn a parallel between Egyptian pyramid construction and many other examples of changes in the relative investment in "waste" of various cultures. In the late Paleolithic-Mesolithic transition, for example, highly crafted stone points, cave paintings, and so forth seem to disappear and are replaced by a "drab" but functionally more complex technology. Both this transition and the decline of pyramid building, he suggests, may be linked to changes in carrying capacity, that is, the number of individual people who can be supported by a given area's natural resources over a long term: Luxury goods, such as gold bowls, pyramids, or even spear points, tend to appear in abundance during the early stages of adaptations because their costs help suppress unstable rates of expansion of these systems – perhaps even population growth (see Sterling 1999 for a good application of this idea to Egypt). However, once the increased carrying capacity – whether through more productive forms of agriculture or more efficient governmental administration through decentralization – is well established, the selective advantages of the "waste" of resources in the form of highly stylized stone tools, pyramids, and so forth diminish.

Similarly, most early complex societies underwent a transition in which labor-intensive, highly decorated pottery was replaced by mass-produced forms of much less aesthetic appeal and labor invested in them (Chazan and Lehner 1990). Various scholars have seen cultural collapse and dissolution in such changes, but, as Trigger notes, such changes do "not indicate a decline in cultural or aesthetic standards. Instead [they suggest] that pottery no longer served as a medium of artistic expression" (1983: 64). In fact, the appearance of these mass-produced forms of pottery seems to be a prime indicator of increasing complexity in the institutions administering and controlling craft production (G. Johnson 1987). As the first states evolved in Egypt and Mesopotamia, unimpressive, mass-produced forms largely replaced earlier highly decorated pottery types. Several factors may explain these dramatic changes in pottery manufacture. The individual and corporate social groups previously identified by regional pottery styles were, in a sense, dangerous to the unity of the larger state. These states may have suppressed some expressions of group identity not derived from the state structures (as opposed to nome symbols, for example, which were derived from the organizational structure of the state, and persisted). The greater efficiency, too, of producing massive quantities of cheap and nearly identical simple pottery vessels would appeal to the state administrators who made cost–benefit calculations.

The examples used here of applications of evolutionary theory to pyramids and pottery are directed at measurable objects, and it remains to be seen whether evolutionary theory can be usefully applied to more abstract issues – like the evolution of complex systems in general. It is one thing to show how changes in pottery styles fit an evolutionary pattern, but how do we apply evolutionary ideas to complex systems in general, from computers to cellular biology to the dynastic state? In fact, it is not even clear what would have been the *unit* of selection: the individual? the extended family? the community? the entire state?

One interesting current trend in evolutionary analyses involves non-linear systems analyses and the "emergent" properties of complex systems. Physicist Steven Wolfram, for one, has suggested (2002) that there are no simple cause and effect explanations of such phenomena as biological entities, and his ideas can be extended to ancient civilizations. He argues that complex systems that have a determinable time span and an evolutionary trajectory can best be understood as algorithms, and he shows how extremely complex organisms, biological or cultural, can evolve from simple elements that reproduce according to simple rules. The usefulness of these and similar ideas in analyses of early states is not clear. Cultural complexity *appears* to evolve in part through Lamarckian – not just Darwinian – processes: That is, people are able to direct the generation of variety that is then selected, such as investments in irrigation systems and other agricultural techniques – changes deliberately introduced to achieve some objective.

At this point it is unclear the extent to which these attempts to analyze "self-organizing" complex systems, whether biological or historical-political, by using evolutionary theory will advance our knowledge of these issues, but they certainly raise important questions. No matter how powerful evolutionary theory might become as a means to understand the dynamics of ancient Egyptian history, it will always be considered a limited form of analysis because evolutionary theory does not focus on human behavior. And most people who do archaeology, and most people in general, want interpretations of the past translated into ordinary human terms, such as the methods used to build the pyramids. Evolutionary archaeology as described in this section will never fulfill that need.

Conclusions

It has proven remarkably difficult to prise apart the many causes and effects that make up Egyptian cultural history, but we are beginning to understand at least some aspects of this history. And, as with other early civilizations, there is much about Egypt that is interesting and rewarding at a level beyond that of the mechanics of its history.

Nonetheless, the review of ancient Egypt that constitutes this book has led me to agree (Wenke (1991, 1995a, 1995b) with Bruce Trigger, who noted (1993: 111–112):

While I do not deny that cultural traditions provide the intellectual material with which individuals and groups approach new problems, and that they therefore exert a significant role in determining the nature of cultural change, my findings indicate that practical reason plays a greater role in shaping cultural change than many postprocessual archaeologists and postmodernist anthropologists are prepared to admit. This encourages me to accord greater importance to an evolutionist analysis and less importance to a cultural particularist one than I would have done when I began my study. A particularist approach is necessary to understand many aspects of early civilizations. But it is clearly a mistake to ignore, or even to underestimate, the importance of evolutionism, as those who privilege cultural reason would have us do.

Perhaps the clearest vision of the future of archaeology is Kent V. Flannery's (2006) argument for the long-term prospects for *anthropological* archaeology. All through the many revolutions in archaeological theory, the concepts and methods of anthropology have persisted in the actual practice of archaeology. This has been particularly true of studies of ancient Egyptian civilization, and such analyses will probably continue far into the future.

Bibliography

Adams, Barbara. 1974. *Ancient Hierakonpolis*. Warminster: Aris & Philips.

Adams, Barbara, and Renée F. Friedman. 1992. Imports and influences in the Predynastic and protodynastic settlement and funerary assemblages at Hierakonpolis. In *The Nile Delta in Transition, 4th–3rd Millennium B.C*, edited by Edwin C. M. van den Brink, pp. 317–338. Jerusalem: The Israel Exploration Society.

Adams, Matthew D. 2005. *Community and Society in the First Intermediate Period: An Archaeological Investigation of the Abydos Settlement Site*. Ph.D. Dissertation. Philadelphia: University of Pennsylvania.

Adams, Matthew J. 2007. *The Early Dynastic through Old Kingdom Stratification at Tell er-Rub'a, Mendes*. Ph.D. Dissertation. Pennsylvania State University.

Adams, Robert McCormick. 1966. *The Evolution of Urban Society*. Chicago: Aldine.

Adamson, Donald A., Françoise Gasse, Frances A. Street–Perrott, and Martin A. Williams. 1980. Quarternary history of the Nile. *Nature* 287: 50–55.

Allen, James P. 1992. *Genesis in Egypt: The Philosophy of Ancient Egyptian Creation Accounts*. New Haven, Conn.: Yale Egyptological Seminar.

———— 2000. *Middle Egyptian*. Cambridge: Cambridge University Press.

Ammerman, A. J., and L. L. Cavalli-Sforza, 1984. *The Neolithic Transition and the Genetics of Populations in Europe*. Princeton, N.J.: Princeton University Press.

Anderson, Wendy. 1992. Badarian burials: Evidence of social inequality in Middle Egypt during the Predynastic era. *Journal of the American Research Center in Egypt* 29: 51–66.

Armelagos, George J., and James O. Mills. 1999. Egyptology and paleopathology. In *Encyclopedia of the Archaeology of Ancient Egypt*, edited by Kathryn A. Bard, pp. 604–607. New York: Routledge.

Arnold, Dieter. 1991. *Building in Egypt*. Oxford: Oxford University Press.

Arnold, Dorothea, ed. 1981. *Studien zur altägyptiaschen Keramik*. Mainz: Verlag Philipp von Zabern.

Asante, Molefi K. 1990. *Kemet, Afrocentricity, and Knowledge*. Trenton, N.J.: Africa World Press.

Assman, Jan. 2002. *History and Meaning in the Time of the Pharaohs*, translated by Andrew Jenkins. New York: Henry Holt.

2005. *Death and Salvation in Ancient Egypt*, translated by David Lorton. Ithaca, N.Y.: Cornell University Press.

Badawy, Alexander. 1967. The civic sense of the pharaoh and urban development in ancient Egypt. *Journal of the American Research Center in Egypt* 6: 103–109.

Badr, Abdel F., Kai Müller, Ralf Schäfer-Pregl, Haddad Abdel Samie El Rabey, Siglinde Effgen, H. H. Ibrahim, Carlo Pozzi, Wolfgang Rohde, and Francesco Salamini. 2000. On the origin and domestication history of barley (*Hordeum vulgare*). *Molecular Biology and Evolution* 17: 499–510.

Baer, Klaus. 1960. *Rank and Title in the Old Kingdom*. Chicago: University of Chicago Press.

Baines, John. 1994. On the status and purposes of Egyptian art. *Cambridge Archaeological Journal* 4(1): 67–94.

2000. Writing, invention, and early development. In *Encyclopedia of the Archaeology of Ancient Egypt*, edited by Kathryn A. Bard, pp. 882–884. New York: Routledge.

Baines, John, and Jaromir Malek. 1980. *Atlas of Ancient Egypt*. New York: Facts on File.

Bard, Kathryn A. 1992. Toward an interpretation of the role of ideology in the evolution of complex society in Egypt. *Journal of Anthropological Archaeology* 11: 1–24.

2000. The emergence of the Egyptian state. In *The Oxford History of Ancient Egypt*, edited by Ian Shaw, pp. 61–88. New York: Oxford University Press.

Bard, Kathryn A., and Robert L. Carneiro. 1989. Patterns of Predynastic settlement location, social evolution, and the circumscription theory. *Sociétés Urbaines en Égypte et au Soudan. Cahiers de Recherches de l'Institut de Papyrologie et d'Égyptologie de Lille* 11: 15–23.

Barocas, Claudio, Rodolfo Fattovich, and Maurizio Tosi. 1989. The Oriental Institute of Naples expedition to Petrie's South Town (Upper Egypt), 1977–1983: An interim report. In *Late Prehistory of the Nile Basin and the Sahara*, edited by Lech Krzyzaniak and Michal Kobusiewicz, pp. 295–301. Poznan: Muzeum Archaeologiczne W. Poznaniu.

Barzun, Jacques, and Henry F. Graff. 1970. *The Modern Researcher*. New York: Harcourt World & Brace.

Bernal, Martin. 1987. *Black Athena: The Afroasiatic Roots of Classical Civilization*, Vol. 1: *The Fabrication of Ancient Greece*. New Brunswick, N.J.: Rutgers University Press.

2006. *Black Athena: The Afroasiatic Roots of Classical Civilization*, Vol. III: *The Linguistic Evidence*. New Brunswick, N.J.: Rutgers University Press.

Bietak, Manfred. 1979. In *Egyptology and the Social Sciences*, edited by Kent R. Weeks, pp. 21–56. Cairo: American University in Cairo Press.

Binford, Sally, and Lewis Binford, eds. 1968. *New Perspectives in Archaeology*. Chicago: Aldine.

Bokonyi, S. 1985. The animal remains of Maadi, Egypt: A preliminary report. *In Studi di paleontologia in onore di S. M. Puglisi*. Rome: Università di Roma La Sapienza.

Bonani, Georges H., Herbert Haas, Zahi Hawass, Mark Lehner, Shawki Nakhla, John Nolan, Robert J. Wenke, and Willy Wölfli. 2001. Radiocarbon dates of Old and Middle Kingdom monuments in Egypt. *Radiocarbon* 43(3): 1297–1320.

Bourdieu, Pierre. 1977. *Outline of a Theory of Practice*, translated by Richard Nice. Cambridge: Cambridge University Press.

Bourriau, J. 1981. *Umm el Ga'ab: Pottery from the Nile Valley before the Arab Conquest*. Cambridge: Fitzwilliam Museum.

Boyd, Robert, and Peter J. Richerson. 1985. *Culture and Evolutionary Process*. Chicago: University of Chicago Press.

Brace, C. Loring, David P. Tracer, Lucia A. Yaroch, John Robb, Kari Brandt, and A. Russell Nelson. 1993. Clines and clusters versus "race": A test in ancient Egypt and the case of a death on the Nile. *Yearbook of Physical Anthropology* 36: 1–31.

Brass, Michael. 2007. Reconsidering the emergence of social complexity in early Saharan pastoral societies, 5000–2500 BC. *Sahara* 18: 1–16.

Brewer, Douglas. J., and Renée F. Friedman. 1989. *Fish and Fishing in Ancient Egypt*. Warminster: Aris & Phillips.

Brewer, Douglas. J., J. Isaacson, D. Haag, and Robert J. Wenke. 1996. Mendes regional archaeological survey and remote sensing analysis. *Sahara* 8: 29–42.

Brewer, Douglas. J., Donald A. Redford, and Susan Redford. 1994. *Domestic Plants and Animals: The Egyptian Origins*. Warminister: Aris & Phillips.

Brewer, Douglas, and Emily Teeter. 1999. *Egypt and the Egyptians*. New York: Cambridge University Press.

Brunton, Guy, and Gertrude Caton-Thompson. 1928. *The Badarian Civilization*. London: The British School of Archaeology in Egypt.

Buck, Paul. 1989. *Formation Processes of Old Kingdom Sediments at Kom el-Hisn, Egypt*. Ph.D. Dissertation. Seattle: University of Washington.

Burkert, Walter. 1992. *The Orientalizing Revolution: Near Eastern Influence on Greek Culture in the Early Archaic Age*. Cambridge, Mass.: Harvard University Press.

Butzer, Karl W. 1976. *Early Hydraulic Civilization in Egypt*. Chicago: University of Chicago Press.

1990. A human ecosystem framework for archaeology. In *The Ecosystem Approach in Anthropology: From Concept to Practice*, edited by Emilio F. Moran, pp. 91–130. Ann Arbor: University of Michigan Press.

2002. Geoarchaeological implications of recent research in the Nile Delta. In *Egypt and the Levant: Interrelations from the 4th through the early 3rd millennium BC*, edited by Edwin van den Brink and Thomas Levy, pp. 83–97. London: Leicester University Press.

Cagle, Anthony J. 2001. *The Spatial Structure of Kom el-Hisn: An Old Kingdom Town in the Western Nile Delta, Egypt*. Ph.D. Dissertation. Seattle: University of Washington.

Caneva, Isabella, Marcella Frangipane, and Alba Palmieri. 1987. Predynastic Egypt: New data from Maadi. *African Archaeological Review* 5: 105–114.

Carneiro, Robert L. 1970. A theory of the origin of the state. *Science* 1169: 733–738.

Caton-Thompson, Gertrude, and Elinor W. Gardner. 1934. *The Desert Fayum.* London: The Royal Anthropological Institute of Great Britain and Ireland.

Cavalli-Sforza, Luigi, and Marcus Feldman. 1981. *Cultural Transmission and Evolution.* Princeton, N.J.: Princeton University Press.

Chazan, Michael, and Mark Lehner. 1990. An ancient analogy: Pot baked bread in ancient Egypt and Mesopotamia. *Paléorient* 16(2): 21–35.

Childe, V. Gordon. 1934. *New Light on the Most Ancient East.* London: Kegan Paul.

Clayton P. A. 1994. *Chronicle of the Pharaohs.* London: Thames and Hudson.

Cohen, G. A. 1978. *Karl Marx's Theory of History: A Defense.* Princeton, N.J.: Princeton University Press.

Coutellier, V., and Jean Daniel Stanley. 1987. Late quaternary stratigraphy and paleogeography of the eastern Nile Delta, Egypt. *Marine Geology* 77: 257–275.

Crone, Patricia. 1989. *Pre-industrial Societies.* Oxford: Blackwell.

Dagnon-Ginter, A., Boleslaw Ginter, Janusz K. Kozlowski, Maciel Pawlikowski, and J. Sliwa. 1984. Excavations in the region of Qasr el-Sagha, 1981: Contribution to the Neolithic Period, Middle Kingdom settlement and chronological sequences in the Northern Fayum Desert. *Mitteilungen des Deutschen Archäeologischen Instituts Abteilung Kairo* 40: 33–102.

Daniel, Glyn. 1967. *The Origins and Growth of Archaeology.* Baltimore: Penguin.

Darnell, John C. (assisted by Deborah Darnell). 2002. *Theban Desert Road Survey in the Egyptian Western Desert: Gebel Tjauti Rock Inscriptions 1–45 and Wadi El-Hol Rock Inscriptions 1–45.* Chicago: University of Chicago Oriental Institute Publications.

Davies, W. Vivian. 1987. *Reading the Past: Egyptian Hieroglyphs.* Berkeley: University of California Press.

1989. *The Canonical Tradition in Ancient Egyptian Art.* Cambridge: Cambridge University Press.

Debono, Fernand. 1956. La civilization prédynastique d'el Omari (Nord d'Helouan): Nouvelles données. *Bulletin de l'Institut d'Égypte* 37: 329–329.

Derrida, Jacques. 1978. Structure, sign and play in the discourse of the human sciences. In *Writing and Difference,* translated by Alan Bass. London: Routledge.

Diamond, Jared. 1999. *Guns, Germs, and Steel: The Fate of Human Societies.* New York: W. W. Norton.

Diop, Chiekh A. 1974. *The African Origin of Civilization: Myth or Reality,* translated by Mercer Cook. New York: L. Hill.

Dreyer, Gunter. 1988. *Umm el Qaab I: Das prädynastische Königsgrab U-j und seine frühen Schriftzeugnisse.* Mainz am Rhein: Verlag Philipp von Zabern.

1992. Recent discoveries at U-Cemetery at Abydos. In *The Nile Delta in Transition: 4th–3rd Millennium B.C,* edited by Edwin C. M. van den Brink, pp. 293–299. Jerusalem: The Israel Exploration Society.

Drower, Margaret S. 1985. *Flinders Petrie: A Life in Archaeology.* London: Victor Gollancz.

Du Bois, William E. B. [1903] 1995. *The Souls of Black Folk.* New York: Signet.

Dumont, Louis. 1980. *Homo Hierarchicus: The Caste System and Its Implications,* translated by M. Sainsbury, L. Dumont, and B. Gulati. Chicago: University of Chicago Press.

Dunnell, Robert C. 1971. *Systematics in Prehistory.* New York: Free Press.

—— 1982. Science, social science, and common sense: The agonizing dilemma of modern archaeology. *Journal of Anthropological Research* 38: 1–25.

Earle, T. K. 1987. Chiefdoms in archaeological and ethnohistorical perspective. *Annual Review of Anthropology* 16: 279–308.

Earle, T. K., ed. 1991. *Chiefdoms: Power, Economy, Ideology.* Cambridge: Cambridge University Press.

Edwards, Stephen I. E. 1961. *The Pyramids of Egypt.* London: Parish.

Eisenstadt, Shmuel N., ed. 1986. *The Origins and Diversity of Axial Age Civilizations.* New York: State University of New York Press.

Eiwanger, Josef. 1982–1992. *Merimde-Benisalâme I-III. Die Funde der Mittleren Merimdekultur.* 3 vols. Mainz: Verlag Philipp von Zabern.

El-Hadidi, Nabil, and Irina Springuel. 1989. The natural vegetation of the Nile Valley at Wadi Kubbaniya. In *The Prehistory of Wadi Kubbaniya*, Vol. 2: *Palaeoeconomy, Environment and Stratigraphy*, edited by Angela Close, Fred Wendorf, and Romuald Schild, pp. 243–251. Dallas: Southern Methodist University Press.

Emery, Walter. B. 1967. *Archaic Egypt.* Harmondsworth: Penguin Books.

Fagan, Brian. 1975. *The Rape of the Nile: Tomb Robbers, Tourists, and Archaeologists in Egypt.* New York: Charles Scribner's Sons.

Fairservis, Walter. A. 1981. *The Hierakonpolis Project: Excavations of the Archaic East of the Niched Gate Season of 1981.* Occasional Papers in Anthropology Number III, pp. 1–23. Typescript, Vassar College, Poughkeepsie, N.Y.

—— 1986. Excavation of the archaic remains east of the Niched Gate: Season of a revised view of the Na'rmr Palette. *Journal of the American Research Center in Egypt* 28: 1–20.

Faltings, Dina. 1996. Recent excavations in Tell El-Fara'in/Buto: New finds and their chronological implications. In *Proceedings of the 7th International Congress of Egyptologists: Cambridge 3–9 September 1995*, edited by Chris J. Eyre, pp. 365–375. Leuven: Uitgeverij Peeters.

—— 1998a. Ergebnisse der neuen ausgrabungen in Buto. Chronologie und fernbeziehungen der Buto-Maadi-Kultur neu überdacht. In *Stationen: beiträge zur kulturgeschichte Ägyptens Rainer Stadelmann Gewidmet*, edited by Rainer Stadelmann, Heike Guksch, and Daniel Polz, pp. 35–45. Mainz: Verlag Philipp von Zabern.

—— 1998b. Canaanites at Buto in the early fourth millennium B.C. *Egyptian Archaeology* 13: 29–32.

Faltings, Dina, and E. C. Kohler. 1996. Vorbericht über die Ausgrabungen des DAI in Tell el-Fara in/Buto 1993 bis 1995. *Mittleilungen des Deutschen Archäeologischen Instituts abteilung Kairo* 52: S. 87–114.

Feinman, Gary M., and Joyce Marcus, eds. 1998. *Archaic States.* Santa Fe, N.Mex.: School of American Research Press.

Flannery, Kent V. 1972. The origins of the village as a settlement type in Mesoamerica and the Near East: A comparative study. In *Man, Settlement and Urbanism*, edited by Peter J. Ucko, Ruth Tringham, and George W. Dimbleby. London: Duckworth.

1976. *The Early Mesoamerican Village.* New York: Academic Press.

2006. On the resilience of anthropological archaeology. *Annual Review of Anthropology* 35: 1–13.

Flores, D. V. 2003. Funerary sacrifice of animals in the Egyptian Pre-Dynastic period. *British Archaeological Reports,* No. 1153. Oxford: Archaeopress.

Foster, John. L., and Nina M. Davies. 1992. *Love Songs of the New Kingdom.* Austin: University of Texas Press.

Foucault, Michel. 1986. *The Foucault Reader,* edited by Paul Rabinow. Harmondsworth: Penguin.

Frankfort, H. 1956. *The Birth of Civilization in the Near East.* Garden City, N.Y.: Doubleday.

Friedman, Renée. 1996. The ceremonial centre at Hierakonpolis Locality HK29A. In *Aspects of Early Egypt,* edited by Jeffrey Spencer, pp. 16–35. London: British Museum Press.

2007. The friends of Nekhen. *Ancient Egypt* 7(3): 45–51.

Friedman, Renée F., Amy Maish, Ahmed G. Fahmy, John C. Darnell, and Edward. D. Johnson. 1999. Preliminary report on field work at Hierakonpolis: 1996–1998. *Journal of the American Research Center in Egypt* 36: 1–35.

Geller, Jeremy. 1992. From prehistory to history: Beer in Egypt. In *The Followers of Horus: Studies Dedicated to Michael Allen Hoffman,* edited by Renée F. Friedman and Barbara Adams, pp. 19–26. Oxford: Oxbow Monograph 20.

Ginter, Boleslaw, and Janusz Kozlowski. 1986. Kulturelle und Palläoklimatishe Sequenz in der Fayum-Despression: Eine zusammensetzende Darstellung der Forschungsarbeiten in den Jahren 1977–81. *Mitteilungen des Deutschen Archäologischen Instituts Abteilung Kairo* 42.

Godfrey Smith, P., and Richard Lewontin. 1993. The dimensions of selection. *Philosophy of Science* 60: 373–395.

Goedicke, Hans. 1988. The Northeastern Delta and the Mediterranean. In *The Archaeology of the Nile Delta: Problems and Priorities,* edited by Edwin van den Brink, pp. 165–175. Amsterdam: Netherlands Foundation for Archaeological Research in Egypt.

Gould, Stephen Jay. 1989. *Wonderful Life.* New York: W. W. Norton.

Grene, David. 1987. *Herodotus: The History.* Chicago: University of Chicago Press.

Grimal, Nicholas. 1992. *A History of Ancient Egypt,* translated by Ian Shaw. Cambridge: Blackwell.

Haarman, Ulrich. 1996. Medieval Muslim perceptions of pharaonic Egypt. In *Ancient Egyptian Literature: History and Forms,* edited by Antonio Loprieno, pp. 605–627. Leiden: E. J. Brill.

Haas, Herbert, J. Devine, Robert Wenke, Mark Lehner, Willy Wölfli, and Georges Bonani. 1987. Radiocarbon chronology and the historical calendar in Egypt. In *Chronologies du proche orient,* British Archaeological Report International Series 379: 585–606.

Hansen, Donald. 1967. Mendes 1965 and 1966. *Journal of the American Research Center in Egypt* 6: 5–16.

Harris, Marvin. 1977. *Cannibals and Kings.* New York: Random House.
1989. *Cows, Pigs, Wars, and Witches: The Riddles of Culture.* New York: Vintage.
Hart, John P., and John E. Terrell. 2002. *Darwin and Archaeology: A Handbook of Key Concepts.* Westport, Conn.: Bergin & Garvey.
Hartung, Ulrich, 1998a. Prädynastische siegelabrollungen aus dem friedhof U in Abydos (Umm el- Qaab). *Mitteilungen des Deutschen Archäeologischen Instituts Abteilung Kairo* 54: 187–217.
1998b. Zur Entwicklung des Handels und zum Beginn wirtschaftlicher Administration im prädynastischen Ägypten. *Studien zur altägyptischen Kultur, Hamburg* 26: 35–50.
2000. Imported jars from Cemetery U at Abydos and the relations between Egypt amd Canaan in Predynastic times. In *Egypt and the Levant: Interrelations from the 4th through the Early 3rd Millennium BC*, edited by Edwin van den Brink and Thomas Levy, pp. 437–49. London: Leicester University Press.
Hartung, Ulrich, M. Abd el-Gelil, A. von den Dreisch, G. Fares, R. Hartmann, T. Hikade, and C. Idhe, 2003. Vorbericht über neue Untersuchungen in der prädynastischen Siedlung von Maadi. *Mitteilungen des Deutschen Archäeologischen Instituts Abteilung Kairo* 59: 149–98.
Hassan, Fekri A. 1984. Toward a model of agricultural developments in Pre-Dynastic Egypt. In *Origin and Early Development of Food Producing Cultures in North-Eastern Africa*, edited by Lech Krzyzaniak and Michal Kobusiewicz, pp. 221–224. Poznan: Polska Akademia Nauk-Oddzial W. Poznaniu.
1985. Desertification and the beginnings of Egyptian agriculture. In *Akten des vierten internationalem Agyptologen Kongress Munchen*, edited by Sylvia Schoske, pp. 325–331. Hamburg: Helmut Buske.
1986. Holocene lakes and prehistoric settlements of the western Faiyum, Egypt. *Journal of Archaeological Science* 13: 483–501.
1988. The Predynastic of Egypt. *Journal of World Prehistory* 2: 135–185.
1992. Primeval goddess to divine king: The mythogenesis of power in the early Egyptian state. In *The Followers of Horus: Studies Dedicated to Michael Allen Hoffman*, edited by Renée F. Friedman and Barbara Adams. Oxford: Oxbow Monograph 20.
Hassan, Fekri A., T. R. Hays, A. A. Hassan, J. Gallagher, A. Gautier, and W. Wetterstrom. 1980. Agricultural developments in the Nagada Region during the Predynastic Period. *Nyame Akuma* 17: 28–33.
Hassan, Fekri, and S. W. Robinson. 1987. High-precision radiocarbon chronometry of Ancient Egypt and comparisons with Nubia, Palestine, and Mesopotamia. *Antiquity* 61(231): 119–135.
Hawass, Zahi, ed. 2003. *Egyptology at the Dawn of the Twenty-First Century.* Cairo: The American University in Cairo Press.
Hawass, Zahi, Mark Lehner, and Wilma Wetterstrom, eds. 2006. *The Giza Plateau Mapping Project: Project History, Survey, Ceramics, and the Main Street and Gallery Operations.* N.P.: Ancient Egypt Research Associates.

Hecker, Howard M. 1982. A zoological inquiry into pork consumption in Egypt from prehistoric to New Kingdom times. *Journal of the American Research Center in Egypt* 1982: 59–71.

Hendrickx, Stan, and Pierre Vermeersch. 2000. Prehistory. In *The Oxford History of Ancient Egypt*, edited by Ian Shaw, pp. 17–43. New York: Oxford University Press.

Highham, Tom, Bronk Ramsey, and Clare Owen, eds. 2004. *Radiocarbon and Archaeology*. Oxford: Oxford University School of Archaeology.

Hodder, Ian. 1991. Postprocessual archaeology and the current debate. In *Processual and Postprocessual Archaeologies: Multiple Ways of Knowing the Past*, edited by R. W. Preceul. Carbondale Ill.: Center for Archaeological Investigations.

Hoffman, Michael A. 1980a. *Egypt before the Pharaohs: The Prehistoric Foundations of Egyptian Civilization*. New York: Knopf.

    1980b. A rectangular Amratian house from Hierakonpolis and its significance for Predynastic research. *Journal of Near Eastern Studies* 39: 119–137.

    1982. The Predynastic of Hierakonpolis: An interim report. *Egyptian Studies Association Publication No. 1*. Cairo: Cairo University Herbarium.

    1989. A stratified Predynastic sequence from Hierakonpolis (Upper Egypt). In *Late Prehistory of the Nile Basin and the Sahara*, edited by Lech Krzyzaniak and Michal Kobusiewicz, pp. 317–323. Poznan: Muzeum Archaeologiczne W. Poznaniu.

Holmes, Diane L. 1989. The Predynastic lithic industries of Upper Egypt: A comparative study of the lithic traditions of Badari, Nagada and Hierakonpolis. *British Archaeological Reports International Series 469*.

Holmes, Diane L., and Renée F. Friedman. 1989. The Badari region revisited. *Nyame Akuma* 31: 15–19.

Hornung, Erik. 1999. *The Ancient Egyptian Books of the Afterlife*, translated by David Lorton. Ithaca, N.Y.: Cornell University Press.

Hornung, Erik, Rolf Krauss, and David A. Warburton, eds. 2006. *Ancient Egyptian Chronology (Handbook of Oriental Studies/Handbuch Der Orientalistik)*. Leiden: Brill.

Houlihan, Patrick. 1986. *The Birds of Ancient Egypt*. Warminister: Aris & Phillips.

Hughes, Langston. 2002. *The Collected Poems of Langston Hughes*. New York: Alfred Knopf.

Ikram, Salima, and Aidan Dodson. 1998. *The Mummy in Ancient Egypt: Equipping the Dead for Eternity*. London: Thames and Hudson.

James, Thomas, G. H. Davies, and W. V. Davies. 1985. *Egyptian Sculpture*. London: The British Museum.

Janssen, Jacques. J. 1978. The early state in Egypt. In *The Early State*, edited by Henri J. M. Claessen and Peter Skalnik. The Hague: Mouton.

Jeffreys, David G. 1985. *The Survey of Memphis I*. London: The Egypt Exploration Fund.

Joffe, Alexander H. 1991. Early Bronze I and the evolution of social complexity in the southern Levant. *Journal of Mediterranean Archaeology* 4(1): 3–58.

Johnson, Andrew L., and Nancy C. Lovell. 1994. Biological differentiation at Predynastic Naqada, Egypt: An analysis of dental morphological traits. *American Journal of Physical Anthropology* 93: 427–433.

Johnson, Gregory. 1987. Nine thousand years of social change in western Iran. In *The Archaeology of Western Iran*, edited by Frank Hole. Washington, D.C.: Smithsonian Institution Press.

Kaiser, Werner. 1956. Stand und Probleme der Ägyptischen Vorgeschichtsforschung. *Zeitschrift für ägyptische Sprache und Altertumskunde* 81: 87–109.

1957. Zur inneren Chronologie der Naqadakultur. *Archaeologia Geographica* 6: 69–77.

1958. Zur vorgeschichtlichen Bedeutung von Hierakonpolis. *Mitteilungen des Deutschen Archäologischen Instituts Abteilung Kairo* 16: 183–192.

1964. Eine Bemerkungen zur ägyptischen Frühzeit. *Zeitschrift fur ägyptische sprache und Altertumskunde* 91: 86–125.

1985. Zur Sudausdehnung der vorgeschichtlichen deltakulturen und frühen entwicklung oberägyptens. *Mitteilungen des Deutschen Archäologischen Instituts Abteilung Kairo* 41: 61–87.

1990. Zur Entstehung des gesamtagyptischen states. *Mitteilungen des Deutschen Archäologischen Instituts Abteilung Kairo* 46: 287–299.

Kaiser, Werner, and Gunter Dreyer. 1982. Umm el-Qaab: Nachuntersuchungen im frühzeitlichen Konignsfriedhof. Vorbericht. *Mitteilungen des Deutschen Archäologischen Instituts Abteilung Kairo* 38: 211–269.

Kaiser, Werner, Gunter Dreyer, H. Jaritz, A. Krekeler, T. Schlager, and M. T. Ziermann. 1988. Stadt und Tempel von Elephantine 13./14. Grabungsbericht. *Mitteilungen des Deutschen Archäologischen Instituts Abteilung Kairo* 43: 75–114.

Kanawati, Naguib. 1977. *The Egyptian Administration in the Old Kingdom: Evidence on Its Economic Decline*. Warminster: Aris & Phillips.

Keding, B. 1998. The Yellow Nile: New data on settlement and the environment in the Sudanese eastern Sahara. *Sudan and Nubia* 2: 2–12.

Kemp, Barry J. 1963. Excavations at Hierakonpolis Fort 1905: A preliminary note. *Journal of Egyptian Archaeology* 49: 24–28.

1967. The Egyptian 1st Dynasty royal cemetery. *Antiquity* 41.

1968. Merimde and the theory of house burial in Predynastic Egypt. *Chronique d'Égypte* 43: 22–33.

1973. Photographs of the decorated tomb at Hierakonpolis. *Journal of Egyptian Archaeology* 59: 36–43.

1982. Automatic analysis of Predynastic cemeteries: A new method for an old problem. *Journal of Egyptian Archaeology* 68: 5–15.

1983. Old Kingdom, Middle Kingdom and Second Intermediate Period c. 2686–1552 B.C. In *Ancient Egypt: A Social History*, edited by Bruce Trigger, Barry J. Kemp, David O'Connor, and Alan Lloyd, pp. 71–174. Cambridge: Cambridge University Press.

1989. *Ancient Egypt: Anatomy of a Civilization*. London: Routledge.

Kitchen, Kenneth A. 1991. The chronology of ancient Egypt. *World Archaeology* 23(2): 201–208.

Kitto, Humphrey Davy F. 1951. *The Greeks*. Harmondsworth: Pelican.

Knapp, A. Bernard. 1988. *The History and Culture of Ancient Western Asia and Egypt*. Chicago: Dorsey.

Kobusiewicz, Michal, Jacek Kabacinski, Romuald Schild, Joel D. Irish, and Fred Wendorf. Discovery of the first Neolithic cemetery in Egypt's western desert. *Antiquity* 78(301): 566–578.

Köhler, E. Christiana, and Dina Faltings. 1996. Vorbericht über die ausgrabungen des DAI in Tell el-Fara'in/Buto 1993 bis 1995. *Mitteilungen des Deutsches Archäologisches Institut Abteilung Kairo* 52: 87–115.

Kristiansen, Kristian. 2004. Genes versus agents: A discussion of the widening theoretical gap in archaeology. *Archaeological Dialogues* 11: 77–99.

Kristiansen, Kristian, and Michael Rowlands 1998. *Social Transformations in Archaeology: Global and Local Perspectives*. London: Routledge.

Kroeper, Karla, and Dietrich Wildung. 1985. *Minshat Abu Omar. Münchner Östdelta-Expedition Vorbericht 1978–1984*. München: Karl M. Lipp.

Krzyzaniak, Lech. 1989. Recent archaeological evidence on the earliest settlement in the Eastern Nile Delta. In *Late Prehistory of the Nile Basin and the Sahara*, edited by Lech Krzyzaniak and Michal Kobusiewicz, pp. 267–285. Poznan: Muzeum Archaeologiczne W. Poznaniu.

1992. Again on the earliest settlement at Minshat Abu Omar. In *The Nile Delta in Transition: 4th and 3rd Millennium BC.*, edited by Edwin C. M. van den Brink, pp. 151–155. Jerusalem: The Israel Exploration Society.

Kuper, Rudolph, and Stefan Kröpelin. 2006. Climate-controlled Holocene occupation in the Sahara: Motor of Africa's evolution. *Science* 313: 803–807.

Lefkowitz, Mary R. 1996. *Not out of Africa: How Afrocentrism Became an Excuse to Teach Myth as History*. New York: Basic Books.

Legge, Anthony J. 1996. The beginning of Caprine domestication in southwest Asia. In *The Origins and Spread of Agriculture and Pastoralism in Eurasia*, edited by David R. Harris, pp. 238–262. London: UCL Press.

Lehner, Mark. 1983a. Some observations on the layout of the Khufu and Khafre pyramids. *Journal of the American Research Center in Egypt* 20: 7–29.

1983b. The development of the Giza necropolis: The Khufu Project. *Mitteilungen des Deutsches Archäologisches Institut Abteilung Kairo* 41: 109–143.

1985. A contextual approach to the Giza pyramids. *Achive für Orientforshung* 32: 136–158.

1997. *The Complete Pyramids*. London: Thames and Hudson.

Leone, Mark, Parker B. Potter, Jr., and Paul A. Schackel. 1987. Toward a critical archaeology. *Current Anthropology* 28(3): 283–302.

Lesko, Leonard H., ed. 1998. *Ancient Egyptian and Mediterranean Studies in Memory of William A. Ward*. Rhode Island: Department of Egyptology, Brown University.

Lévi-Strauss, Claude. 1963. *Structural Anthropology*, translated by Claire Jacobson and Brooke G. Schoepf. Harmondsworth: Penguin.

Levy, Thomas E. 1993. Production and social change in the southern Levant. In *Spatial Boundaries and Social Dynamics: Case Studies from Agrarian Societies*, edited by A. F. C. Holl and Thomas E. Levy. Ann Arbor, Mich.: International Monographs in Prehistory.

Levy, Thomas E., and Edwin C. M. van den Brink. 2002. Interaction models, Egypt and the Levantine periphery. In *Egyptian-Canaanite Interaction: From the 4th through Early 3rd Millennium B.C*, edited by Edwin C. M. van den Brink and Thomas E. Levy, pp. 3–38. London: Leicester University Press.

Libby Willard F. 1955. *Radiocarbon Dating*, 2d ed. Chicago: University of Chicago Press.

Lichtheim, Miriam. 1973. *Ancient Egyptian Literature. A Book of Readings I: The Old and Middle Kingdom*. Berkeley: University of California Press.

Lovell, Nancy. 1999. Egyptians, physical anthropology of. In *Encyclopedia of the Archaeology of Ancient Egypt*, edited by Kathryn A. Bard, pp. 277–280. New York: Routledge.

Lumsden, Charles, and Edward O. Wilson. 1981. *Genes, Mind, and Culture*. Cambridge, Mass.: Harvard University Press.

Lustig, Judith. 1994. Kinship, gender, and age in Middle Kingdom tomb scenes and texts. In *Anthropology and Egyptology: A Developing Dialogue*, edited by Judith Lustig, pp. 43–65, Sheffield: Sheffield Academic Press.

Lyman, R. Lee, and Michael J. O'Brien. 2000. *Applying Evolutionary Archaeology: A Systematic Approach*. New York: Kluwer Academic/Plenum.

Mackey, Damien F. 1995. *The Sothic Star Theory of the Egyptian Calendar*. M.A. Thesis. Sydney: University of Sydney.

Maisels, C. K. 2001. *Early Civilizations of the Old World: The Formative Histories of Egypt, the Levant, Mesopotamia, India and China*. London: Routledge.

Malek, Jaromir. 1997. *The Cat in Ancient Egypt*. Philadelphia: University of Pennsylvania Press.

——— 2000. The Old Kingdom. c. 2686–2160 B.C. In *The Oxford History of Ancient Egypt*, edited by Ian Shaw, pp. 89–117. New York: Oxford University Press.

Malek, Jaromir, and Werner Foreman. 1986. *In the Shadow of the Pyramids*. Norman: University of Oklahoma Press.

Manniche, Lise. 1991. *Music and Musicians in Ancient Egypt*. London: Dover Publications.

Marcus, Joyce. 1998. The peaks and valleys of ancient states: An extension of the dynamic model. In *Archaic States*, edited by Gary M. Feinman and Joyce Marcus, pp. 54–94. Santa Fe, N.Mex.: School of American Research Press.

Maschner, Herbert D. G., ed. 1996. *Darwinian Archaeologies*. New York: Plenum Press.

Mathieu, Bernard. 1986. Les hommes de larmes, à propos d'un jeu de mots mythique dans les textes de l'ancienne Égypte. Hommages à François Daumas, 2, pp. 499–509. Montpellier: Publications de la Recherche, Université de Montpellier/OrMonsp, 3.

Mauss, Marcel. 1979. The notion of body techniques. In *Sociology and Psychology: Essays*, translated by Ben Brewster, pp. 97–123. London: Routledge and Kegan Paul.

McArdle, John. 1982. Preliminary report on the Predynastic fauna of the Hierakonpolis project. In *The Predynastic of Hierakonpolis: An Interim Report*, edited by M. A. Hoffman, pp. 116–121. Cairo: Egyptian Studies Association Publication No. 1.

McGuire, Randall H. 1983. Breaking down cultural complexity: Inequality and heterogeneity. In *Advances in Archaeological Method and Theory*, Vol. 6, edited by Michael B. Schiffer, pp. 91–142. New York: Academic Press.

Meskell, Lynn. 1999. *Archaeologies of Social Life*. Oxford: Blackwell.

Midant-Reynes, Béatrix. 2000. The Naqada period. In *The Oxford History of Ancient Egypt*, edited by Ian Shaw, pp. 44–60. New York: Oxford University Press.

Midant-Reynes, Béatrix, and Nathalie Buchez. 2002. *Adaïma I: Économie et Habitat*. Cairo: Institut Français d'Archaeologie Orientale.

Midant-Reynes, Béatrix, Nathalie Buchez, Eric Crubezy, and Thierry Janin. 1991. Le site prédynastique d'Adaïma rapport préliminaire de la deuxieme campagne de Fouille. *Bulletin de l'Institut Français d'Archaeologie Orientale* 91: 231–246.

Midant-Reynes, Béatrix, Nathalie Buchez, A. Hesse, and C. Lechevalier. 1990. Le site prédynastique d'Adaïma. *Bulletin de l'Institut Français d'Archaeologie Orientale* 90: 247–258.

Miller, Naomi. 1992. The origins of plant cultivation in the Near East. In *The Origins of Agriculture*, edited by C. Wesley Cowan and Patty J. Watson. Washington, D.C.: Smithsonian Institution Press.

Miroschedji, Pierre de, Mohamad Sadeq, Dina Faltings, V. Boulez, L. Naggiar-Moliner, N. Sykes, and M. Tengberg. 2002. Les fouilles de Tell es-Sakan (Gaza): Nouvelles données sur les contacts égypto-cananéens aux IVe–IIIe millénaires. *Paléorient* 27(2): 75–104.

Mithen, Steven J. 1996. *The Prehistory of the Mind: A Search for the Origins of Art, Religion and Science*. London: Thames and Hudson.

Moens, Marie-Francine, and Wilma Wetterstrom. 1989. The agricultural economy of an Old Kingdom town in Egypt's West Delta: Insights from the plant remains. *Journal of Near Eastern Studies* 3: 159–173.

Morenz, Sigfried. 1992. *Egyptian Religion*. Ithaca, N.Y.: Cornell University Press.

Mortensen, Bodil. 1991. Change in settlement pattern and population in the beginning of the historical period. In *Ägypten und Levante II*, edited by Manfred Bietak, pp. 11–37. Wien: Österreichishchen Akademie der Wissenschaften.

1992. Carbon-14 dates from El Omari. In *The Followers of Horus: Studies Dedicated to Michael Allen Hoffman*, edited by Renée F. Friedman and Barbara Adams, pp. 173–174. Oxford: Oxbow Monograph 20.

Neiman, F. D. 1995. Stylistic variation in evolutionary perspective: Inferences from decorative diversity and interassemblage distance in Illinois woodland ceramic assemblages. *American Antiquity* 60(1): 7–36.

O'Connor, David. 1989. New funerary enclosures (Talbezirke) of the Early Dynastic Period at Abydos. *Journal of the American Research Center in Egypt* 26: 51–86.

1995. The earliest Egyptian boat graves. *Egyptian Archaeology* 6: 3–7.

1997. Ancient Egypt: Egyptological and anthropological perspectives. In *Anthropology and Egyptology*, edited by Judy Lustig, pp. 13–24. Sheffield: Sheffield Academic Press.

Parkinson, Richard. B. 1995. Homosexual desire and Middle Kingdom literature. *Journal of Egyptian Archaeology* 81: 57–76.

1997. *The Tale of Sinuhe and Other Ancient Egyptian Poems, 1940–1640 B.C.* London: Clarendon.

2002. *Poetry and Culture in Middle Kingdom Egypt: A Dark Side to Perfection.* London: Continuum.

Pearson, Gordon. 1979. Precise 14C measurement by LS counting. *Radiocarbon* 21(1): 1–22.

Petrie, William M. Flinders. 1920. *Prehistoric Egypt.* London: British School of Archaeology in Egypt.

1939. *The Making of Egypt.* London: Sheldon.

Petrie, William M. Flinders, and James E. Quibell. 1896. *Naqada and Ballas.* London: British School of Archaeology in Egypt.

Pfaffenberger, Bryan. 1988. Fetishized objects and humanized nature: Towards a social anthropology of technology. *Man* (n.s.) 23: 236–52.

Pollan, Michael. 2007. Unhappy meals. *New York Times*, January 28, 2007.

Pollock, Susan. 1999. *Ancient Mesopotamia.* Cambridge: Cambridge University Press.

Quibell, James E. 1898 Slate palette from Hieraconpolis. *Zeitschrift für Ägyptische Sprache und Altertumskunde* 36: 81–86.

Quibell, James E., and Frederich W. Green. 1902. *Hierakonpolis. Part II: London*: Egypt Research Account 5.

Quirke, Stephen, and Jeffrey Spencer, eds. 1992. *The British Museum Book of Ancient Egypt.* New York: Thames and Hudson.

Redford, Donald. 1986a. *Pharaonic King-Lists, Annals, and Day-Books: A Contribution to the Study of the Egyptian Sense of History.* Ontario: Benben Publications SSEA Publication IV.

1986b. Egypt and western Asia in the Old Kingdom. *Journal of the American Research Center in Egypt* 23: 125–143.

1992. *Egypt, Canaan, and Israel in Ancient Times* Princeton, N.J.: Princeton University Press.

2004. *Excavations at Mendes*, Vol. I: *The Royal Necropolis*, pp. 32–33. Leiden: Brill.

Reeder, Greg. 2000. Same-sex desire, conjugal constructs, and the tomb of Niankhkhnum and Khnumhotep. *World Archaeology* 32(2): 193–208.

Reeves, Carole. 1992. *Egyptian Medicine.* Buckinghamshire: Shire Publications.

Reeves, Nicholas. 1990. *The Complete Tutankhamun.* New York: Thames and Hudson.

Rice, Michael 1990. *Egypt's Making: The Origins of Ancient Egypt.* London: Routledge.

Richards, Janet, and Mary Van Buren, eds. 2000. *Order, Legitimacy, and Wealth in Ancient States.* Cambridge: Cambridge University Press.

Rindos, David. 1984. *The Origins of Agriculture.* New York: Academic Press.

Rizkana, Ibrahim, and Jürgen Seeher. 1984. New light on the relation of Maadi to the Upper Egyptian cultural sequence. *Mitteilungen des Deutschen Archäologischen Instituts Abteilung Kairo* 40: 235–255.

1985. The chipped stones at Maadi: Preliminary reassessment of a Predynastic industry and its long-distance relations. *Mitteilungen des Deutschen Archäeologischen Instituts Abteilung Kairo* 41: 235–255.

1987. *Maadi I. The Pottery of the Predynastic Settlement*. Mainz: Philipp von Zabern.

1988. *Maadi II. Lithic Industries*. Mainz: Philipp von Zabern.

1989. *Maadi III. The Non-lithic Small Finds and the Structural Remains of the Predynastic Settlement*. Mainz: Philipp von Zabern.

1990. *Maadi IV. The Cemeteries of Maadi and Wadi Digla*. Mainz: Philipp von Zabern.

Robins, Gay. 1993. *Women in Ancient Egypt*. London: British Museum Press.

Roth, Ann M. 1991. *Egyptian Phyles in the Old Kingdom: The Evolution of a System of Social Organization*. Chicago: The Oriental Institute of the University of Chicago.

1995a. Buried pyramids and layered thoughts: The organization of multiple approaches in Egyptian religion. In *Proceedings of the Seventh International Congress of Egyptologists*, edited by Christopher John Eyre, pp. 991–1003. Leuven: Peeters.

1995b. *A Cemetery of Palace Attendants*. Boston: Museum of Fine Arts.

2003. Social change in the Fourth Dynasty: The spatial organization of pyramids, tombs, and cemeteries. *Journal of the American Research Center in Egypt* 30: 33–55.

Sahlins, Marshall. 1976. *Culture and Practical Reason*. Chicago: University of Chicago Press.

Salzman. 1999. Is inequality universal? *Current Anthropology* 40(1): 31–61.

Schmitz, Bettina, ed. 1985. Untersuchungen zu Idu II. Giza: Ein interdisziplinares Äygyptologische Beitrage, 38. Hildesheim: Gerstenberg Verlag.

Schoch, Robert M. 2005. *Pyramid Quest: Secrets of the Great Pyramid and the Dawn of Civilization*. New York: Jeremy Tarcher.

Seeher, Jurgen. 1990. Maadi – eine prädynastische Kulturgrupper zwischen Oberägypten und Palastina. *Prähistorische Zeitschrift* 65: 123–156.

1991. Gendanken zur Rolle Unteragyptens bei der Herausbildung des Pharaoenreiches. *Mitteilungen des Deutschen Archäologischen Instituts Abteilung Kairo* 47: 313–318.

Seidlmayer, Stephen. 1987. Wirtschaftliche und gesellschaftliche Entwicklung im Übergang vom Alten zum Mittleren Reich: Ein Beitrag zur Archäologie der Graberfelder der Region Qau Matmar in der Ersten Zwischenzeit. In *Problems and Priorities in Egyptian Archaeology*, edited by J. Assman, Gunter Burkard, and Vivian Davies. London: Routledge & Kegan Paul.

Shafer, Byron E., ed. 1997. *Temples of Ancient Egypt*. Ithaca, N.Y.: Cornell University Press.

Shanks, Michael, and Christopher Tilley. 1987a. *Social Theory and Archaeology*. Oxford: Polity Press.

1987b. *Reconstructing Archaeology*. Cambridge: Cambridge University Press.

1989. Archaeology into the 1990s. *Norwegian Archaeological Review* 22(1): 1–12.

Shaw, Ian, ed. and introd. 2000. *The Oxford History of Ancient Egypt.* New York: Oxford University Press.

Shennan, Stephen. 1988. *Quantifying Archaeology.* San Diego: Academic Press.

——— 2004. Culture, society, and evolutionary theory. *Archaeological Dialogues* 11: 107–114.

Sjoberg, Gideon. 1965. *The Preindustrial City: Past and Present.* New York: The Free Press.

Smith, Bruce D. 2006 Domesticating domesticated plants in the archaeological record. In *Documenting Domestication: New Genetic and Archaeological Paradigms*, edited by Melinda Zeder, Daniel G. Bradley, Eve Emshwiller, Bruce D. Smith, and Karin Sowada. Berkeley: University of California Press.

Smith, Harry Sydney. 1991. The development of the A-Group culture in northern Lower Nubia. In *Nubia from Prehistory to Islam*, edited by W. Vivian Davies, pp. 92–111. London: British University Press.

Spence, Kate. 2000. Ancient Egyptian chronology and the astronomical orientation of the pyramids. *Nature* 408: 320–324.

Stadelmann, Ranier. 2003. The Great Sphinx of Giza. In *Egyptology at the Dawn of the Twenty-First Century: Proceedings of the Eighth International Congress of Egyptologists Cairo, 2000*, Vol. 1: *Archaeology*, edited by Zahi Hawass, pp. 464–469. Cairo: The American University in Cairo Press.

Sterling, Sarah. 1999. Mortality profiles as indicators of lowered reproductive rates: Evidence from ancient Egypt. *Journal of Anthropological Archaeology* 18: 319–343.

Steward, Julian. 1949. Cultural causality and law: A trial formulation of the development of early civilizations. *American Anthropologist* 51: 1–27.

Stockstad, E. 2002. Early cowboys herded cattle in Africa. *Science* 296: 236.

Strudwick, Nigel. 1985. *The Administration of Egypt in the Old Kingdom: The Highest Titles and Their Holders.* London: KPI.

——— 2005. *Writings from the Ancient World: Texts from the Pyramid Age*, edited by Ronald J. Leprohon. Atlanta: Society of Biblical Literature.

Taylor, John H. 2001. *Death and the Afterlife in Ancient Egypt.* London: British Museum Press.

Teeter, Emily. 1997. *The Presentation of Maat: Ritual and Legitimacy in Ancient Egypt.* Chicago: Science Academy of Chicago.

——— 1999. Kingship. In *The Archaeology of Ancient Egypt*, ed. Kathryn Bard, pp. 411–414. New York: Routlege.

Terrell, John Edward, John P. Hart, Sibel Barut, Nicoletta Cellinese, Antonio Curet, Tim Denham, Chapurukha M. Kusimba, Kyle Latinis, Rahul Oka, Joel Palka, Mary E. D. Pohl, Kevin O. Pope, Patrick Ryan Williams, Helen Haines, and John E. Staller. 2003. Domesticated landscapes: The subsistence ecology of plant and animal domestication. *Journal of Archaeological Method and Theory* 10: 323–368.

Tompkins, Peter. 1971. *Secrets of the Great Pyramid.* New York: Harper Colophon Books.

Trigger, Bruce Graham. 1983. The rise of Egyptian civilization. In *Ancient Egypt: A Social History*, edited by Bruce Graham Trigger, Barry John Kemp,

David O'Connor, and Albert Bushnell Lloyd, pp. 1–70. Cambridge: Cambridge University Press.

1984. Archaeology at the crossroads: What's new? *Annual Review of Anthropology* 13: 275–300.

1989. Monumental architecture: A thermodynamic explanation of symbolic behavior. *World Archaeology* 22: 119–131.

1993. *Ancient Civilizations. Ancient Egypt in Context.* Cairo: American University in Cairo Press.

2003. *Understanding Early Civilizations.* New York: Cambridge University Press.

van den Brink, Edwin C. M. 1988. The Amsterdam University Survey expedition to the northeastern Nile Delta (1984–1986). In *The Archaeology of the Nile Delta, Egypt: Problems and Priorities*, edited by Edwin C. M. van den Brink, pp. 65–114. Amsterdam: Netherlands Foundation for Archaeological Research in Egypt.

1989. A transitional Late Predynastic–Early Dynastic settlement site in the Northeast Nile Delta. In *The Nile Delta in Transition: 4th–3rd Millennium B.C*, edited by Edwin C. M. van den Brink, pp. 317–338. Jerusalem: The Israel Exploration Society.

1992. Preliminary report on the excavations at Tell Ibrahim Awad, seasons 1988–1990. In *The Nile Delta in Transition: 4th–3rd Millennium B.C*, edited by Edwin C. M. van den Brink, pp. 43–68. Jerusalem: The Israel Exploration Society.

van den Brink, Edwin, and Thomas Levy, eds. 2002. *Egypt and the Levant: Interrelations from the 4th through the Early 3rd Millennium BC.* London: Leicester University Press.

Vermeersch, Pierre, Etienne Paulissen, S. Stokes, and C. Charlier. 1988. A middle Paleolithic burial of a modern human at Taramsa Hill, Egypt. *Antiquity* 72: 475–484.

Vermeersch, Pierre, E. Paulissen, and W. van Neer. 1989. The Late Paleolithic Makhadma sites (Egypt): Environment and subsistence. In *Late Prehistory of the Nile Basin and the Sahara*, edited by Lech Krzyzaniak and Michal Kobusiewicz, pp. 87–114. Poznan: Muzeum Archaeologiczne W. Poznaniu.

Von der Way, Thomas. 1988. Investigations concerning the early periods in the northern Delta of Egypt. In *The Archaeology of the Nile Delta: Problems and Priorities*, edited by Edwin C. M. van den Brink, pp. 245–249. Amsterdam: Netherlands Foundation for Archaeological Research in Egypt.

1989. Tell e-Fara'in-Buto 4. Bericht. *Mitteilungen des Deutschen Archäologischen Instituts Kairo* 45: 275–308.

1992. Excavations at Tell e-Fara'in/Buto. In *The Nile Delta in Transition: 4th–3rd Millennium BC.*, edited by Edwin C. M. van den Brink, pp. 1–10. Jerusalem: The Israel Exploration Society.

Weeks, Kent, ed. 1979. *Egyptology and the Social Sciences.* Cairo: American University in Cairo Press.

Wegner, Josef. 1998. Excavations at the town of Enduring-are-the-Places-of-Khakaure-Maa-Kheru-in-Abydos: A preliminary report on the 1994 and 1997 seasons. *Journal of the American Research Center in Egypt* 35: 1–44.

Wendorf, Fred. 1968. *The Prehistory of Nubia*, Vols. 1 and 2. Dallas: Southern Methodist University Press.

1985. Prehistoric settlements in the Nubian Desert. *American Scientist* 73: 132–141.

Wendorf, Fred, and Romuald Schild. 1976. *Prehistory of the Nile Valley*. New York: Academic Press.

1998. Nabta Playa and its role in northeastern African prehistory. *Journal of Anthropological Archaeology* 17: 97–123.

Wendorf, Fred, Romuald Schild, and Angela E. Close, eds. 1980. *Prehistory of the Eastern Sahara*. New York: Academic Press.

1984a. *Cattle-Keepers of the Eastern Sahara: The Neolithic of Bir Kiseiba*. New Delhi: Pauls Press.

1984b. Some implications of Late Paleolithic cereal exploitation at Wadi Kubbaniya (Upper Egypt). In *Origin and Early Development of Food-Producing Cultures in North-eastern Africa*, edited by Lech Krzyzaniak and Michael Kobusiewicz, pp. 117–127. Poznan: Polska Akademia Nauk-Oddzial W. Poznaniu.

1989. Summary and synthesis. In *Prehistory of Wadi Kuabbaniya: Late Paleolithic Archaeology*, Vol. 3, pp. 768–824. Dallas: Southern Methodist University Press.

Wendrichs W., and R. Cappers. 2005. Egypt's earliest granaries: Evidence from the Fayum. *Journal of Egyptian Archaeology* 27: 12–15.

Wengrow, David. 2006. *The Archaeology of Early Egypt: Social Transformations in North-east Africa, 10,000 to 2650 BC*. Cambridge: Cambridge University Press.

Wenke, Robert J. 1980a. *Archaeological Investigations at el-Hibeh 1980: Preliminary Report*. Undena: Malibu.

1980b. Egypt: Origins of complex societies. *Annual Review of Anthropology* 18: 129–155.

1991. The evolution of early Egyptian civilization: Issues and evidence. *Journal of World Prehistory* 5: 279–329.

1995a. City-states, nation-states, and territorial states: The problem of Egypt. In *The Archaeology of City-States*, edited by D. Nichols and T. Charlton, pp. 27–50. Washington, D.C.: Smithsonian Institution Press.

1995b. Anthropology, Egyptology, and the explanation of culture change. In *Anthropology and Egyptology*, edited by Judith Lustig, pp. 171–136. Sheffield: Sheffield Academic Press.

Wenke, Robert J., and Douglas J. Brewer. 1992. The Neolithic-Predynastic transition in the Fayyum depression. In *The Followers of Horus: Studies Dedicated to Michael Allen Hoffman*, edited by Renée F. Friedman and Barbara Adams, pp. 175–184. Oxford: Oxbow Monographs 20.

1995. The archaic–Old Kingdom delta: The evidence from Mendes and Kom el-Hisn. In *House and Palace in Ancient Egypt*, edited by M. Bietak, pp. 260–284. Vienna: Austrian Archaeological Institute.

Wenke, Robert J., Paul E. Buck, Hany A. Hamroush, Michal Kobusiewicz, Karla Kroeper, and Richard J. Redding. 1988. Kom el-Hisn: Excavation of an Old Kingdom settlement in the Egyptian delta. *Journal of the American Research Center in Egypt* 25: 5–34.

Wenke, Robert J., Janet E. Long, and Paul E. Buck. 1988. Epipaleolithic and Neolithic subsistence and settlement in the Fayyum Oasis of Egypt. *Journal of Field Archaeology* 15: 29–51.

Wetterstrom, Wilma. 1993. Foraging and farming in Egypt: The transition from hunting and gathering to horticulture in the Egyptian Nile Valley. In *The Archaeology of Africa: Food, Metals and Towns*, edited by Thurston Shaw, Bassey Andah, Paul Sinclai, and Alex Okpoko, pp. 165–226. London: Routledge.

1997. Pre-agricultural people of the Nile Valley. In *The Encyclopedia of Pre-colonial Africa*, edited by Joseph O. Vogel. Walnut Creek, Calif.: Alta Mira Press.

White, Leslie. 1949. *The Science of Culture*. New York: Grove.

Wildung, Dietrich. 1984. Terminal prehistory of the Nile Delta: Theses. In *Late Prehistory of the Nile Basin and the Sahara*, edited by Lech Krzyzaniak and Michal Kobusiewicz, pp. 265–269. Poznan: Muzeum Archaeologiczne W. Poznaniu.

Wilkinson, Richard. 2000. *The Complete Temples of Ancient Egypt*. London: Thames & Hudson.

Wilkinson, Toby A. H. 1999. *Early Dynastic Egypt*. New York: Routlege.

2000. Political unification: Towards a reconstruction. *Mitteilungen des Deutschen Archäeologischen Instituts Abteilung Kairo* 56.

2003. *Genesis of the Pharaohs*. London: Thames and Hudson.

2004. Before the pyramids: Early developements in Egyptian royal funerary ideology. In *Egypt at Its Origin: Studies in Memory of Barbara Adams*, edited by Stan Hendrickx, Renée F. Friedman, Krzysztof M. Cialowicz, and Marek Chlodnicki, pp. 1129–1142. Leuven: O.L.A.

Williams, Bruce. 1986. *Excavations between Abu Simbel and the Sudan Frontier. The A-Group Royal Cemetery at Qustal: Cemetery L*. Chicago: The Oriental Institute of the University of Chicago.

Wilson, Hiliary. 1988. *Egyptian Food and Drink*. Princes Risborough, England: Shire.

Wilson, John. A. 1951. *The Culture of Ancient Egypt*. Chicago: University of Chicago Press.

de Wit, H. E., and L. van Stralen. 1988. Geo-archaeology and ancient distributaries in the Eastern Nile Delta. *Reports of the Laboratory of Physical Geography and Soil Science* 34, University of Amsterdam.

Wittfogel, K. A. 1957. *Oriental Despotism: A Comparative Study of Total Power*. New Haven, Conn.: Yale University Press.

Wolfram, Steven. 2002. *A New Kind of Science*. Champaign, Ill.: Wolfram Media.

Wright, Henry T., and Gregory A. Johnson. 1975. Population, exchange, and early state formation in southwestern Iran. *American Anthropologist* 77: 267–289.

Wright, Rita P. In Press. *The Ancient Indus: Urbanism, Economy and Society*. Cambridge: Cambridge University Press.

Yoffee, Norman. 2005. *Myths of the Archaic State: Evolution of the Earliest Cities, States, and Civilizations*. Cambridge: Cambridge University Press.

Zeder, Melinda, Daniel G. Bradley, Eve Emshwiller, Bruce D. Smith, and Karin Sowada, eds. 2006. *Documenting Domestication: New Genetic and Archaeological Paradigms*. Berkeley: University of California Press.

Zibelius, K. 1978. *Ägyptische Siedlungen nach Texten des Alten Reiches*. Wiesbaden: Reichert.

Zivie-Coche, Christiane. 2002. *Sphinx: History of a Monument*, translated by David Lorton. Ithaca, N.Y.: Cornell University Press.

Index

Abadiya, 193
"Aborigines," 23
"Abu Bagousheh" ("father of pots"), 195
Abu Roash, 278
Abusir el-Meleq, 225, 290
Abydos
    allegations of artifact destruction at, 85
    bronze vessels in Khasekhemwy's tomb
        at, 246
    burials at, 206, 245
    c. 3500 BC, 205
    c. 4000 BC, 212
    funerary enclosures at, 247
    Predynastic, 111
    richness of site at, 252
acacia, 65, 66
accelerator mass spectrometry (AMS),
    102, 105
Actium, Battle of (31 BC), 81
Adaïma, 224–7
Adams, Matthew D., 282
Adams, Matthew J., 211
Afghanistan, 49
Africa, 33, 49
afterlife. See also religion; soul
    Egyptian conception of, 2, 20
    elites aspiring to an, 242
    provisioning for, 13
    and the pyramids, 297
Agamemnon, 136
agriculture
    c. 4000 BC, 4
    c. 5000 BC, 42–4
    c. 5000–3500 BC, 212
    c. 9000 BC, 138
    c. 9000–6000 BC, 139
    and community development, 72
    early, in Faiyum, 159–66

efficient, in the Nile Valley, 293
and environmental modification, 151–2
farm animals in, 72
farming system in Ancient Egypt, 56–64
and fertilization, 42
versus hunting-foraging, 144
land ownership in Old Kingdom
    (2686–2160 BC), 287
origins of Egyptian, 137–41
and population, 339
preindustrial, and climate, 38
seasonal cycle of, 52–6
social status of farmers, 57
specialized tools and techniques in, 57–8
subsistence, 57, 141–3, 214
in Syro-Palestine (c. 8500 BC), 164
use of wooden plows in (c. 2500 BC), 44
Aha. See Menes, King
Aida (Verdi), 9
Akh (enlightened spirit), 269. See also mut
Akhenaten, King (c. 1352 BC), 337
akhet (time of inundation), 53
alcoholic beverages, 59–61, 143
Amélineau, E., 85
Ammerman, A. J., 176
AMS. See accelerator mass spectrometry
amulet, 67, 268
Amunhotep I (1525–1504 BC), 55
analysis
    faunal (animal remains), 121
    paleoethnological (plant remains), 122
Anatolia, 165
Anedjib, King (c. 2850–c. 2700), 244
anemia, 73
animals, use of, in Ancient Egypt, 64–5
Ankh (life force), 269
anthracosis ("black-lung disease"), 74
antiquity, Egyptian, rediscovery of, 81–5